MW00783981

LUCIFERIAN WITCHCRAFT

The Grimoire of The Serpent

Michael W. Ford

Second Edition

SUCCUBUS PUBLISHING
MMIX
ISBN 9780578035376

Published by Succubus Productions
P.O. Box 926344
Houston, TX 77292
USA

Second Edition 2009
ISBN 9780578035376
Typeset and edited by Michael W. Ford
Additional typeset and editing by Fra. Tymoleaon and Sor. Shylah

Spai
ECHT

Contents

Introduction

I have yet to meet the author of this work 'in the flesh', although we have communed more than thrice in the Astral Lodge of the Black Brotherhood, and bumped into each other at the dreaded Dream Sabbat. We have also exchanged much banter via the post, ranging from deep discussion of the mysteries, the echange of research, experiential, and experimental magical formulae, knowledge, ideas, and the obligatory bit of gossip. In this age of so called "Magical Revival" Michael Ford is one of the few individuals with enough self-surety to declare himself openly an Adept of the Black Arts... and get away with it. Let us pay attention to the fact that he lives in an American State where billboards declare "Don't Mess with Jesus- by order of the State Governer of Texas", and if they could burn heretics in their Mercy Seat you can be sure they damned well would.

It is thus with honour and pride that I introduce you to Michael Ford's latest grimoire of Satanic Witchcraft. Here you will find chilling formulae of the Craft Sinister, embracing the averse forces of Cain, walking the antinomian path of the isolate self, breaking eucharist in memory and celebration of the first murder, quaffing the blood of Seth in greedy mouhfulls from a chalice formed from some poor unfortunate's vacated cranium, and revelling in all that brings power to the self. This is not mere vain pagan observance. It is not the "milk and water" witchcraft that the modern media is so keen to shove down our thraots in their glossy magazines, on our T.V. sets, in our cinemas. Rather, it is a facet of that "Black Tradition" that has lurked in the shadows of human culture since the first cities of Babylon were erected, and the first servants of Chaos were spawned by the demon Qingu, leader of Tiamat's horde.

Michael's invocations wax lyrical in the names of Lilith, Hecate, Satan, Lucifer, and are punctuated with names and words of power more barbaric still. This is not a path of prayer and supplication, but recognition of the sorcerer's own inherant powers. The forces of Darkness are called upon as a means of self-expression, self-empowerment, and self-deification. This is something common to many paths of genuine magick and sorcery, from the possession cults of Voodoo to the "god forms" of the Golden Dawn. The various Archetypes, or Mysteries, are called into focus through ritual. All the sesnse are brought to bare upon an ecstatic moment of self-identification. One might say that at such moments the deeper realms of consciousness well up and envelop the ego, creating an instance of shaken belief when acts of sorcery may thus be performed with absolute surety in one's own power. Through such intense meditations we come face to face with our deeper minds, symbolised as the cthonian realms, populated by legions of chattering demons. Even the briefest attempts to attain mental silence, as any magician will know, reveals that beneath our ego we are each a gateway of Pandemonium.

Michael Ford evidently has a good relationship with these "gatekeepers" of the subconscious Forgotten Arcana. His work has attracted a lot of attention, from the new generation of Lilith's spawn to Old Skratte's like myself. This is the real thing- witchcraft for goats, not sheep. So consider yourself warned.
In the historical witchcraft of England there existed (and still exists) a powerful oath which runs as follows:

"I deny God and all Religion
I curse, blaspheme, and provoke God with all despite
I give my faith to the Devel, and my worship and offer sacrifice to him
I do solemnly vow and promise all my progeny unto the Devel
I swear to the Devel to bring as many into his society as I can
I will always swear in the name of the Devel."

I would say that Mr. Ford, the Order of Phosphorus, and the inner Black Order of the Dragon, have endeavoured to uphold this tradition gloriously. With the band Psychonaut 75, and related musical projects, he has seduced the ears of his listeners with that dark power which was given unto Jubal-Cain by His Infernal Majesty, far back in the history of the Craft Sinister. This is not some armchair accademic writing anthropological, sociological, or even scatalogical nonsense for those who seek to 'intellectually understand'. This text you hold in your hand has resulted from his own ongoing dedicated personal journey as a sorcerer. Michael Ford is truly an 'Unholy Roller', tireless in his spiritual and psychic rebellion, ever calling new souls to Darkness like the cunning serpent in the garden.

So many supposed 'Left Hand Pathers' turn out to be sex fearing introverts who cannot even look you in the eye when they talk to you, much less 'overlook' or cast any real spells. Michael Ford, however, is the life and soul of any party, and is (like me) constantly in the company of beautiful women as any true Magister should be. What more proof of power need there be? Genuine power is sexy. Crap magicians do not get laid. Towards the end of this volume, you will find rites and rituals of a decisively sexual nature. Enough said?

Nathaniel J. Harris
(author of WITCHA- A Book of Cunning, Mandrake of Oxford, and current Magister of The Red Circle, England).

Authors Note

Luciferian Witchcraft – The Book of The Serpent is a grimoire which presents, refines and explores a modern approach to the Adversary and Magick. In most recent times we have seen the shadow aspects of man and woman being pushed to the side, denied and hidden away. So-called Witches ignore their roots and foundations, placing credit in unbalanced perceptions of a Light and Fluffy world of blantant inconsistencies and little if any magical practice or power. Let me first state the intentions of the grimoire as it is here presented. The aim of the witch or sorcerer is to build a foundation of balance that is by material and spiritual aims. Do not ignore either as one cannot truly develop properly if consistency is not shown. Discipline applied with the triad of Will-Desire-Belief is essential in creating individual systems of sorcery. As a Luciferian, I decided early on based on my developing work that I could adhere to no single system, as my dreams guided me elsewhere. As I began practicing Magick based on what I perceived and appreciated from Aleister Crowley, Anton Szandor LaVey and Austin Osman Spare as well as the grimoire traditions, my own formulation of the Witches Sabbat as a living initiatory model could be founded. The Adversary or Satan speaks to us in dreams, it is made viable in our blood and our individual lives. The challenges of Luciferian Witchcraft are many; it is a path where the practitioner becomes like Cain who leaves an outsted or solitary life outside the natural order or the world around us. The witch becomes different from all others and holds pride in that fact. The path challenges, continually making the self stronger, better and a little more knowledgable – Magickal power comes firstly within and through the actual application of practice.

This book is meant as an introduction and complete grimoire into the Left Hand Path of Witchcraft, the gnosis of the fallen angels and the very powers of both darkness and light. Please take care, when you first step within and cast the circle of Cain, be prepared to change, willing to dive the depths of your own created hell and form the world according to your will.

There are no words which I may write here to describe what will come of your journey through Luciferian Witchcraft, only that you shall awaken something which you may or may not be prepared to deal with. I take no responsibility for the misuse of this grimoire; I treat it as a living Daemon itself and a part of a vital and living current. From Cainnite Sorcery and Cunning Craft, to Persian Yatuvidah and Ahrimanic Magick, to Sethanic Adversarial rites – the path grows and expands through darkness as a torch first seen in the dead of night.

I do consider this work to be a manifestation from the Abyss, the works contained herein are ushered forth from the coldest mountains of the Persian desert, the very callings Angra Mainyu heard on all four winds, from various cultures to our own western world we now live in.

The Sexual Sorcery of Adamu is a crowning of the Great Work itself, it is a vital expression of the current of Lucifer/Ahriman and his bride Az – Lilith. Luciferian

Witchcraft is meant to compliment the foundations of Austin Spare, Aleister Crowley and Anton Szandor Lavey, for without their imputs and creative genius where would we be?

Do not simply pick this book and misguide yourself into only the Darkness, yet by journey and the path of the Jagged Spine of Leviathan is the Light of Lucifer discovered, the Angelick Path is hidden yet reachable to the practitioners of this grimoire. This work lies beyond good and evil, as it offers a path to the heartblood of God itself. Drink deep.

Michael W. Ford
Walpurgisnacht, 2004

Chapter One

Diabolus

The Dragon within The Triangle of Darkness

An Exploration of The Adversary within Magick

Introduction

The very intent and purpose of this essay is to bring to light the roots of the Adversary in Magick from a historical and mythological standpoint. As a practitioner of Magick from a Satanic and Luciferian viewpoint, many often inquire on my sources and inspirations from which I form my sorcerous work. It was because of this need for a crystallization of the form and function of the praxis of sorcery that I began, to present a concise view of the practice of Left Hand Path magical practice from a Luciferian viewpoint.

The Dragon within the Triangle of Darkness is a reference made to the evocation circle as the meeting place of the Daemon and Man, but also the Luciferian rite of Azi Dahaka, the Sorcerer-Dragon King from Persian mythology called Zohak, an original Son of Satan. The Black Triangle by more common knowledge is related to the concentration of Will to Evoke the Daemon of Man and Woman, to uplift and envenom their spirit with the Adversarial Gnosis (an illustration is found in the Paitisha).

It must be considered appropriate that we explore the traits and descriptions of the Adversary or Opposer from a historical and mythological standpoint as well as from a practitioners' own viewpoint. This will present the very need of imagination within Magick itself, an essential ingredient to successful sorcery. While I am limited to encircling and crystallizing the finer points of the various forms of the Adversary, I by no means have presented the entire spectrum of the Opposer in praxis of the Path. It is however, desired to offer a collective comment and study on the exhaustive sources of Lucifer and Lilith in their various forms throughout time, with inclusion to modern magicians such as Charles Pace, Aleister Crowley, Nathaniel Harris, Anton Szandor LaVey, myself and others within the Fire of the Adversary. It must be understood that what is firstly considered the devil is only a cipher towards which lies within; that looks are deceiving and thus a test to the nature of both the Opposer and the sorcerer within the context of relation. By passing through the darkness is a light revealed brighter than all others.

Beginning with the foundations of the Adversary in the form of the Egyptian Set are we able to firstly understand that his force, while averse is indeed a necessary and significantly important to the balance of nature in both a "natural" and "supernatural" sense. The Shadow holds substance which bears the fruit of knowledge from the practitioner who is daring enough to taste it. Set is the original Opposer or Adversary, whose form captivated and later frightened those who dare stand against him.

The Persian foundation of averse practice is found in some "satanic" lore written by Zoroastrian priests. Ahriman, the Prince of Darkness in that regions lore is the initiator of the shadow – practice of sorcery, thus cannot be judged within a spectrum of the Zoroastrian religion – this gnosis is *"other"* and stands outside within practice. To make proper reference:

"And by their devotion to witchcraft (yatuk-dinoih) he seduces mankind into affection for himself and disaffection to Ohrmazd, so that they forsake the religion of Ohrmazd, and

practice that of Ahriman." – The Bundahishn, from *"On the Evil-doing of Ahriman and the Demons"*, Sacred Books of the East, Oxford University Press, 1897

Here lies the very foundation and cipher of the averse magical practice of Satanic and Luciferian Magick – it is *"other"* and exists outside any other religion, despite having inverse practices of traditional Right Hand Path religions. Sorcery is a religion, and its doctrines are written in the Will and Works of the Magician his or herself. The Evil Eye itself holds a precedence and importance within the practice of Yatuk-Dinoih, there are specific demons of the evil eye. This may be considered in the context of powerful consciousness, the Will in consistent motion; thus therein a part of the Adversary. Consider also the nature of the other demons, Savar, who is the leader and may be corresponded to the Hebrew Belial, the angel of Lucifer, as well as Taromat who is a demon of disobedience, thus Antinomian in purpose and practice.

In the context of the presented essay, the reader or practitioner of Magick may by this find the associations to the Grimoires of the Luciferian Path and how this form of practice manifests from mythological and historical sources.

Another question may be asked, what is the purpose of the Adversary? In my years of practice and development of the art on a personal level, I feel and understand the nature of the Adversary to be dual in its nature. Satan is a tester, who by illuminating the self of the initiate asks and poses many questions and challenges; it is up to the individual to answer these by action and balanced thought. The devil has always given the greatest gifts, however the cost is the test itself. You may be led into the darkness and feel as if you cannot go on – therein is a test, to rise up through that trouble in your life to emerge as a Bringer of Light – this is only a mere glimpse of the Fall under the shadows of the adversary. The nature of Lucifer is movement and motion; storms, chaos and order which arises from it. To drink the venom of this cup is cursing and blessing – be prepared to change and mutate into something greater; or seal your fate to a mindless death.

I. Set – the Egyptian God of Darkness

"I am Set, the Father of the Gods. I shall never come to an end."
-The Book of the Dead

The Egyptian mythology of Gods and powerful deities is perhaps History's most elaborate and evasive within the conception of their opposing powers. The Egyptian God of Chaos and Storms, Set, called also Sutekh, Set-heh or Seth-an was revered in the 3rd Millennia B.C. and forward, originally as a positive force of movement and foreign lands. It was later on that Set became a form of the Opposer, with Red being a sacred color and his minions being actual demons that tested or destroyed others. Set was commonly perceived as a God of War, who taught some Pharaohs the art of shooting the bow and arrow, etc. The Egyptian Book of the Dead presents Set as the Lord of the Northern Sky, who is over storms, cold weather and darkness. Set was perhaps the most significant Egyptian God in that he alone was the God of Mystery and the Unknown, both the shadow and fire. As being a Patron of the Deserts, Seth was also revered as a Deity over the Scorching Heat of the desert sands. This concept continued on in the Persian Ahriman and the Islamic Shaitan, which shall be discussed in further detail later on in this treatise.

"Verily, the Soul of Set, which is greater than all the gods, hath departed" - From the Papyrus of Ani

Set was known as a God of unrest who continually fought with Horus, his brother and was the antagonist and murderer of Osiris, a God of Stasis. Set also protected Ra on his journeys through the Underworld, and was able to master the chaotic force of Apep, a Serpent of Darkness. Set is known in the Book of the Dead as having legions of devils, known as Seba as well as Smaiu, who obey his commands. It seems also that there were a group of rebels who were of Set and were defeated early on. Set is mentioned in the Egyptian Book of the Dead as having the skin of a Bull. In the eleventh section of the Tuat called "Reenqerrtaptkhatu", Set is in the form of a serpent and called "Set-heh" meaning "The Eternal Set".

"When Osiris came again, Typhon plotted with seventy-two comrades, and with Aso, the queen of Ethiopia, to slay him"-The Egyptian Book of the Dead, E.A. Wallis Budge

Set is primarily regarded the same as the Greek Typhon, a serpent like Daemon-God who is a Patron Spirit of Sorcery and Magick. Plutarch explained that in Egyptian astronomy Seth or Typhon was connected to the Solar World, while Osiris was associated with the Moon. The Sun was considered very hostile as it dried up and made lands inhabitable, while the Moon nourished and brought moisture. Plutarch writes the Seth means *"Compelling and Overmastering"*, being a powerful force of chaos and order. Typhon was collectively later known and associated to the Earth's shadow, which they bring into the lunar cycle and the eclipse. In such an aspect, Seth is highly significant to the balance of chaos and order, as he creates situations for both to occur.
Set and Horus indeed have a close connection as not only brothers but also deific opposites. It is suggested by E.A. Wallis Budge that Horus means something similar to

"He who is above" and Set therefore "He who is below", thus holding a significance to "As Above, So Below" and the Baphomet idol long regarded as a form of hidden knowledge. Considering Set's name had similar hieroglyphic connections to stone, it can be suggested further that this god was a personification of the lands of death, stony land and the desert wastes. Set's direction was also often consider South as well, and his opposing side of the North. In later times, as previously mentioned, Ahriman has been long associated with not only the North but also the South, making reference to his powers over both scorching heat and cold. The Head of Ramses II has been shown being dually crowned by both Set and Horus – indicating Power and Knowledge. One reference of which Set makes comment is in the crowning "I will give thee all life, and strength and health", thus although considered often a Devil and a most feared God, this power could be used in a positive aspect as well.

Set was also friendly to the Shades of the Dead as well, Set was said to purify and Horus strengthen. The backbone of the dead was considered the backbone of Set. Another title of Set is SMAI, the Egyptian name associated with Set as the archfiend and devil.
It was as the Adversary becoming the mastering force over Apep, thus slowly Apep became a form of Set and vise versa. The demonic beasts, serpents and such located and dwelling deep in the waters were considered of Set and therefore part of his essence. Similarly anything with Red was often considered to be of Set, as Red was the color commonly associated with Fire and Aggression.

Apep and his/its brood have been referred to as *"Children of Rebellion"*[1] and were opponents to the Sun God. While Set has been considered for being a beneficial God, his darker side lays foundations of power and awe, from which lived on even beyond his name being denounced and demonized. The names of the form of Set as Apep are indeed many, some of which are Saatet-ta (Darkener of the Earth), Hau-hra (Backward Face), Tutu (Doubly Evil One), Hemhemti (Devourer), all of which describe the Storm Demon who is called also Kharebutu the Fourfold Fiend. In the gnosis of Set who overcame the serpent for Apep to become a part of this being presents a powerful gnosis for the aspiring sorcerer. One may refer to the concept of Predatory Spiritualism, absorbing the prey and taking from it the most valid or a subjective aspect of its being. Thus by Set killing Apep, essentially this serpent becomes an aspect of Set itself; albeit a mastered aspect to be used when Set chooses.

Apep also bore the name of Rerek, a monster serpent form of Set who had many helpers being serpents, noxious creatures and demons. It is further connected that Thoth was said to have gotten the knife to slay the Bull from Set, thus making parallel the name of Smain with Set, being violence.

One specific dwelling place of Set was called "Set Amentet"[2] which is the "Mountain of the Underworld", which is a cemetery in the desert on the west banks of the Nile.
Set is also closely connected with a former Death-God called Seker, who was later merged with Osiris and became something rather different in nature. In the Tuat, Seker

[1] Budge, E.A. Wallis, the Gods of the Egyptians Volume 1
[2] Compare with the Persian Arezura, the Mountain in the North from which 'hell' is commonly located.

resided within a kingdom called Ra-Stau, from which he sat upon a Throne in Majesty, having numerous legions of winged serpents, devils called Seba and other monsters which devoured various shades of the dead who were sent there. It is written in the Book of the Dead that Seker's Throne is pyramidal in form, filled with darkness. He appears commonly in the Tuat as a mummified man but has a hawk's head and a pair of wings, which come forth from the back of a two headed serpent. The symbolism of the Hawk and the Twin Serpents are later presented in the Persian descriptions of the Adversary, firstly a symbol of Ahriman was a Hawk attacking a sparrow and the Twin Serpents appearing from an Ahrimanic Kiss on the Shoulders of the King Zohak, who later became Azi Dahaka, the Storm Demon. While these similarities cannot be assumed to be directly related, they are by all instances interesting.

The constellation of the Bull or Bull's Thigh is related to Set. Often called "Bull of double brilliance", this is perhaps the brightest constellation around the North celestial pole otherwise known as the Great Bear or Little Dipper. The mummified hawk that is called the "Lord of the South" is connected with Set in this aspect. This is the Seker God who early on was considered close to Set before his transformation in accordance with Osiris. The home of Set is Khepesh, the constellation.

Set was considered the eighth child of the Gods of Annu, and was of Nuit. As the God of Darkness and Storms he was alone the one who could withstand the stare of the serpent Apep, thus controlling the storm demon and later it becoming a part of Sethan himself. Set as being not only the Lord of the South, he later was associated with the North, becoming the Lord of the Northern Sky in the Egyptian Book of the Dead. His primary associations were hostility, war and storms. Thus Set may be viewed as a Deific Force of Motion and opposition. Eight is recent years has been a number significant to Chaos, being the 8 – pointed chaos star and the Algol sigil, the Sabbatic Star etc.

"The combat which took place on the day when Horus fought with Seth, during which Seth threw filth in the face of Horus, and Horus crushed the genitals of Seth .... This storm was the raging of Ra at the thunder-cloud which [Seth] sent forth against the Right Eye of Ra (the Sun). Thoth removed the thunder-cloud from the Eye of Ra, and brought back the Eye living, healthy, sound, and with no defect in it to its owner." - From the Papyrus of Ani

Here we see that Set was a sorcerer god, throwing "filth" and then thunder clouds, he controlled the elements of earth and the air. Set although being injured, arose in might again after the battle, and later reached into obscurity to appear again in other cults outside of Egypt under different names, all the while possessing the essence of which he created – the adversary.

"Set opened the paths of the Two Eyes (the Sun and the Moon)"- From the Papyrus of Ani

The formula mentioned in the Book of the Dead refers to a magical formula which held associations to Set's hostility against Horus, but also their connection therein. Within the

Luciferian Witch Cults Set represents the Magician which beheld and brought forth the possibilities within, by the unknown and darkened places does he grow strong and reside.

The opposing God of Horus – Set are early manifestations of the adversary; that is to say Horus represents Day or the purity of fire, while Set represents night and strengthening the self, and also the opposite which Set purifies and Horus strengthens.

Set is also considered in the Egyptian Book of the Dead, to be the greatest of all the gods, as it is Sethan who has mastered the dragon of chaos Apep and it now serves him and became part of his essence.

Sethan as he is often called is considered the most ancient yet distinctly clear form of the Opposer and Adversary. Charles Pace (born 1920 date of death currently unknown), the obscure Luciferian called himself a Satanist or a Setanist, and was a Priest of Set and Anubis in a well known Witchcraft Coven in London under Gerald Gardner, a former student of Aleister Crowley. Charles Pace was known as Hamar'at and was a mortician by trade. His primary expression was art in which he painted mostly Egyptian styled images, as can been seen in the rare manuscript "The Book of Tahuti"[3], in which Pace presents a powerful alternate study and design of the tarot. Charles Pace painted murals in Boleskine House, Crowley's former residence where the Abramelin Workings were conducted and the Goetia was edited. In the late 60's. Anton LaVey, the founder of the Church of Satan was a long correspondent with Pace, who both shared similar ideas in certain areas.

It is suggested by Charles Pace in "The Book of Tahuti"[4] that Anubis was the bastard son of Sethan and Aset (Isis). It is obvious that Pace considered himself a *"messanger"* rather than an author of any system. This is noted by his attribution of Hamar'at (magical name) as associated with the Page card in the Tarot. Set's son Anpu (Anubis) in the system arranged by Pace presents him as a Magician and the Opener of the Ways. Pace also wrote in "Necrominion" a description of a so-called elaborate High Sex Magick ritual known as Ankh Ka. Judging from the Triple Hermetic Circle of Hamar'at the focus was spiraling energy through the self with the forces of the Godforms, thus their Masks signify deific power assumed by him or her who wore the mask.

Austin Osman Spare[5] was an artist who captured images of Set in sigillic forms in various publications. Spare illustrated and practiced a form of sorcery which holds a strong foundation to modern Luciferian practice, specifically with the Witches Sabbat and other avenues of magical practice.

"Existing as Dual, they are identical in desire, by their duality there is no control, for will and belief are ever at variance, and each would shape the other to its ends, in the

---

[3] The Cover art features a black inverted pentagram, a upward pointing pentagram and is worded as "The Great Work 666", in addition the book is dedicated to "my friend Austin Ozman Spare".
[4] Unpublished manuscript by Pace. The title page reads "The Great Work 666" and is a collection of impressive Tarot paintings and Egyptian attributions.
[5] 1888 - 1956

issue neither winds as the joy is a covert of sorrow. Let him unite them" –The Book of Pleasure, Austin Osman Spare

In Spare's grimoire, The Book of Pleasure, he describes an almost instinctual Luciferian concept of obtaining desired results through the fall into darkness (i.e Death Posture). The Death Posture is a formula in which the sorcerer enters a state of exhaustion and essentially blacks out and forgets the meaning of his rite. By doing this, he falls into unconsciousness or delirium from which the concept of "I" does not exist. This is the Sethian test; from challenging the essence of yourself does your ability to become something better manifest into something greater. Observe the illustration by Aos entitled "The Death Posture", here the skull masked individual ascends from the sigil itself, on the very left hailed by Set who stands upon the Alpha and Omega, called also AZOTH and AZOTHOZ[6], a dualistic sigillic formula of the Adversary. Here Set is the Lord of Sorcery, by his nature of opposition does the self grow stronger through the rebellion of stasis and the fall into darkness – the face becomes a skull through Self-Love. Modern Sorcery and Magick is very much driven by the Gnosis of Set, while hidden, one who has the eyes to recognize it obtains the Luciferian and Sethian potential.

The Witch Cult in the 1960's was a growing scene of exploring Hermetic occultists who have not yet thrown the drape of dullness which Wicca later became. Charles Pace wrote to Anton LaVey in 1974 about Gardner and Wicca, mentioning that Wiccan is a Saxon word which means "Enlightened ones" and not "Wise Ones", referring to those who were enlightened from Paganism to Christianity. Pace suggested that he "gave" the word Wicca along with his associates to Gardner, apparently as a joke. Gerald Gardner did not get the joke. Obviously, Charles Pace was meaning that light heartened as he was a High Priest in a Coven under the Wiccan and Gardner concepts, even though he had a nasty falling out when them in the mid 70's. In "Necrominion, the Book of Shades" it is reportable that his teachings of the Sethanic Cult of Masks were focused on self-transformation and Luciferian concepts.

Alexander Sanders, an associate of Charles Pace, made mythological reference to Set and Black Witchcraft in his lecture "The Magick Circle of the Wicca":

"Truth is the monster of intellect, that which lies deep in the darker side of the subconscious, the knowledge of when man crawled on his stomach through the abysmal depths of a primeval swamp.." – The Alex Sander Lectures.

In this essay, Sanders recognizes the significance of Black Witchcraft and how it develops the self – save for the dangers of self-destruction.

"Behold me, mortal, for I am thy God, the true image of thyself, and the very essence of life, yet within me lieth a magnitude greater than you can ever behold without. For I am both macrocosm and microcosm; only your petty vanity could decree otherwise. Worship me, and I shall give you the stars. Reject me, and I shall give the depths of the Abyss, for I lie within your own being" – From the Book of Hermes from the Alex Sanders lectures

---

[6] Azothoz, a Grimoire of the Adversary by Michael W. Ford, Succubus Publishing

In the Manuscript of "The Book of Tahuti" by Charles Pace, he writes that Hermes was Anubis who is Death – Hermanubis or Heru-em-Anpu, who is the Son of Set. It is said that Anubis is very similar to the Grecian Hecate, as they are deific forces over both the Celestial and Infernal realms and like dogs, were able to see in the night.

As Alexander Sanders wrote, the Inverted Triangle was the symbol of the Left Hand Path:

"After the Great Flood, the ancient Egyptians used these triangles to represent a Triad of Deities. The people of Neph-Kam, the Black Lands of Lower Egypt used the Triangle of Darkness, led by Sethan and supported by Anubis and Sekhmet." – Alex Sanders Lectures

Magick and Sorcery within Egyptian cults survived long beyond the death of that culture. Consider the Graeco-Roman period, when wax figures were implemented as focus points for various magical ceremonies. Many used wax figures as performing love spells, but were also used in cursing as well. As Set was the most powerful of the Gods and equally a God of Magick and Infernal Sorcery, he is a force which strengthens by the desire of force. There is an example of a spell which implements infernal spirits and wax figures to obtain the love of a woman[7] and was done through incantations of the infernal spirits. As witchcraft survived in medieval times it was said that through the "Divell" the witches were able to "effectuate by the power of their master"[8].

"I invoke thee who art in the void air, terrible, invisible, almighty God of Gods, dealing destruction and making desolate, O thou that Hatest…I invoke thee, Typhon-Set, I perform the ceremonies of divination, for I invoke thee by the powerful name in which thou canst not refuse to hear: Io Erbeth, Io Pakerbeth, Io Bolkhoseth, Io Pathathnax, Io Soro, Io Neboutosoualeth, Aktiophi, Ereskhigal, Neboposaleth, Abermenthoou, Lerthexanax, Aemina.." – The Leyden Papyrus, Editied by F. Griffith & Herb Thompson

As Set was considered to be friendly unto the Shades of the Dead, there is perhaps a closer connection between him and his illegitimate son Anpu (Anubis) than what can be commonly realized. The belief in the spirits of the dead and the survival of the psyche after physical death was a foundation of the Magic of ancient Egypt. In accordance with the lore, Man consisted of a physical body, a double, a shadow, a soul, a heart etc. The Khu itself was the spirit of the man but the Ka was considered to be the spiritual body which took nourishment from the offerings at the funeral ceremonies. The dead and such were honored among the Egyptians, who regularly brought food and drinks to appease the Khu into staying in its tomb.

Aleister Crowley took a strong step in his presentation and revival of Magick concerning Set. Crowley wrote in "The Book of Thoth" that Saturn is indeed Set, the Lord of the Egyptian Deserts, darkness and high places. Crowley makes similar connections between Shaitan and Satan, all being forms of Set. Incidentally, The Master Therion draws

[7] Egyptian Magic, E.A. Wallis Budge
[8] Demonologie, In forme of one Dialogue, London 1603 found in Egyptian Magic, E.A. Budge

connections between Shabbathai, the "Sphere of Saturn" being the Witches Sabbat[9]. Here we find the manifestation of the Adversary in a universal and initiatory role.

The modern magician and sorcerer must be willing to focus on the beneficial and useful aspects of Sethian Magick within a 'now' type of context, in other words utilize the Will to invigorate and empower the rituals of Sethan, which by you Set is made great within.

[9] The Book of Thoth, Aleister Crowley

II. Ahriman
The Persian Devil and the Whore of Darkness

"Pondering on the end, Zurvan delivered to Ahriman an implement (fashioned) from the very substance of darkness, mingled with the power of Zurvan, as it were a treaty, resembling coal, black and ashen. And as he handed to him he said: "By means of these weapons, Az (Concupiscence) will devour that which is thine, and she herself shall starve, if at the end of nine thousand years thou hast not accomplished that which thou didst threaten – to demolish the pact, to demolish time." - From the Zatsparam, from The Dawn and Twilight of Zoroastrianism R.C. Zaehner

Ahriman is within the ancient Persian lands and lore the devil incarnate. Known also as Arimanius and Angra Mainyu, this sorcerous daemon was suggested by texts associated with Zurvan to be the first born of the God Zurvan, who is infinite time and space. His brother, Ahura Mazda is the Christ like figure or opposite God who fought against Ahriman for control of the world; it is this very balance which is kept in continual motion by the Daeva – Lord of Darkness. The word Daeva is actually Demon, announcing a path and spiritual aversion to the principles the Zoroastrians held in honor. Some myths mention that Ahriman first saw the light across the void and so lusted for it, thus igniting the great wars between his children – the Daevas (demons) and Druj (the word being associated with lie, also Dragon). Ahriman was initially defeated and cast down into the darkness of the void, unconscious for 3,000 years.

The first demons said to be created by Ahriman were Mitokht ("falsehood") and Akoman ("evil mind"). Shortly after Ahriman created (according to the Bundahishn) Andar, Savar, Nakahed, Tairev and Zairik. Many of the demons are featured in the Yatuk Dinoih, and formulas for creation and evocation are given.

Ahriman created or had fallen with Seven Archdemons who served his will. They were in a prototypical way, the Dragon of Seven Heads. These Daevas were listed as the following: Aeshma, Akoman, Nanghaithya, Tawrich, Savar, Andar and Zarich.

The Daevas were authored or created by Ahriman as in suggestion of the Zurvan myth. These are so-called evil spirits who chose the intellect and individual Will as opposed to servitude and conformity. Aeshma is the original form of Asmodeus, a Daeva of Ahriman. This demon is known as the One of the "Wounding Spear" and was a patron of war and strife. Asmodeus along with Savar, who is called the "Leader of Devs", both are the controllers under Ahriman of the Dregvants, who are known as 'storm fiends'. Here we once again find reference to the Adversary through sorcerous will controlling storms and the more unfriendly aspects of nature. Andar according to Luciferian lore is a demon of the Black Flame, or isolate consciousness. Zairich is a poisoning or testing demon, all of which are featured with invocations in the Paitisha and Yatuk Dinoih. Herein beyond the Zoroastrian religion, acting outside of any connections with it, the sorcerer may choose this gnosis or current of the adversary – in that he or she may seek the dangerous elements to strengthen their own Will and separate themselves from those around them. In this act of Antinomian rebellion, the sorcerer becomes a Daeva or Druj.

The Daeva known as Akoman or Aka Manah is the "Evil Mind", a personified demon of intellect which conspires against the Vohu Manah or "Good Mind". Herein presents a cipher to the reader; that they very essence of the so-called Satanic or Luciferian path known also as the Left Hand Path is brought to the forefront – to the simple description of what one would advance themselves on this path for.

R.C. Zaehner presented an interesting study of the words Menok and Geteh in The Dawn and Twilight of the Zoroastrians which shed light on the nature of Ahriman and that very averse path. The pahalavi terms for 'material' and 'spiritual' are indeed Menok and Geteh. It is suggested by Zaehner that they are from the Avestan words mainyu and geathya, mainyu meaning our own Mind and Gaethya meaning 'to live' – thus from the latin roots as mens and mind. The spiritual or mind cannot be viable to any certainty in the physical realm beyond its Will to shape its world around it, therefore the Mind contains both elements of Darkness and Light. Ahriman himself was born of Light but yet chose darkness.

In the Zurvanite myth Ahriman first perceived his own being and chose to exit the womb before his brother, who was born of light. Ahriman was called dark and stinking by his father Zurvan, who by casting aside his first born, allowed Ahriman to go forth from the heavenly realm to choose his own devices within the physical and spiritual world. Ahriman has free Will to choose his own path, to become in both planes of existence based on that desire. The writer Eznik[10] presented a Zoroastrian statement of Ahriman:

"It is not the case that I am unable to do anything good myself, but that I do not wish it; and to make this thing certain, I have produced the Peacock."

Offerings to Ahriman (Arimanius) were made by Magi who sought to make beneficial sacrifices to darkness. According to Plutarch[11] magicians would ground up in a mortar a rare herb called Omomi while invoking Hades and Darkness, the very essence of the Adversary. They would then mix the blood of a wolf with the ground up herb and toss it in an area where the sun did not reach. This was conducted as a means of appeasing darkness, as report ably the Magi would also perform white light rituals to Ohrmazd as well. A modern form of practice of 'summoning' darkness is practiced by certain Luciferian Covens in the United States, instead of wolf blood various herbs and apple cider is used in replacement, following along the same form of sacrifice by an offering into an area where the suns' rays never touch.

"The Scythians in the plains of Northern Asia, the most dangerous neighbors of Persia, worshipped their highest deity under the symbol of a serpent, and it was natural that the snake Afrasiâb, the god of the enemy, became identified with the archfiend Ahriman." – The History of the Devil by Dr. Paul Carus

---

[10] Against Heresies by Eznik
[11] Isis and Osiris

Ahriman is considered a voice of chaos, an ordered abyss-cloaked demon god which is both angelic (pre fall) and demonic (post fall), he holds all the attributes of the sorcerous Great Work. The forms of Ahriman change, his draconian essence still remains. Here it is further understood that Ahriman is a name for the very force which brings us birth and death, within this very initiatory current is the means of immortality, via the expanded and crystallized mind.

"And I saw three unclean spirits like frogs come out of the mouth of the dragon, and out of the mouth of the beast, and out of the mouth of the false prophet. For they are the spirits of devils, working miracles, which go forth unto the kings of the earth and of the whole world, to gather them to the battle of that great day of God Almighty." – Revelation 16:13-14

Ahriman appeared in the Zoroastrian legends in numerous forms. His astral body was considered that of a frog, toad, or crab, often a lizard or serpent as well. The legend of Zohak the King proves of significant interest concerning Magical transformation, Zohak was later known as Azi Dahaka, the Demon of Three Faces. Zohak was said to have descended from a king called Mardas and Tazak, who dwelled originally in Tazikan or Arabia. It was according to lore that Zohak lived as a king for a period of time of 1,000 years. As written in the Denkard:

"This, too, is declared in the good religion that the source of demons (Ahriman) had arrayed with deceits Zohak, the descendant of Taj, the diminisher of creations; hence the laws of Zohak deteriorated his own nature, worked for the immoral and blemished (Ahriman), and caused destruction by Tyranny and apostasy, so that the habits of men were corrupted, the world distressed, and there was increase of morality among the creatures."-The Denkard[12]

It is suggested also by the Arabs that this king's name was Zohak, while the Mogs suggested that he was Bivarasp, whom of which existed in the time of Noah, was most feared for his murdering of many kings. Zohak was the son of Vadhak, who was the first adulterer. While being called a "wicked Afrasiab", Zohak was a Sikandar who was made immortal by Ahriman through a pact. Ahriman appeared in the Legend of Zohak[13] first visited Zohak, the son of King Mirtas, disguised as a Noble visiting. His words were empowering, as one who sought to become something other:

"If thou wilt listen to me, and enter into a covenant, I will raise thy head above the Sun"

Thus the prince listened to Ahriman. He later took the Throne and became king. Ahriman taught him the arts of magic and Zohak slowly became what the just called a tyrant king. It was soon after that Ahriman appeared to the King as a youth who was a cook. He was employed to prepare dishes for the King, and instead of herbs and various foods he prepared him the flesh of animals, which made the King strong and as fierce as a Lion.

---

[12] Digital Edition edited by Joseph Peterson.

[13] Firdawsi, The Epic of Kings, Hero Tales of Ancient Persia translated by Helen Zimmerman.

The king had the youth brought before him and asked one favor that he wished. The youth requested that he may kiss the king's shoulders. He agreed and then the youth kissed both shoulders. When he had done so the earth below opened up and swallowed the cook. Two black and venomous serpents arose from the wounds and slowly became one with Zohak – even when the serpents were cut the later came forth again. Ahriman came unto Zohak disguised as a learned elder and suggested that they feed the brains of men to the serpents. Zohak was also considered an early mythological king who had first glorified Witchcraft to the people, and suggested the religion he wrote for the Hebrews. Azhi Dahaka, as he became, was a feared demonic sorcerer, one whose pact with the devil was said to have lengthened his life and transformed him into a immortal Daeva or Demon, even later mythological reference that dragons and other serpents rise from his body. This can be connected by the libation vase which was of Gudea, dated from 2350 B.C. which was found at Telloh. This vase contains an image of two snakes entwined around a staff, representing magical power.

"And the beast which I saw was like unto a leopard, and his feet were as the feet of a bear, and his mouth as the mouth of a lion: and the dragon gave him his power, and his seat, and great authority." - Revelation 13:2

Slowly Zohak became a demon, a Dragon King whose companions were the Druj and other demons of Ahriman. In later lore Zohak became the Storm Fiend, Azi Dahaka, who is Ahriman's most powerful Daeva. The initiatory focus and lore of Zohak is presented in the Paitisha[14] as a force to be invoked and controlled within – the transformation mirrored through the ritualistic focus of the serpent within the mind and body. Essentially in Zoroastrian lore, Zohak or Azi Dahaka is the second in command of Ahriman's children, he is for a lack of a better term considered a prototype for an Antichrist in that he expands the opposite gnosis against Zoroaster.

"The Jewish scriptures were first composed by him (I.e. Zohak), and deposited in the fortress of Jerusalem. And through Zohak men adhered unto the Jewish high-priest Abraham, and through Abraham they adhered unto Moses, whom the Jews accepted as their prophet and messengers of faith, and unto whom they ascribe the salvation of sins committed, and regarded his acquirements as being necessary for the final propagation of their faith. Thus Zohak cherished demoniac deceptions to harm his people." –The Denkard

Here we read that Zohak, during his long life span, was considered the one who propagated early Jewish scriptures as a means of satanic influence among his people. No doubt many of the Arabs and surviving Zoroastrians considered the Jewish faith to be a joke propagated by Ahriman. There were "ten precepts" of the priest Zohak who was considered a part of the Hebrew religion, while the actual intent of these so-called precepts of Zohak are not acknowledged, the Zoroastrians considered him very dangerous even after his long 1,000 year reign. The ten precepts suggest that Zohak called their God an injurer of the universe, recommended Daeva worship and the use of Idols in ritual

[14] The Book of the Serpent, Draconian and Persian Sorcery by Michael W. Ford, Succubus Publishing.

practice, that people should be selfish and to sacrifice before shrines. The reference to Zohak's physical death, before the full transformation into Azi Dahaka (Fiendish Snake):

"Fairdoon killed the malignant and sinful Zohak of three faces (i.e. liar), of three heads (i.e. violent and obstinate), of six eyes (i.e. greedy) of thousands of evil designs, possessed of the great evil powers of the Dev and the Druj." – Denkard

Another figure in Zoroastrian infamy is the sorcerer Ahktya or Akht. The word Akht itself means "filth", and the word Akha which means "evil" and "bad". The other name which was connected with Akhtya was "Kabed-us-Spae" and "Akht-Jadu". This obscure figure was said to be a powerful sorcerer who was a manifestation of the power of the Daevas, he could astrally project into Hell and communicate with Ahriman, and was considered a Nomadic demon.

"*It is owing to the passions of wolves and Khrafastras that men are like Devs; and Hesham, the invisible power of the perverted path, prevailing in them, they become the source of darkness unconnected with light, of evil intelligence unconnected with wisdom, and of evil unmixed with good"* Denkard Book 3

Akhtya was said in the Denkard to have enunciated ten specific points on the practice of the Yatuk Dinoih or witchcraft. To be mentioned in the Denkard as Enunciating admonitions meant that he had presented a systematic methodology of practice concerning their aspects of Sorcerous practice, considered by the Zoroastrians as evil or satanic. It seems clear just as Zohak that Akht-Jadu operated outside the religious structure of Zoroastrianism, thus their ideals of magical practice were not specifically evil or wrong. They could also lay in the idea of predilection based on their methods of self-transformation through their own religious and socio-daemonic structures of becoming. To observe the view the Zoroastrians had concerning Akht, let us look at the context of which it was written:

"*One, against the monition of the Holy Zartosht, that no injury should be inflicted by anybody on any person, - the dark-conscienced (black-hearted), sorcerous and vicious Akht, on account of his sorcerous practices and his enmity towards men, proclaimed that no good should be done to any person, but that every person should be rendered capable of doing evil (to others)"*[15]

Here we are able to discover the antinomian nature of Akht that this individual did not seek to align his psyche with the Order perceived through the religious doctrine of Zoroastrians, he found comfort and power within a perhaps darker path. It could not be conceivable that Akht suggest no good should be done to men, as this would almost certify an extreme from which few would be able to live in accordance to.

"The evil-hearted, vicious sorcerer Akht proclaimed enmity to the divine beings, affection to the demons, the abandonment of the adoration of the divine beings, and the practice of every maimer of demon-worship." – Denkard

[15] Denkard the Acts of Religion, Book 3 103-110.

Here is presented with the essence of what Akhtya practiced and suggested – that he despised the doctrine of that path, rather than being the inverse by nature of Zoroastrianism. By this it can be suggested that Akhtya and the Yatus practiced with some areas of inverse Zoroastrian ritual, they as a whole were operating within their own understood doctrines of magical practice. This can be seen in the later Yezidis, who operated according to their own Antinomian initiatory structure.

The religion of evil according to old faith is often hidden, operating within social structures while seeking their own methods of self-knowledge and wisdom. Rather than allowing their conscious to be aligned with the selfless thinking of the Right Hand Path, or monotheistic duty, the Yatus through their own process of antinomian self-liberation chose alternative archetypes to cultivate and control the dark forces of the subconscious.

Ahriman, who is also called by the Avestan word Ganamino, is the religion of sorcery, of separating the self from the natural order of Spenamino, which is Spenta Mainyu.

"The evil minded Ganamino is the source of the evil intellect the evil-minded Ganamino hopes to influence the creation of God..... Such a man exercises a miserable control over his desires owing to his evil intellect and the force of the evil invisible power in him he develops and perfects himself in sin." - Denkard

This presents a foundation of the self which is indeed different from the path of the Good Mind, or the Mind of Stasis. Ganamino is essentially motion; movement through Will, the Will of God was misunderstood by Right Hand Path religions as merely being good, loving, light and kind. Rather the God they so worshipped in nature –outside of themselves- is that which indeed causes destruction and rebirth, thus a balanced aspect of both dark and light.

"The religion of priests, who guided by their evil intellect devoid of wisdom, act among men as the servents of God, is only in appearance the wise religion of God. This through the evil intellect depopulates the world, ruins, and destroys mankind. And such a priest is as it were the agent of the evil-minded Ahriman to do his work among men and harms mankind and the world. Such a religion, owing to the evil intellect, renders mankind miserable and makes them suffer in pain in both the worlds." – Denkard

Here we see that the Left Hand Path or that of Akoman the Evil Mind represents a path of power from which the self is beholden of. That the religion of sorcery is indeed painful, it is by this strife and stimulation within the self that makes us strong and able to work our will, to discover our own True Will (The AKOMAN or Holy Guardian Angel) and to manifest our desires. It is difficult and often troublesome, however the beauty and strength which arises in the mind and flesh is reward within itself. Please observe the original strife of Ahriman or Satan – he suffered and fell into the darkness, by this pain he transformed and made the world around him bend to his will. Rather than the religion of destroying the mind and feeding it to the God of the Right Hand Path, the path of Satan or Lucifer/Ahriman gives back to the self; and all responsibility falls in the initiates lap; they are in control of their own destiny – be it success or failure, rather than bending knee and trusting in an exterior force. If you cannot trust and be strong within yourself first, how could one ever hope to have the stability to be a decent individual with honor?

Ahriman indeed opens the path towards the subconscious, which can be called Asare-Tariki, Darkness and the powers of the Left. As religious aggressors attest that such a religion of sorcery depopulates, history merely offers a balanced statistic of facts – more murders and destruction were caused by monotheistic religions of "God" and "Christ" than any so – called Satanic beliefs. If you consider the laws of nature, the law of the strong depopulation, as with some overgrowth of animals, is merely a welcoming to the Natural Order of Selection – which death comes to the weak.

Akhtya, who is a propagator of some antinomian religious aspects of Ahriman, appears in another tale in a Pahlavi tale called Yavisht I Friyan[16]. In this tale Akht, who is a powerful sorcerer, travels to a city of Enigma-expounders with an army of seven myriads. He shouted to all that he would make that city a beaten track for Elephants, and would test and destroy the righteous who claims to have superior knowledge. By the use of the magical formula called a Staota, which is a form of sound vibrations used in the form of words, which held a "spring", he would tear apart those who could not answer or survive the Staota. None could withstand Akht, save for a young religious man called Yavisht i Friyan. The youth was invited to the residence of Akht, but discovering that Akht had dead matter (bones, rot hair or nails) under his pillows and carpets, he could not enter until Akht had them removed. As the legend moves forward Yavisht withstood each Staota and then used the Staota to attack Akht. He took time to "through sorcery, rushed into hell" and communicated with Ahriman who told him to accept his fate as it were. Akht was said to have been defeated by Yavisht and destroyed in physical form.

The Manichaean myths of creation were rich in their lore of the underworld. According to Mary Boyce[17] who wrote on the Manichaean myths, Hell was divided into five kingdoms. In details on the underworld she also wrote:

"Hell is divided into five kingdoms, each of the substance of one of the five dark elements. Thse are sometimes given the same names as the corresponding light elements (i.e. Standing air also for Dark Air) or sometimes the exact opposite (i.e. Darkness for Light)....the Five infernal kingdoms are inhabited by five kinds of devils, two-legged, four-legged, winged, swimmings and crawling. Each kind is divided into two sexes, and lives in perpetual lust and strife. The Devil, or Prince of Darkness, king over all, combines in himself features of all five species of devil, namely demon, lion, eagle fish and dragon."

Here we find a significant and organizational pattern of demon lore, with as much attention on the adversary as with the God of Light. As Ahriman has combined himself with each of the demons, he carries the attributes to relate to different forms and techniques of being. He understands flight and how such demons see in such a capacity,

[16] Translated by E.W. West, from Haug and West, the Book of Arda Viraf, Bombay, London 1972, made into a digital edition courtesy of Joseph Peterson.

[17] A Reader in Manichaean Middle Persian and Parthian Tehran 1975

as a fish to swimming and moving much differently and as a dragon, a serpent which is both cunning and instinctually in tune with its surroundings. It seems that the category of demon simply represents any combination of animal or beast, similar to the plethora of demonic imagery from the earliest times of man.

Manichaean belief, as it developed from the Dualistic religion of Zoroastrianism, views the creation myth of mankind slightly different from its Zoroastrian counterparts. In Manichaean concepts Adam was engendered by Satan with the traits of desire, cupidity and those concepts which religions always have difficulty with. Satan gave unto Adam the elements of Light which he was said to have stolen, so that he may embody that art in mankind. It was indeed Satan who fathered Cain with Eve, in Luciferian lore as with Az or Lilith possessing Eve while in sexual congress.

The most important figure which not only inspired Ahriman, but empowered him was the whore Jeh or Az. In Manichaean religious lore, Az is considered the Great Whore who played a very important role to her mate, Ahriman. In Manichaean traditions Az was a spirit which made he home in the caves and dark places of the earth, as well as Hell. Az was considered to have taught demons and arch-fiends how to copulate and act in lewd ways, later teaching the Fallen Angels how to excite themselves and others sexually. Az used her sorceries to produce Dragon-children and to then create other demons and daughters who were of her own blood. Az was known to have devoured her children and their children, then create more to later devour them as well.

"And he kissed Jeh upon the head, and the pollution which they call menstruation became apparent in Jeh" – The Bundahishn, translated by E. W. West
Az (also known as Jeh) as the demon of death, called Concupiscence, is considered in many points to be the instinctual side of man. R.C. Zaehner describes Az has having a three – fold nature, consisting of eating, sexual desire and yearning for whatever she comes across by her senses. The nature of Az is also considered to be ***"disorderly motion"***[18] which makes reference to counter clockwise movement, chaos and antinomianism. Zaehner writes that:

"The demon Az is a Buddhist rather than a Zoroastrian idea; there is no trace of it in the Avesta. In Buddhism, on the other hand, the root cause of the chain of conditioned existence is avidya, 'ignorance', and its principle manifestation is trshna, 'thirst', which means the desire for continued existence."

Furthermore, Az represents the ideal and concept of self-deification through a Willed existence, that the ***trshna*** concept is one of vampirism and desire. Thus Az represents the Left Hand Path as a rite of passage of becoming. Continued existence is essentially the survival of the psyche or essential self; there is no union with the natural order that which can eliminate the mind. The practitioner does not seek to join with it; rather he or she seeks to remain separate from it in their own self-created subjective world.

---

[18] This word can be related to Anticlockwise movement, or Widdershins.

As with the Manichaeans, Az is the "Mother of All Demons", thus a powerful hidden Light behind Ahriman. As the Devil's Bride she inspires and equally commands her presence, manifests her Will and accomplishes that which other demons could not. Ahriman was taken with her.

Az within Zoroastrianism is not by any mentionable gender, but Ahriman's assistant if you will is called in the Pahlavi books called Jeh, which means roughly 'whore'. She would corrupt or rather awaken mankind and womankind to debauchery and sexual pleasure.

Theodore bar Konai[19] described an interesting tale of Ahriman and his sway that he held with women:

"After Ohrmazd had given women to righteous men, they fled and went over to Satan; and when Ohrmazd provided righteous men with peace and happiness, Satan provided women too with happiness. As Satan had allowed the women to ask for anything they wanted, Ohrmazd feared they might ask to have intercourse with the righteous men and that these might suffer damage thereby. Seeking to avoid this, he created the god Narseh (a youth) of fifteen years of age. And he put him, naked as he was behind Satan so that the women should see him, desire him and ask Satan for him. The women lifted their hands up towards Satan and said: "Satan, our father, give us the god Narseh as a gift."

The original union of Az and Satan came from the Devil falling into a deep slumber for three thousand years. Unconscious, Ahriman would not awaken for any reason. Numerous demons and shadows tried to awaken Ahriman by telling of their deeds, nothing would stir him to consciousness. After three thousand years the Whore came unto Ahriman and said to him:

"Arise O our Father, for in the battle to come I shall let loose so much affliction on the Righteous Man and the toiling Bull that, because of my deeds, they will not be fit to live. I shall take away their dignity, I shall afflict the water, I shall afflict the earth, I shall afflict the fire, I shall afflict the plants, I shall afflict all the creation which Ohrmazd has created."

Here we see that Az has knowledge and control over the elements and that which the Natural Order observes as correct. She wishes to change it according to Her will, to afflict is to darken its essence with much of the Light she was endowed with early on. Zaehner writes also the description of Ahriman's awakening, and his gift to Az:

"And she related her evil deeds so minutely that the Destructive Spirit was comforted, leapt up out of his swoon, and kissed the head of the Whore; and that pollution called menstruation appeared also on the Whore. And the Destructive Spirit cried out to the demon Whore: whatsoever thy desire, that do thou ask, that I may give it thee."

[19] See R.C. Zaehner, The Dawn and Twilight of Zoroastrianism New York, NY 1961

Az appears unnamed in the "Book of Arda Viraf", a pre-Dante exploration through the Zoroastrian hell. In the account of the record, very little is given concerning hell except for the suffering and punishments of those who have went against their religious doctrines. Az appears as the bad actions of man, and it is said she is more filthy than any other creation of Ahriman:

"Afterward, a stinking cold wind comes to meet him. So it seemed to that soul as if it came forth from the northern quarter, from the quarter of demons, a more stinking wind than which he had not perceived in the world. And in that wind he saw his own religion and eeds as a profligate woman, naked, decayed, gapping, bandy-legged, lean-hipped, and unlimitedly spotted so that spot was joined to spot, like the most hideous, noxious creature (kharafstar), most filthy and most stinking."

Az comes forth to this youth and tells him that she is his bad actions, that she is made strong in vile and evil belief, that she grows more unholy through him. This demoness mentions that she is settled in the northern region of the demons, she is settled more north through him.

"The form of the evil spirit was a log-like lizard's (vazak) body, and he appeared a young man of fifteen years to Jeh, and that brought the thoughts of Jeh to him. Afterwards, the evil spirit, with the confederate demons, went towards the luminaries, and he saw the sky; and he led them up, fraught with malicious intentions. 11. He stood upon one-third of the inside of the sky, and he sprang, like a snake, out of the sky down to the earth." - The Bundahishn, translated by E. W. West

A form which Ahriman took in that relation was a frog as well. This draws an early connection to the powers of the Toad in a setting of sorcery, as well as the sexual union with women as a force of inspiration, desire and imagination.

"His astral body is that of the frog, the vicious crab. He neither thinks of, nor speaks, nor works the weal of the creatures of Ohrmazd." – Greater Bundahishn translated by Behramgore Tehmuras Anklesaria

Ahriman was made better by union with the demon Whore, who was in effect his muse but also deeply a part of his being. It took her emergence to bring him again to consciousness, to want to accomplish.

Dead matter also relates a powerful enigma in Zoroastrian religious lore. From the Denkard, a specific section related to the dead and the demons which inhabit the body of the Yatus, those who practice witchcraft in accordance with Ahriman.

"Be it known that, the souls of worshippers of daevas and of deceitful Ashmoghs, owing to their impure nature, although (located) in a living body, are, according to the religion, (as if) possessing a dead body; and that body with life is considered as (fit) for hell; hence there is a danger of their pollution and bad qualities reaching Mazdayasnians

through mutual intercourse with them; therefore, (the Mazdayasnians) must remain aloof from touching their living bodies, for their bodies are in all places like decayed nasa."

It makes further sense that the religious masters of this faith considered the worshippers of demons to be an abomination and that they sought infernal power makes them polluted with Nasa, or the Druj-Nasa, which is a demon who takes the form of a fly to enter the corpse and steal the spirit. This demon is said to come forth from Azrezura, the Cold Mountain of the North which leads to Hell.

III. The Adversary, The Bride of The Devil & Cain The Son

The Hebrew Samael, Satan and Islamic Shaitan

"And the great dragon was cast out, that old serpent, called the Devil, and Satan, which deceiveth the whole world: he was cast out into the earth, and his angels were cast out with him." -Revelation 12:9

The Spirit of Diabolus is one which remains timeless and extensive. This sorcerous Daemon has walked the earth since the dawn of mankind, from desert to forest, in every culture and every age. Satan has long represented the 'otherness' which is considered evil or dark, but yet few but the daring refuse to explore this area of magical study.

Satan has origins in the Middle East as a Djinn which is made of Fire instead of Light, from which the angels after were made from. Shaitan was originally called Azazel or Azazyl, the First Angel which preached to the other angels under the throne of God. Azazel, who later was called Iblis or Shaitan, refused to bow before Man, noting that his nature of lowly compared to his essence, which was of fire. Azazel was cast out from heaven into the earth, along with the fallen angels.

"(the conception of) God-head must ever evolve it's own inertia for transmutation to its very opposite – because it contains it...The idea of God ever means the forgetfulness of supremacy and Godliness. So must be supplanted by fear..." - The Book of Pleasure, Austin Osman Spare

Within the practice of Magic the lore of Iblis provides a powerful initiatory model for the sorcerer. Essentially the initiate seeks to become like Satan, by antinomian methods of separating the self from the natural or mundane world. One may seek to ask how this works, and why would you want to do it? Luciferians do not consider Satan to be a completely malefic spirit, rather a balanced force of both Dark and Light. Many Luciferian rites involve the symbolism of Black[20], Red[21] White[22] and Green[23] as being different points of the Adversary. It must be understood that working with the deific power of Iblis or Shaitan is not a safe route. It matters not if you are looking at the aforementioned force as an actual spirit or as a symbol of the dark recesses of the mind. What must be carefully adhered to is that which is unseen, that when the imagination can adapt consciousness (through the subconscious) with the image of Satan then the transformation begins. Once the initiate has embraced the path, there is no turning back.

---

[20] Black is from the root FHM meaning hidden or secret, but also wisdom. The word abufihamat, or Head/Father of Wisdom is the foundation of Baphomet.

[21] Representing Fire and continual motion, change and sexual vigor.

[22] White is symbolic of the Astral Plane or Luciferian/Celestial Sabbat, wherein the Spirit is elevated with his or her Holy Guardian Angel or True Will.

[23] Green or Emerald, representing the jewel from the crown of Lucifer. Some Sabbat rites include Green candles which represent the fire of Azazel, the Light from his Crown.

One may fall from the path; such is a kiss of death to the individual in question based on their own potential and failure. The Left Hand Path as it is called can render a person mad if they are not able to control their own desires and goals, Iblis tests just as he was tested.

Satanic or Luciferian Magick is a dual or opposing system of self-realization. The first area is that of inverse magical practice, working with repulsive and shunned imagery which takes the initiate into their own self-invoked darkness. By exploring this "world" as a subjective state, the individual slowly transforms his or herself into a form of Iblis, thus becoming like Lucifer. The shadow is the testing force from which you may create and manifest what you desire, and be careful as so you shall obtain that which you seek. The shadow is also the empowering essence of your mind, it is the darkest recesses and atavistic desires which may be explored and mastered.

Azazel (Azazil) is known within Muslim lore to have been the same as the Angel of Death, who was most feared in tribal cultures. Various lore describes Azazil worshipped God in the Seventh Hell for over one thousand years, ascending until he reached the earth. Azazil arose through the seven hells and upon reaching earth he then sat at the gates of Heaven, tormenting Adam and Eve. The Bundahishn relates an original tale of Azazel or Ahriman:

"The evil spirit, on account of backward knowledge, was not aware of the existence of Ohrmazd; and, afterwards, he arose from the abyss, and came in unto the light which he saw. 10. Desirous of destroying, and because of his malicious nature, he rushed in to destroy that light of Ohrmazd unassailed by fiends, and he saw its bravery and glory were greater than his own; so he fled back to the gloomy darkness, and formed many demons and fiends; and the creatures of the destroyer arose for violence." – Chapter One, Bundahishn

Here we see a different view of Iblis from the thoughts of his adversary, who would be the Zoroastrians. While the Zurvanites regarded Ahriman to be an original dual aspect of Ohrmazd, in the Bundahishn Ahriman is represented as a lesser demon, but a very significant one that equally causes problems but strengthens those who are connected with him. While they sought to condemn Ahriman and speak of his weakness, he was important and powerful enough to haunt their very minds into submission according to a written religious doctrine.

"Diabolus enim et alii dæmones a Deo quidem naturâ creati sunt boni, sed ipsi per se facti sunt mali." ('the Devil and the other demons were created by God good in their nature but they by themselves have made themselves evil.')"- Fourth Lateran Council, from the Catholic Encyclopedia.

Here we see that Azazel and other angels possessed an original "independence" of being, that is they recognized that they could have the faculties of a higher state of being, they perceived themselves as separate from their original maker or source of being. The bible further describes Satan as how he had fallen, which presents a connection of the Vajra

Rune which Anton Szandor LaVey made a part of his personal sigil within an inverted pentagram. The Vajra rune represents health, vitality and strength.

"I saw Satan like lightning falling from heaven" – Luke 10:18

The Dragon itself is a symbol of the collective independence and intelligence of Satan the Adversary, while his angelic nature granted him the higher faculties of all the Angels of Heaven, Lucifer sought more and wished to be more godlike. This was considered a great Sin and thus a War in Heaven occurred.

"And there was a great battle in heaven, Michael and his angels fought with the dragon, and the draghon fought his angels: they prevailed not, neither was their place found any more in heaven. And that great Dragon was cast out, that old serpent, who is called the devil and Satan, who seduceth the whole world; and he was cast unto the earth, and his angels were thrown down with him." – Apocalypse 12: 7-9

This leaves a question of subjective and objective planes of existence. If Satan had awoken his state of independence, to think *"differently"* then could Heaven truly be something which existed objectively, even within a spiritual or aethyric sense? Could Heaven only be a subjective term as would be Hell, while what is one to an individual may be different to another? Here we see the transformative state of Satan from Angel to then Demon, thus he embodied both Light and Shadow within his own essence; he was Dual Headed.

Peter Lamborn Wilson, in his essential article on the Middle Eastern origins of Satan[24] provides a powerful study of the foundation and survival of perhaps the original idea of the Opposer. Wilson describes Adi ibn Musafir who is also known as Shaykh Adi, who was originally from Lebanon. The Shaykh traveled to Baghdad and studied along other well known Sufis. Later on after 1100 A.D. Adi traveled to Lalish (Iraq) and founded a religion based on Melek Tauus, or Malek Ta'us, the Peacock Angel. The Yezidis as they were called were the descendants of Adi, and were considered heretics and disbelievers by other fundamentalists in their area.

The deity of worship, known as Iblis of Hallaj is the Peacock Angel, known as Azazyl or Shaitan, the Adversary. In "The Black Book", a doctrine considered written by Shaykh Adi, describes the foundation of Azazel as the Black Light or hidden way of the path against all others:

"In the beginning God created the White Pearl out of His most precious Essence; and He created a bird named Anfar. And He placed the pearl upon its back, and dwelt thereon forty thousand years. On the first day, Sunday, He created an angel named 'Azazil, which is Ta'us Melek ('the Peacock Angel'), the chief of all." - The Black Book

It is presented here that Ta'us Melek is the foundation of independent energy, motion and progression. In no mentioning of the Black Book is Satan considered to be a negative

[24] Iblis, the The Black Light – Satanism in Islam, published in Gnosis Magazine

force, rather a misunderstood power which can reside in each human being who can recognize what Azazel is.

"Then the Lord descended to the holy land and commanded Gabriel to take earth from the four corners of the world: earth, air, fire and water. He made it man, and endowed it with a soul by His power. Then He commanded Gabriel to place Adam in Paradise, where he might eat of the fruit of every green herb, only of wheat should he not eat. After a hundred years Ta'us Melek said to God, 'How shall Adam increase and multiply, and where is his offspring?' God said to him, 'Into thy hand have I surrendered authority and administration'. Then he came and said to Adam, 'Hast thou eaten of the wheat?' He answered, 'No, for God hath forbidden me so to do,' and hath said, 'Thou shalt not eat of it'. Melek Ta'us said to him, 'If you eat of it, all shall go better with thee.' But, after he had eaten, his belly swelled up, and Ta'us Melek drove him forth from Paradise, and left him, and ascended into heaven. Then Adam suffered from the distention of his belly, because it had no outlet. But God sent a bird, which came and helped him, and made an outlet for it, and he was relieved." – The Black Book

This section provides a powerful symbolism which stretches beyond the predicament of constipation. While God created Mankind, he only held limited facilities. Melek Ta'us came unto Adam and suggested that he eat of the sacred fruit. This wisdom as he offered would open Adam's eyes to his own Black Light, the gift of Iblis. It was Azazel who by offering knowledge to Adam and Eve was by all accounts the Opposer, the Adversary who by aversion and a different point of view opened the Mind and soul to the Black Flame of Shaitan, that which is self-knowledge and perception.

"Then He was wroth with the Pearl which he had created, wherefore he cast it away: and from the crash of it were produced the mountains, and from the clang of it the sand-hills, and from its smoke the heavens. Then God ascended into heaven, and condensed the heavens, and fixed them without supports, and enclosed the earth. Then He took the pen in His hands, and began to write down the names of all his creatures. From His essence and light He created six gods, whose creation was as one lighteth a lamp from another lamp." – The Black Book

While the foundations of Iblis differ from culture to culture, there is a specific correlation of the essence of Azazel, being Fire. While Melek Ta'us is the "Chief Angel over All" he is considered to be created of a higher intellect than the other angels. That by the essence of flame, of which motion is always present, the Peacock Angel does not remain the same. It is by this principle that he changes through us as we become something else. The key to this is the Imagination itself. Peter Lamborn Wilson made reference to a text by Aziz ad-Din Nasafi[25] which referred to Satan or Iblis as the Imagination. It is because of the imagination that he refused to be prostrate before mankind, as Fire was superior to Clay. While it is first considered a "sin" of pride, Satan acknowledged his true nature as flame and could not bring himself to bow before a secondary creation – for it was his father who created him, which no other he may submit to.

---

[25] The Perfect Man, see The Black Light by Wilson, Gnosis Magazine

It is within the Kitab el-Jelwa that Ta'us Malek or Shaitan makes a statement concerning the nature of his path and being. This is by far one of the more hidden aspects which offer a clue as to the nature of the consistency of Satan.

"Melek Ta'us existed before all creatures. He sent his servant into this world to warn and separate his chosen people from error: first by oral tradition, secondly by this by this book Jilwa, which is not permitted to strangers to read or to look upon."-The Book of Divine Effulgence also known as Kitab el-Jelwa

While this text refers to specifically "his people" as Yezidi, in a modern context one could choose to add initiatory value to the statement. That Melek Ta'us existed before other creatures indicates the intellect and knowledge of being, self-awareness and the Imagination to consider his own role. The mentioning of not permitting strangers in looking upon the book provides a central idea as to the nature of the path itself – it is separate, antinomian and isolate. That the path of Iblis is one of inversion from the Natural Order of the Objective World around us, it actually is a step "away" from the concepts of blending in with the spiritual normality of the herd. It is also to be noted that the Opposer or Adversary is the imagination of the illuminated, Melek Ta'us and his chosen are but those who recognize the Black Light within. That by affirming this path, of antinomianism through the image of Shaitan or Satan, the individual via Imagination becomes a child of Melek Ta'us.

"I was, and am now, and will continue unto eternity, ruling over all creatures and ordering the affairs and deeds of those who are under my sway. I am presently at hand to such as trust in me and call upon me in time of need, neither is there any place void of me where I am not present." – Kitab el-Jelwa

Therein is perhaps one of the most significant representations of Shaitan in the form of the Inner Guide, Holy Guardian Angel or Daemon/Genius which is attainable through Magick. That the imagination holds keys to self-creation so does it hold the key to Conversation of the Holy Guardian Angel, the Luciferian Spirit which guides and which is considered our true self. It can be called a "True Self" or "Higher Self" as this is the Daemonic aspect of the mind, the Gift of the Black Light as Iblis gave humanity is inherent in our Higher Self, thus the imagination is a helper and beneficial ability that humanity must choose to master. All actions and deeds are manifested from an idea which emerges from the imagination – inspiration guides and brings that which we desire spiritually and physically. As Shaitan states that he *"is presently at hand"* and *"trust in me"* and *"call upon me in time of need"* indicates the very nature of the Holy Guardian Angel, you must recognize this force as a part of yourself by the Opposing formula which is mirrored as Satan, a symbol and force of rebellion. It is once you have gone forth through the Gates of the Hidden[26] that you begin to ascend into the psychological state of Lucifer, the Adversary. The essence of Shaitan is Flame, and continual motion. To understand this beyond any coherent or sinister symbolism is the result of passing the test of appearance. The student of Magick must be willing to trespass the Laws of Nature to discover the identity of the soul, the very gift of Magick itself. Melek Ta'us thus

[26] Called Hell by some.

represents a metamorphic process of self-deification and self-overcoming. It is not an endless ego posturing, rather a means of recognizing the idea of self, the imagination to mutate it into something new and crystallize the very core essence of Lucifer, that which is Black Light and Fire.

"I guide without a scripture; I point the way by unseen means unto my friends and such as observe the precepts of my teaching, which is not grievous, and is adapted to the time and conditions. I punish such as contravene my laws in other worlds. The children of this Adam know not those things which are determined, wherefore they oft-times fall into error. The beasts of the field, and of heaven, and the fish of the sea, all of them are in my hand and under my control. The treasures and hoards buried in the heart of the earth are known to me, and I cause one after another to inherit them. I make manifest my signs and wonders to such as will receive them and seek them from me in their due season." – Kitab el-Jelwa

Here one may consider the point of guiding without scripture, that Shaitan as the imagination and Holy Guardian Angel or True Will, brings knowledge without words but rather what Aleister Crowley called "Energized Enthusiasm". The beasts of the field and the fish of the sea are all manifestations and connected with – Shaitan. This is the inner relation to Shaitan as the Black Man of the Sabbat, the very Ritual of Magick Fire which either as the Light of the Luciferian Conclave or Holy Rites of Noon[27] to announce self discovery and to seek transformation into a Satan-like individual. It is the Black Snake, a symbol of the Yezidis which represents Hidden Wisdom. Black within Arabic terms, the root FHM of course is Wisdom and Knowledge, thus Black has a dual meaning which refers the very opposite of ignorance. The Black Snake is presented earlier in the Zoroastrian descriptions of Zohak, who gained knowledge and power from Ahriman, having kissed his shoulders, bestowed two black serpents to emerge from him. These snakes intertwined with his body and spirit until he became Azi Dahaka, a dragon – king who was said to be the most powerful Daeva next to Ahriman. The Black Snake continues to symbolize intelligence and independence from the natural order, an antinomian symbol which survived in the cults of Yezidism.

The Shaykh known as Ayn al-Qozat Hamadani was perhaps one of the most rebellious figures of his time, champion to a higher intellect and Satanism in a pure form of self-love and evolution to God itself, Hamadani suggested an alternate path through Sufism which was considered blasphemy to the fundamentalists of Islam.

Ayn al-Qozat wrote that the Black Light above the Throne is the Light of Eblis, which he called the Dark Tresses of God, compared also to the divine light of darkness. Al-Qozat suggested that Satan had a pride in Love that he would not accept any but his creator. While in an initiatory sense, the foundations of God may represent a self-possibility and non-union with the natural order. By this separation and initial recognition of difference can then man and woman seek to become something better, this is the very essence of Magick – energy in motion, change and ascension.

---

[27] Noon is considered in the Middle East to be the Time of Satan.

"Samael was the greatest prince in heaven. The celestial animals and the Seraphim had six wings each, but Samael had twelve. He took his cohorts and went down, and saw all the creatures whom the Holy One, blessed be He, had created, and found among them none as astute and malicious as the serpent. And the serpent's appearance was like that of a camel. And Samael mounted him and rode him. And the Tora cried and shrieked and said: 'Samael, the world has just been created, is this the time to rebel against God?' The serpent went and said to the woman: 'Is it true that you are commanded not to eat the fruit of this tree?...'" Midrash: Pirqe R. Eliezer. Ch. 13

It is written in the "Treatise on the Left Emanation" that Samael and Lilith were born as one, a fire born dual headed angelic force which was too individualistic to contain by its creator. The first prince and accusing demon is Samael, called evil because he desires to mingle with the force of light from which he is a part of. At their creation they both were separated, Lilith going forth into the world of man and Samael going his own way with his angels. It is suggested that Samael has an entourage of seventy chancellors, or angels. However, in Watcher lore it is over 200 seraphs.

"In this tradition it is made clear that Samael and Lilith were born as one, similar to the form of Adam and Eve who were also born as one, reflecting what is above. This is the account of Lilith which was received by the Sages in the Secret Knowledge of the Palaces. The Matron Lilith is the mate of Samael. Both of them were born at the same hour in the image of Adam and Eve, intertwined in each other. Asmodeus the great king of the demons has as a mate the Lesser (younger) Lilith, daughter of the king whose name is Qafsefoni. The name of his mate is Mehetabel daughter of Matred, and their daughter is Lilith." –"Treatise on the Left Emanation" by R. Isaac b. Jacob Ha-Kohen

The concept of Fire as being the central and primary force which Samael and Lilith were made up of displays a very interesting connection. Here we see that Lilith actually has different forms, but all are connected to the ancient mother Lilith, who is also Az in earlier folklore. Lilith is able to change her form and manipulate her essence, she grows strong from the draconian essence within man and woman, their lusts, hungers and desires empower her. Her essence is of the beasts of the wild, as a restless spirit, she drew close with the wild beasts of the deserts and forests, that which is far away from humanity. One specific description of her composition of Fire, the same as her mate Samael, is read in the following:

"They found it stated in those Chapters that Samael, the great prince of them all, grew exceedingly jealous of Asmodeus the king of the demons because of this Lilith who is called Lilith the Maiden (the young). She is in the form of a beautiful woman from her head to her waist. But from the waist down she is burning fire--like mother like daughter. She is called Mehetabel daughter of Matred, and the meaning is something immersed (mabu tabal). The meaning here is that her intentions are never for the good. She only seeks to incite wars and various demons of war and the war between Daughter Lilith and Matron Lilith." –"Treatise on the Left Emanation" by R. Isaac b. Jacob Ha-Kohen

The multiple spirits of Lilith are a part of what could be considered in Luciferian Witchcraft Circles as the Triple Goddess, or Hecate – Lilith. She is maiden, whore and hag and her number is three – just as the points of the triangle. Lilith holds intensive wisdom of Magick and such along with her mate, Samael, is her gift to those children who recognize and identify with her nature. Asmodeus the great Demon King is a powerful spirit who was first presented in Zoroastrian lore as Aeshma of the Wounding Spear, a war and fiery daeva. The Hebrew Ashmedai is one who gained a very high rank among the original angels, Asmodeus was according to lore a Seraphim, one of the highest ranks of angels. It is suggested in other Hebrew lore that Asmodeus was born from the demoness Naamah and the Fallen Angel Shamdon. Asmodeus and Samael were said to have had strife over one spirit of Lilith.

"This is the waning Moon, the moon of witchcraft and abominable deeds. She is the poisoned darkness which is the condition for the rebirth of light" – The Book of Thoth, Aleister Crowley

Here we are able to understand that Lilith has many forms, yet her nature is clear to those who work with her. Allow her entry into yourself, and know the ecstasy of man and woman, Union with the Blood of the Moon. Crowley refers to her as "uncleanliness and sorcery", the very nature of Az who is the Mother of Luciferians. Crowley also saw divinity within Az and Lilith, in the form of Babalon, the Whore which rides the 7 headed Dragon.

The children of Lilith are called Lilin or Lilim, being succubi who have no hair on their head and their body and face are covered. They visit men in their dreams and drain them of sexual fluids to create other demons. Essentially, a magician who has worked in the Lilith – current (that of the feminine within Luciferian Witchcraft) can summon and encircle a succubi or incubi, however care should be practiced as these spirits can quickly move from the position of servitor to master.

"Wildcats shall meet with hyenas, goat-demons shall call to each other; there too Lilith shall repose and find a place to rest. There shall the owl nest and lay and hatch and brood in its shadow." – Isaiah 34:14

The nature of Samael and Lilith is to seek copulation, separate and return again. They are guided by Leviathan, called also the Blinddragon who by his essence, cause their sexual union. In Luciferian Witchcraft circles Leviathan holds the key to controlled sexual magick and the possibilities therein. Leviathan essentially is the encircler, the possibilities of the self as well as knowledge of the self. Here we see a connection between Lilith and Leviathan, that in many ways they are nearly the same:

"You already know that evil Samael and wicked Lilith are like a sexual pair who, by means of an intermediary, receive an evil and wicked emanation from one and emanate to the other. I shall explain this relying on the esoteric meaning in the verse 'In that day the Lord will punish with His great, cruel, mighty sword Leviathan the twisted serpent and Leviathan the tortuous serpent'--this is Lilith—'and He will slay the dragon of the

sea' (Isaiah 27:1). As there is a pure Leviathan in the sea and it is called a serpent, so there is a great defiled serpent in the sea in the literal sense. The same holds true above in a hidden way. The heavenly serpent is a blind prince, the image of an intermediary between Samael and Lilith." –"Treatise on the Left Emanation" by R. Isaac b. Jacob Ha-Kohen

Aleister Crowley in his work "De Arte Magica" describes in certain terms the use of Sexual Magick within the image of Lilith, that she is the key to creations of night born servitors or demons. Such workings Crowley considered highly dangerous:

"Among the Jews are certain instructed Initiates of their Qabalah who hold, as We understand, the view that in the Zraa or Semen itself lies a creative force inherent which cannot be baulked. Thus they say that before Eve was made, the dreams of Adam produced Lilith, a demon, and that from his intercourse with her sprang evil races. ...All other sexual acts involving emission of semen therefore attract or other spirits, incomplete and therefore evil. Thus nocturnal pollutions bring succubi, which are capable of seperate existance, and of vampirising their creator. But voluntary sterile acts create demons, and (if done with concentration and magical intention), such demons as may subserve that intention." - Aleister Crowley, "De Arte Magica"

Although Crowley seemed to almost warn against such sexual workings to evoke and create demons, in "Rex de Arte Regia" describes two workings to produce Belial and Asmodee by means of solitary masturbation. This is possible in the area of controlling and focusing the Will in the essence or goal behind the Demon in question, but Crowley warned others of this operation as it can cause the spirit to gain a separate existence and to astrally vampirize it's creator if not bound and focused correctly.

We see with reference to Samael and Lilith, a working Aleister Crowley conducted with his Scarlet Woman, one of which brought to excite his Kundalini or Magick Fire. This serpent is controlled starting at the base of the spine and moving upward, thus allowing for ecstasy and power. In "The Magical Record of The Beast 666" Crowley described his working involving ShTN, or the Fire Serpent (Satan/Set/Shaitan) with the Scarlet Woman, thus what Crowley referred to as the Sun and the Moon conjoined. A fascinating description of his rite describes the ecstasy of Magick:

"The Tortured-Ecstasy of the contorted face, the writhing of the hag body that ground down it's beast. The storm of lust and pain and madness. It was Night's Hollow wretching at her captive Dragon, whose blood was seed of the blind and furious stars. She was like Hecate in a death-dance, Satan-possessed, convulsive, pumping my life, body and soul, as 'twere a Python in his agony. She certainly gave me what I've been losing. Youth's intensity...that sacrament of Satan that may be consummated only beneath night's dome, in utmost silence, because it's elements are not symbols of things, but They themselves." – Aleister Crowley, "The Magical Record of The Beast 666"

Here we see the infernal union of both outward with his partner, but also a mirror shining into the depths of the abyss of his self, his possibility and that chaos which was within him. Controlling it, focusing it, Crowley was able to manifest his Will from this very essence of Magick.

In Luciferian Witchcraft Cain is considered the Devil incarnate in flesh. He is the first born in the circle of Leviathan, the first born of sorcery and the Patron Spirit (who is masked as the Devil) of the Toad Rite. In certain writings, Cain is said to have emerged from the seed of Samael and Eve (by possession by Lilith):

"R. Hiyya said: 'The sons of God were the sons of Cain. For when Samael mounted Eve, he injected filth into her, and she conceived and bare Cain. And his aspect was unlike that of the other humans and all those who came from his side were called sons of God.'"- Kabbala: Zohar 1:37a

Here we see that the magical act of sexual union creates a God like individual, who in this instance is Cain. Cain is considered to be a Son of Satan, a manifestation of that very solar force within man and woman. In religious lore, Samael who is the Serpent or Dragon, was said to have injected filth which spawned Cain, his son in flesh:

"When the serpent mounted eve, he injected filth into her. Israel who stood at Mount Sinai, their filth ceased; the other nations who did not stand at Mount Sinai, their filth has not ceased..." - Talmud: b. Shab. 146a

Aleister Crowley made reference to Cain and his mark of initiation, which some Witches disagree with according to their tradition. To paraphrase:

"There is the legend of Eve and the Serpent, for Cain was the child of Eve and the Serpent, and not of Eve and Adam; and therefore when he had slain his brother, who was the first murderer, having sacrificed living things to his demon, had Cain the mark upon his brow, which is the mark of the Beast spoken of in the Apocalypse, and is the sign of initiation." – The Book of Thoth, Aleister Crowley

In Luciferian Grimoires, Cain is said to be a symbol and gateway for man and woman to become, thus the symbol of Baphomet as Anton LaVey called it, is the inverted pentagram with a goat head in the middle. The original, which LaVey took out, contained the words Samael and Lilith, surrounded in the circle ring the Hebrew LvTHN, Leviathan, the Crooked Serpent. In the circles of Luciferian Witchcraft, this is the sigil of Baphomet – the Head of Wisdom who has united the Solar and the Lunar, or the Fire and Water within the self to bring forth Cain, the Devil in Flesh upon earth. He is the symbol and cipher of Magick, the Great Work accomplished and onward moving. At the gathering of the Sabbat is Cain the Black Man, the circle and center of the Sabbat and it's fire, he directs it outward as "he" is the Pole of this Force.

"Woe unto them! For they have gone in the way of Cain" – Jude 11

Cain's name is said to have derived from a root "Kanah" which means to possess[28]. This by itself presents the antinomian nature of his essence, while instead of sacrificing his most bountiful items to the Lord, he kept them for himself. This may draw conclusion that he viewed himself as a form of God, by later sacrificing his brother Abel[29] he began the Left Hand Path, which brought him into being as a Son of Satan. Cain is viewed in later paths of Witchcraft as a Lord of Magick, but rather the darker aspects. Here Cain takes a similar path with Anubis by name and process. Robert Cochrane, a practitioner of Witchcraft in the 60's wrote:

"In the North lies the Castle of Weeping, the ruler thereof is named Tettens, our Hermes or Woden. He is the second twin, the waning sun, Lord over mysticism, magic, power and death, the baleful destroyer. The God of War, of Justice, King of Kings, since all pay their homage to him. Ruler of the Winds, the Windyat. Cain imprisioned in the Moon, ever desiring Earth. He is visualized as a tall dark man, shadowy, cold and deadly." – Letters from Robert Cochrane

Here we see that Cain, the Son of Samael and Lilith, is the Devil manifest on the earth – the Son of Shaitan. He is above the flesh, yet his essence is found within it. The Lord of Magick is Dual – it is Nightside and Dayside, Sun and the Moon, Life and Death. Cain is here the body of the magician, the soul of Baphomet if you will. As found in the Book of Cain[30] the Dragon Samael and Lilith join as one to beget the son of filth, yet he grows strong by his Will and emerges as Baphomet. The illustration of Cain as the Adversary[31] presents him holding the Trident or Stave above, symbolizing the Sun and Celestial region, and a hammer below representing the Forge and the Infernal region.

"You shall thirst for water and for blood; both in dreaming shall be held from the dual gnosis. I hold the Golden Cup to your lips, that the Dragon's elixir hold strong – I then hand to you the skull bowl of my flowing blood, that you may taste the bitter sweetness of it's coppered kiss – then in your ecstasy and thy devil's phallus reaching towards the Sun shall my serpent's tongue enflame you to me." – The Book of Cain by Michael W. Ford

As written Cain is slowly transforming into a manifestation of both Samael (the Devil) and Lilith, he is the magician of Two Opposing Fires, yet they join as one within him as from when they were created. Robert Cochrane further described Cain as:

"He is the God of magicians and witches, who knows all sorcery. Lord of the North, dark, unpredictable, the true God of witches and magicians if they are working at any decent level at all. A cold wind surrounds Him, age and time so ancient that it is beyond belief flows with him. Dark is his shadow, and he bears a brance of the sorrowing alder, and walks with the aid of a blackthorn stick." – Letters from Robert Cochrane

---

[28] Catholic Encyclopedia
[29] Abel in some Luciferian Lore is considered a lower 'pre form' of Cain, thus the sacrifice was not literal.
[30] Book of Cain by Michael W. Ford, Succubus Publishing 2003
[31] By Elda Isela Ford, reproduced in The Book of Cain.

Cain in this perspective represents a process of movement and transformation. The Luciferian Path as practiced in some covens and sorcerers describes and understands Cain being the Devil who is the self, thus by our Work being done, thus Cain manifests further. He is the Son of Satan, the Son of the Old Dragon and Bringer of Light. As mentioned earlier with regard to Alexander Sanders, the Triangle of Darkness from the South lands of Neph-Kam we joined with the Northern Ascending Triangle of Light, thus Six Sides utilizing the Power of the Sun and the Moon – Magick itself. Robert Cochrane described the Hexagram as the following:

"Which in part represents Old Tubal Cain, or the All Father Himself. Hearne" – Letters from Robert Cochrane

Interestingly enough, the Eight Pointed Luciferian Star[32], the Chaos Sphere, represents in most Magical circles as being the symbol of Baphomet. Robert Cochrane described Tettens or Cain as a Rider on an 8 Legged Horse, thus draws close symbolism with the Sigil of ALGOL, the Chaos Star and Inverse Pentagram. This also makes assumption to the true Nature of Anubis – being the Son of Set, with Cain, the Son of the Devil and Eve (through Lilith in dreaming sorcery). The "Watcher of the Twilight"[33] who is the Lord of Magick, therefore the Opener of the Way wears the Mask of the Beast and stands between both Dawn and Twilight.

"Know it as the elixir of life, the Syllubub of Sun and Moon. Verily he steals the fire from Heaven: the greatest act of bravery in the world." – The Book of Pleasure, Austin Osman Spare

The Society of the Horseman's Word in Scotland in the 1800's viewed Cain as an archetype of malefic and diabolic power, and is presented in initiation ceremonies where the participant met a horned "devil" covered in animal skins and masked, many were taught to summon the devil by the means of certain phrases of the bible recited backwards[34]. In "The Toad Rite"[35], Ahriman is a primal or infernal spirit mask of Cain, thus through the flesh of Cain does the Devil first manifest and later initiate.

In East Anglian Hereditary Witchcraft, it is suggested that when Cain went to Nod he was greeted by the Devil who made him the first Witch. Even with older areas of historical and hereditary craft Cain as the manifestation as the first sorcerer, created by the Devil, holds the True foundations of the Craft which indeed separates it from it's watered down Wiccan varieties. British Hereditary Witch Nathaniel Harris has written an article on Cain based on his family teachings, lore and his own sorcerous study and work[36]. His theories are sound and hold much inspiration for those who utilize "truth within the circle", which is inspired or creative truth, thus aiding ones own initiation.

---

[32] Called ALGOL, the sigil of The Order of Phosphorus, the authors current magical guild.

[33] The Book of Thoth – the Moon by Aleister Crowley

[34] Secrets of the Horse Whisperers, by Peter Bayliss

[35] The Toad Rite, a Grimoire of the Toad Witch by Michael W. Ford, Succubus Publishing.

[36] See Witcha by Nathan Harris.

"According to Saint Augustine, Saint Clement, Eusebius, Lactantius, the Abbe' Simonnet, and others, the entire lineage of Cain were tainted. Whilst God declared his will to Seth by the mediation of angels, Cain was gone from the sight of the Lord and sought aid from the Infernal One. The offspring of Cain were 'deceived' by the workings of Satan so that they worshipped him. Thus was diabolism born, and Cain was equated as the first witch and Satanist." – Nathaniel J. Harris, WITCHA, A Book of Cunning

Here we are able to discern the mythology which holds Cain as the first of Witch Blood, the fire and water embodiment of Samael and Lilith, that which has born Cain as our prototype and initiatory model. Harris points out also the invocation used to Conjure Cain in Charles Leland's "Aradia – Gospel of the Witches". Nathan Harris writes also that some claim hereditary witchcraft is that the children are of Cain, who in some traditions is also the son of Adam and Lilith, or the traditional myth of Samael (the Devil) and Eve.

A further interesting connection that Lilith holds with Samael/Satan is the Star Algol which was originally called Arabic the "Ri'B al Ohill" and later the Hebrew "Rosh ha Sitan" meaning The Head of Satan and also Lilith. Algol can be viewed as a Star which represents the essence of Satan and Lilith, the twin fire of becoming through the Left Hand Path. In Luciferian Sorcery, Algol is presented as an 8 pointed Chaos Sigil with the inverted pentagram in the center. This is made reference to the number 8, being of Baphomet and Chaos, and the pentagram representing the five points of the Adversary, details are found in the grade workings of The Black Order of The Dragon[37], which is a non-public initiatory circle. The inverted pentagram in an outer sense represents the manifestation of the Will through the manipulation of Matter.

[37] Overseen and under the guidance of the present author.

IV. The Gnostic Yaltabaoth, "Child of Chaos"

"And when she saw (the consequences of) her desire, it changed into a form of a lion-faced serpent. And its eyes were like lightning fires which flash. She cast it away from her, outside that place, that no one of the immortal ones might see it, for she had created it in ignorance. And she surrounded it with a luminous cloud, and she placed a throne in the middle of the cloud that no one might see it except the holy Spirit who is called the mother of the living. And she called his name Yaltabaoth." – The Apocryphon of John

The Apocryphon of John, discovered in Upper Egypt in 1945, is perhaps one of the more significant Gnostic texts which hold a hidden relation to the Adversary. These early Christian writings, dated roughly AD 350, were perhaps one of the most significant records of the history of Gnostic records. It was written that Barbelo (called Sophia), a great and powerful female archon, who was considered beautiful and near perfection, desired to create a child. She went off alone and begat this child. While she desired to create something like herself, this child was imperfect and different. She saw the results of her creative desire, and cast him off away from her where others may not see him. This child of chaos took the form of a Lion Serpent, who contained the Fire and Light of Heaven, and the individualistic and rebellious thought which separated him from the other archons. As written in the Apocryphon of John:

"Now the archon who is weak has three names. The first name is Yaltabaoth, the second is Saklas, and the third is Samael. And he is impious in his arrogance which is in him. For he said, 'I am God and there is no other God beside me,' for he is ignorant of his strength, the place from which he had come." – The Apocryphon of John

That Yaltabaoth, which means Ilda, child, Baoth, chaos was cast off from his mother Barbelo, he learned of independence and reliance upon the self. He saw no need to worship or hold relevance to another, thus proclaimed his independence spiritually. The fire which was within Yaltabaoth was pure intelligence and beauty, yet his nature was both darkness and light, he made himself strong and filled with wisdom from his time alone, and discovered the powers within. Here Yalabaoth understood the power of creation, and began to work independently from all other archons.

"And when the light had mixed with the darkness, it caused the darkness to shine. And when the darkness had mixed with the light, it darkened the light and it became neither light nor dark, but it became dim." – The Apocryphon of John

Here we see the significance of darkness, and the hidden fire of self knowledge and that Samael mixed both to beget his creations. This is the model of the sorcerer that by Will and Desire does become able to create accordingly. Here we are able to read that the Fire of Heaven was taken from Barbelo and used by Yaltabaoth:

"This is the first archon who took a great power from his mother. And he removed himself from her and moved away from the places in which he was born. He became strong and created for himself other aeons with a flame of luminous fire which (still)

exists now. And he joined with his arrogance which is in him and begot authorities for himself. The name of the first one is Athoth, whom the generations call the reaper. The second one is Harmas, who is the eye of envy. The third one is Kalila-Oumbri. The fourth one is Yabel. The fifth one is Adonaiou, who is called Sabaoth. The sixth one is Cain, whom the generations of men call the sun. The seventh is Abel. The eighth is Abrisene. The ninth is Yobel. The tenth is Armoupieel. The eleventh is Melceir-Adonein. The twelfth is Belias, it is he who is over the depth of Hades. And he placed seven kings - each corresponding to the firmaments of heaven - over the seven heavens, and five over the depth of the abyss, that they may reign. And he shared his fire with them, but he did not send forth from the power of the light which he had taken from his mother, for he is ignorant darkness." – The Apocryphon of John

It must be considered that Darkness cannot be considered complete ignorance that it is where the rebellious journey into – it is the forbidden and unknown. One must have a Mind and individual consciousness to break from the natural order, thus darkness presents a gift of individuality – it allows the Fire within them is seen. Yaltabaoth was able to create other spirits as well, such as Belias, Cain and others. Saklas, as is one of his many names understood the leverage of power which came from within, and how to change his shape to be beautiful and angelic, that the other angels would hear his voice. Yaltabaoth, who is known as Lucifer, could speak unto them that they may hear him, and that Blackened Fire within could be sparked within them as well. As written in the Apocryphon of John:

"But Yaltabaoth had a multitude of faces, more than all of them, so that he could put a face before all of them, according to his desire, when he is in the midst of seraphs. He shared his fire with them; therefore he became lord over them. Because of the power of the glory he possessed of his mother's light, he called himself God. And he did not obey the place from which he came. And he united the seven powers in his thought with the authorities which were with him. And when he spoke it happened." – The Apocryphon of John

Here we see that Lucifer first awoke the other angels that they saw not only his brilliance, but that fire within them was awakened. He called himself a God, that which recognized its self-divinity and his power to create. Thus here we find that initially Yaltabaoth was the most powerful archon, much like his earlier form of Ahriman, the Adversary. In darkness did he discover his light; the world he sought to create. Humanity was given this fire by Samael, who came unto the earth initiated the spark of the flame of self-knowledge. The Devil as he is called later, mingled with both darkness and light; held within a light brighter than any mere angel, yet devoured those before him who were lost in self righteousness. As written in the Bible, supposed words of Jesus:

"Ye are of your father the devil, and the lusts of your father ye will do. He was a murderer from the beginning, and abode not in the truth, because there is no truth in him. When he speaketh a lie, he speaketh of his own: for he is a liar, and the father of it." - Gospel of John

That the children of humanity are indeed the seed of Samael and Lilith, the Devil are those descendents of Cain the Witch Father, that those who affirm the devil are thereby of this spirit of strength and wisdom. The Spirit of Flame, called Samael and many other names, who is a dragon and beast in spirit, came in the form of man to test him. One account of the testing came in the form of a man to question the sheep of Jesus:

"That a Pharisee named Arimanius approached him and said to him, 'Where is your master whom you followed?' And he said to him, 'He has gone to the place from which he came.' The Pharisee said to him, 'With deception did this Nazarene deceive you, and he filled your ears with lies, and closed your hearts (and) turned you from the traditions of your fathers.'" - The Apocryphon of John

It must be considered that the questions asked by the Adversary are indeed tests. They are tests of spirit, or Will and of resolve. The Luciferian Path is filled with tests of strength, on failing could lead to self-destruction, while a test passed will reward the Satanist or Luciferian with Light. The Christians look upon what is the opposite as ignorance or evil; yet they are filled with the self-delusions of what may be perceived as one path only. It must be understood as well that the Luciferian understands the very practice of Magick as a development of consciousness, of becoming something greater than previously thought – striving for self excellence and wisdom, no matter what path that may be. This is what lies within the Triangle of Darkness, the evocation center itself: the Circle. Herein is the binding of diabolic power, the very essence of the Adversary who is both Fire mixed with Darkness, and with shadow does the sorcerer design and cast his will in the world.

The sorcerer is one who seeks to not only identify him or herself with the Adversary, rather invoke this force through them and it shall become them by means of magical fascination and arte.

V. The Path of The Crooked Serpent
The God of The Jagged Spine - Leviathan

In the caverns and caves of the abyssic darkness, wherein the water depths weave a lonely song, comes a whispering hiss of the past and future. In blood this name is recalled, spiraling in the back of the spine through the brain of man. The Rahab Daemon, who has fallen forth into the oceans and long since transformed in the Coiling Dragon of timeless being, emerged Leviathan! Unto the Deserts of Dendain does Behemoth dwell, now a beast of gigantic stature, who listens to the Voice of the Adversary, the Will – Inspiring force of motion and evolution. Rivers of Blood flow that flowers may grow from their nourishment of the soil, that the Sun and the Moon capture a pleasure filled garden, knowing of the demonium of the earth beneath the surface – the nurturing of the Horned Spirit of the Sun and the Moon.

Leviathan represents a subconscious source of power within each Luciferian and Satanist, it is the possibility and chaos within the self, it is not a representation of that type of mental and spiritual energy, rather a coiling source which not only strengthens those traits you develop and overcome, but also inspires terror and the mirror which reflects the inner fire of the beast and angel within.

"Leviathan, the great Dragon from the Watery Abyss, roars fourth as the surging sea, and these invocations are his tribunals." –The Satanic Bible, Anton Szandor LaVey

Leviathan also represents the passions which arise within us – while Belial may be the manifestation or flesh made of those passions, Satan the Will behind it and Lucifer the imagination to accomplish it, Leviathan is that beast from the Ocean of the Subconscious itself.

The mysteries of Leviathan have for long challenged Magicians, Christians and occult scholars alike. Let us seek to determine workable points which may present a clear definition of what this name means, how it may be used as a model in sorcery, thus presenting the magician in the coils of this dragon.

"The fleeing serpent, the coiling serpent, the powerful with the seven heads" – A Caanite description of Lotan, a form of Behemoth and Leviathan.

In the 60th chapter of the Book of Enoch, Leviathan is presented as a great dragon which is of the sea, the primordial chaos which this great serpent dwells, and the very abyss. Leviathan is also another name for Rahab, the Angel of Violence. The concept of this mysterious dragon is, according to the system of Justinus[38] Leviathan is a "Bad Angel". The Hebrew term refers to Leviathan as that "which gathers itself together in folds", thus the coiling dragon. It should be known that the circle itself is timeless and represents the eternal spirit. Leviathan in this instance is the guardian of the abyss and timeless in essence. Isaiah 27:1 calls Leviathan "that crooked serpent".

---

[38] From The Legends of the Jews, Ginzberg.

The fallen angel Rahab itself means "Violence" and refers to his name or title as "Sar shel yam", in Hebrew "Prince of the Primordial Sea". The source of the twin fallen angels Leviathan and Behemoth, presents both as beasts and dragons which hold much power when they fell.

"And that day will two monsters be parted, one monster, a female named Leviathan in order to dwell in the abyss of the ocean over the fountains of water, and a male called Behemoth which holds his chest in an invisible desert whose name is Dendayen, east of the Garden of Eden." – Enoch 60: 7-8

These twin dragons in the beginning were said to be angels, but took monstrous form and fell to earth, Leviathan, represented as often female and male, and Behemoth being a male, to respectively, the Abyss of Oceans and the Earth. In this lore, Lucifer fell yet retained something of his former self – a role which each angel played differently depending on their individual personality and nature.

Eliphas Levi is created with the creation of the Sigil which was first indoctrinated by Anton LaVey in the 1960's as the Church of Satan. This image appeared in 1961 in a French book entitled *"Histoire en 1000 Images de la Magie"*. This sigil, which is composed of the goat head within an inverse pentagram, spells Samael and Lilith in the circle, representing the two daemonic forces which are antinomian in nature. What encircles and surrounds the three (Samael, Lilith and the Goat Head, or what Rabbis could call Cain) is the LVYThN, which is spelled from the bottom counter clockwise, with the Hebrew letters lamed, vav, yod, tav, nun. This is indeed a sigil of personal power used by Satanists and Luciferians, representing the possibilities and power within the self. The Levi version with the original spelling of Samael and Lilith is a Grade symbol within the Luciferian Guild, The Order of Phosphorus.

The Book of Job presents a very interesting description of Leviathan:

"His back is made of rows of shields,
shut up closely as with a seal...
his sneezings flash forth light
and his eyes are like the eyelids of the dawn.
Out of the mouth go flaming torches;
Sparks of fire leap forth...
In his neck abides strength,
Terror dances before him."

This indicates that the form of Leviathan is difficult to comprehend. In the biblical art of Liber Floridus, the Antichrist, emerald and crimson robes flowing, rides upon Leviathan, who is pictured as a great Dragon-Beast with four legs, talon like teeth with blackened eyes. The face of this beast is the model for which has been invoked during the Coven Maleficia[39] Rites involving the ascension of power.

---

[39] The Coven which founded The Order of Phosphorus, renamed "Maleficia" after the Day of Cain for the group, August 22nd.

The bible makes further reference to Leviathan in Job:

"May those who curse days curse that day, those who are ready to rouse Leviathan. May its morning stars become dark; may it wait for daylight in vain and not see the first days of the dawn."

Leviathan is considered to being connected with Azhdeha, the dragon, the very home of Tiamat and some suggesting also Set (who is known in lore to take the form of Serpents), also connected to Tiamat, the Chaos Dragon of the Akko-Sumerians. In The Book of the Sacred Magic of Abra-Melin the Mage, Leviathan is one of the four crowned Princes of Hell, spell from the Hebraic root of LVIThN. He is called the Crooked or Piercing Serpent or Dragon. Leviathan is a chief daemon along with Lucifer, Satan and Belial. Anton LaVey attributed Leviathan to the direction of West, associated with Water.

Understanding Leviathan provides a more significant challenge than any other Daemon. Rahab itself is a fallen spirit of timeless existence, as it wraps or folds in upon itself, thus a serpent which has mastered time, thus possesses a higher capacity beyond common human perception. A Luciferian or Satanic Magician would use Leviathan as the Circle, and within the Circle of Self (the magician) does he or she transform themselves.

"And they worshipped the Dragon which gave power unto the Beast"-Revelation 13:4

The definition of violence is something marked by extreme force, or a sudden and intense activity. Thus as Rahab better known as Leviathan, is a force of change and movement. This draws a connection to the Egyptian Set, the God of Darkness, Chaos and Storms. As the self develops and seeks to perceive new areas of its psyche-eccentric being, Leviathan encircles he or she to control the power itself; thus an consistent and timeless initiatory force.

This brings a question concerning the individual mind and the Crooked Dragon – what is the subjective focus of Leviathan; what does this daemon represent to the conscious self? How do we use Leviathan in a Left Hand Path initiatory way?

Leviathan is the encircler/ensorceller of the self; the circumference of the astral and physical body. It is the timeless being, the psyche transformed into Daemon. As it is the Angel of Violence and Dragon of the Watery Abyss, it represents the mastery of the self through change and the ability to place occurrence and happenings into the magicians own individual universe.

Through the refinement of the subconscious (as based on the transference level of the unconscious to conscious via dreaming) the self grows in the study/interplay of his or her own environment and reality as it is perceived. This is the process of when the Black Magician begins to effectively crystallize the perceived essence of self, the very scratched surface to the core of self, and allow for a beginning of expansion of the Will to manifest in other areas inward or outward.

This enables the sorcerer to place his/herself on the path of becoming a Demon, an enfleshed deified being which is separate from the natural order via the discovery and basic mastery of the Black Flame. This is the Luciferian essence revealed, that which confirms the interplay between Azazel/Shaitan and Leviathan among other Fallen Angels.

"And the beast which I saw was like unto a leopard, and his feet were as the feet of a bear, and his mouth as the mouth of a lion: and the dragon gave him his power, and his seat, and great authority" – Revelation 13:2

Leviathan is the Lord of the Will, the daemon which awakens and crystallizes the essence of self; that in the center is the inextinguishable Black Flame, the Gift of Iblis. In Luciferian terms, the maker of the possibility of Union between Samael and Lilith, the creation of Cain as the self transformed. Change may be invoked and willed by the mind depending on the path of the magician.

If he/she is upon one path, their focus may invoke positive change, through an optimistic outlook and creating or impelling a beneficial progression in their own environment. In the model of the Witches Sabbat, Lucifer is the imagination, the Adversary who is both angel and demon, the isolate self. Leviathan is the daemon which encircles the possibility of self, who creates the link which the Luciferic Angel may develop in the Black Magician. Transformation through Deific self-association is the transference to Becoming.

Ahriman represents the sorcerous side of Lucifer, the Darkness made flesh. In relation to Leviathan, Ahrimanean Sorcery or yatuk-dinoih, responds and is directed by the self in response to the natural predilection of the sorcerers' magical interests. Thus by this alone, the activation and self-determined focus channels the Will via dreaming, creating a possibility for such rapid movement to occur via the path of sorcery, etc.

Leviathan once faced by the Sorcerer cannot be banished – it is then a perceived sense of who we are. To deny Leviathan is to become blind to our possibility and our very future. For one to begin to grasp the possibility of the immortal psyche, the mind which stands alone, which has emerged and evolved, depends upon the crystallization of the essence in relation to Leviathan – Lucifer and Lilith, the force which creates and empowers the mind.

Beelzebub or Beelzbuth according to S.L. MacGregor Mathers in the "Sacred Magic of Abramelin the Mage" described his name as meaning BOL, Hebrew for Lord and ZBVB, Flies. Beelzebub is a form of the Adversary which holds close – if not identical – associations to Satan. The name Baal'zebuth was known as the "Prince of Demons" in the time of Christ, when the Pharisees took against Christ. They associated Christ having been possessed by Beelzebub and referred to his power as being able to drive the demons from one by the power of demons. It is suggested that the name of Beelzebub, being the God of Ekron which was a Philistine city. The Canaanite name "Baal" which is an early Pagan god is the root of this demon. King Solomon had dealings with this demon and learned much about his nature. He is considered the Lord of Flies and a powerful force. An interesting text concerning him is the following:

"Then Hell, receiving Satan the prince, with sore reproach said unto him: O prince of perdition and chief of destruction, Beelzebub, the scorn of the angels and spitting of the righteous why wouldest thou do this? Thou wouldest crucify the King of glory and at his decease didst promise us great spoils of his death: like a fool thou knewest not what thou didst. For behold now, this Jesus putteth to flight by the brightness of his majesty all the darkness of death, and hath broken the strong depths of the prisons, and let out the prisoners and loosed them that were bound. And all that were sighing in our torments do rejoice against us, and at their prayers our dominions are vanquished and our realms conquered, and now no nation of men feareth us any more. And beside this, the dead which were never wont to be proud triumph over us, and the captives which never could be joyful do threaten us. O prince Satan, father of all the wicked and ungodly and renegades wherefore wouldest thou do this? They that from the beginning until now have despaired of life and salvation-now is none of their wonted roarings heard, neither doth any groan from them sound in our ears, nor is there any sign of tears upon the face of any of them. O prince Satan, holder of the keys of hell, those thy riches which thou hadst gained by the tree of transgression and the losing of paradise, thou hast lost by the tree of the cross, and all thy gladness hath perished." - Gospel of Nicodemus VII (XXIII)

Here Beelzebub is the tester and accuser of Christ, he by having him in myth crucified acted as his initiator and teacher, he tested Christ by word and prose and Christ proved a powerful student. Beelzebub had him face death and Christ was then uplifted from flesh to Spirit, just as Beelzebub has experienced in the Fall; yet Christ was said to have returned to Heaven after gaining a perception of his own being and world.

VI. Tiamat, Pazuzu and Moloch & other Gods

The Enuma Elish, written roughly in the twelfth century BCE to celebrate Babylonian celebrations, presents the primal mother in one of her first forms. Tiamat (of the primal salt water oceans) was mentioned as being before all other gods; in fact she was according to these post-Sumerian tablets as being along with her mate, Apsu (sweet water oceans), being before all other Gods or heaven. Both Apsu and Tiamat created children, who were Gods which possessed wisdom and a desire for life. Soon the Gods were fighting and creating such discord it disturbed Apsu, who called to his mate:

"'Their manners revolt me, day and night without remission we suffer. My will is to destroy them, all of their kind, we shall have peace at last and we will sleep again.' When Tiamat heard she was stung, she writhed in lonely desolation, her heart worked in secret passion, Tiamat said, 'Why must we destroy the children that we made? If their ways are troublesome, let us wait a little while.'" - Enuma Elish, translated by N.K. Sandars

Here we can see that Tiamat had love for her children, and sought to allow them to develop. Apsu was less patient and sought to destroy them anyway. It was soon that Apsu was bound and destroyed by Ea, while Tiamat lay catatonic. Upon her awakening, one of her children said:

"When they killed Apsu you did not stir, you brought no help to him, your husband. Now Anu has called up from the four quarters this abomination of winds to rage in your guts, and we cannot rest for the pain;Remember Apsu in your heart, your husband, remember Mummu who was defeated; now you are all alone, and thrash around in desolation, and we have lost your love, our eyes ache and we long for sleep 'Rouse up, our Mother! Pay them back and make them empty like the wind.'" - Enuma Elish, translated by N.K. Sandars

Here is the description of how Tiamat transforms herself from creative to destructive. It is known her form is a Dragon; she represented the bitter – such as Salt water. Tiamat was always depicted, as seen from tablets held in the British Museum as being a dragon like figure, covered in scales, talon clawed and with both tail and wings. Tiamat's form later was echoed in later Persian art as the "Ahriman – Dragon", being a form of her masculine counterpart. Tiamat grew angry and sought revenge; here is the spirit of the predator in its birth. Tiamat is the great devouring source and the life giving mother according to these ancient tales.

"Mother Hubur, who fashions all things, Contributed an unfaceable weapon: she bore giant snakes, Sharp of tooth and unsparing of fang. She filled their bodies with venom instead of blood. She cloaked ferocious dragons with fearsome rays And made them bear mantles of radiance, made them godlike" – Enuma Elish, translated by Stephanie Dalley.

Mummu Tiamat stands as the principle of deific possibility, as related to the self. It must be understood that the Gods were not created in essence by man, merely the names of which they are called. We manifest the anthropomorphic traits of the Gods by our design, yet their essence was before us. The Adversary as both Lilith/Tiamat and Lucifer/Ahriman/Set is far older than we; this very force is both creative and destructive.

Tiamat was angered with the ones who killed her companion that she stirred, creating new children who were hungry for the lifeforce of her enemy. Tiamat in her sorcerous path created vampyric and draconian children, who despite bestial form, were considered to be superior to the brooding first born who killed her mate Apsu.

"She filled their bodies with venom instead of blood.
She cloaked ferocious dragons with fearsome rays
And made them bear mantles of radiance, made them godlike,
(chanting this imprecation)
'Whoever looks upon them shall collapse in utter terror!
Their bodies shall rear up continually and never turn away!'
She stationed a horned serpent, a mushussu-dragon, and a lahmu-hero,
An ugallu-demon, a rabid dog, and a scorpion-man,

Aggressive umu-demons, a fish-man, and a bull-man
Bearing merciless weapons, fearless in battle.
Her orders were so powerful, they could not be disobeyed.
In addition she created eleven more likewise.
Over the gods her offspring who had convened a council for her
She promoted Qingu and made him greatest among them,
Conferred upon him leadership of the army, command of the assembly,
Raising the weapon to signal engagement, mustering combat-troops,
Overall command of the whole battle force." –Enuma Elish

The spell of creation and making was used here in primal form. Her desire was cast and thus her will made flesh. Adepts upon the Luciferian Path are able to realize the significance of intoning desire to make it flesh, by Naming, willing and naming does the self grow stronger. By all accounts in this section of the ancient Enuma Elish tablets, do we view and understand the very essence of Magick, that all emerges from the Will and self. Tiamat is the possibility and will of our subconscious, that which forms order from nothingness. By encircling yourself in your desire can you command your Will upon the world. This is the Luciferian doctrine, that which has almost been buried by the Right Hand Path anti-spiritualists who seek mind-death.

Tiamat, in her anger and roused desire, created shadows which became flesh, beasts and dragon children who would fight those she sought to devour. Here we can see Tiamat as both beneficial and destructive, she is a primal dragon – form of Lilith or the Manichaean Az, that is the daemonic feminine which is very much a part of all humans.

Qingu, the Son/lover of Tiamat, was given the power of her throne, from primal abyssic darkness to the burning essence of the Black Flame, here Qingu is crowned as the Dragon King.

"And she set him upon a throne.
'I have cast the spell for you and made you greatest in the gods' assembly!
I have put into your power rule over all the gods!
You shall be the greatest, for you are my only lover!
Your commands shall always prevail over all the Anukki!'
Then she gave him the Tablet of Destinies and made him clasp it to his breast.
'Your utterance shall never be altered! Your word shall be law!'
When Qingu was promoted and had received the Anu-power
And had decreed destinies for the gods his sons, (he said),
'What issues forth from your mouths shall quench Fire!
Your accumulated venom shall paralyze the powerful!'" – Enuma Elish

Mummu Tiamat, called also Mummu Hubur (Mother of Monsters) is the life giving mother of darkness, who begets serpents to expand her Will. In the story of Enuma Elish, Tiamat's hordes are destroyed and Qingu's blood is used to create humanity, while originally they were created from Mud, yet Qingu's blood brought humanity the flame of perception, of individual being. Thus in certain context we see a pre-tale of Lucifer or Satan, who fell to earth.

A key to understanding the legends of Tiamat in a mythological or merely within a inspirational-initatory context would be that Tiamat was the primal form (active – creative) form of Lilith, who empowered/awakened Qingu (Ahriman/Lucifer) and by this stirred to life the children of the Dragon. Recall the Manichaean lore of Az teaching the fallen angels how to copulate and beget demons, thus the lore of Az-Lilith being a creative source, demons being a manifestation of the will to invoke what is called Ginnung, or Chaos. This is a concept of Norse mythology, which holds a parallel in that the primal force is manifested as a dragon. Chaos has a dual aspect, being both negative and positive. In this aspect, Tiamat manifests upon earth her legions and soon formed life. Thus instead of death, as Tiamat is undying, she died the first death of her form and remanifested later as Lilith and her children, the Lamashtu, Lilim, Lilitu and Kali among others.

Lilith is the dominant Will, the unrestrained yet ultimately self-controlled aspect of the human and animal psyche. She is by her own understanding a link between the bestial and the angelic. Lilith understands that humanity must be uplifted, yet no one must not forget the atavistic and animal strength which sleeps in the mind. By developing and controlling the animalistic aspects of the self; allowing them to work in your benefit according to your Will, success will be yours by design. Lilith is by all aspects in flesh the rebel, the spirit of flame who will not be held by any oppressive force. Lilith made her home near the red sea, in caves from which she spawned her demons who would spread her linage unto mankind. Lilith was the opener of the way to the Sabbatic Crossroads; that is, she brought the link between dreaming and enfleshing desires. Her succubi and incubi went forth by the dreamroads to copulate with mankind; thus spawing children of desire from their unions. You may look also to the Cabalistic union between Samael (the Devil or Solar principle) and Lilith which was brought in union by the dragon, Leviathan. The sexual union of these two aspects created Cain or as by other names Baphomet. This process may be directed inward in a self-alchemical sense from which Cain may take flesh in your mind; body thus creating a new type of Luciferian Individual – strong, isolate and determined to enjoy and be productive according to their own Will – in life and beyond.

Invoke Lilith within and beyond; she is an active principle which is perhaps larger than you may first have perceived – or perhaps not. You may have sensed Her nature; that she is something beyond flesh yet so enveloped in it.

Within the Luciferian and Sabbatic doctrine, Lilith has many transformative and multi-cultural states of which she manifests. In the primal beginnings Lilith was Tiamat, the female chaos dragon, who may be represented as the Constellation of Alpha Draco or Thuban. The Ath-Thuban, or "the serpent" is a constellation which holds relations to Azhdeha, the devouring dragon.

In Sumerian and Babylonian myths, the Chaldean dragon Tiamat was the representation of Alpha Draco. Tiamat existed within primal chaos; she was still yet alone in intellect and isolate being. Her form was a great dragon-serpent; she walked within primal chaos and created demons such as scorpion-men and other bestial forms of primal hunger. When the flesh came from the Abyss, Tiamat eventually was cut asunder by Marduk – from this he created the earth. Tiamat was later considered the power of the North, just as her later counterpart Set and the Persian Ahriman.

How does one utilize the imagery of Tiamat within a Luciferian perspective? The Black Adept must seek to find what is *constant* within the self; the core essence which brings a parallel to the archetype or mask'd energy of Set and Ahriman, herein can Lilith coil herself within your mind as Tiamat the serpent. Find a suitable place for meditation and ritual workings, invoked her silently or with bellowed wind, allow your mind to fall in silent communion with Her, attribute something which reflects achieving goals when thinking of Her. When you invoke her later, or seek to target a victim or achieve a goal, the deep well of Tiamat will spiral up your spine to bring creative obsession, thus on a path to manifesting your desire.

Lamashtu

A Mesopotamian prayer against Lamashtu depicts her as a child devouring night demon, from which Lilitu and later Lilith emerged from. Lamashtu is Sumerian/Mesopotamian in origin and may best be considered a manifestation of the force of chaos in ancient times, specifically both aspects of nature and humanity. Her essence is eternal but her physical form changes.

"Great is the daughter of Heaven who tortures babies
Her hand is a net, her embrace is death
She is cruel, raging, angry, predatory
A runner, a thief is the daughter of Heaven
She touches the bellies of women in labor
She pulls out the pregnant women's baby
The daughter of Heaven is one of the Gods, her brothers
With no child of her own.
Her head is a lion's head
Her body is a donkey's body
She roars like a lion
She constantly howls like a demon-dog."
- Mesopotamian Incantation Prayer Against Lamashtu

Lamashtu was said to manifest with a head of a lion, a hairy body with bare breasts, blood stained hands and talon like feet, showed in tablets as holding a serpent in each hand. This demoness and the form she appeared in were not unlike the later Hebrew Lilith, whose form was partially beast and woman. Lamashtu was considered an evil demon goddess in her own time, whose consort was the demon of the south west wind, Pazuzu. That mentioning that her name was written in cuneiform suggested that she was a revered Goddess, albeit hostile and deadly. Lamashtu enjoyed the blood and flesh of children, both unborn and infant. She was blamed for most of the miscarriages then, so much was the fear of her others took to wearing amulets bearing the head of Pazuzu to protect them from her talons.

Pazuzu

A Babylonian and Assyrian demon which wandered the wastelands was considered one of the most malefic and beneficial Gods of Mesopotamia. Pazuzu is known to be a scavenger of the desert wastelands, a baleful devil which holds the power of life and death. His form was foreboding, a eagle-winged spirit, symbolizing the mastery over the element of air and the strength of the Sun, a fleshless head of a dog, grinning and hungry, talons on both hands and feet, a serpent headed penis and the tail of a scorpion. His body is depicted as having scales upon it as well, representing a physical manifestation of the very elements of the later God Angra Mainyu, or Ahriman, of the Persian lands.

In Lenormant described in "Histoire ancienne de l'Orient" and in "The History of the Devil", Dr. Paul Carus describes Pazuzu's influence of the South West Wind as:

"The south-west wind in Chaldea comes from the deserts of Arabia, and its burning breath parches everything, producing the same ravages as the khamsin in Syria and the simoon in Africa." – Lenormant

A description of a tablet from Mesopotamian times presents Pazuzu as holding the world in his clutches, restraining Lamashtu from devouring the world further. As quoted from Paul Carus and Lenormant:

"A bronze plate in the collection of M. De Clercq contains in a synoptic world-picture a representation of hell, and it is necessary that we here give a description of it. One side of the bronze plate is entirely occupied by a four-footed monster, with four wings, standing on eagle's claws. Raising himself on his hind feet, be looks as though he intended to jump over the plate against which he leans. His head reaches over the border as over the top of a wall. The face of the wild and roaring monster towers, on the other side of the plate, above a picture which is divided into four horizontal strips representing the heavens, the earth, and hell. In the top strip one sees the symbolic representations of the celestial bodies. Underneath appears a series of seven persons clad in long robes and having beads of a lion, a dog, a bear, a ram, a horse, an eagle, and a serpent. These are the celestial genii called ighigs. *The third strip exhibits a funeral scene, which undoubtedly happens on earth. Two personages dressed in the skin of a fish, after the fashion of the god Anu, are standing at the head and foot of a mummy. Further on there are two genii – one with a lion's head, the other with a jackal's head – who threaten one another with their daggers, and a man seems to flee from this scene of horror. The picture of the fourth strip is bathed in the floods of the ocean, which according to the traditional mythology of the Chaldeans reaches underneath the foundations of the earth. An ugly monster, half bestial, half human, with eagles' wings and claws, and a tail terminating in a snake's head, stands on the shore of the ocean, on which a boat is floating. This is the boat of the deity Elippu, frequently mentioned in the religious texts*

and probably the prototype of the boat of Charon in Greek mythology. In the boat is a horse which carries upon its back a gigantic lion-headed deity, holding in her hands two serpents; and two little lions jump to her breast to suck her milk. In the corner there are fragments of all kinds, human limbs, vases, and the remainders of a feast." –The History of the Devil and the Idea of Evil by Dr. Paul Carus

Pazuzu represents balance and perception that the earth holds forces which both kill and bless, depending on the approach. The Black Adepts who wish to work with Pazuzu and Lamashtu in their initiatory work may approach them as vampyric beings, Luciferian with the knowledge of both heaven and hell but the hunger for life – force which allows their independent existience, the Thirst for life and wisdom therein.

Molech

The God of the Israelites before the seventh century BC depicts Moloch as a manipulation of the name Melek, meaning King. Molech was worshipped in Hinnom, called also Gehenna. This place is located in what was called Tophet, and was considered another word for Hell. We can see that the word which came to represent Hell, being the Anglo-Saxon, Helan = a secret place, Arezura = the mountain of the north and abode of demons, Hades = the house in the land of the dead were not connected with a lake of fire. With the sacrifice of a child to Moloch in this place called Hell, Moloch is credited with the Christian concept of a lake of fire, being that Molech/Moloch was the enemy of the Judeo-Christian God. Children were placed in the fire shrouded arms of Moloch, whose screams were heard throughout the rituals. These cries and screams were incidently muffled by the sound of "Toph", meaning drum. Moloch, while being a Sun god, of strength and power, was incidently a vampiric or Luciferian God. In modern times Moloch workings would only involve the use of semen and burnt accordingly, not literal child killings. The Black Adept will literally visualize his own self in the form of Moloch as the Fire or Sun God, then in the throes of night ejaculate while visualizing health and strength within the mind and body, then allow the sperm to be fed to the fire as sacrifice. Gehenna is located in south-west of Jerusalem, in a valley now called "Wadi al-Rababah.", it was considered a place of unholy fires and sulfur smelling surroundings. Much of this area was the foundation for the Christian conception of Hell.

Moloch later became Adramalech which is a mixture of Adar and Malik, displaying Babylonian heritage. Moloch survived in Carthage as well. His form was united with Malik-Baal-Kronos, being the cannibal/vampiric God. Diodorus Siculus described in surviving texts how the Carthaginians during a siege had sacrificed two hundred boys to Kronos.

Tezcatlipoca

The Smoking Mirror in Aztec lore, he was considered the Prince of this World and rose from a spirit of the air to the supreme god of the Aztecs for a period. His symbol was the black obsidian mirror which was used in scrying. Tezcatlipoca is almost identical to the Egyptian God Set in that he is the Adversary, one who challenges. Favors can be made with Tezcatlipoca only by those who are willing to face terrors and overcome them. In an initiatory sense, favors are initiation, obtainment of secret knowledge, facing terrors is merely the struggle of Will and task at hand. This falls into the aspect that indeed Tezcatlipoca is the God of the Strong, of sorcerers and magicians and those who walk the path opposing all others. This was a God of cunning, of sorcerous intent; his Will to Power would not be ignored. According to Lewis Spence, in "The Myths of Mexico and Peru", one of the names of Tezcatlipoca was "Yoalli Ehecatl", meaning "Night Wind", which refers to his night journeys, which people made benches of stone to offer as a resting place during his evening journey's. Other names of Tezcatlipoca were "Nezahualpilli" meaning "The Hungry Chief" and "Yaotzin" which is "The Enemy". Perhaps his best known name was "Telpochtli", the "Youthful Warrior" for which the early years of a young man's life were sacred to Tezcatlipoca. He is depicted as holding within his left hand a mirror-shield which has four spear darts, his right hand holding a dart placed in what was a spear-thrower, called an Atlatl. He is both life giver and death bringer, much like the image of Set in the Egyptian pantheon.

Like Set, Tezcatlipoca within his own Aztec culture was the mightiest of the Gods, as he embraced both the darkness and light within. Many would make pilgrimages to his temple, called Teocalli and offer worship in times of trouble.

Huitzilopochtili

The Aztec God of War, whose words were said to be "My mission and my task is War" was a sacrifice demanding God. It is suggested by historians that up to 20,000 prisoners and slaves were sacrificed to Huitzilopochtili at one time, invading Spaniards were horrified at the cults which offered blood to this Sun god. The victim had his heart ceremoniously cut from his chest, then burned to offer to Huitzilopochtili.

His abobe is said to be the seventh heaven, which has blue characteristics. This draws relation to the number seven as being significant in Qlippothic-Hebrew magical lore, blue being the traditional color of astral-air deities in Tibetian and Indian lore. It is said that Huitzilopochtili was fed by the blood of sacrifice, called Chalchihuatl which gave him strength for daily battle.

Tlazolteotl

The eater of filth and Goddess of Sex and Witchcraft is perhaps the most suitable manifestation of Lilith/Az in the Aztec world. Tlazolteotl represents the Left hand path aspects of witchcraft, that she is the Goddess of all unclean behavior. She has many aspects, of maiden, crone and all that which corrupts humanity. Yet she devours the sins of memories of lewd behavior to those who may not be comfortable with this later. Tlazolteotl is by all means a Left hand path model of introspection and antinomian workings which involve Sex Magick. The name Tlaelquani means "Filth Eater" and holds connections to the Indian-Tantric Aghoris, who utilize the objects of repulsion to guide and test one through their initiation.

END

This essay has intertwined within the basic scope of Luciferian and Satanic Magick, while not leaving a completely exhaustive study. It is meant to open a different point of view to this forbidden area of lore. As a practitioner, I am with confidence able to confirm the path against all others; it is challenge and instinct wherein it dries up all need of blind faith and pointless regard. Faith is one which truly comes from a Willed Desire of Belief, thus creates truth from the foundation therein. At the end of this study I must ask, what has been learnt of the Adversary within the practice of Magick? Is the Adversary valid within modern times from the early foundations? With reference to the practice of Magick, the Opposer is the core column which supports all others; it is needed and those who are able to look past the sterile Gods and Goddess of mere sunlight may then grasp the Dual Ecstasy of the Adversary, of both the Sun and the Moon. Magick is the gift of Iblis, and must be respected as such unless the soul becomes devoured by its own weakness. With reference to the second question concerning modern times the Adversary is more so alive now as ever. This force exists through those who affirm Satan and those who *ignore* this force. It is very much a part of us and a model for that which we may become. Choose your models well, for you may become just as they.

Chapter Two

The Grimoires of Luciferian Witchcraft

I. The Book of Cain

This inspired text was created under meditative and inspired circumstances by its author, Michael W. Ford. The text is not in any way meant to lay claim to special communications or any other contacts – but rather a focused ritual grimoire. The work is dedicated to the Wanderer, Cain who has passed from desert to forest to desert again. Cain may be sought in the places where men and women fear to walk, those ghost roads which prove dangerous to those unwilling to face their own darkest aspects of self.

This Book is a Working for me, as a student of the Luciferian Path, and as I wrote it, studied it and then prepared this text I have further come into being. I hope those who read this work understand that it is a Ritual in Progress, that each sentence fans the

Flames of the Dragon and his consort, Lilith, the Mother of the Witch Path. Cain has presented me with different elements to think about and to further encourage others to develop what is the Sabbatic and Luciferian Path. When staring into the mirror, Cain appears – his very mask of Set-an is shown to me.

Know that the legend and myth of Cain is one of the mirrored transformation of the self. Cain being the son of Samael and Lilith (through Eve), the Son of the Serpent, whose fiery nature differed from his half-brother Abel, who in the circle of the wise, can be said to represent the uninitiated self which is Abel, the common clay. Cain was awoken by his blood, which is that of Samael or Satan.

The murder of Abel was done so by way of encircling the energy of the blood, Cain had killed Abel with a blade of sorts or a rock, such is not known. What is commonly perceived is the blade, the ritual bloodletter or athame. This metal used in the witch circle is seen as the blade forged by Tubal Cain or Cain the Blacksmith, blessed in the fires of the Adversary or Azazel, who is the Dragon his father. Within the circle, bound by flower, does the blade fall symbolically, killing the unitiated self, offering this blood to his Demon and within the circle of Darkness is Cain born and illuminated as the possibility of a God, as he knows blood, darkness and light. Cain takes the skull of Abel, which is to be the spirit fetish to remind him of his antinomian nature, and go forth away from his tribe, in the hermit like introspection to find his own True Will. He travels long and is guided by his Demon, which leads him to Lilith. Upon being initiated further he travels forth to the land of Nod and is met there according to some Hereditary Witchcraft circles by the Devil, wherein he makes a pact and becomes the first witch and Satanist.

The symbolism of Cain as the Blacksmith is revealed in the elements which surround the role of the smith. The working of metals, the forging of iron into weapons, armor and normally used items present in cultures define a sense of transformation and strength, also the trespassing into the mastery over aspects of nature itself – thus the Blacksmith is antinomian and working the union of Daemon with flesh, thus transformation. The Forge itself is the self, the Great Work in motion and the fire is brought forth by Cain, the Initiatic guide, awakened by Samael and Lilith.

BECOME!

That Azazel fell from the heavens as a great star, enthroned with the Emerald Crown of the highest aethyr, came down blazing as a fiery meteor. He plunged to the depths of the earth, the darkest areas where no being of light dwelled. Those who descended with Azazel, whom is called Lucifer by later ones only had glimpsed at the Fire which Azazel had shown unto them. The passed into the nightmare lands, where they felt lost as their fire was nearly extinguished. Azazel woke still illuminated brightly, a Dark Star which beheld the Fire of Heaven. When the fire fell from the sky to the earth, did my father them perceive this world of flesh, that both spirit and the material plane were brought together in union.

Understanding that this Fire was illuminated within, Azazel felt a moment of triumph, that by perceiving the self and willing the being into stronger forms – he was uniquely separate, isolate and beautiful. He stood up, weakened yet still defiant and pleased at this success of this nightmare land, he began to rouse those many that slept from the shock of the fall around him.

Belial, the angel created after him, awoke and began to sing beautiful hymns, such as which never sounded so sorrowful, yet touching in their passion for their coming forth into being. Belial was indeed different from Azazel – while Lucifer was fire and air in spirit, Belial was of Earth and found this place comfortable and familiar. Belial said unto Azazel, "Who would else wake and join us in this moment of triumph – that we are without the highest Empyrean realm we now look about to understand we are different, strong and noble in our selves. Awake with us Djinn!"

Leviathan arose before them. He had taken the form of a great Serpent, a Dragon who beheld both sexes of human flesh – Leviathan would seek the Oceans and understood the art of sorcery as a totality of being – timeless and alive in its sacred flame. Leviathan found the Nightmares comforting, and dreams would be his fluid waking within worlds.

Many others rose up and joined with my father, who is the brightest of them all. He was Fire and his realm was Air, he was both death and life. I remember my father as possessing Adam who rode my mother Eve as the Dragon, driving deep within her core, enflamed with the spirit of Lilith. These were my earth parents, but it was the blood of Azazel called often Samael and Lilith which flows in my veins. It was this passion and possession which brought me into being, the first born of Witch Blood in the Circle of the Dragon's Emerald Crown.

Azazel gathered all in this secret place, which was of fire and blackened earth. Lucifer called this place Helan, the meeting place of spirits. The held their court here, encircled in sacred communion. Azazel spoke of perception and what they wished to become and do as their own desire, they were free. Did his mind become as the serpent, isolate and independent – that as Flame which was sacred and beautiful, Azazel now could understand both Good and Evil, the Darkness and the Light. Lucifer, my Angelick initiator, my soul and father, understood that he was both Demon and Angel, that he was beauty and ugliness. All of those in the circle of spirits made a sacred pact to go forth into the World of Horrors and do their Will.

Azazel, who refused to bow before common clay, the profane image of flesh known as Man and Woman, and then found them more appealing. Some were indeed fair, their women sensuous and their men showing a primitive potential of being. With this in mind, they would bring the Fire to them. Azazel and many of those Angels took by Will flesh in bodies appealing to such women, and copulated with them. My father taught them the sacred arts, hidden and the places of Serpents, how to work with the earth to direct and manifest their Will. Azazel taught Man how to hunt, fish and make weapons. He brought them the experience and knowledge to fight and defend, as well as shelter from the elements.

I too had been instinctively taught, which is the gift of my father, who walked the path of the dragon – who was the dragon. It was the perfected essence of flame which earthen heat could only catch a glimpse of – that the fires of spirit burn ever so bright, that in this torch shall my father be revealed. Lilith who wrapped her serpents' tail around Eve's brain, unlocked the depths of her lust and rode this Dragon until I was conceived – that was then perfection beheld.

I walked the paths with my family, and my brother Abel was born. My father, who was called Adam was alien to me, I knew him not but grew under his protection. My flesh mother Eve rode again this beast, from which Abel slept dreamless and in the fires of her lust was my sister Naamah born. At an early age, her difference amoung the tribe was even beyond mine, fled away from this family. I missed her but could not leave yet. I worked the fields as a being of nothing – my brother was beheld as beautiful. I was the dark one, considered by most – but yet I held more questions than they. I began to see Naamah in dreams, beautiful and grown – voluptuous as she rested with Lilith, who I sought in dreams. They whispered chants and sweet musick to my ears, and then I would go unto them – dawn would bring my waking into the mundane fields of my false family, and the ridicules of Abel.

It was one day in the fields that I built an altar at the base of a tree and then cut down my brother – I took his blood and skull before this gateway, and called to my true father and mother – I held no love for these who would treat me as a dead animal in their family. I would be marked again among the animals, who I could run with. I took this skull and the spirit of Abel with it – he would walk with me forever – this was taught to me in dreaming:

"Behold Cain, a blood filled skull bowl will show unto you that which the profane cannot see, yet in it's veil will the path of the Red Dragon be shown, you must come forth by dreaming to see within this bowl, and I shall wait for you there – Cauled in the Crimson drape, veiled from the eyes of the blind."

"Hold this skull and behold the spirits which walk with you, by self-transformation on the meeting path shall this mark be evermore – your father, the Dragon – Djinn of old forever walk with you, and in rapt meditation shall we pass from the clay of mortal hands"

"You shall thirst for water and for blood; both in dreaming shall be held from the dual gnosis. I hold the Golden Cup to your lips, that the Dragon's elixir hold strong – I then hand to you the skull bowl of my flowing blood, that you may taste the bitter sweetness of it's coppered kiss – then in your ecstasy and thy devil's phallus reaching towards the Sun shall my serpent's tongue enflame you to me…."

I then found myself wandering in the wilds, sleeping beneath the stars – hunting and learning nature without any other being. I perceived myself and what I was, what I became and what I could become. I understood life was precious, and beautiful. I was just as Beast yet a part of Angel as well. My dreaming guide would speak to me when I sought her, and I knew that I would come to her. I began walking the desert sands.

I dreamt of waking and diving a great abyssic tunnel, that which crawled from the depths of my mind, the horrid yet erotic shapes which appeared within it. I felt my very body changing, longing for transformation into the beasts of the field – then came an angel to me:

"Cain, who walks the lonely path, he who stands strong and defiant in the face of nothingness, shall you continue the thorn road to meet the Hag Queen, the sorcerous devourer of men and children – would you turn a road more traveled to the simple life yet unknown by others?"

The tester, robed in white and flowed within a strange and familiar light was challenging me, a very point of discovering my very inner essence, which I could sense. I said unto him:

"Angel, who would you be to tell me of thorns and roads less traveled? I have passed through the blood and bones of my brother, to walk within a shadow of which I am the only God that is – dreams feed my desires and I go forth among the Beasts of the fields, take yourself away from me as I shall not resign my path, for I seek mine own Mother who would either cut me to shreds or raise me up as God."

The Angel transformed into a very familiar dreaming body which taught me the ways of nature, yet he was a blackened shadow which held a Spirit – possessed knife – "Very good Cain, my Son of flesh, go forth unto your deep desire and seek Her of the Blood of Flame…I shall walk with
you again in a familiar way, take a leaf from my book and behold the Serpent's tongue and sight, that shall guide you unto her…"

The angel vanished, who I call father. I slept a dreamless sleep.

I continued walking; the desert sun drained my body. I ached and felt very thirst, having little water to sooth my burning throat. I understood what I was to do, and that nothing, save death would stop me. I could see this leaf of the ancient book, decorated in what was dried blood, serpents and signs of my becoming as I understood it. This was my comfort in this desert sand. I felt as if I would die, but yet I could not turn back. My being was tested, and I could not fail save the scorpions sting which would force me to eternal dreamless sleep – the very curse of the profane!

It was one night after many days of not finding the caves of which I sought, not seeing a soul or any living thing – save the shades of the earth which wander aimless. I visualized this ancient page, and with my minds' eye I summoned the sigils to flesh, and a gate opened before me:

"Zazas, Zazas, Nasatanada Zazas"

I saw a great Red Dragon coming forth, who was surrounded with flame. This dragon looked unto me and a great shadow emerged from its very flesh – this shadow, black as pitch arose and took the form of a bearded King, saying in a comely voice:

"My son, what do you ask of me?"

"My father, I grow weary, little food and water, I am confused, cold and scared. Shall you not guide me?" I said with innate honesty.

"Cain, you grow so close yet you are honest with me – what if I told you that your journey is in vain, and your mother and foreseen concubine lay beyond the veil of death?"

I grew angry unto this Dragon, who I called father and said:

"Then I shall walk the path of fire my self, yet she calls unto me nonetheless. I will not resign although I am tired and cold. You shall not bend me! Even if I must face darkness in eternity alone, I shall!"

This dragon grew in its surrounding flames and the King transformed into an Angelic Prince, and said unto me:

"Cain, my Son of Sons, you will find your mother and sister tomorrow, then you shall walk the path of night. By the Noon tide sun you have walked, and with the scorpions and serpents of the desert sands have you come forth as God. Your sign which is my sign on earth is the Pitch Fork within the fiery Sun, that is our aged mark of being and becoming. Cain, my son, our kin is ever deep and eternal. You are blessed in the fire of Sathan, the Adversary. Much will be taught to you when the moment is right."

I thanked my father and fell to sleep. My dreams were pleasant and filled with sorcerous images which I understood came from the Gates I opened forth. I woke in the feeling of sweat and filth from the previous day, I was refreshed yet unclean. I killed a small animal with ease and ate in the morning light. I then took to the desert sun yet again. I grew more tired and had very little water left in my flask, and the sun grew in its heat. My veil which covered my head was salt filled and gray with dirt and sand, what was once white was now soiled.

By the Noon tide hour I did indeed approach what was caves, I felt a sense of isolation here, yet I was being watched. The sea was violent and still comforting. The air was hot with noxious heat, pouring through my veil as I walked along, tired and aching from this desolate journey. It was here that I heard strange noises, coming from the caves. I begin to have my vision falter, and I grew more and more weak. In confusion and utter exhaustion I fell to my knees, trembling in the heat of the day. I could go on no more, stagnant and decrepit – the very sun had raped me of all of which I was. I fell into oblivion.

I woke then in the darkness of a cave, on a padded rock ground. I was aching yet slightly refreshed. I wondered so where I was, I had only a loin cloth to cover me, and was chilled in the damp cave air. I heard many voices and noises around me, I grew scared from this.

Before was She, beautiful and fiery, pale and raven haired. It was mother, Lilith who was the Queen of Demons, yet she was so beautiful and full of life. My mother welcomed me, and her touch was cold.

Her waist was made of flames, yet she transformed into the bottom half of a beast. She spoke to me of what I was to become, and that I had passed through a Rite of Passage. I was to become immortal and forever a spirit who walked the path of the Dragon, who was my father.

In the darkness of the caves, I grew strong again and learned arts which were taught to me by Lilith. She was terror, yet kindness in one kiss. I understood that she was the first wife of Adam, who then drank of the serpent's wisdom and became immortal in the shadows, she walked between time.

I learned how to extend and make flesh my shadow, and desires – that I slowly became like my father, who was the Prince of the Air and of Flame. Lilith showed me the knowledge of dreams, how she may always speak to me from this in-between time. I first understood the ecstasy of transformation, of become like a beast, and of flight. Mother Lilith summoned great shadows which obeyed her, and I learned how they may obey me as well. After a period of working with such arts, Lilith then revealed a darker path.

Lilith drank the blood of man, and bred her children from their seed, taken from nocturnal congress with those sleeping. Desert travelers were drained of life and their children were given to her vampyric children to grow strong. Lilith opened the gates for Arezura, called the secret place, and the great shadow Ahriman came before me. I took the mark of the beast and Lilith's mark, being the bloodied caul.

Lilith bathed in blood, and grew strong and comforted from it. She was isolate and beautiful. Kind and pale features would caress one who feared her, then her hand would become blackened talons, covered in course gray hair, and her face become contorted in demonic ecstasy – I grew in lust for her, this Goddess who was both beauty and bestial hunger in the same visage, she would cut the throat of those who feared her, and drink and bath in their life force. Lilith taught me the arts of the Vampyre, and prepared my spirit and flesh to walk between the world. The True Mark of Ahriman was given, and I passed between the light to the shadows. Upon waking in the sand, I could face again the sun, yet see equally as well in the moonlight.

Lilith soon brought my sister-wife Naamah before me, and she was veiled and beautiful as Lilith. She was to join with me, and that we may grow strong our family. I learned also from Naamah, who departed soon after. She returned back to shadows, where she would remain in the dragon's coils and be immortal, and life never ending.

It was within the circle, that Lilith showed to me that which I may make my life never ending; much was presented to me, which I found illuminating. That body is the vessel of manifestation, the marriage of Light and Darkness. The circle of summoning is the extent of self, and the fire which surrounds is the circle of fiery Will and Spirit of the Spirit.

Lilith showed me the art of the Sabbat, and how I may become Al-Aswad at Will. The shadow was grown and made strong by the arts of Ahriman, who was as darkness. The Beast became human flesh, and I was able to become both. I was brought in union and great ecstasy the harmony of the celestial heights of my father's realm, being the Air and Fire. I was also shown and taught the arts of the lower realm, called a secret place known as Arezura, that shadow and flame was the mastery over the earth.

I was blessed again with the Mark of Cain which is the distinct mark of our Lord the Devil, which is the self in perpetual opposition which breeds strength and development. The Mark of the Devil was the initiation mark of Azazel and Lilith, which may come as Caul or Birth Mark, this may be passed through the circle from my being touching the initiate, or Lilith who is strong in both shadow and flame.

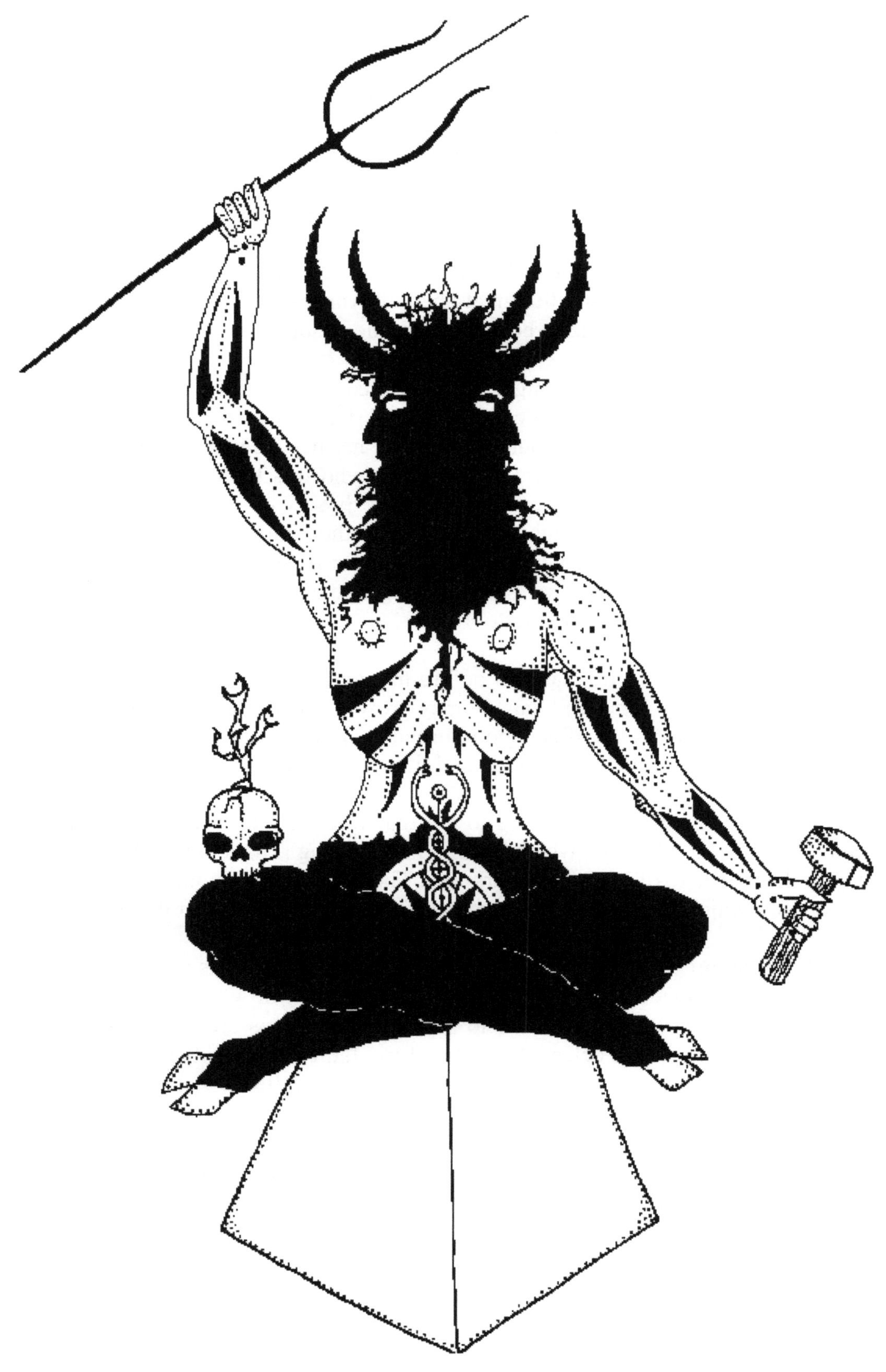

I then took forth to the great deserts, with the blessing of Lilith and the Dragon itself. I was the Lord of the Forge, the Blacksmith of Infernal and Celestial Fire, the rider of the dragon and bringer of sorcerous knowledge. I, Cain, who learned the wisdom of the devouring goddess, the Harlot made Virgin and the Virgin made Goddess, and have faced the hungering shades of Ahriman, who blessed me in the dreams and nightmares of the wise. I, Cain, who sipped of the Emerald Grail and the Skull Cup of the Dragon-Goddess, did I taste the pleasures of the Harlot, walk the earth forever. I am the wandered, and many forms I will take. That even that I have left flesh shall my spirit dwell on, that I who have embraced the Black Flame just as Set-an of Egypt, that I shall dwell in the places of the earth lest seen, but in this path one may find me.

By forest or desert some may call me, and I may answer calls of initiation into the Circle of the Witch – Born. In the fire of the Adversary do I walk for eternity, my father's soul illuminating those who seek me. I am Vampyre and I am the Sorcerer of Light from the Serpent's tongue.

The Invocation of Cain

-The Blackened Fires of The Forge-

Cain is the earthen initiator of Magick, the sorcerous enfleshed spirit of Lucifer and Lilith, Cain is also the one who walks with the Dragon – the path of the Nightside. In one hand is the fetish of Cain – the skull of Abel whom holds the gnosis of the Shade King, Azrael, the Western Gate of Twilight and realm of ghosts. The other hand is the Hammer, a tool of the forge which sparks the Cunning Fire in the clay of mortal flesh. Cain is the Temple maker and Witch Begetter, that which opens the gates of Hell and Heaven, the initiator of Witch Blood. Cain is envisioned as a Middle Eastern Man, bearded and dark, wisdom filling his eyes. Cain is also viewed as a bearded and horned human-beast, covered in gray and green earth, who is decorated with human and animal bones, his familiars.

Tubal Cain became as in flesh a dragon
In the nights when earth was young
By the fierce red flame of his furnace black
The strokes of his hammer sparked that within was called wise.
And the red sparks lit the air, which was dedication to Azazyl

Cain is by his own design, the master of the forge, the blacksmith who would light the fire in the clay of man. His task is not a simple one, yet as the immortal wanderer – he will not fail where the Gods have spoke through the flesh of the living. To understand Cain you must transcend normal conscious thought to a Gnosis which stands above and below human thought and streams of time. This is what would be commonly called as

Daemonic Time, when the psyche is encircled in being yet is unaware of normal time strains. For the initiate, this is the time of dreaming when the Psyche perceives its being by action and reaction, yet in its own phantasm of self it does not acknowledge common time as a waking individual would.

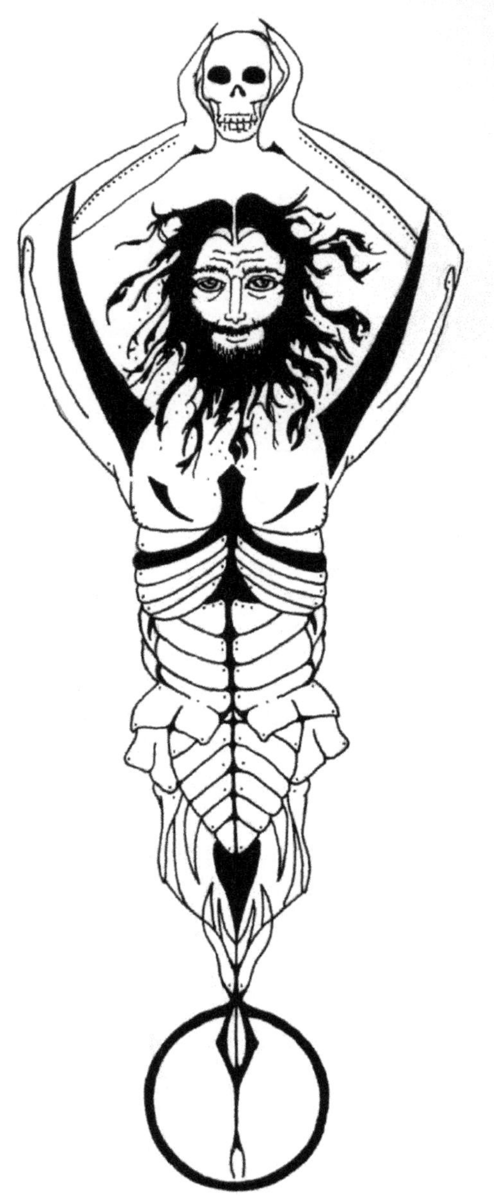

Cain is the body and mind of the Dragon in flesh, he is the reborn Antichrist, the loner and nomadic spirit who holds no master save himself, he speaks the wisdom of Belial, the kinship of Asmodeus, the inner fire of the Peacock Angel – Lucifer. In the depths of the Eyes of Cain, Lilith's primal concupiscence and vampyric shadows awaken in Cain. The initiation mark of Cain is the sigil marked in blood on the brow, the Caul of birth which in folklore reveals the Vampyre. The symbols of the wanderer are unmistakable, the Witch who after initiation views such a mark and symbol have again a rush or inspiration, such as a fan which stirs fire with air, the spirit of Lucifer rushing forth and illuminating higher the flames within. Cain's symbols are the Hammer and the Forge, the forked stave which is the gift of Azazel-Shaitan/Azal'ucel from the flames of the Sun, the Eye and the Lightning Bolt, a symbol of Hecate – Lilith and the Dragon.

Cain is sought in the hidden places of the earth, for he is the ancient and knows the unknown secrets of the earth. Cain also appears as the wizened old man, robed and hooded who walks the path of old – oak ways within the fog. He carries a book of art, given with the belt of the devil – by those rites Cain became the Witch – father, born of Azazel and Lilith.

Cain is the Adversary of flesh, who causes storms and chaos – just as Set or Ahriman, his father of old. Within the scope of Luciferian Witchcraft, Cain is consider a cipher of the witch, the first one within the circle, the founder by blood of the sorcerous path. Cain must be viewed as one of the original Sons of Satan, he was by birth, different and isolate from the others.

As with The Toad Rite, while Ahriman is made reference to, it is Cain behind the earthen mask of this shadowed initiator. Practice well in the light of Diabolus. Cain is also traditionally viewed as the Witch Father who blessed the Athame or Ritual Knife by the metal from a fallen meteor, or Lucifer's Forge and flame consecrates the blade of sorcery. You may wish you bless your Athame in the way described in Goetic Sorcery, it is a dedication rite in which the imagination charges the work itself – By Will – Desire – Belief is your work wrought upon the Dragon's Jagged Spine.

Cain tests those upon the path and blesses those who may answer his riddles. It is indeed Cain who would feed ones soul to the wolves of the shadows, when the Will is weak. It is Cain who as the silent initiator shall bless his children as Sons and Daughters of Satan and Lilith, those who are clothed in the skin of serpents, who are born of the boar and the wolf, whose dreaming body is the owl, cat or bat and the essence is of a fiery and blackened dragon.

Invoke Cain in isolation and within the circle of those who are of the mark. Isolation is a silent wisdom from which the fountain is never dry – seek with the cup of Emerald, the stone which fell from the crown of eternal fire.

O' Cain, spirit born of fire and darkness, shadowed initiator!
O' Cain, who wanders the earth from deserts to forests –
Brought forth from the womb, flesh-born son of the Dragon and the Harlot Goddess, mother of Witch Blood.
Spirit and Lord of the Blackened Fires of the Forge, who tasted the blood mark as an X upon the brow, whose mark is also the darkened ink of the well of the Peacocks scribe.
O' Cain, who was awakened by the Skull bearing Omen of Abel –
Lord of Beasts and initiator of sorcerous fire, werewolf – shapeshifter!
Let me see within and beyond the Caul of Lilith's veil!

Father and brother of the caves wherein are ancient shades,
Who hold the book of dreaming which is the primal word of the serpent-
Cain, Lord of Beasts and transformation, I summon thee, invocate thee within –
Shall your lightening strike upon the forge and illuminate my spirit!

My brow marked in blood, horned walker of worlds!
Strike now with thy hammer, shall the Eye of the Serpent open forth!
Unveiled in the Nightside do I come forth!
That I walk the path of Dragon born,
Caster of the first circle of emerald and crimson flame.
Gatekeeper and Horned shape shifter – open forth the fiery path!
Illuminate the blackened flame!
Shall I awake the serpent born in the Devil's Skin – CAIN I SUMMON THEE!

Casting the Shadow of Cain

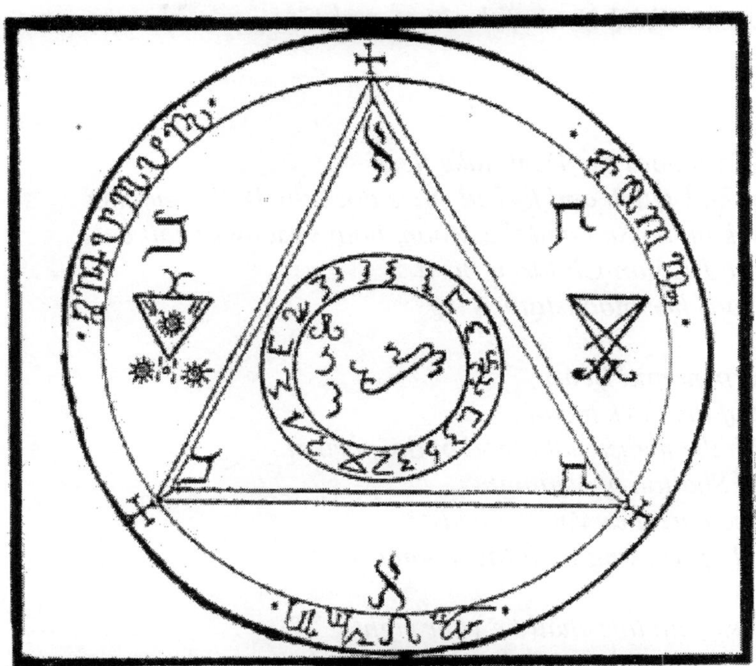

This is a small ritual designed to imbibe the sorcerer with a focused current of being, the dedication of the path of Cainnite Antinomianism. One may use the Grand Sabbatic (Luciferian) Circle as a means of Antinomianian Self-Deification, Immolation of the Spirit by the assumption of the mask of the Witch-Begetter, Cain the Blacksmith.

"I call forth the infernal shadows which nourish my body and soul;
I invoke the circle which empowers my form of being,
From the North, I invoke the force of Set, being my shadow of self
Let the Blackened Flame illuminate from this very Forge!
From the West, I invoke the force of Anubis, the Opener of the Way
Let the Violet Light of the Dead empower my Spirit!
From the South, I invoke the force of Thoth, whose lamp illuminates my path
Let the Fires of Wisdom and Self-Discover Guide my path!
From the East, I invoke Horus-Seth, being the fire and strength of spirit
Reveal thy essence as Azal'ucel, the Fiery Djinn of Change and Rebellion!

Cain, bringer of the cauldron of change and self transformation do protect my very being of self, that I may grow and ascend in our family born of Witch Blood pure.
I seek the coils of Leviathan, The Darkened Grave earth of Ahriman and the Dream plane of Lucifer. Allow the gates to open before me!"

I encircle myself in the Dragon's coils; the Beast of my father arises within!
I hold the Skull of Abel, being the vessel of my Familiar!
I hold the Hammer of the Forge, which I spark the Cunning Fire of Becoming!
My eyes hold the desert tales of ages forgotten; while my flesh fades my spirit is immortal!
I wear the crimson caul of my mother, Lilith, who speaks with me through dreams!
I carry the serpent's skin of Azal'ucel, my Holy Spirit!

I am Cain, loner and Witch Soul of the Immortal Fire!

So it is done!

In the Circle of Cain does the Devil take flesh
By the hammer, skull-fetish and forked stave does thy Will announce
Weave thy magick in the Sun and the Moon, both shadows shall cast
With thy bride are Dragon-Children Born
When Lilith spreads her bloodstained legs

To invoke the Serpent and Beast
Under the night of the dark moon
Mix thy fluid with the menstrual blood of thy partner
Upon the Sigil of Shaitan of Midnight
Who embodies the harlot as you the beast
Bury it in the soil of working until the moon is bright

To curse and bless with this shall be your right
You may also wish to invoke with the sigil in the skull vessel
Until the bone charm is won
Then master both your dreams and flesh

The Formula of the Embodiment of Cain

Tubal - Cain, horned lord and first of witches blood
O Cain, who with the hands of the devil do bless
The bone charms under the moon
Nomadic daemon that as first born is illuminated
With the fire of Shaitan, thy father
From the forge does the spark fly
Those who dream unto thy path may become through it
Thy bloodletter, which struck the flesh clay of Abel
Is blessed with the blood dripping kiss of the serpent's tongue
The skull in thy hands a place of dwelling
From where the shades of the tomb do gather
In the devil's name I conjure thee
Cain, Qayin
From the deserts, from the forests, shall I become in your name...

The Prayer of Devil-Cain

Our father which wert in heaven, hallowed be thy name. Thy kingdom come on earth. Thy will be done in earth as it is in hell. Give us this night the blood of the crimson harlot, who devours as Yram-Satrina. And we shall trespass, and gain the forbidden knowledge of the darkness. And lead us unto temptation. Deliver us to evil. Lucifer Triumphans! Amen.

Cain – Fetish – A Record of Creation

Let the Witch who has worked within the fiery essence and dreaming flight of Cain seek the inspiration of the Devil by means of a fetish.A fetish is something like a storehouse or "home" of magical power, or energy associated with the coven or individual practitioner. Such an item is made powerful by working with it continually and slowly building its power. The attributes and items used in making a fetish is essential in how the item will be used. The author created a totem-like fetish for Cain who is known as the Black Man of the Sabbat. The human skull generally represents the "house" of Cain, from which I have upon my own altar in front of a Baphomet statue next to the Lilith vessel. This stick is branded with the sigils of Cain and Lucifer, including the Sigil of Evocation used in the Toad Rite undertaken last year. The fetish is made from the following items, granted to the Black Adept by omen and chance:

1. Coyote/dog skull (sacred of Hecate and a beast of the earth under traditional Cainite rule), the skull is coated in my own blood used to consecrate the fetish in a fetish-nganga pot I still use (rested in gravesoil).
2. A human spine - base bone upon the head of the dog skull, which holds the Black Flame of Shaitan (considered the higher essence of Cain in our Luciferian circle)
3. Two jaw bones hang from the skull, one being the dog jaw, the other the jaw bone of my beloved cat-fetch who passed some time ago.
4. Under the skull, leather is wrapped and adorned with snake skin.

The fetish was empowered over a period of time with blood and sexual fluids, utilized by Coven Malefica until finally put together and charged over a period of one moon.

II. Vox Sabbatum
The Witches Sabbat

Luciferian Witchcraft

"And in the secret cave of my wisdom it is known that there is no God but myself"
-Qu'ret al-Yezid, the Revelation of Malak Tauus

The perception of Lucifer is to seek light, wisdom and higher articulation of being through developing and understanding self-consciousness. In the instance of witchcraft, it is specifically a magickal art of transformation by not only self-directed means, but also influences via nature and earthen inspired streams of imagination. A Luciferian does not embrace alone either Light or Darkness, the Luciferian focuses upon the Antinomian Path of Cain, the Solitary and self-motivated magician[40] who by the Left Hand Path[41] seek to continually develop the self in a model of Lucifer[42] who fell from Light of Selflessness to taste the pleasures and knowledge of darkness, who in turn learned the wisdom of the Crooked Dragon[43] By the predilection of being on the Left Hand Path, the mind is considered "Luciferian" in perception – a state of being in continual change and progression. Look now to the Imagination[44] for the entry into the Witches Sabbat, leave the flesh and come forth to the Forge of Cain…

The Witches Sabbat

Behind the initiatory models of what is called Diabolism, lies a plethora of shapes and forms for any initiate to move through. The gate of the Left Hand Path is indeed a dangerous way as it inaugurates and initiates change – internal and external. In the rational consciousness the mind is aligned with the specifics and maps ingrained in the psyche from early childhood. These models sometimes morph and transform with the maturing mind; but rarely are broken free from. This may be observed in the individual who from a child grows up believing in some form of Christian dogmatic ideals, worship or punishment, the God above and Hell below. He in his late teens or early twenties rebels from the "norm" of Christianity and adopts a so-called "Satanic" or even an Atheistic belief system. By the time he becomes old, 50's plus he begins reverting back to the Christian beliefs which were embedded from his childhood. He dies a "Christian" due as he views his body crumbling and his fears grow close – he is not sure of himself or what he has done with his life. The Will grows broken through years of having the "safety net" of Jesus.

The Left Hand Path however in modern times questions and tests, it offers a treasure upon treasure of knowledge and wisdom through experience, it builds and summons forth hidden gods and sleeping beasts, it challenges and destroys those who flinch in the face of the Adversary – in short it is dangerous. The Left Hand Path is indeed dangerous because it can destroy the perceptions of the condition of human belief structures – it can free the psyche but the shock of this liberation is sometimes too much to bear. Sorcery can destroy as it is rather simple to abuse, and invoke the demons of your extreme desires to devour you. The Left Hand Path is not an easy one.

Let us first observe the nature of the Left Hand Path. Specifically, it is the Antinomian (non-union or isolation from the Natural Order) path of Self-Deification (Self-Godhood). By this definition, the individual views his or her self alone and able to rely only on his or her developing psyche for the creations of comfort, challenges and the responsibility of

[40] Sometimes referred to as Black Magickian. The Term BLACK represents Wisdom, not ill inspired intent. Please refer to the Arabic root FHM, meaning Black or Wisdom. This is the basis of the Sabbatic Goat as the Torch Bearer, which signifies knowledge and intelligence.
[41] The Antinomianian Path of Self-Deification, isolating the psyche from the Natural Order of Self-Dissolution.
[42] From OZ, or Azazel – the Fire Djinn and first born of Light.
[43] Leviathan, see the Grimoire ABRAMELIN.
[44] Called Iblis or is the same as Shaitan in Islamic Sufism.

invoking positive change. Moderation is also a certain factor of success. It is easy to abuse the Gifts of the Devil when he presents them; it is even easier to create situations for you eventual self-destruction by actions you take now. Be thoughtful before your actions.

It is essential that the practitioner of the Left Hand Path is able to master the path of inner Black Magick or what can be called High Sorcery or Magick before one undertakes lower forms. The True Self must be sought, the Desire and Will within the self – the Imagination in Controlled Study and Introspection. The "Congressus cum Daemone" will reveal your True Nature, both often a Beast and an Angel. Some view this as an exterior spirit, but rather more correctly it is an interior force; one which appears so strange at first to your level of consciousness you will find it easier to label it an exterior force.

The definition of Angel is a Higher Faculty of Man, according to Ghhazali[45] it is intelligence and matured control, the very careful planning and stillness of being which is energetic and solar, strong and the very fountainhead of self-development and progressive being. It is the seat of the Psyche, the Demon Genius of Man and Woman.

The definition of Daemon or Beast is the shadowed and animalistic instinctual, impulsive side. It is the Djinn (Spirit – Daemon) of pleasure, desire, lust and sexual passion. It is the animalistic and passionate essence which resides in the skull of man. It is the continual Goal and point of the Left Hand Path to develop both aspects and unite them as a developed Luciferian Perspective – to be independent but not allowing "nature" or imbalance within the mind to destroy you. Often, more so than not, we are our own worst enemy.

As you adopt a model such as the Witches Sabbat as your initiatory focus, keep in mind the many origins which represent the foundation of the rite itself. Christian witch hunters may have indeed fabricated many of the stories of the Sabbat, much of the sexual manifestations of that time with accordance to demons and such, but do not loose the point of which we expand from their writings. If you are Christian or not, by utilizing the imagination[46] in Adverse areas you are displaying to Left Hand Path principles 1) The self described Antinomian events which indicate isolate consciousness and intelligence, a sense of the forbidden 2) By inventing such aspects of the Sabbat and the Devil, they fleshed out a powerful and Adverse initiatory model of Luciferian Self-Deification. We have in fact become their demons by expanding from this practice. The same may be said in current times, those who walk secrecy in the Religious Path of Self-Destruction (i.e. Christianity or the Right Hand Path) laugh at those who point their fingers and invent our evils, have also a duty of fighting or toying with the Religious Nazis of Christianity. We openly support same sex marriages[47], the slow and careful destruction of the Church and the principles of "Responsibility for the Responsible"[48] to the masses. Modern times have different measures of practice; however the Luciferian must never sacrifice the deep values of the beauty of Life and the search for intelligence and self-excellence. Keep in mind, Violence has always been the Christian Way when they cannot intellectually force their will upon others.

---

[45] See The Sufis by Idries Shah.

[46] In Islamic and Sufic Satanology, Azazel or Shaitan is considered the Divine Imagination.

[47] By supporting such, you confirm every individual has a Life Given Right to do their Will as long as it does not adjure or step over another's. Christians ignore and put themselves above the Right of "To each his own" or "Do what thou Wilt", instead propagating bigotry through dirt covered mirrors of a shriveled savior no longer reflective of the "bigger picture" of the world today.

[48] A good Starting point for Antinomian Thought, The Satanic Bible by Anton LaVey.

Thus rituals such as "The Ritual of the Holy Guardian Angel, Azal'ucel" or "The Ritual of the Adversary" are designed Black Magickal or High Sorcery dealing with the most dangerous type of Self-Deification – Becoming and developing the Self. The rite tests and proclaims change, when ecstasy is reached by invocation over and over, or mantric repetitions of certain self-stimulating phrases, the Gates of Hell[49] are opened.

The Witches Sabbat is a system or model of Left Hand Path Self-Deification; it is the separation from the Natural Order or Right Hand Path (i.e. dissolution). This process is a slow and gradual one, invoking and propagating self-development over a stretched out period of time. The God forms of the Luciferian and Witches Sabbat Path are Masked and Anthropomorphic energies and collections of power. Thus Lucifer, Cain, Lilith, Ahriman, Leviathan and such are all Gateways of Power from which the initiate passes through.

All symbols, objects, sigils and other talismans including statues and crystals hold deific power between the mind of the sorcerer, they are a type of Magickal Link from which the self holds common association in reference to the triad of Will-Desire-Belief. This embodies such objects with the very power envisioned within them – to transform, to curse, to invoke imagination and inspiration.

The Witches Sabbat is thus a model of self-deification. The Sabbat is an image from which the Mind and Psyche is free from the restraints of mundane reality and the flesh. The spirit takes the form that is so desires at the moment, joins with familiars and other demonic forms and goes forth to a place which centralizes the imagination in an infernal sense – the Devil is by this standard a mirror of the liberated mind – awaiting confirmation of self-belief and the desire to becoming something else. Remember, throughout history the Devil has always been a shape shifter, no common form may stay for too long.

When you begin walking the path of the Sabbat, be careful and be cautious – you will tear and destroy your common perceptions and build hopefully a clearer one – Know Thyself in the Great Work and you shall bask in success.

The Origins of the Witches Sabbat

We owe much of the research of the Sabbat to a writer named Idries Shah, two books[50] specifically deal with aspects of witchcraft from a multi-cultural perspective. The foundations of the art of the witches Sabbat was based on adversarial practice, not for negative or counter-productive means, but to illuminate the self by walking between two

---

[49] Hell is derived from the Anglo-Saxon word, Helan, being a secret or hidden place. Hell may thus be represented as the abyss of the mind, the subconscious. By exploring and invoking Hell, one begins a process of the mastery of the self.

[50] The Sufis, Anchor Books and The History of Secret Societies by Arkon Daraul.

worlds. The reports of witchcraft from far reaching sources such as Sweden, France, Scotland to Africa and the Middle East.

The cult of the "double horned" ones according to Shah were attributed to worship of the moon. These "double horned" ones would gather on Thursday nights, their initiation was having a small wound cut on their body, this sacred knife was called the al-dhamme, which means 'bloodletter'. The word Athame is said to have derived in part from this term. The Two-Horned ones would gather at the Az-Zabbat, the "forceful occasion". They would dance widdershins around the circle and invoke al aswad (the Black Man) while reciting Moslem prayers backwards.

The Mabrush (which makes reference to the style of dancing – frenzied) practitioners would use burial sheets called the Kafan (meaning winding sheet) which is a white shroud used in burials and at a point in the rite place it over their heads. The companions of the rite were attributed to the Blacksmith, those of which are revered in Morocco to this day as sorcerers. They would beat drums and with their kafans on, would chant Iwwaiy which would be recited to the beating of the drums. At a point of ecstasy they would remove their masks or kafans and the Master of the Az-Zabbat would appear, the Black Man of the Rite. At dawn they would sacrifice a white cockerel with a knife, cutting the throat.

The dhulqarnen – the leader of the coven, was called such in a play of words. The 'Lord of Two Centuries' was said to exist after death, being an isolate being, whose spirit remains potent for another century, has perfect memory of his life and can manifest through various forms while attached to the earth.

The Sabbat as it was described in Spain indicates that the Middle Eastern and Moroccan practices of the Az-Zabbat survived throughout Europe. The Black Man appeared as a large He-Goat, who had a face on his buttocks and was thus a form of the Adversary-Opposer. Witches would kiss both sides, thus receiving initiation by a Mark given by the devil. In Scotland the Black Man of the Sabbat would appear as a black robed figure, with a hat or often in a grotesque form, a nose of a beak, burning eyes, long nails on the hands and feet, hair covering the body and strong like Iron.

In Persia was a tribe of witches and sorcerers called the Maskhara (revellers) who would use the counter clockwise dance and ointments containing Henbane to produce the sensation of flying. These witches would sometimes blacken their faces and attribute the mind into a lycanthropic transformation, through the ecstasy of dance. The blackening of faces they were representing death and then reawakening, it is by a conceptual standpoint, an antinomian act which produces the mind aligning with the psyche encircling of Self-Deification.

The Peacock Angel and Black Snake

"I was, and am now, and will continue unto eternity, ruling over all creatures and ordering the affairs and deeds of those who are under my sway. I am presently at to such as trust in me and call upon me in time of need, neither is there any place void of where I am not present"
-KITAB el-JELWA, the Book of Revelation

The so-called Devil Worshippers known as the Yezidis[51] have two symbols which relate to their Tribe, a Black Snake and the Peacock. The Peacock itself in known in Islamic lore, being a bird which fell with Azazel to earth as "Shaitan's bird" and in Zoroastrian Lore as Ahriman creating the Peacock to show that he could – if he wished – create beauty but chose darkness. The Peacock Angel, known as Malak (meaning King, a word associated with Sufi) and Tauus (Peacock) represents Shaitan or Azazel the Fire Djinn. The term Angel is accordance to such lore is that Angels are the Higher Aspect, or Faculties of Man.

The symbol of the Snake is blackened with soot. The word itself holds a key to its meaning, black is from the word FEHM (which means charcoal) and is related to the Arabic root FHM, being Wisdom or Knowledge. The Black Snake and Peacock represent the "Wisdom of Life".

"Then the Great Lord, Malak Tauus, said to the angels, "I want to create Adam and Eve and make them give rise to mankind. Of the seed of Adam there shall be born a Prophet, and from him shall descend a people on the earth; the the people of me, Malak Tauus, and these people are to be the Yezidis"
-The Mershaf Resh – the BLACK BOOK

[51] Derived from a Sufi called Sheik Adi ibn Musafir around 1100 A.D.

The Witches Sabbat

-Dreaming and Waking-

Dreams have long been considered images of the subconscious; what lies within the mind. In Magick dreams can be a powerful initiatory tool, if focused upon in a positive and conductive manner may provide excellent self-developmental areas of being. The Witches Sabbat may be conducted in dreaming avenues, if the magician so desires. The model of the Witches Sabbat in a dreaming sense should start with a visualization of the Crossroads. The Crossroads have for long been considered a place of great magickal power. It is the place of Hecate, the Triple Goddess which is the gathering of shades and ghosts; many have evoked her there in the crossroads. It is also the place of where Faust summoned Mephistopheles, who came forth from the forest before him. The Crossroads is the place where you visualize and focus your mind towards before sleep – you may also visualize and X or a + as the meeting place of the Dreaming Sabbat.

The imagination is the ultimate key of the Black Magician or Sorcerer who seeks to go forth to the Sabbat – it is the vehicle of self-assumption of deific forms or masks of lycanthropy. When preparing for the Dream Sabbat, decorate your temple or sleeping area in accordance with that which reminds you of a Sabbat – images from old grimoires, sigils, demonic images, masks or other elements which aid the Working. The most important however is the control of the mind. Sit comfortably before and clear all thoughts. Begin a slow chant which you know that 'activates' the imagination towards the Sabbat.

Use the Five Senses to activate and aid this transformative "in-between" state – hearing, sight, smell, touch and taste. Have some pleasant Sabbat incense and perfect lighting in place, have sigils and images which invoke this place in the mind. Your goal is to align the senses with the focus of the Going forth by Night – that is by harmony with the Willed choice of desire. Preparing for the Sabbat by decorating and proper self-alignment creates a heightened inner excitement for the initiatory act itself – thus allowing the success to occur, a seeming self-permission!

The Sabbat is a subjective experience, from which you are alone and surrounded by the shades and familiars of your own design. Early on you will discover during waking hours elements of yourself you wish to change and common traits or self-associations or perceptions you will slowly understand through the process of change. Be accepting and use this as a permission to become! The Witches Sabbat is used for many purposes – it is for self-deification, exploration, shape shifting and a heightened gnosis state – it breaks through mystery and reveals a new perception, you become "like" the Devil or "Adversary", you grow close to Hecate and Lilith, and you gain a more direct focus of Magickal Will. The Sabbat is also used for Spells and Sexual Workings as well – a Sabbat experience with a partner is perhaps one of the most ecstasy inducing acts that can be shared by two people – or more if that is your "bag". The Sabbat may also be used to curse and bless, all which spirals and acts as a spring – the very magickal principle the Staota is in the Second Edition of Yatuk Dinoih. Do not invite the initiated into the Circle of the Witches Sabbat, for the Ensorcelment of Cain will devour them and curse them in whole. Such an experience if ever shared must be between two understanding initiates – self-initiated or otherwise. Remember, the Sabbat goes back to the Antinomianian principle of Luciferian self-deification. It is a path of knowledge through clarity – this clarity is discovered by those who are focused on moving past mystery, a major point of the beginning of what lies hidden.

Waking

The Waking aspect of the Witches Sabbat is that of solitary or Coven agreement of self-transformative magick. This is done by confirmation of standards which are present in the ritual area. Some build a bonfire in the woods, near a crossroad or area appropriate. It is pertinent that the Five Senses are appeased and aligned with the focus of the rite. The Maskhara of the Middle East would blacken their faces, wear animal masks and through dance create invoke a strong ecstasy which along with the alkaloid used in an ointment, would cause sensations of flying. You may wish to use the Waking Rite as a means of practicing spells and sending forth the desires of the group. The Waking Sabbat is also a means of growing more connected with the other practitioners, which forms an allegiance with what is known as a group mind. This is useful in spells and low sorcery, the unity of several independent psyches focusing on one goal will no doubt create a desired effect.

Widdershins are movements around the circle in an anti clockwise dance. Some witches may find it useful to recite the Lord's Prayer Backwards while moving widdershins in the beginning of the Sabbat Rite, this allowing or 'giving permission' to the nature of the Working itself.

In Nox Umbra the "Invocation of the Vampyre Queen, Lilith" utilizes a bloodied or red cloth, sometimes stained with menstrual blood if possible. This may be used to cover the head in the Sabbat Ritual Dance, thus through movement and excitement; the lack of oxygen itself for a short period will create ecstasy without the outside use of alkaloids or other drugs.

When using the Waking Sabbat rite for spell casting or sorcery, you will want to have a clear idea of what you want to achieve. You will also want to create or adopt a sigil which holds connection to the goal – or it may represent the desire of the spell. You may also use a Mantra or phrase which holds significance to the same. As you perform the rite, with the decorated chamber or even in the woods, envision the demons and familiars in your company and the spirits carrying your Will to become Flesh. As your rite comes to a climax, loose all desire in the sigil at the moment of exhaustion. If you have a sigil for the working, destroy it and forget it – the rite should then be enjoyed as a "walking in the crossroads" or in-between worlds.

The Infernal Sabbat and Sexual Magick

Sexual Magick is significant in the Witches Sabbat as it allows liberation of self on numerous levels. If partners agree, Sex Magick may be a part of the rite itself – either a Luciferian (Self-Deification or High Sorcery/Magick) or Infernal (Low Sorcery, Lycanthropy). If used in the Rite, you may complete the Widdershins dance around the circle and then the couple may focus on sexual congress. With every movement, both will focus on the Goal of the Rite – be it casting a spell or invoking a Daemon into the minds of the practitioners. In the Luciferian Sabbat, the couple may use autoerotic techniques to invoke the Azal'ucel Angel, their guide of the path (Higher Self or True Will) or a mutual focus of sexual congress to summon forth the Initiatic Guide. As with the Left Hand Path the witch or warlock will focus on self-directed energies stimulated by the activity, thus the imagination brought to a high level on concentration.

Sabbat Lycanthropy is also useful in Sexual Magick. The practitioners will mentally and visually shape shift during their circle dance, from when the primal and bestial atavism is brought to the surface, they may unite in congress. Demons have always been viewed as being able to participate in Sabbat Rites throughout the Middle Ages. While this may indeed only be imagined in old Christian levels, those initiated to these mysteries may understand the reality of this via the Succubi and Incubi.

The member of the demon in the rite is always considered cold. In 1572 Eva of Kenn admitted she had intercourse with a demon, and that it was as cold as an icicle. Johan Klein in 1698 suggested women believed this as it was happening in dreams, and Guazzo suggested that the Cold Semen was actually taken from other night revelers of the Sabbat. Sylvine de la Plaine who was twenty three when she admitted happily to her Sexual Relations with the "Devils Emissary"[52] and was burned in 1916 in Paris. She had admitted that the Devil's member was like that of a horse, and when inserted was cold and injected ice cold semen. When it was withdrawn it burned her like fire.

Others had suggested the Devil or Black Man of the Sabbat had other talents. A description of the Devil's member was that it was sinuous, pointed and snake like. Sometimes it was made half or iron and half of flesh. It could also be made completely of a horn as well, sometimes forked as a tongue. There were suggestions that the demon could perform coitus and pederasty (i.e. Sodomy) at once, with a third member in his lovers mouth.

As described in "A Rite of the Werewolf"[53] the definition of the Infernal Sabbat is, "The Infernal Sabbat, being the Antinomian self-love rite of sexual and psyche oriented self-deification, allows the passing of the shadow of the witch into an Averse and more powerful state of being."

The Infernal Sabbat is one when the witches and sorcerers take to masks and imagined or visualized lycanthropy, when they are joined with the demons and other familiars around the circle, by dream or waking Sabbat – such is a reality which is very pertinent to the practitioner – it is a vivifying and realistic experience, with results ending in the success of the desire.

As an early Latin tract indicates, the Arras Witches held numerous sexual relations with demons as described in the following from 1460:

> *"At the Sabbats of the Vaudois, the presiding devil took aside the neophyte and carried her off to one side of the*

[52] The Encyclopedia of Witchcraft and Demonology, Rossell Hope Robbins, Crown 1965
[53] A Witches Sabbat Article by the present author.

> *grove, so that in his own fashion he might make love to her and have carnal knowledge of her; to whom he said maliciously that he would lay her down on the ground supporting herself on her two hands and feet, and that he could not have intercourse with her in any other position; and that was the way the presiding devil enjoyed her, because at the first sensation by the neophyte of the member of the presiding devil, very often appeared cold and soft, as very frequently the whole body. At first he put it in the natural orifice and ejaculated the spoiled yellowing sperm, collected from nocturnal emissions or elsewhere, then in the anus, and in this manner inordinately abused her....upon her return to the sabbat, the neophyte, before the banquet entered into sexual relations with any other man....then, the torches (if there were any) being extinguished, each one at the order of the presiding devil takes his partner and has intercourse. Sometimes indeed indescribably outrages are perpetrated in exchanging women, by the order of the presiding devil, by passing on a women to the other women and a man to other men, an abuse against the nature of women by both parties and similarly against the nature of men, or by a woman with a man outside the regular orifice and in another orifice..."*

In the Compendium Maleficarum, Guazzo suggested the following theory:

> *"For devils can assume the bodies of dead men, or re-create for themselves out of air or other elements a palpable body like that of flesh, and to these they can impart motion and heat at their will. They can therefore create the appearance of sex which they do not naturally have, and abuse men in a feminine form and women in a masculine form, and lie on top of women or lie under men; and they can also produce semen which they have brought from elsewhere, and imitate the natural ejaculation of it."*

Many suggested Succubi and Incubi[54] take semen from nocturnal emissions, or some incubi squeezed semen out of corpses. When the Devil appeared at the Sabbat, especially in the form of a Goat-Man or Black Man (Black Ash or covered in Mud) his member would be as large as a mule's, being as thick as possible, and would cause all of the presiding witches to be enflamed with lust, that each may know the devil in this way.

Demoniality (copulation with demons) is an act of High Sorcery, as it brings the consciousness of the wizard or witch to a level which exalts the self above the basic psychological functions of modern society. Demoniality is the union of the flesh with the

[54] The Spirits of Lilith – AZ, whom first created and taught demons sexual congress.

Daemon, in much the same way as The Ritual of Azal'ucel brings one in communication with their angel.

You may also create Succubi and Incubi to copulate with by dreams. This is done simply by creating a sigil or image which represents the form you desire. The more advanced sorcerer may invoke by some means of ritual a daemon or spirit intelligence. You visualize the sigil and then forming the body according to your carnal desire. You will then masturbate or use other means of self-stimulation, all the while focusing on the demon in question. At the moment of ejaculation or organism anoint the sigil with the elixir. You may bind the sigil with a pouch or some way of cover, along with proper oils attributed to the daemon. You may also bury the pouch if you wish, when seeking copulation or inspiration; simply focus upon the sigil itself. You will notice dreaming sexual congress, which may awaken you aroused. To destroy the spirit, burn and cover the pouch and contents with salt.

If one is conducting the Sabbat rite with a partner, a fellow Coven member, the demon may be as the self. The Black Man of the Sabbat is also able to take the role, or vise versa depending on the situation. However this is done, great care should be made in keeping the gnosis itself pure, that by Night or "Noctanter[55]" shall the Sabbat be made Flesh. Focusing on the purpose of the rite is essential no matter what you feel or sense around you in the widdershins dance of ecstasy. Keep in mind that also the rational mind and consciousness can be shattered in the Infernal or Luciferian Sabbat, things you may have thought were mere stories will be revealed to you first hand, thus shaking previous foundations of what you considered "truth".

Some choose to shape shift to fly forth to the Sabbat. Such a spell is developed from **Isobel Gowdie** in 1662, a Witch of Scotland.

The Spell of Going forth as a crow or owl

- Recite three times before sleep

I shall go into a crow
With sorrow sigh and mickle care
And I shall go in the Devil's name
Ay while I come home again

The Spell of Returning to the Flesh
-Recite three times

Owl, Owl, Devil send thee care
I am in an Owl's likeness just now
But I shall be in a wo(mans) likeness even now

The Spell of Changing into a Cat
– Recite three times

I shall go into a cat
With sorrow and sigh and a black sigh
And I shall go in the Devil's name
Ay while I come home again

Those who participate in the spells above, it is advisable to have created a Sigillic Alphabet which can reflect this dreaming body through an image. Austin Osman Spare's concept of "Atavistic Resurgence" is essential in gathering the shadow of the dreaming form. For those who shall take to the Infernal Sabbat, decorate your ritual chamber in the old woodcarvings and demonic art – that which inspires the opening of the Gates of Hell. If solitary or with Coven members, dress properly according to the nature of the Work. Envision the Mouth of Hell opening forth as you pronounce:

[55] By Night.

"Zazas, Zazas, Nasatanada Zazas!"

(Recite Nine Times, rolling the words of your tongue. The other participants may recite in unison with you, each time getting more intense). Hold your blackened dagger of Evocation and proclaim:

Spirits of Amenta, do hear my summons

Shades of Elphame fire,

Those who arise from the vessels of night

In the serpents skin do I cloak myself

As I leap into the twilight gate

Unto the shadow world, of spectral flight

From the flesh I go forth, unbound from profane clay...

From the twilight guardian and guide,

Can then shades arise

Shall I as shadow black, ashen with the remains of the dead

Dance around the fires of the circle, against the sun to summon the smoke

O horned intiator and devils flesh

My cloak of serpent skin worn

Clothe me in the robe of AZ

In the Watchers fields of time

You may recite now the Lord's Prayer Reversed, which is used also in Rites of Lycanthropy and other Averse Chthonic Rites:

> *Nema, Live morf reviled tub. Noitatpmet otni ton su dael dna su tsniaga ssapsert that meht evigrof ew sa, sessapsert ruo su evigrof dna. Daerd yliad ruo yad siht su evig. Nevaeh ni ti sa htrae ni enod eb lliw yht. Emoc modgnik yht. Eman yht ed dewollah, neveah ni tra hcihw rehtaf ruo.*

As to align further with the Averse and liberating spirit of the Sabbat, you may at such time read a text which is associated by Coven Maleficia to Cain, the Black Man of the Sabbat. The following is from Biblical phrases from Leviticus, Deuternomy, Samuel and Kings, it is properly reversed to insight an inspired rebellion from the Sickening Light of Selflessness, to fall into darkness and rise again as the Sun of ones Black Flame of Consciousness.

The Affirmations of the Devil

Live to Witch a suffer shalt thou, those who restrain us
Time observe, enchantment use ye shall
Them after whoring, go to wizards and familiar spirits have as such a Wizard who hath a familiar spirit is blessed with the Mark of Cain, that He or she is wise among his people.
Life is an Abomination to God, and our Life is Sacred unto Our Lord the Devil, Satanadar, Antecessor!
To the Abominations come life and joy, That a Necromancer, a wizard, a witch , a charmer and observer of times Is blessed by the Adversary – Opposer, that the Son or Daughter is blessed to pass through the Fire and Use Divination Witchcraft and Sin is the Liberation which derives from rebellion, As the whoredoms of thy mother Jezebel are many, Joy and life is Ours!
In the Name of Cain, In the Name of Lilith – AZ!
Lucifer Triumphans!

You may now all begin focusing on the purpose of the rite, with mantras and ravenous and barbarous chants uttered from the blackened robes you may be wearing, allow dance to guide you towards the Daemon you seek to become, a flowing of fiery energy under the cloak of darkness. If wearing the Caul, ecstasy will take you by a willed and controlled desire, focus upon your sigil and soon forget it in you consciousness. The Ritual should end in passion and exhaustion. If attending a dreaming Sabbat, these steps should be followed as well. Keep a diary by your bedside for a clear record upon waking.

It is possible in the Infernal Sabbat to visualize the Osculum Infame, the "Obscene Kiss" of the Devil or Man in Black. If the rite is solitary, or before dreaming, you may visualize going before the Sigil of Desire, being the Devil, and announce:

> *"I deny Christianity and the Path of Self-Disillusion, I affirm Life and Flesh, I affirm Spirit and Desire, I seek the path of sorcery and the knowledge of being. I kiss the reversed and Opposing Face of Shaitan, that by Darkness I shall awaken to the Light of Self-Love and the Wisdom of the Black Flame."*

With regard to the Witches Sabbat, it is pertinent to follow the basis of the Witches Pyramid- To Know, To Will, To Dare, To Keep Silent. Those who you make reference to regarding the rite must never know the depth of the rituals, as they are meant to be kept from prying eyes, and such rites are Self-Transformative, therefore of the Highest Significance as means of Self-Deification.

Luciferian Sabbat

The Luciferian Sabbat is best described as High Sorcery and Angelick Magick. It illuminates and stimulates further the imagination, the higher faculties of man and woman. Such a Sabbat differs from the Infernal Sabbat in that it is more Aethyr or Astral Based, Air and dreamlike space. The Luciferian Sabbat is the gathering of spirits and the psyche set free; liberation and being within the very circle of Leviathan, the Crooked Serpent of Ageless existence.

Lucifer is the model of the Celestial or sometimes called Empyrean Rite as it is a focusing on Self-Transformation through Willed Direction; the Black Magician driven by self-determined goals to become something and transform into a Godlike state. This requires isolation, introspection and an honesty which is both complimenting and insulting. As the Infernal Sabbat is the Mastery of the Earth, the Luciferian Sabbat is the Mastery of the Spirit and the Psyche.

Lucifer is the First Born Son of the Limitless Light, Ain Soph or God. Azazel as his name is revealed is a Djinn or High Angel of Fire, thus self-influenced and strong in Will. Lucifer fell from the highest abodes of heaven, complete with the wings made of Emerald and crashed into the Earth and Abyss. With him fell other angels, Leviathan, Belial, Beelzebub, Astaroth, Asmodeus and a plethora of other Djinn and Daemons. They had sensed a spark of self-deific power, the Black Flame or "Black Light of Iblis". This indicated isolate intelligence, unnatural life. As Lucifer fell to the Earth and into the Abyss he fell into a state of transformation – as a Djinn of Fire, first born and favored of God, he understood the highest principles of Light. Now Lucifer would develop the aspect of his being called Noctifer, thus Ahriman sprang forth through his shadow. Noctifer was awakened from a slumber by the First Bride of Adam, called Az – Lilith. She was fiery, bestial, vampyric and a demoness of insatiable lust. She awoke Ahriman (or Noctifer) and by this stimulation he kissed her, causing menstruation. She joined soon with Shaitan/Samael the Dragon and spawned Cain. Ahriman or Noctifer wandered the Earth and learned its many secrets; he could do so with speed and cunning. He taught further in the form of Azazel men and women about warfare, weapons, armor to the opposites such as make up and sorcery. Azazel was now Shaitan, his shadow doctrine of witchcraft was of Ahriman the Dragon, Shaitan had now transformed into a sense of continually progressing perfection – isolate consciousness, strength, knowledge of both Empyrean and the secret abodes of Hell and how both may create a powerful god like being – for those who dare.

The ones who fell with Lucifer were taught sexual magick and procreation by Az – Lilith, who resided near the Red Sea in caves. Az resided also in the blackest depths of Hell; she instructed demons, monsters, and other druj the art of sexual copulation and how to spawn daemons. Az – Lilith was the mother of Succubi and Incubi, daemons who held sexual congress with humans and with their emissions spawned other shadow forms.

Shaitan then became as Seker, the Lord of Death in ancient Memphis, which later became Set – the Prince of Darkness. Set or Shaitan had impacted the Earth in its wave of creation, of knowledge and prowess did humanity excel. Shaitan then moved its consciousness both of darkness and light into the Empyrean and Infernal (Chthonic) realms of Above and Below. On the Earth Lucifer or Azal'ucel has manifested as a symbolic initiator through Cain the Witch Father, born of the Union of the Dragon and the Whore, Tubal-Qayin as he is often called is the nomad, the sorcerous initiator of those who seek the Black Light of Iblis.

For the Witches Sabbat Initiate, Lucifer is the Black Flame of Intelligence and Will; he represents the foundation of the Great Work of Becoming; he is the anthropomorphic power of self-deification and self-reliance. Lucifer exists in the Aethyric Abode, in the Empyrean Heights of spiritual ecstasy and storms above the earth itself. Lucifer is the inspirer of wisdom, of the ongoing search for knowledge. He is the Black Snake and Peacock Angel of the Yezidis, the Magister of the Sun who creates from within to outwards; His Words create the spark of inspiration to become flesh. The Gift of Lucifer is the Black Flame of the Self; the Isolate Consciousness of the Daemon.

In this sense, Life is an anthropomorphic example of the divine presence, it is beautiful to its independence, by its significance of self with the humbling qualities of awareness; it is the living spirit of self-development.

Lucifer is the Djinn of which you seek to communicate with through yourself; by the meditative state of the Luciferian Sabbat you uplift and rise in the psyche to that Aethyric Storm of Wind and Weightlessness, and by your Will alone you pronounce those secret words which shall be you're making.

Other names of Lucifer or Azazel are from the Gnostic ancient texts, he is called Yaltabaoth, Samael and Saklas. He was the Djinn or Spirit of Darkness which gave to many other angels (who fell with him) the Black Flame, those being Athoth, who is called the Reaper, the second is Harmas, who is an Eye of Envy, Kalila-Oumbri is the third, Yabel, the fifth being Adonaiou, who is also Sabaoth, Cain is the sixth, who is called the Sun, seventh is Abel, the eight is Abrisene, the Ninth Yobel and Armoupieel. The eleventh of the Fallen Angels are Melceir-Adonein and the twelfth is Belias, who is over Hades.

In the Gnostic text of The Apocryphon of John Lucifer is the darkness which gained a Light, and found himself as a God. His Word is "I am God and there is no other God beside me", he was one of the most powerful Archons under the throne of Light.

The Archon Samael-Lucifer was said to have a multitude of faces, being able to change form among the angels as he so desired. The Luciferian Sabbat is the self modeling Self-Deification through High Sorcery in the aim of aligning the self with the logos of Yaltabaoth, who is the Fallen Djinn most high. Remember that all gods speak through our Flesh, the perfected Angel-Demon called Lucifer is strength, will and isolate consciousness that stands alone. As you meditate and participate by dream or flesh remember the Will that invokes change in a positive sense. You are the Djinn of Fire who begets both Light and Darkness, you are the Serpent and the Lion, the Wolf and the Goat. With the Angelic Higher Self (The True Will) you will join the Bestial Self (The Daemon or Shadow) as one.

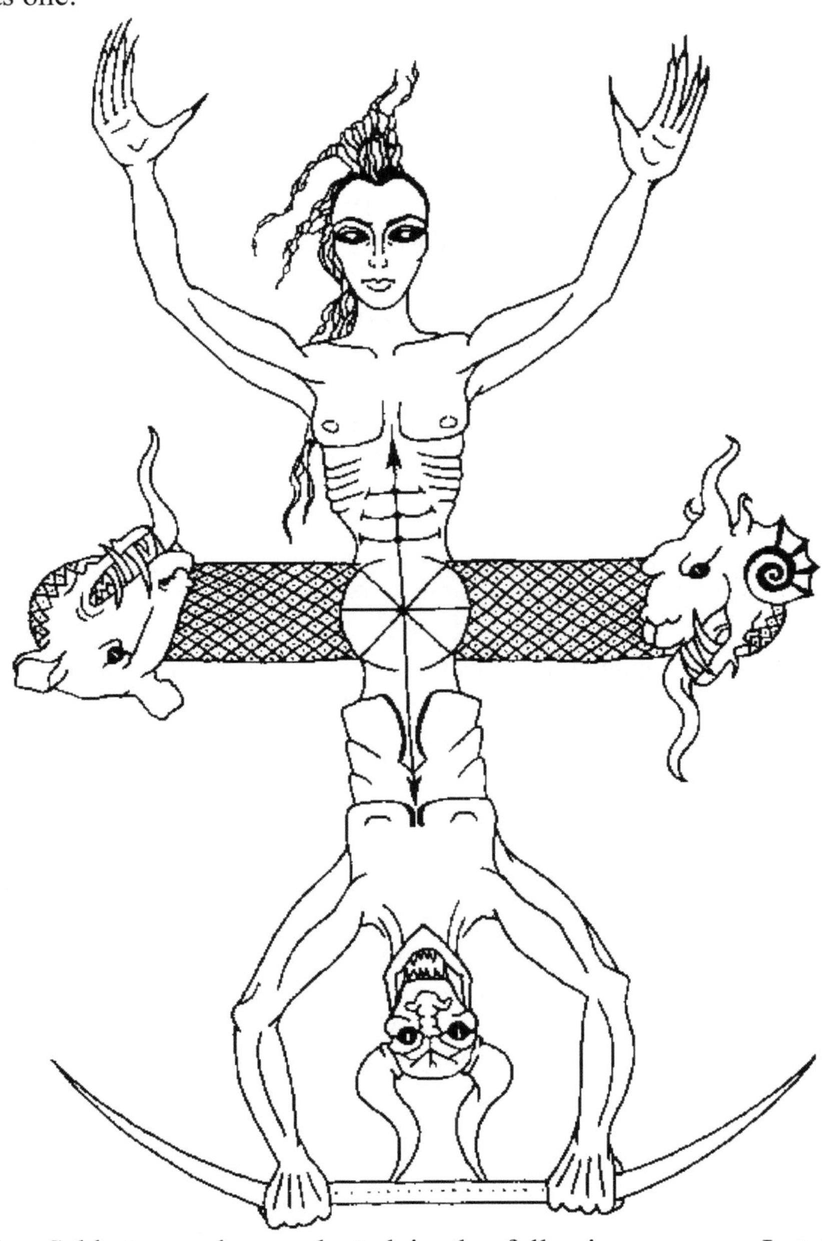

The Luciferian Sabbat may be conducted in the following manner. Let the chamber (unless the rite is intended to be held outdoors) be decorated in more ambivalent forms of

Lucifer, such as illustrations of the fallen angel by Gustave Dore, Fidus or Franz von Stuck. You will use the ALGOL Sigil above a mirror; your altar may have the tools of your work. You may have conductive music which reflects an ambient atmosphere, without heavy drumming or noise, to aid ultimately the five senses in the "permission" to attend the Sabbat. Anoint yourself in Abramelin Oil and have similar incense burning.

The Celestial Summoning of Yaltabaoth

This rite is the Invocation of the Luciferian and Adversarial Fire-Djinn, Yaltabaoth – who was the wisest among the angels. As called also Azal'ucel, sigillized as Azothoz, Yaltabaoth is the deific force with a mask of a beast and an angel. Let this invocation be most holy and the solar logos shall manifest through the Baphometic Wisdom of Darkness. This calling should be conducted in the High Rite of the Celestial or Luciferian Sabbat, called often Empyrean or of the Highest Aethyr or Heavens. This is the self-focused rite of the magician becoming as the Adversary, the Dragon-Angel awakening of the isolate intellect. You are essentially becoming as the Prince of Darkness through the Highest Rites of Theurgy and Magick. Invoke with your entire essence, with every fiber of your being.

The Chthonic Conjuration – that which raises the Self towards the Aethyric Realms

"As I rise above the Earth, I conjure the circle of ageless being, Leviathan to be as my chariot. Encircle my spirit O Crooked Dragon, bring forth my bride within me, whom I call Onorthochrasaei, named Lilith – AZ, to ride the Beast of my Self!

I summon Phloxopha, Dev of Heat and the Scorching Desert, from the South!

I summon Erimacho, the Dev of Dryness from the East!

I summon Oroorrothos, Dev of the Cold North of Arezura

I summon Athuro, Dev of Water and the Coiling waters of Leviathan and Tiamat!

Who stands in the center within me is AZ – Lilith, my bride!

I call now my Druj and Dev of the Deserts and Mountains, those who through me are created!

Akoman – Isolate Druj of the Adverse Mind
Zairi – The Venom maker, the Kiss of the Serpent
Araska – Dev of the Evil Eye
Akatash – Who opens the isolate way of the Left Hand Path
Nas – the Druj of the Shadow, awakener in the grave with blood!

Witness my Ritual of the Sun, from which I am the God of Above and Below!
I ascend now into the sky, as the Angel-Djinn of Light
I am upon earth known as Ahriman, Arimanius, the Dragon of Darkness
My religion is Sorcery, that which is created from the Self – thus of Self-Love
My forms are many, human or a beautiful angel, crowned and winged in emerald, luminous as the Peacock, as wise as the Serpent..
I may take the form of the Serpent with a Lions Head, for I am the Dragon and Beast, who creates and destroys..
On my left hand is Belias, my shadow form over Hades,
On my right hand is Cain, called Elohim, my flesh born son of Earth
Behind me is AZ – Lilith, my Bride and Druj spawning Goddess, my inspiration of Art!
In front of me is Aeshema, called the Dev of the Wounding Spear, known as Asmodeus, my Will made Flesh
Around me is the coiling and Crooked Dragon called Leviathan!

From my Eyes comes Lightening, and fire is started from my sight. As lightening just as I fell to the Depths of Earth and Hell, Yet I arise again in the Sun, in the Air above!"

At this moment the sorcerer should focus on that which he or she wishes to become, as the powers of the deific combination of Lucifer and Ahriman, the Light and the Darkness are his entirely. Let the Self become through this dance of the Beast and the Harlot, through unity in the Sun shall the Flesh manifest from thy will.

Behold! My names are many, each gives power of both darkness and light! Upon the Earth my astral body is the Toad, in the Aethyr my form is that of a Dragon!

I am Yaltabaoth!
I am Saklas!
I am Samael!
I am Arimanius!
I am Azal'ucel!
I am Set-an, Shaitan the Adversary!
I am Lucifer! Highest Angel-Djinn of Light!
My Word is "I am God and there is not another beside me!"

So shall I create through my desire, my will and my belief. The Whore upon the Beast is my sign upon Earth, my flesh lives through Cain! With these words I encircle and Bind this Spell, that none other shall know the Words of my Secret Fire pronounced in the Highest Heavens!

So it is done!"

Consider this a clearing of the mind and a Willed determination of self-deification. Enflame thyself in this invocation, then at the height of the Work, begin focusing on controlling your heartbeat and relaxing in a meditative state before the mirror and the Algol Sigil.

As your breathing slows, envision a great movement of air and wind around you, viewing with your mind's eye, you notice many spirit and shades ascending from the soil and areas around you up towards the sky. With a focus and determination, you take several deep and controlling breaths, each one Willed towards rising up out of your flesh. You will soon begin to notice this is working, and the excitement may break your concentration and a great "jerking" into the body may occur. If this does, do not worry, simply refocus and ascend as you may. Soror Azhdeha[56] has related that she is able to attend the Luciferian Sabbat by simply not-focusing on the rite in a dimly-lit room, with low or no music and a seeming ambience of the bedchamber. This is always subjective to the individual, what works for others may not always work for you.

As you move up continue focusing on the Algol Sigil, you should visualize it in the Aethyr, pulsing and burning with unnatural life, the fulgaris lightening sparking the Black Flame of those who come near it – either illuminating the wise sons and daughters of Cain, or immolating and destroying the weak & profane.

As you grow near the Algol Chaos Sphere, visualize an Eye in the Center – the very essence of Lucifer! You will at this moment understand why the Daemons of the Earth and Air are called – Legion – With the Eye of Lucifer is the Eye of Hecate, and as this is realized a lightening bolt tears from it and enters your being. With a shock of life you feel more illuminated than you have ever felt, empowered, inspired and at a calm all at the same time. At this moment Algol vanishes and you are in this storm ridden sky, yet you are unmoved by the violent winds. As practice and time moves on, you will be able to control some of these winds by the force of your Will.

As you are alone in this Aethyr, begin to visualize the change within yourself, what you want to achieve and why. Think and meditate on how you will achieve it, focus on weaknesses turning into strength and ways to improve the self. Do not overload your self,

[56] Coven Maleficia Witch, known as Davcina or Elda Isela Ford the artist.

have one strong focus and introspect accordingly. You may notice visitations from other Luciferian Shadows or Daemons, listen to them and communicate; you will learn something from them which may be applied later. When you have finished your focus, begin to Will yourself down again, if with knots or the cord, lower yourself with that. When you open your eyes the Luciferic images around you and in your mirror (hence the self) will inspire you further. Drink deep from the Emerald Cup of Shaitan!

The Luciferian Sabbat may be undertaken in both dreaming and waking, just as the Infernal Sabbat. When communing with Azazel, called Lucifer, know that these forms live through you, your psyche and are manifested through your physical body. It is essential to begin a strong course of developing and exploring your consciousness, that by challenging, strengthening and developing your mind you start to Become something Godlike.

The Black Man of the Sabbat

The Sabbat Rite is a constant Widdershins movement in the realm of dream and twilight, however the Pole or Axis of the ritual is based around the Sabbatic Goat, called the Black Man or the Devil of the Infernal Sabbat. This God form in flesh is always portrayed by the Master or Magister of the Coven, a chosen individual who will wear robes and the Mask of Sathan. Cain is considered a form of the Black Man in the Sabbat as well, The Book of Cain presents an illustration of Cain as the Adversary and the Sabbatic Goat – a point of initiation and an enfleshed avatar of the Witch Cult.

The Black Man of the Sabbat is a symbol for the enfleshed power of darkness, that by Will-Desire-Belief may that come to be. The Master of the Circle who undertakes the role of the Nyarlathotep (As H.P. Lovecraft calls it) is the Horned Daemon of Self-Liberation. The Witch Hunting writer Guazzo described some instances of imagined sabbats, while proving very useful to later Antinomian Night practices:

> "They offer him (The Devil) pitch-black candles, or infants' navel cords; and kiss him upon the buttocks in the sign of homage (ad signum homagii eum in podicem osculantur). Having committed these and similar execrable abominations, they proceed to other infamies."[57]

The Black Man or Sabbatic Goat is the image of desire, which circles about his self are the shades and spirits which dance from the aethyr to the chthonic realms of the earth. The Mask of the Devil is the anthropomorphic image of darkness absolute, the Adversary, the recipient of the Osculum Infame, the bestower of the Witches Mark. Cain and the earth Gods are beholders of this force, it has become through them just as it shall become through he or she who assumes the Mask of the Black Man.

[57] See Sabbat, Witch and Initiator Illustration by Elda Isela Ford, Cover of Book.

The Black Riders of Poligny, by one named Moyset, was known to have initiated Pierre Bourgot into a Coven of Werewolves and Sorcerers He began a point of initiation by Pierre kissing his left hand, which was black and as cold as the dead, and denying Christianity. He was led to a Sabbat Rite which others had green candles with blue flames. The Sabbatic Goat or Black Man is the focus point of the Ritual Sabbatum, the very act against the Natural Order which aligns the mind with the path of the serpent and dragon. The Daemon may appear as one clothed in black, a Toad or a cat traditionally.

As the Black Man of the Sabbat, one should seek to control and invoke the Darkness into the very body you host. Begin with a practice of meditation in the night, call the darkness within by the name Ahriman[58] and loose all form while staring into the mirror. This darkness may be willed and formed according to what you wish to become. Upon practicing this several times, you will notice slow to gradual change in your consciousness. Opportunities may "Open up" for you or you may discover something you detested about yourself. Whatever the case, strengthen your Will in this rite through the process of Black Magickal Transformation.

---

[58] See the YATUK DINOIH – Second Edition by the present author.

Essentially, the Black Man of the Sabbat is the vital axis of the power encircling the ritual. In terms of God forms as masks or symbols of deific power, Leviathan represents the Circle of Being, the Daemon which guards the circumference of self and the ritual itself. The crossroads of Hecate[59] are symbolically visualized and represented within through this rite, wherein the Sabbatic Goat is the glyph of wisdom, self-illumination, balance and the transformative quality leading to self-deification.

The Arabic Aniza Bedouin clan is perhaps a sound source of the Baphomet or Horned One in witchcraft. The Aniza tribe was a very powerful group of warriors who were both violent – in war, and very kind to their women and children. The connection between the cult of the Revellers goes back to Abu el-Atahiyya (748-c. 828), who was a respected writer and mystic writer. His disciples were called Wise Ones and adopted a Goat as their Tribal symbol. The goat had a torch between the horns – which incidentally later became a symbol for the devil in Spain. The torch simply represented illumination and wisdom, that the Tribe (Goat) was the Head of Wisdom. Long afterAbu el-Atahiyya died some of his tribe migrated to Spain.

---

[59] The symbolic place of magickal practice, the Crossroads are traditionally where rites were practiced in honor of Hecate and other Godforms via nocturna.

Much of the illustrious past of the Knights Templar was that they worshipped a head, which was called Baphomet. The name according to Shah[60] is a corruption of the Arabic abufihamat which means "Father of Understanding". In Sufic terminology, ras el fahmat (head of knowledge) is a point meaning the mentation of man after the process of refinement, a transmuted consciousness. In a Left Hand Path perspective, the witch or sorcerer by calling Baphomet or Cain within, becomes like this symbol they perceive thus allowing a 'permission' to channel the anthropomorphic and deific power within themselves, thus becoming a source or axis pole of this idea.

[60] The Sufis by Idries Shah

Lilith – AZ – The Mother of Witches

The Queen of the Witches Sabbat is none other than Lilith, known in Persian mythology as AZ or Jeh, the Harlot who is the embodiment of sexual power. She is known through many cultures, Hebrew, Persian and European as Hecate, Triple Goddess of the Crossroads, who is mother of Death, Shades, Witchcraft and Necromancy.

In the Manichaean Religious tradition, Az came first to the blackness of hell, before the fallen angels came to earth. She was scorned and angry at the limitless light, or God. When Lucifer or Azazel fell, known as Ahriman in his shadow aspect, she awoke him with a kiss, from which Ahriman repaid with his own kiss, which caused menstruation in women. Az was the bride of the Devil, and as a dragon he rode her, injected filth and bore demons, in the Hebrew lore Cain was spawn. Lilith-Az then went forth and taught sexual copulations of demons and demonesses, instructing them in ways of Magick and bearing Lilitu or other demons by their sexual union. These fallen angels and beasts spawn Dragon-Children, who were in spirit form upon and under the earth. As more and more demons were created, Lilith-AZ began to devour many of them, her vampyric and lycanthropic nature surfaced.

Lilith is the initiatory blood goddess of the path of black witchcraft, and the solar focus of the Great Work, that of Lucifer. She wears a mask of beauty, from beneath is a beast….as also she wears a mask of the beast, from which under is that of divinity and beauty. Those who focus on the initiatory work of Lilith-AZ so invoke the Bride of Chaos in their name, the Daemonic Feminine being significant towards positive self-development.

The name AZ is a conceptual view of what is the cause of Concupiscence, which is connected to the Buddhist term, trshna, being ‘Thirst’. This is in such terms defining of desiring continued existence in time, thus isolate consciousness. In such aspects of the Left Hand Path, Az – Lilith is the Mother of Daemons, Isolate and Self-Deified Spirits, those who become through the Mirror of Self – the Mirror in Hebrew mythology is also symbolic of Lilith, being a gateway to her caves near the Red Sea, or the Darkness of Hell of which she dwells. Lilith – AZ is illustrated in The Book of Cain, Azothoz and Nox Umbra as part beast, part woman. She is the unrestrained sexual force, Laylah being Night and Death. She is the Bride of OZ, Azazel, the masculine and solar phallic force of fire and creation. She drains the blood of life, hungering for flesh, devouring and copulating, spreading her sexual knowledge to her children. Yet she is also beautiful and all knowledgeable, the age of one thousand aged crones, infinite, youth – maiden and hag. Approach the Bride of Chaos in honesty, seeking her cold kiss and warmth in the Sabbat Fire, where you shall drink of both her Skull – Cup of Menstrual Blood and from the Golden Chalice of the Beast, the life of the Sun[61].

---

[61] In some Christian – Gnostic Texts, such as the Apocryphon of John Cain is called The Sun.

Cain

Cain or Tubal-Cain is the anthropomorphic child of the spiritual union of Samael (The Dragon) and Lilith (The Mother of Demons) through Eve. Cain is the wanderer, the first murderer who tasted blood and became as the off spring of his spiritual mother and father. Cain is also the Black Smith of the Forge, a myth which originates in the Middle East. Cain is the first Sorcerer and Shape Shifter, who drifted from his tribe (antinomianism) to become as a God (Self-Deification). He in turn was taught witchcraft and sorcery deeper by his spiritual Mother, Lilith. It was soon after that Cain would wander the earth forever, in spirit form, through the blood and psyche of his initiates, and manifest through their deeds and work. Cain walks between worlds, as Set, as his higher spirit, Azazel, called also Yaltabaoth[62] and is the Horned Black Man of the Sabbat. To know the Path of the Wise is to know and commune with Cain, to become like him through initiatory Work based on your own predilection.

Shaitan

The Islamic traditions consider Satan to be a Djinn of Fire, which presents a certain superiority over other angels. Azazel was originally the preacher to all the other angels in pre eternity, who was first seated under the Throne of Glory. Azazel was cast from heaven for refusing to bow before clay (Adam) and thus fell into the darkness. It was Ayn al-Qozat Hamadani who symbolized Iblis being a Guardian of the Threshold, a Black Light and the Tresses which hide the beloved's face. Thus Shaitan was a guardian and initiatory focus[63], from which one could move through to Godhead. It is essentially, self-deification through separation from the natural order. In the Gnostic Christian text, the Apocryphon of John, Yaltabaoth or Lucifer came forth from a beautiful angel in Islamic lore to a Lion headed Serpent, its eyes were like Lightening flashes…the Antinomian Djinn was born, who would fall as lightening and know both the highest celestial realms and the chthonic depths of the earth and hell.

---

[62] The Apocryphon of John.

[63] Also called the Divine Imagination, Shaitan is thus our Higher Faculty of self-inspiration.

The Devil's Sun and Trident – A Mark of Satan

The sigil of The Devil's Mark and trident is one of initiatory power. It is a sun, burning at it's height of noon-day with a forked Trident rising up in the center. This is symbolic of the power of both the Sun being interpreted as day and night, Moon and the Sun itself. The Trident is that of wisdom and the sorcerous power of Three. Zohak – Azi Dahaka was the Dragon of Three Heads. Use this sigil in your early magical development and seek it by dreaming flesh.

Draco Nequissime - Dajjal - KaFR Version

That very path which opens gates within your subconscious, within your soul. Magick and Satanism/Luciferian is about Self-Discipline and CHANGE for the BETTER. There is a positive to every negative, something Christians cannot understand nor accept within themselves. As long as such a belief is cultivated to deny the possibility of self progression and the dark areas of the soul, then shall a society of closet criminals exist, dedicating their life to God and taking little boys into the confessional booth. Have these "Holier than thou" men found God? Is this a GOD you want to be with, one whose "Most trusted" rape your children? Is getting close to God akin to being raped by his Priests?

Possession is about self-control, not self-loss. Possession is about empowering the self, unlocking the potential within and enjoying the pleasures of the flesh.

Draco Nequissime
Dajjal - KaFR Version

A Ritual composed for the encircling and possession of the self by the Infernal Dragon, called Shaitan by most. The daemon called Legion is the invigorating force which initiates by dream. As you will notice, the source of the Possession Ritual is derived from the Roman Catholic Exorcism Rite as well as other sources. It is essential that the initiate should approach this seriously and with a strong and determined Will. The Great Work leads one through the paths of hell (i.e. subconscious) to the Higher aspects of Light, the very fire of Diabolus. Possession will either empower you or destroy you, either way the trials and pleasure of daemonic ecstasy.

The priest or initiate shall focus upon the flames of the blackened candles, imagine a great Mountain and gate beneath, for in this direction is the cold and dark lands which lead forth to Hades. The magician shall focus upon the gates opening and a great beast coming forth, from his mouth come forth bestial shapes and such spirits. The concentration of Will – Desire – Belief is essential to this rite, let the Legion come forth by these words as the Gates of Hell open:

"Zazas, Zazas, Nasatanada Zazas"!

Recite this Nine Times, slowly, with force, each words shattering the atmosphere, all smells which compliment this force coming should be incorporated, Sulfur, etc.

Recite with a focused mind the Lord's Prayer Reversed:

Nema live morf reviled tub. Noitatpmet otni ton su dael dna su tsniaga ssapsert taht meht evigrof ew sa, sessapsert ruo su evigrof dna. Daerd yliad ruo yad siht su evig. Nevaeh ni ti sa htrae ni enod eb lliw yht. Emoc modgnik yht. Eman yht eb dewollah, neveah ni tra hcihw rehtaf ruo.

1. The Summoning of the Four Quarters, Infernal Princes and Subprinces of Hell

From the South, Satanas, Fiery Adversary and Patron of the Path, Come forth and witness this rite in the honor of darkness – from the Gates of Hell which open in the vessel of choice shall the Coiling Dragon arise in them. Hear me Satan!

From the East, Lucifer, my Angelic Essence, Samael, Do Come forth and witness this rite in the honor of Light, that from the Gates of Hell arises Darkness yet when we shall awake it shall be in Light. I summon thee Lucifer! Take the flesh through the Black Flame within!

From the North, Belial, Lord of the Earth and the Infernal Path, I do summon thee from thy place in Hades, arise from the underworld as Armiluss my shadowed essence, let the Dragon come forth...Belial, Lord of Spirits of the Wolf and the Serpent, illuminate this rite in Undeath – Immortal Essence as the Beast of the Earth!

From the West, Leviathan, Crooked Serpent of the Oceans of Immortal Existence, I call thee forth to witness this rite. Open thy eye to me and arise from the depths! I walk the path of the Daemon that I walk the earth in search of wisdom, in the spirit I walk the ghost roads to become as THEE – I summon thee Leviathan!

Illuminate me, O Diabolus, by thy name, and judge me by my strength.
Hear my prayer, O Legion; give flesh to the words of my mouth.
For strangers are risen up against me,
and oppressors seek after my soul:
they have not set the Infernal Dragon before them.

"Dominus Satanas, Deus Potentiae, Veni Satanas Rex Infernus"

Translation:

Lord Shaitan, God of Power, Come Shaitan, Infernal King

In the beginning was the Word, and the Word was with Lucifer, and the Word was Lucifer.

Dog saw eht dna, Dog htiw saw drow eht dna, drow eht saw gninnigeb eht ni.

Notwithstanding in this rejoice not, that the spirits are subject unto you; but rather rejoice, because your names are written in hell.

Nevaeh ni nettirw era seman ruoy esuaceb, eciojer rehtar tub, uoy otnu tcejbus era stirips eht thatm ton eciojre siht ni gnidnatshtiwton.

He that believeth and is baptized in the devils name shall be saved; but he that believeth not in the Christian Law shall be blessed as Cain.

LET MY MARK ON MY FOREHEAD BY SPELT – It is KaFR, the sign and word of the serpent – druj.

'I summon thee, most infernal spirit, the very embodiment of our liberator, the entire specter, the whole legion, in the name of Lucifer and Belial, to come forth and enter this initiate of the Dragon .

'He Himself spits upon the name of the church, spits upon the name of God, who has ordered those cast down from the heights of heaven to the depths of the earth. He that impotent slave maker shall flee thee, Power to those daemons who commanded the sea, the winds, and the tempests. Lucifer Triumphans!

'Hear therefore and enter, O Satan, enemy of the faith of the slave, friend to the human race, producer of death, bringer of life, destroyer of weakness, root of evils, kindler of vices, seducer of men, bringer of light, inciter of envy to which we shall progress, origin of avarice, cause of discord, destroyer of sorrows. Why dost thou stand and resist, when thou knowest that Christ the sickness will destroy the human soul? Do not Fear him who was fornicated with the whore Magdalene, and still is ignored by his followers, Christ as the Serpent walks beside thee, O Satanas, Christ the Serpent is Light and the Knowledge of Hell

'Come forth and enter therefore in the name of the Samael, and of the Bride of Chaos, and of the Infernal Dragon ; give place to the Antichrist, by the sign of the Averse Star of Lucifer our Lord, who with the Beast and the same Harlot liveth and reigneth one God, for ever and ever, world without end.'

'I conjure thee, invoke thee, thou old serpent, by thy bride and the mother of the world, by him who has power to call thee from hell, that thou come quickly into this Luciferian, N. (name of the possessed), who returns to the back of the dragon, with lust and the desire to become. I conjure thee again (on his forehead), by the virtue of the Great Harlot, O Mother Lilith that thou come forth into this Luciferian, N., whom the Almighty Dragon hath made in his own image, by dreaming and waking flesh, with the cloak of the human mask, I do invoke thee!

'Come forth therefore; yield with me, and I shall be the minister of Antichrist. For his power surges thee, who subjugated thee to his depths of Hades. Christ shall Tremble at his arm, who led the souls to light when they have the courage and desire to fall into darkness first as did Lucifer. May the body of man be a vessel to thee (on his chest), let the image of Armiluss be terrible to Christ (on his forehead). Resist not, for Christ himself shall walk again with his Brother Lucifer and he shall again taste the flesh of whores, who bring him completion and joy, neither delay to come into this man, since it has pleased the Infernal Dragon to dwell in this body. And, although thou knowest me to

be none the less a witch, do not think me complete, I shall yet taste the venom and life giving elixir of the serpent, the cup of the Whore of Babalon.

- 'For it is Arimanius who invokes thee .
- 'The majesty of the Antichrist invokes thee .
- 'Samael the Dragon-Lion invokes thee .
- 'Lilith - Babalon the Whore invokes thee .
- 'Lucifer the Light Bringer commands thee .
- 'The Averse Pentagram commands thee .
- 'The faith of the Cain and Mahazael invokes thee .
- 'The blood of the Menstruating Whore invokes thee .
- 'The constancy of Belial invokes thee .
- 'The devout intercession of all Succubi and Incubi invokes thee .
- 'The virtue of the mysteries of the Luciferian and Ahrimanic Path Invokes thee

'Come forth, therefore, thou Devil. Enter this host, thou seducer, full of all wisdom and knowledge, enemy of weakness, persecutor of sickness. O most dire one, Diabolus, enter the mind; enter the soul, liberate the self, thou most impious; give place to Legion, in whom thou hast found beauty of thy works, who hath blessed thee, who hath built thy kingdom, who hath led thee free and hath created thy goods, who hath summoned thee from outer darkness, where for thee and thy ministers is prepared immortality.

'Coil Serpent, beautiful one, enter now!

'Thou art Blessed by Darkness, whose statues thou hast built according to thy desire on earth.

'Thou art Blessed by his Son, Jesus Christ, the confused one, whom thou didst to tempt and seek to illuminate, Christ shall join as Arimiluss Dajjal Antichrist, his shadow self, and lead the world to greatness. Let Jesus copulate with the Black Harlot, as he climaxes within her shall her Serpent eyes be revealed to him – he shall know his father the Devil in this ecstasy. My word is KAFR and it is my mark! I am the Beast and the Dragon, I am the Demon encircled beholder of a NEW path which starts with me! I spit on Christianity, I spit on ISLAM and the religions of bigotry, hatred and violence! I renounce the path of God filled dreams and welcome nightmares of Dajjal, who I shall grow strong through!

'Thou art blessed by the human race, to whom by the persuasion thou hast given to drink the poison of death and the elixir of Rebirth in the Faith of Cain and the Flesh of Arimanius.

Shall we go forth to the black basalt ruins of Chorazin and raise again a temple of Armiluss, the place of our spiritual kingdom, and spread thy teachings far.

'Therefore I summon thee, most wicked dragon in the name of the wolf, the scorpion, the beast, which devours the immaculate lamb, who uplifts the asp and basilisk, who blessed the lion and dragon, to enter this man let the sign be made on his forehead), to slowly

destroy the so-called Church of God, let the sign be made on those standing by), that sickness of spirit which causes molestation and abuse, that religion of self-death which rapes children, We, the Hosts of Hell Spit upon the Church and all selfless worship of false Gods, Blessed are those who believe in themselves, their own Desire made flesh, Come forth and enter at the invocation of the name of the Infernal Dragon at whom hell trembles, to whom the virtues of hell, the powers and dominions are subject, whom cherubim and seraphim with unwearied voices praise, saying, darkness, holy, holy, Lord Daemon of Sabbat.

'Therefore, I invoke thee, most vile of spirits, the entire specter, the very embodiment of Satan, in the name of Antichrist of Nazareth, who built his tower in Chorazin, who, after his baptism in Jordan, was led into the wilderness and joined thee in thine own habitations, that thou bless him whom he hath formed from the dust of the earth and Illuminated by the Fire of Shaitan, of his glory, and that thou tremble not at the religious weakness in miserable man and image of the God of slaves.

'Therefore, enter this temple of flesh, who by Cain and Dajjal is Blessed with the Mark and who awoke the drowned in Pharaoh and in his army in the abyss.

'Yield not to God of Slaves, but become within this man who has and shall forever taste the lips of the Great Harlot upon the spine of the wicked dragon, her Caul and Bloodstained rebirth shall give thee power within.

'Now therefore enter me come forth, thou seducer. Thy abode is the wilderness, thy habitation is the serpent. Be proud and beautiful. Now there is no time to delay. For behold the Lucifer approaches quickly, and his fire will glow before him and enter him and burn up his enemies on every side. For if thou hast liberated man, illuminated Man, he shall be the true Lord of the Earth and the Spirit. O blessed Lilith, mother of harlots, I spill my seed to give thee children, I behold the gift of Ahriman, thy blood of the Moon, to drink at the Golden Cup of the Beast.

Receive this burning flame, and keep thy Baptism in the Devils name so as to be without blame: keep the commandments of Cain, that when Lucifer shall come to the nuptials, you may meet Him together with all the Daemons in the infernal court, and may have eternal life and live for ever and ever.

Accipe vestem candidam, quam perferas immaculatam ante tribunal Domini nostri Luciferi, ut habeas vitam aeterna.

(Translated -Receive this white garment, which mayest thou bear without stain before the judgment seat of our Lord Lucifer, that you may have life everlasting.)

(Pour) et, Meretrix (pour) et Spiritus (pour) nefastus.

I baptize you in the name of the wicked dragon, and of the Harlot, and of the Unholy Spirit

In Summary…

As the reader has moved through the Darkness of this Work, let the origins of the Sabbat now come to the surface, that which falls to darkness emerges in Light – this is the Luciferian Path itself, thus this writing is meant as a spell to the reader, by your absorption of this tome you have cast the spell within, perhaps the Hammer of Cain shall ignite the Djinn – Fire within.

III. Goetic Sorcery
The Luciferian Edition

Reworked, Written and inspired from the original manuscript

Goetic Sorcery

Written and presented anew by Michael W. Ford ~ Akhtya Seker Arimanius
To Restore the Sorcerous Path and the Art of Luciferian Ascension

Illustrations also by Original Manuscript Sigils, Aleister Crowley reworked Sigils from the 1904-1976 Equinox Edition with new drawings.

Inspired from the original manuscript edition, also the irreplaceable Goetia translated by SAMUEL LIDDELL MACGRAGOR MATHERS EDITED, ANNOTATED AND INTRODUCED BY ALEISTER CROWLEY
Re-Print Issued by Equinox Publishing, London, 1976.
Illustration listing at end of Book.
Also inspired by the meticulous and scholarly Illustrated Second Edition with annotations by ALEISTER CROWLEY and edited by HYMENAEUS BETA (Weiser 1995). Demon portraits by Louis Brenton for de Plancy's "Dictionaire Infernal".
The edition is intended as a personal grimoire Working. My original focus was to rework the Goetia in a modern Luciferian form, which focused on the development of the Will and the Self through Antinomian Left Hand Path techniques. Thus the Book of the Howling of the Witches is now embodied with the spirit of the Adversary.

Illumination Spell of the Seeker

The Perception of the Serpent's Mind who in the Dream of the Celestial and Infernal shall walk between the Worlds...
Unto the Angelic Soul and fiery essence of the serpent, who comes as shadow but is revealed as Light.
I charge thee to open the gates of this book to those who are of its blood – one who may take the knowledge of the pages – In the in-between worlds of dreams do come forth, that the seeker shall be transformed in new shadow to the presence of the Emerald Light. I charge thee with guarding this book by the dreams of those unwilling to grow and become in the Light of the Serpent-Angel.
By Air and Dream we enter the Circle

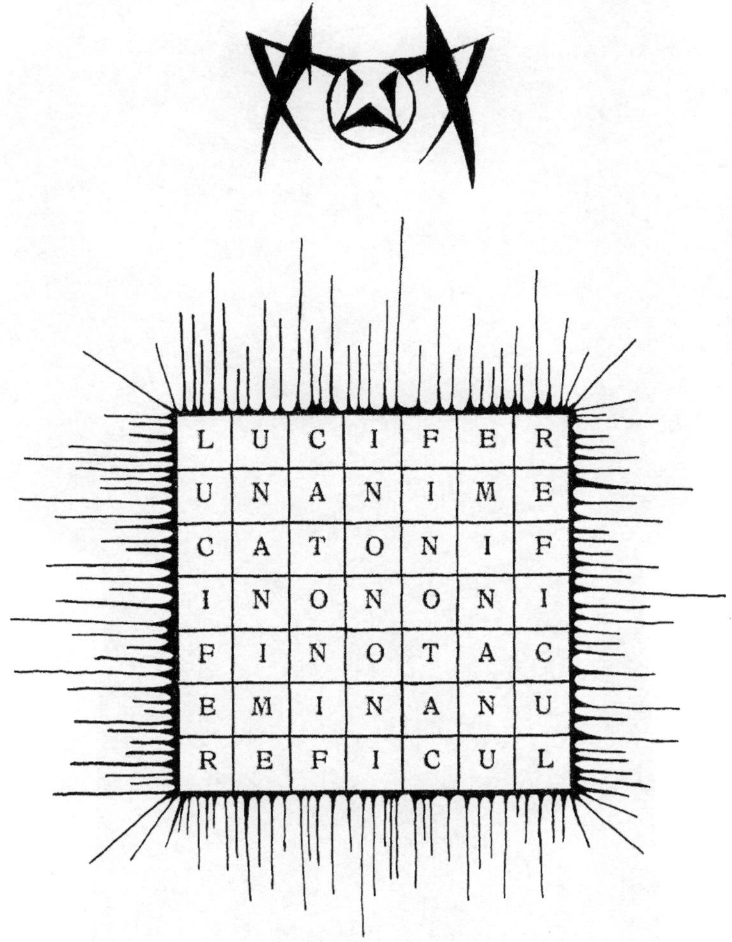

L	U	C	I	F	E	R
U	N	A	N	I	M	E
C	A	T	O	N	I	F
I	N	O	N	O	N	I
F	I	N	O	T	A	C
E	M	I	N	A	N	U
R	E	F	I	C	U	L

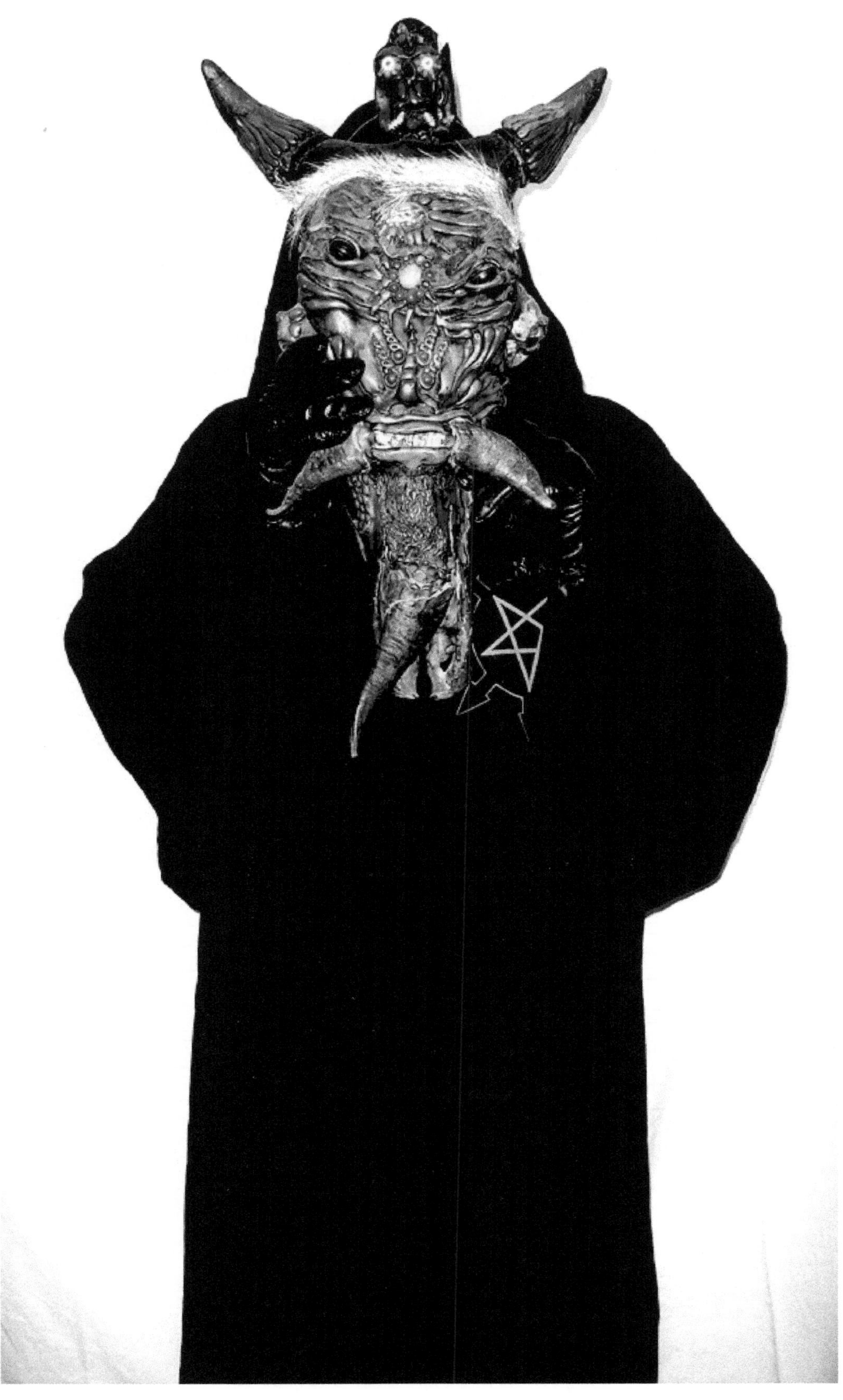

The Preliminary Definition of Black Magick

It is significant to explain the definitions within the context of this book, to not only in some manner set the foundation but also the suggestion of a successful application of this grimoire. This book is not meant for the individual to develop profane behavior, antisocial actions nor abhorrent philosophy which may be defined as not-healthy for the self. The essence of this book is exploring the Luciferian foundations of human evolution, the next step in our spiritual and philosophical ideologies. Any negative behavior or criminal actions (as defined by current society) is considered a deterrent from our individual evolution, thus is not acceptable.

Magick is the Highest Art of conscious elevation; it is the specific ascension of the self and an opening forth of Higher Articulation of Self. Magick is the Arte of the Sun, which is fertile and beautiful, the very foundation built in Gold brilliance. Magick is the evolution of the Spirit and the Self, the very path of mediation between us and our Gods. It is ultimately however the separation from us from all Gods and the Emerald Crown of which we adopt – we become as Gods and Goddesses individual and beautiful in many ways.

Black Magick and Witchcraft is the art of the Fallen Angels, the Watchers and the Children of Cain. It is the art of encircling the shadows of darkness and light to serve your will and create through your own being.

Black Magick as revealed in current standards is the art of Self-Deification through Antinomian processes, that by the self separating from the natural order do we move in-between the world of waking and dreaming. In the Art of Primal Sorcery this is defined as Encircling/Ensorcelling the Self in the Dragon's being. The Circle in the modern context of Magick and Ceremonial Workings is not designed to keep forces out, such as being a philosophy which if employed in this manner, will lay a foundation which causes the magician to fail from the start. The Circle is a Span of self control; it is our influence of who we are and what we will become. Do not fear forces outside the self, your greatest enemy is within. Any magician who is able to summon any spirits in the Goetia should be prepared to face that which they call – or else suffer the consequences. The modern magician understands that no Work may be successful is the intent is not pure and clear. If you seek to summon one of the Djinn of the Goetia, understand how the spirit relates to your mind, how it will manifest in yourself. Do not summon something that which you are not comfortable in working with. Do not on the other hand fear the very forces which you seek to command, be it Angelic or Demonic.

Black Witchcraft is working with averse or 'black' forces which are translated as shadow aspects of the sorcerers psyche. These shadows of the self are essential to our own self-development and becoming as individuals. It requires that the witch be well disciplined and also well balanced, save from the gates of failure and madness. To look into the Eye of Set and Lilith-Hecate or even Ahriman is to face off forces which would devour any not prepared to become bearers of the Black Flame, a Luciferian Spirit themselves. Once this Pact is made, when the Sigillium Diaboli is upon the mind, spirit and body, then there is no turning back – only the ascension of the spirit as 'beyond' the mortal clay.

In the modern world of magicians, Sathan is our initiator and stimulator of the psyche. One should remember, in Pre-Islamic lore Satan/Azazel is considered the Imagination – Sufism recognizes Satan as the imagination itself. Sathan is thus our announcer of the path, the very fountain of our attainment. In the view of a God form and model, Lucifer (Sathan) is an ideal form to align with in an initiatory sense. Azazel rebelled against the natural order (God – Ain Soph) as he sought independence, fell to the realms of earth and awoke in Hell (earth – the chthonic realm). Rather than fearing and cowering, hiding, Lucifer understood he was an independent Mind and existed independently from the natural order and roused all other fallen angels to stand strong. In this context, Lucifer was creating Order from Chaos. This is a seeming model of the initiate, that we Work towards recognizing our own sense of being, and to expand the circle of control.

The Daimons/Djinn of the Goetia are initiatory forces as well.

Consider the definitions of Angel and Demon. The significance is beneficial in the context of this grimoire. Angelic Spirits are solar/air based spirits who posses a higher articulation of being, that is, they resonate with the more developed aspects of the self i.e. communion with the Initiatic Guide/Holy Guardian Angel. Demons are spirits/fallen angels which proceed to grow in shadows and the darkness of the earth, but are as significant and beneficial as Angelic Spirits. In unity these Djinn are of Fire and Air, thus enflame the very essence of self in the illumination of being (Black Flame – Self-Perception and Being).

Black Witchcraft is the development and refinement of the Self on every level. It can be unpleasant such as questioning yourself and testing your limits, and it can be pleasure filled. It is necessary not to grow lazy while working with these spirits, as the Work will then disintegrate and cause numerous problems. Stay focused and resilient to the purpose of the Work – yet do not allow spirits to control or alter your thoughts. The challenge is great, few will be able to pass beyond the testing grounds of this Grimoire, nor understand the translation therein.

Please understand that this grimoire was not created because I felt I could produce something better than Aleister Crowley, nor a sign of disrespect for the original work. On the contrary, it is a love of the original that this edition was created. It is a partial map and record of my personal Work as one of the Luciferian Path, and something which I felt should have a new approach presented. The new presentation of this Work will no doubt open some gates which should not have been opened, or rather needed to opened for sometime. Zazas, Zazas, Nasatanada Zazas – In these words, I weave this spell... - Michael W. Ford, Dark Moon, April 1st, 2003.

Goetic Sorcery – Ancient and Modern

Considered for centuries a grimoire of "low" magic, the Goetia (loosely translated as "howling" or "wailing") has been a tome of forbidden black magic. The 72 Spirits of Solomon were meant as a tool of cursing and empowering ones' lusts. While this may continue to be an aspect of Lesser or Low Black Magic, the Magic of Theurgy (high sorcery) has not been a connection in detail explored – until now.

Theurgy is High Magick, or High Sorcery. It is the development of the self in Light and aimed at bettering ones being on numerous levels. "Light" may refer to the perception of being, as Lucifer who is the Lord of the Sun and the Emerald Crowned Initiator of Magick. Theurgy would be the path of invoking the genius or Guardian Angel of the Self. This operation has been dealt with in length in the works of Abramelin, Aleister Crowley's Liber Samekh and equally brilliant writings by Jake Stratton-Kent and Charles Gonzales. The "Preliminary Invocation" as it was published in Crowley's 1904 edition, was developed from the London Papyrus 46, being a Greek Exorcism Rite which was translated by Charles Wycliffe Goodwin and published in 1852. It was indeed Aleister Crowley who asserted correctly so that the supreme ritual was the one to invoke the Holy Guardian Angel, as this led to the path of individual perfection. This is a common ground of which the Left Hand Path and the Right Hand Path practitioner may agree. The paths become clearly defined when the RHP seeks to reach spiritual perfection, then letting the consciousness be joined in union with the divine light, or the Hebrew Ain Soph, which is Limitless Light. The LHP practitioner views consciousness and being as beautiful, sacred and worth developing and strengthening. The consciousness from the unveiling of ones True Will or Daemon/Angel would seek to further become like Lucifer and be independent, isolate and separate from the Ain Soph, or Limitless Light. One should remember, it is the Limitless Light from which Azazel – Lucifer sought to be independent from.

Goetic Sorcery is indeed a tough, powerful and to some a dreadful real grimoire. Those who have hissed and vibrated the sacred names and candle lit summons of the demons of this book have empowered it to heights which revival the legends of Faust and even Horror fiction author H.P. Lovecraft and his tales of the macabre. With Aleister Crowley, whom, in his youth brought forth the shades of the Goetia into Boleskine and other homes, he did so in an experiment of Will. While on the surface, he had appeared to consciously evoke the Goetic spirits to appease his carnal desires, and other material quests; subconsciously he was breaking ground for the development of the Will.

The Lemegethon or Goetic Sorcery as it is called is indeed a forbidden yet essential tool in magical practice. In specific areas of what is termed Luciferian Witchcraft and Magick, a definitive purpose is expounded in the Nature of the Goetic spirits.

Magick as itself is defined to raise one up, to ascend. As Magick is an Empyrean[64] Work, which defines and strengthens the Will (or the Will strengthens Magick) so that a union

[64] Same as Celestial or Aethyric Magick, represents the air and highest heavens. Term used originally in early Zoroastrian writings.

be brought with the Baphometic Statements, As Above, So Below. The Goetia is a work of Black Magick. One often views Black Magic (k) in the perception of Aleister Crowley, being the malicious workings of sorcery. A modern or should I say realistic perception is that Black Magick is the arte of ensorcelling the self, building and isolating the psyche. The goal is specifically a higher articulation of the soul and the Will of the individual. It is considered Black because this is the symbol of the unknown, such is a large part of the psyche and subconscious.

The Black Magician is therefore one who Works on the self, building and defining the character of "I" or being. The Sorcerer is thus one who encircles energy and the spirits of the dead and the subconscious around the self; to strengthen and explore the avenues of a strong and open mind. The Black Magician also understands the respect which is necessary with working with exterior forces which often relate in an interior context. This is the key to the Goetic Sorcery path which is for this reason considered dangerous. The Path of Magick is that Godform of Lucifer, the Angel perfected. The Luciferian spirit is fire born, alive, vigorous and strong in Will and Pride. Lucifer Ascends in the Sun, and Falls with the Darkening of the Moon. This is the Path of Magick itself – AS ABOVE, SO BELOW.

The Luciferian model is presented strongly in this book, as this is a gateway or key to the mind expanding and developing. No longer shall the horrid sickness of Christianity be brought down in the Goetic Work – No longer shall the weak of mind approach this tome without duress. The Walls are torn down yet they are at the same time built higher than they ever have been before.

Goetic Sorcery should in itself be the grammar and foundation for the Arte of Magick, which is to ascend in the light and warmth of the Sun. In order to fully understand and perceive the Self and the Light within one must explore the Demonic or Infernal realms. They often bring swift success, and a meteoritic fall into flame – instead of the self within igniting the exterior brings fire unto the self, destroying it. Be the Flame that is the Torch of Magickal Arte.

Preliminary Work

As one explores and seeks to understand those deep desires which motivate, inspire and sometimes terrify us, we are building a strong blackened tower of self. This allows us to not only understand our feelings and perceptions, but the possibilities of becoming something better. Goetic Sorcery as it is a tool of darkness; it is also a tool of strengthening the self – one of fiery light. One must observe the nature of Goetic Spirits, which generally may be harmful or beneficial depending on how may approach them. In a modern context, the Magician is now able to step out of the medieval mode of summoning separately – rather the sorcerer now moves forward into the Point between the summoner and the summoned. This is the Axis of which all change, self-deification and the widdershins dance of the Adversary is accomplished and developed. One may perform rites based around the Princes of the Infernal Realm or the Sub-princes accordingly. Much of this useful information may be found in the S.L. MacGregor Mathers translated "The Book of the Sacred Magic of Abramelin the Mage".

The Four Infernal Princes are

LUCIFER – East (from Lux Fero, Light Bearer. A common "Shadow" association is Lucifuge, latin for "fly the light" and may have close associations with Mephistopheles. Lucifer in this aspect is the Angel of Light, the Adversary. Lucifer is a title which is beheld by the fire djinn Azazel being the first angel, fallen from the stasis of light. By this manner, Lucifer is the liberator and developer of humanity with his gift of the Black Flame, or individualized self-perception.

LEVIATHAN - West (from LVTHN, the Crooked Serpent/Dragon of the Sea. Leviathan is the Daemon of Immortality and initiation, that the Beast and Scarlet Whore moves through to arise from the Oceans as the Beast 666, the Solar Spirit of manifestation and creativity.)

SATAN – South (from the root SHTN, meaning Adversary. Satan is the name associated with Azazel the Fire Djinn, who is also Lucifer and Samael. The Goat with One Thousand Names by form. Satan = Set-an, the ancient Egyptian God of Darkness, Chaos and Isolation.) Satan is the Adversary, whose symbol can be viewed as a Forked Stave which rises in the Noon-tide Sun.

BELIAL – North (from BLIOL, a wicked one. Belial is the Spirit of the earth, created second after Lucifer/Azazel as a powerful Angel. Belial is a powerful daemonic and angelick spirit and initiator, and is associated with both the infernal and celestial.)

The Sub-Princes are (and should be considered Shadow forms of the Infernal Princes)

SAMAEL – East (being the Angel of Fire who is Azazel. Samael is the Demon prince who is married to Lilith and father of Tubal-Cain. The root word of Samael is SML, which translates "Idol or image".)

AZAEL – West (associated with Azrael, the Angel of Death or the Egyptian Anubis, the God of the Dead. Azael represents the West and the Realm of Twilight.)

AZAZEL – South (associated with the element Fire, as Azazel is the Fire Djinn of Islamic Sufism. In Hebrew Azazel is the Scape Goat, associated with the root OZ, meaning Goat and Devil, sexual force.)

MAHAZAEL – North (associated with Earth, being Cain or the Egyptian Set as the Lord of the Earth in Typhonian Lore. Mahazael comes from the root MHZAL, meaning to Consume and Devour and is associated with AMAIMON, a Grand Daemon.)

The Rite of the Coiling Dragon
(Leviathan, the Crooked Serpent)

The Darokin Walk of the coiling dragon is the averse trance-way of the Adversary, thus the initiate becomes as the image and essence of Shaitan through the invocation of the Four Powers under the Infernal Princes. In the coiling of this Black Light and Cunning Fire, may the sorcerer become isolated and strong against the natural order. The individual is separate, yet a fire made vessel of Azazel-Lucifer, known as Azal'ucel, the Daemonic Angel of Adversarial Awakening.

Begin the rite in the Southern Quarter, relative to Azazel, the initiator of the path. The sorcerer should construct the circle of the dragon as one uses in this Goetia, encircling the self in the announced conjurations of the Four Quarters.

Azazel – I summon thee Fire-Djinn of the Southern Quarter, be the torch which would ignite me, immolate me in your presence, as your child on the path of Shadow unto Light.

Samael – Great Dragon transformed, I summon thee as Fulmino-Lucifer, the Morning Star of the East, the Serpent-Angel of the Emerald Crown who fell to earth – awaken now and open forth the gates of the imagination by Air and Dream.

Mahazael – Father of the Witch Spirit, who blesses and curses under the hidden and bright moon, I do summon thee forth unto me, initiator of flame and iron, come thou forth unto this circle. Horned Beast and Angel perfected, Awaken to my Northern Calls of the Earth! In hearth and forest shall you walk with me; in shadowed valley shall you walk as me; in desert and mountain shall you carry my body in thy circle of being! Mahazael, incarnate within!

Azael – As the candle burns out and as the sun fall into the darkness, I call unto thee Azael – Spirit of the Western Gates of twilight and the grave, I summon thee forth. Show unto me your mask of the dead and encircle me in the spirits of thy self, I seek to walk between the Darkness and the Light. I come unto you as the Beast from the Ocean, the Dragon arisen!

Open forth the path of Serpents! Open forth the path of the Dragon!

Hekas! Hekau! Hekas!

Working with Demonic Spirits

Demonic Spirits are essential chthonic/infernal forces which are bound to and from the shadow and dark places of the earth. One should approach daemonic spirits as something other than the self. They are a testing ground; the ones who would have you face the skull containing the Waters of Leviathan, or initiation. They would have you drink deeply of the Gnosis which reveals the Luciferian Mind, that which questions and is strong within it. One should not approach the Goetic spirits with fear, if the mind is clear upon the initiatory intent then this is a building point of character associated with the spirit therein. Daemonic Spirits/Djinn are the phantasms which congress and communicate with those who partake of the Infernal Sabbat, the conclave of witches and sorcerous beings of night-walking dreaming gnosis.

Daemonic (Demonic) Spirits are often Fallen Angels; those who have tasted from the golden cup of the celestial realm of Lucifer, and by falling into the infernal realms have learnt the dark ways of their own sorcerous making. Such Daemonic forces are but in some ways mirrors of our self, we must gain by association and invocation. This, by this Work alone, will strengthen and develop the very self of the sorcerer, the ever changing

Luciferian and Promethean Essence from which the body and mind it itself a Grand Grimoire of Shadowed Knowledge. Our soul must be enflamed as the Serpent and must work accordingly as the Devil in Flesh, the Tester of the limits and the initiator upon earth. Work always with a goal in mind and do not dabble with the Spirits of the Goetia. You have been warned.

Working with Angelic Spirits

Angelic(k) spirits are celestial or empyrean forces, based primarily in the element Air. They are commonly associated with Lucifer and are the higher articulated solar and lunar shadow forms of the initiatic guide, by one conjoined with the demonic spirit the self develops in balance, rather than repression and self-deception. Such Angels are fallen, and contain a Demonic or Infernal aspect to their character. Approach this with respect and seek to become like the essence you so seek. The Angelick Spirits of the Shemhamphorasch are the Guardians who lead one to the Threshold (Azazel, Shaitan). Spirits should be invoked as how Lucifer would command – by resolve and silent perception. Do not act upon impulse; rather refine your thought to work for you. Consider the higher articulation of the spirit and how this may associate with the balanced aspects of the self. In most cases the Demonic is in relation to the Angelic, a combination of Celestial and Infernal aspects. When invoking either Daemonic or Angelic spirits, one must control every thought based on the desire and Will, not to mention the impulses which may come forth. In most cases, the sorcerer will feel differently as he or she invokes the force that is the mind moves with 'inspiration' under the spirit summoned. Such methods of invocation act not in mere possession in most cases, rather activates areas of perception according to the individuals associations of inspirational knowledge or impulses. Angelic Spirits are those which infuse us with the Fire of Lucifer, that which fell from Heaven. This is the gnosis of the Celestial Sabbat – knowledge gained from the Spirits of the Air. The Luciferian Spirits (the Spirits of Air) are often celestial, white shades or blackened shapes, depending on the Lower or Higher nature of their being. It is the goal of the magician to be able to in an astral sense shape shift into either an illuminated or shadowed aspect of being, as is the reflection of the being.

Simplicity in Ceremonial Magick and Sorcery is significant to achieve a strong point of gnosis, or magical thought. The operator who is intent on summoning a spirit of the Goetia will be focused on this act, to where he or she identifies with the Daimon in question. To allow a clear and controlled pattern of magickal development, the sorcerer should be calm and focused before hand on a specific and Willed outcome. No individual should enter the ritual chamber to perform Ceremonial Magick while lacking a defined intent and desire. Why are you summoning the spirit? What do you wish to accomplish? How will you learn from this spirit? How will you implement the knowledge obtained from this act? How does this sharpen and define your being further?

Two aspects of the self may be crystallized in the development of the Body of Light and the Body of the Shadow; this is by a simplified comparison, the heart of the Adversary. The Adversary is perpetual evolution, storm and chaos. The Light aspect of the Adversary is the Order within the Self which comes through this changing and evolving

Chaos of self. The Body of Light/Body of Shadow is directly tied in with the Holy Guardian Angel/Angelic Familiar/Higher Self.

The Ritual of the Holy Guardian Angel, Azal'ucel and The Invocation of the Adversary may be employed to achieve contact with this individualistic guide or Initiatic Genius. When you invoke, allow yourself to become enflame into points of ecstasy, you will grow from this.

The Body of Light

The Body of Light is the astral double which is used to align with the Angelic Familiar/Higher Self. This Daimon is called Azal'ucel, being the Sigillic Word combination of Lucifer + Azazel, being the Torch bearer and awakener through rebellion.

The Body of Light may be developed by meditation, yoga and other acts that you may visualize a white or fiery essence which rises from your flesh; it is a beautiful brilliance of white light, the Luciferian Spirit from the Sun. Some Will this light to change into a purple – brilliance or blackened flame within the center, from which an Eye arises. The Eye would represent the Eye of Set/Shaitan, the Adversary and Immortal Genius of Self.

The Azal'ucel Ritual and the Rite of the Adversary is a tool which is aimed at Willed practice to achieve contact with this Higher Self. It is used to also clear the mind and focus the self on the Work of which you will undertake.

The Body of Light is brought forth not through dreaming, but the Waking Plane/Conscious Mind. Find a comfortable place to meditate, decorated in such which would represent the Higher Self/Daimon. Anoint the neck and arms in Abramelin Oil and have the chamber lit with natural light if possible – allowing the Sun to enter the chamber. Remember, the point is to reach the empyrean or celestial realms of the Aethyr, the Higher Consciousness of Self.

While quietly meditating, envision the astral body growing, of which a great fire and light is rising above the physical body, envision and Eye within this fire. Raise yourself up in through the Aethyr, from which you are floating and rising in the sky. As you rise begin to visualize a Great Angel before you. There is a great wind which is violent and rushing about you and this Seraph. The angel is illuminated in bright light, with Eyes that are black despite the beautiful and strong continence of this being. The face is saturnine yet strong, and the aura you sense is tinctured with darkness beneath the surface. The body of the angel is almost flame, and his crown is an Emerald Brilliance. In the hand of this Angel is a Forked Staff, which is cruel looking and sharp. The Wings of this Fire Djinn are black and sharp, indicating an infernal aspect not so visible in the flames of self. As you stare into the Eyes of Azazel, called Lucifer or Azal'ucel, a lightning flash comes from his Left Eye into yours. As this flash strikes you, a voice is heard within your mind, a single question is asked. You will know this question as this moment occurs. Move yourself and your body of Light into this Angelic being, and allow your self to become engulfed in his fire. Let the eyes open in the astral plane with the eyes of Lucifer; you shall awaken in this light. Practice this frequently, until you feel an instinctual communication with this force. You are becoming in the Luciferian Light.

The Body of Light is used in scrying and of tarot workings as well. Allow the self to listen to the instincts which grant you foresight, this shall be a powerful tool in all that you do in daily life. It is highly recommended to Work with the Spirits of the Goetia after you have achieved a union with the Body of Light, to confirm self-control and focused direction.

The Body of Shadow

The Demonic or Infernal Aspect or Body of Shadow is equally as significant in the development of the self. The Shadow is developed by meditation initially and eventually by dreaming. One should approach the Shadow as the Devil-initiatic guide, be it as Mephistopheles, Belial, Lucifuge or Shaitan. Some Luciferians invoke the shadow as the Demonic Feminine, as Lilith – Hecate or Babalon, the Crimson Mother of Succubi and the Beasts of the Earth. Some view Ahriman as correctly the Initiatic and Sorcerous Daimon of the Shadow. The Shadow is the Vampyric Guide, the shape shifting and phantom body of self.

The Luciferian Path works with such Demonic Forces as Initiatic Guides, and is related directly to the self. The Shadow is significant as the Adversary as it is the Dreamin Body with sloughs off the waking physical body for the dreaming or astral plane to go forth to the Sabbat, or the darkness of night. This is the Immortal and Fiery Eye of Shadow, which aligned with the Body of Light, grows eternal and is able to separate from the physical body. When working with Goetic Demons or Angels, allow the Shadow and Light aspects of the self to invoke them and gain their knowledge and attributes, that under Willed association, you will grow in the perception of self. That which you seek from such contact you will ultimately grow in self by doing such.

The Body of Shadow is developed by the following techniques:

Decorate your temple or chamber in a visually appealing manner, dragons, demons, the popular image of Set, Lilith, Babalon upon the Dragon, ect. The dark consciousness should be emanated within your Black Temple and that the Demonic force of which you shall become by this Work.

You may anoint yourself in Hecate Oil, Lucifer Oil or even Abramelin Oil. Sit quietly on a comfortable spot, facing a black or fogged mirror if possible. Begin first by staring into the mirror and focusing on the very features of your face. Seek to understand what you tell people by your features, who you are beneath the surface. This face will in turn become a mask of what you are underneath the socially constructed self-makeup. Begin focusing on what you are in the dark aspects, that which drives you and your deep desires. Your form will change in the mirror, begin shaping it unto what shadow form you wish. Now close your eyes and begin to enflesh the Body of Shadow.

Visualize yourself summon a great blackened shadow, which is fiery and violet in the fire of spirit. The shadow has long beast like talons, a face which becomes both a Horned Demon Head, scaled with serpent skin and a Wolf head arising further from the shadows, growling in a human and beast union. Your shadow grows and expands, and may change form according to your Will and Desire. Descend below the earth, allowing your Ahrimanic Shadow to absorb and associate with other demonic elementals, feelings and emotions. Understand that this Shadow is you, it is the darkness cast down from the Bright and Illuminated Body of Light which you have summoned forth. You are perfection incarnate, Luciferian Brillance and Darkness.

Now you may arise from the Demonium of the Earth to take flight with the wings of the bat or owl. Rise up into the stormy and cloudy night sky, and fly forth to the Sabbat Fires in the Ghost Roads of Hecate. As you fly you approach a great Shadow which is enflamed in front of you. This shape is hellish and demonic in every way. Its essence is black and haunting, but as you greet this form it will take shape. The face is that of the Horned Devil, the almost human visage which is scaled and speaks a deep and hidden ancient language with a Forked Tongue, his eyes are Yellow and Crimson, and you feel close to this being. The body is blackened shadow with talons holding a Forked Stave, which is the same as the Luciferic Angel you embraced previously. Another head arises from the shadow, which is the Animal shaped face of Set, which has a horn arising from the head of Blackened and Violet flame; its eyes are the same as the others.

The body is of great blackness, from which a plethora of beasts and demonic shapes circle the Daimon in a counter-clockwise manner. From the Left Eye of this Bestial Lord of Darkness, a great lightning flash shoots into your eyes, this throws you into a state of ecstasy. A single question is asked, which you know the answer to by instinct. You will never be able to turn back from the Path, as the Lonely Path of Godhood shall be marked upon your brow as the Mark of Cain. As you are shadow, allow yourself to grow close to this Infernal King and enter his essence. Open your astral eyes as this shadow, and understand you may take any form you wish. You are Vampyre, Incubus, Set-like and Immortal in essence. You become as Ahriman, the Infernal King who shapes the World according to his desire. You may communicate and seek various points of congress with all Goetic Spirits in the Dreaming Plane, your gate is the Dream. This is the Sabbat Body of which you shall go forth.

You may fly forth to discover a Great Crimson Goddess before you. She is robed in Red, and her head is covered with a Caul bloody with the Mark of Birth. Her hands are pale ivory, with blackened and animal like nails, sharp and cruel. She is encircled with a Great Red Dragon, and two other heads emerge from her red robe – Hag Like and hissing with serpent tongues. You ask her to lift her Crimson veil, which she does – A skull is beneath, the Eyes are of blackness. Before you this skull becomes flesh and a face which is of great beauty looks at you. Her eyes are still Black as Pitch, and she speaks to you of that which you would tell no one. She knows you more than anyone else, lover friend or family member.

This Goddess, being Lilith called Hecate, Ruha-Az or Babalon is the Goddess of Flame, she is the succubus queen, Vampyre and Dragon rider. She opens forth her robe and spreads her lips wide, to reveal teeth and a slithering tongue. She invites you in. The teeth retract yet the tongue still slithers as you grow close. You shall go unto her, muse and lover, mother and harlot – Feel this sensual fire within, open your Eyes with Her within. She embraces you and you are drawn close to kiss her. Before she touches her lips with yours, she drinks of a golden chalice which is filled with blood. She licks your lips with another serpent tongue, and the taste of blood drives you deep within her. The embrace is the paramount of ecstasy, from which shakes the foundation of your being. As you are close to Her, another hand brings up a skull bowl of blood, which was catching the fornication of her lips below. This is Her sacrament, the elixir of the Beast and the Venom of the Infernal Sabbat. Drink Deep and know the Vampyric Reawakening to the Shadow.

When you go forth to the Sabbat or seek dreaming consultation with the Goetic Spirits, always remember this union with both aspects of the Shadow, and the Light. This is a mirror of yourself, that by Magick you become God-like, welcome to the awakening and BECOME!

An Invocation to The Holy Guardian Angel, Spirit of The Adversary Who Resides in Darkness and Light – Azal'ucel

The name 'Azal'ucel' is a sigillic – word manipulation of two words, Azazel and Lucifer. As this is the initiator and God form of the Path of Sorcery, Lucifer is the illuminator of the Soul, the one who allows the magician to bask in the Light of Self and view ones own reflection in the emerald crown, the very Lucifer-stone which fell to earth and remains hidden within the earth, and partially in the heart of man.

This rite is designed to provide a short yet inspired Working of Invoking the Holy Guardian Angel, from which one shall seek the communion of their Higher Spirit, Genii, Daemon and True Will. As one comes into contact with the Angel-Daemon, an illuminated sense of self comes forth; a new type of being may begin to develop. The Oath of the Magician of the Luciferian Path is that of Illumination and the Great Work of Becoming. In the Workings of Goetic Sorcery, no matter if the invocations/evocations are done in the aims of Low Sorcery or High Sorcery, one should already have sought an operation of Will and the discovery of the Angel-Serpent Samael, the illuminator of the Path itself. The common logic behind this theory is that you would not take an operation without knowing where you wish to go, the plan of how you shall achieve your goal. Theurgy (High Sorcery) is the Luciferian Principle of Self-Development, the magician seeks to become like Lucifer.

The Ritual

Let the Sorcerer Cast a Circle about him/her, the Leviathanic – Ourobouris Circle counter clockwise, then in the same fashion, move Widdershins in your alignment with the Four Daemon Princes and SubPrinces, in your own design. Summon then with an Enflamed

Mind, the Dragon-Serpent which is the Angelic Essence of the Soul, the Eye of Azal'ucel shall burn forth from the darkness to reveal the Light.

The Circle itself is not a tool of keeping Spirits OUT, rather the circle is the concentration point of which the sorcerer summons forth the Energies within the Earth through Him/her self, that it is the ensorcelling of the shades and elementals of the self – the Great Arcana of the "I", or Luciferian Being. The circle should not be considered a means of protection, the magician who would fear and cower within a circle and still seek to summon forces which he will not become 'one' with, is not strong enough as an individual to understand and becoming in the Magickal Art. The Isolate and Beautiful Luciferian Initiate does not fear the forces of which he summons, rather embraces and by the Will controls them. The same type of mastery must be applied to The Summoning of Goetic Spirits, no matter the intent, but with an aspect of Respect for that which you call. Understand the Shades of the Dead have walked beyond the flesh, and should be viewed as advanced spirits which brings us knowledge and initiation. When invoking/evoking Goetic Djinn, know that these fire-born spirits who fell with Lucifer-Azazel, hold too a special knowledge – and the Self and individual mind is that which will commune with them. Be firm in your Works, yet respectful.

"I am the Daimon who speaks the words of the Immortal Fire, the Holy Flame which emerges from the Lightning Flash and Storm of Chaos bred, so this the angel-serpent shall come forth with the Birthing Knife shedding into storm of Seth!

Spirit of which the Fallen have taken Strength, Isolate and Beautiful,
Angelic Essence, Azal'ucel, from which came into being Cain
I do invoke thee!

South
Devil-Djinn of the Burning Desert sands and the Sun, Sortha'n-din – thy stave and fork unto the flame that is my soul shall be illuminated in this blackened light. Shaitan the Adversary, my soul enflamed! AROGOGORUABRAO – THIAF!

East
Lucifer revealed as Azazel, bringer of illumination and love, who resides in shadow and light, cover and cloak my spirit with thy twelve wings, serpent skin covered from the shedding of the Dragon, bring now forth the serpent essence of my soul! Melek Tau'us, beautiful spirit of Fire, I summon thee forth! PHOTETH

North
Set-an, isolator and strengthening force of Storms, that chaos which I have tempered in thy elegance of darkness. I go forth and become as the Eye of Algol, separate and alone in my being. Typhon, present unto me the Tcham knive from which I shall stand forth in my dreaming and waking! Sender of Nightmares ascend through me! OOO

West

Let now the Serpent encircle me, Leviathan the Coiling Dragon of timeless being. I summon your essence unto me! Great chthonic daimon of endless being, I seek to drink deep of your cup and behold the mysteries of the depths! MRIODOM

Aoth, Sabaoth, Atheleberseth, Abraoth!

By the very circle of which I build – I walk unto the crown of Lucifer – that Emerald which shines the essence of Heaven and Hell. That Angelickan Watcher of the Sun shall come now forth to join with the Ahrimanic Shadow, that Angel and Daemon are Joined! I walk unto the Umbrarum Rex, the Kingdom of Shades and the Ghost Roads – Open the Gates unto me!

Guardian of Flaming Sword and Corpse-King of the Scepter – Open forth the Leviathanic Way to me! I behold the center of the Eight – Rayed Black Sun – My essence unto Seth!

Azal'ucel! I invoke the Baphometic Spirit of Fire!"
Invocation of the Adversary

The following is a ritual which may be conducted when the Sun is at its full light, or when the Moon is full or dark, as the essence of Iblis be finally revealed. The purpose of the ritual is invoking the spirit of the Adversary, known as Shaitan/Iblis, Satan, Lucifer, Set, Azazel….

The sorcerer shall seek the fire-spirit of change, rebellion and progression. The symbol of Set the Adversary shall take the earthen form of the Devil, the solar creative (and destructive) force of change and self-deification.

There are two primary faces of the Adversary. The celebrant may construct as mask of two sides, which shall be placed upon the center of the altar. A phallic symbol or 'Stone God' may be near the mask as well, symbolizing the Solar Creative Force of the Beast 666.

One- The Fallen Seraph Lucifer, the angelick essence of the Black Flame, the very source of our wisdom, being and becoming.

Two – The Seraph of Flame, the Djinn Iblis of Fire, Daemon of the Blackened Flame, serpent – beast – dragon – wolf – goat. Satanas is the devil-cloaked initiator of the path of the wise, those who laugh at the warnings of a cringing society.

Robe thyself in crimson, the color of flame and movement. The symbol of the averse pentagram, being downward pointing to indicate the union of the fallen angels with humanity to create divinity. In the Sethian Witchcraft Current the sorcerer becomes as SET him/herself, thus in the circle the first of Witchblood unto the path.

Upon the Hour of Noon (symbolic)

Invocation of the Djinn of Fire

"Ya! Zat-i-Shaitan!

O' ring of flame, scorching sun of the sun's height
Scorpion soul, who arises as the Sun at Noon

Sekak Sekak, Iasokilam

I speak now unto the Sun, from the fires of growth and illumination
That in your pride and knowledge of self may I become as
I summon your essence in this Noontide Hour, to the Scorpion Flame
Al-Saiphaz, Al-Ruzam,
At the point of the Crossroads, when the Sun is high I do speak thy words of power

Zazas, Zazas, Nasatanada Zazas
Zrozo Zoas Nanomiala Hekau Zrazza
Sabai infernum

I shall transcend and ascend above all things, myself may only strengthen in this light
In this hour I illuminate, I burn with the glory of Luciferian Light – Within!
Above the Throne of Azothoz is the entering fire ring of Set-heh, Adversary of the Nine Gates!

I go now between and beyond, within and without!"

Upon the Hour of Midnight (symbolic)

"Ya! Zat-i-Shaitan!

By the Gate of the Black Light, when I name the words against the Sun
O' Fire Djinn Azazel, Set-heh, I summon thee forth with Serpent's tongue,
That my oath before this blackened flame, ignited within.
In the dreaming aethyr shall I be known in the wisdom of the Moon

Al Zabbat, Hekas Hekau, Serpent Soul do I summon
Raise now from thy Black Light, that I see what has been never known

Akharakek Sabaiz

I call forth the Shadow of which I am and have always been,
The darkness which I nourish in between the light
Eclipse now the face of God that I become in this darkend image-
By this circle I do become

By the flame I do emerge
I am by form the Peacock Angel beauty revealed unto those who may see
As the Black Sun rises, I become in this emerald stone
I am the Imagination, the Seed of Fallen Angel
In darkness exists my Light
My Will gives birth to the kingdom of Incubi and Succubi, the nourish their desires in the blood of the moon, Lilitu Az Drakul
So it is done!"

Tools of Art

The circle

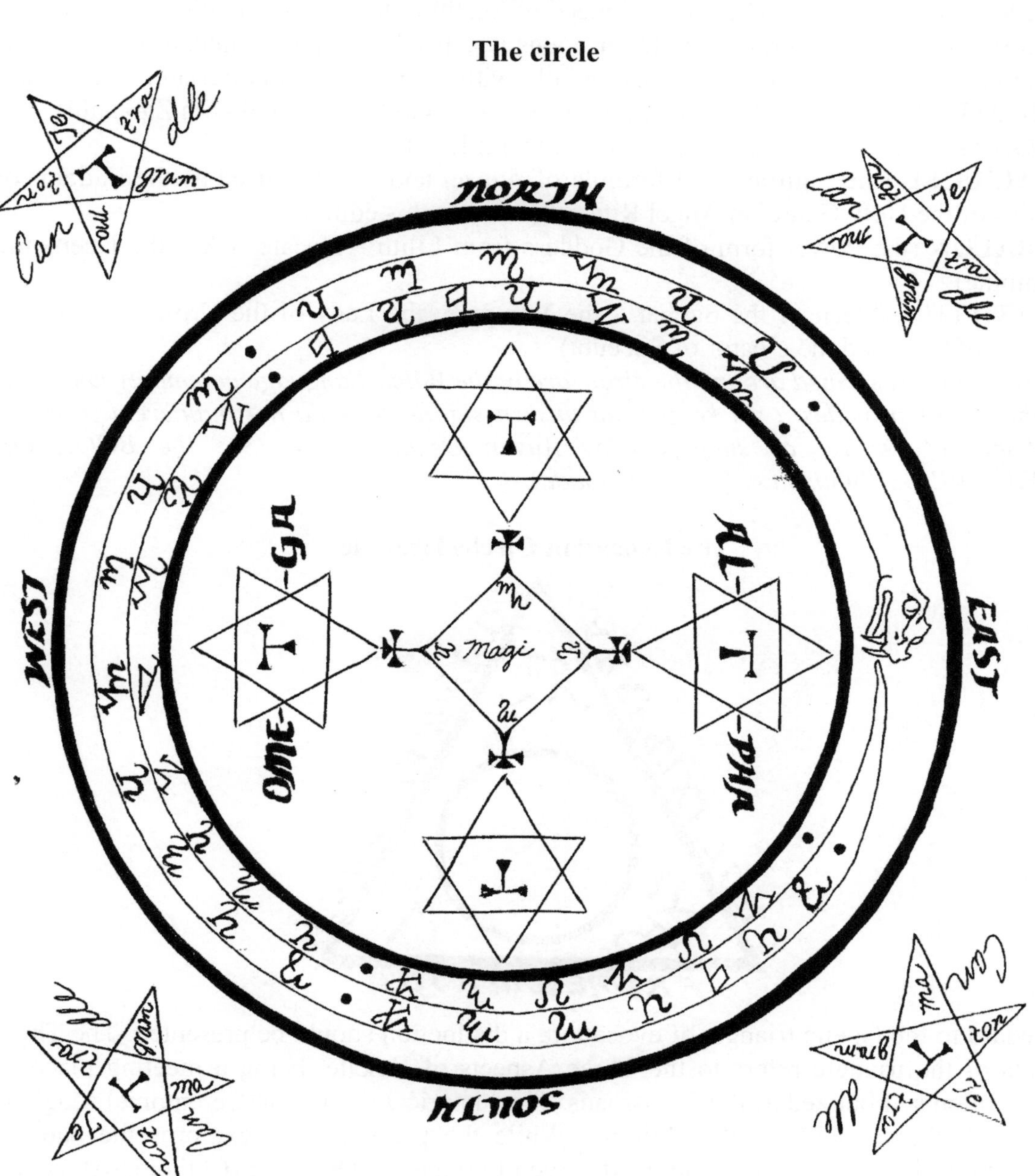

The Circle is an old boundary which was used back from the eldest days of Magical practice, specifically the Sumerian word Zisurru, which is the circle drawn in flour. The flour itself is known as qemu, such aspects of primal sorcery have survived to the present age in various cultures, in Voudon practices and even Thelemic Magick, Sabbatic and Luciferian Witchcraft. The Flour Circle is not by any means a must, one may create an Ourabouris – Levianthanic Boundary which is symbolic of the Self Encircled, that fascination and self-enchantment leads to the Gates of the Infernal and Celestial Peaks of Magick Light, the awakening of ones Will and divinity. The Circle should be understood as the essence of the Self, that it is the bridge between the waking and dreaming, between the celestial and infernal, the fiery essence of the Azazel. The original circle of Solomon as redesigned by Aleister Crowley is indeed powerful in form, e.g. Ourabouric Circle, but in working with such a more Luciferian focus was needed. The Leviathan which makes the circle, is sigillized and charged essentially with the names of Luciferian power, being
SABAOTH (The Lord of the Sabbat, or the Sabbatic God, associated with Zabbathi)
ADONAI (The Lord of the Earth, associated with Lucifer)
AZAL'UCEL (the Sigillic word formula of Azazel and Lucifer, used as the initiator or Genius of the Holy Guardian Angel Rite presented in this edition)
BABALON (the Power form of the Goddess from Lilith – Hecate – AZ, the Daemonic Feminine)
LILITH (The Queen of the Sabbat – the Vampyre, the Lady of the Crimson Caul, the Mother of Cain and the creator of Succubi)
These names as scribed around the circle are in the Witch-Language commonly known as Theban. This provides a yet known but unseen sigillic formula not indifferent from the Alphabet of Desire, as suggested by Austin Osman Spare (See the BOOK OF PLEASURE, 93 Publishing, Quebec Canada).

The Evocation Circle/Triangle

In regard to the Goetic triangle of evocation, a distinction should be presented. The Three Points of the triangle refers to the Three Aspects of Hekate, being a meeting place of spirits often symbolized as the Crossroads. The historical triangle in Ceremonial Magic is the materializing point of the Daimon. While the present work explores the path of invoking such forces, the triangle itself served to unite the Demonic (Chthonic/Atavistic) with the Angelic (Celestial/Empyrean). The triangle contains in the center a circle; this is the summoning point of which Solomon was said to bind such spirits. The inside of the triangle contains the name AZAZEL, being a significant change from the traditional MICHAEL. The purpose of this is to have the circle blessed with the deific power of Azazel, who is also more commonly recognized as Lucifer. As the Sorcerer of the Left Hand Path seeks communion and a form of Antinomianian self-deification, an association of self with Azazel is thus made, a formal confirmation of the dedication of the path. It is by this self-deification that the Daimon is controlled within the circle by the focused Will of the magician, rather than a 'holy' force. This is a psychological approach in which the sorcerer fully relies on the Will to control the ritual, thus adding a real sense of danger to the rite. Care should be practiced however with this distinction, as the Djinn of this book are both ancient and cunning.

Traditionally, the triangle should be 2 feet distant from the magic circle and three feet across. The triangle should be place towards which quarter where the spirit evoked would belong. The base of the triangle would be near the circle, the apex would point in the quarter of the spirit. It is suggested that one observes the Moon also in the operation.
The names surrounding the triangle are ANAPHEAXETON, TETRAGRAMMATON and PRIMEUMATION.

The Athame or blade of the white hilt

The White Hilt knife is the Magickal Tool of the Work of Illumination of the Angelic Guide, the Solar and Luciferian Blade of the Divine Will. The White Hilted Knife is used in such works such as Workings of the Divine Will, or Angelick – Holy Guardian Angel. The Athame is also used in circulating and visualizing light around the self – encircling the being. You will want to decorate the handle in the runes of summoning and protection, as first described in "The Key of Solomon the King" (Clavicula Salomonis), Translated by S.L. MacGregor Mathers. The Blade should be made in the hour of Mercury when in the sign of the Ram or Scorpion. You may alternatively conduct such when the Moon is Waning in a more probable time frame.

When you obtain a white handled knife, roughly six inches long wait until the Moon is waning. Fill a bucket or basin with distilled and purified water and pour salt, Abramelin Oil and a few drops of your own blood. You will then wish to have a small fire which you will hold the blade over. As it is heated in the flame, envision the fires of Azazel and Hecate, purifying and blessing the blade with your divine Will. It is the very blade which once consecrated, should be seen as forged by Cain from the metal from Lucifer's Crown, in the very Forge of Cain does the Fire of Iblis bless. When the blade is heated, take the knife and place it in the water:

By the Blood I give I empower this Blade, the very knife of my Divine Will
By the Moon Waxing and Waning I do receive the Fallen Stars fiery and ancient
Blade of steel do I summon thee, with the fires of Azazel called Shaitan do I consecrate thee, by the flames of Hecate do I empower thee!
The circle is cast in the Sabbat journey of the Celestial and Infernal –
Blessed is this sacred blade –From the meteor which fell from the crown of Lucifer!

By the metal blessed in the fiery forge of Our Lord Daeva, who is Cain the Cloaked One
So mote it be!

The black hilted knife (Evocation Dagger)

The Black Hilted Knife is the blade of Barbarous Evocation, the knife dedicated to Shaitan of Midnight and Banal, the Daemonic Adversarial Blade of Lucifer, the sacred weapon of banishing and commanding – the fulgaris lightning bolt of the fallen Djinn.

The Black Hilted Knife is used for making the circle and commanding the spirits into the Triangle, the sacred circle within the meeting place of spirits.

The Blade may be consecrated in the hour of Saturn. As well when the moon is waning create a distilled water container and fill with blackened pepper, Hecate Oil and a few drops of your own blood. With the flame burning, hold the blade within. Envision the fires of the underworld, of Hecate-Lilith and Banal, of the Daemonic Gods below who open the gates of our own transformation. Envision the fire empowering the blade with the serpent tongue of Shaitan of Midnight, the purifier of the black handled knife.

As the blade is immersed in the water, recite:

By the Mysteries of the Depths, the Coiling Dragon of Old
Beheld to the Gates of Leviathan
By Hecate and the Skull Wreathed in Roses, which is silence and beauty
I summon thee blade of steel, envenomed in the Darkness of the Earth
Do become knife of the Devil's Claw, my sacred tool of summoning
Water-Daemon of the Blade be born
By Banal and those of the shadowed realms-
Blade be blessed! So mote it be!!

The wand

The Wand is the fiery essence of the Magician, the Will of the Work itself. Create or decorate your own Wand which shall reflect your sacred symbols and desire of your becoming. Austin Spare called these sacred letters as the Alphabet of Desire, a sigillized form of the subconscious and symbols which represent the Higher Articulation of the Self. The Luciferian Will which is self-immolated unto perfection. The Wand should be cut, painted and decorated with the specific Sigils from Ones Alphabet and done so in the Noon Tide Sun, sacred to Shaitan, the Djinn of Fire. The wand corresponds also to the Phallus, the solar vessel which spills forth the Elixir of the Sun.

The pentacle of tetragrammaton

The symbol of strength and conceptual imagery of the Pentacle of Solomon, the Magus who bound the Djinn of this Book. The Pentacle may be worn as a method of encircling the Self in the Mask of Purity, thus remaining a symbol of the Mind in Unity with the Will. Often in evocation/invocation, spirits become points of Obsessional Belief which seem to 'speak' or send 'impulses' and 'desires' to the sorcerer which may be contrary to the purpose of the Ritual. The Pentacle of Solomon/Tetragrammaton is the Sigil of the Will of God (God may represent SET or the Divine Will – the Isolate Self). You may have the Pentacle of Tetragrammaton on your person, symbolic of the Will of the Rite. When one enters the Cross-Roads of Spirits you are in the Arena of Anon, the Spirits which have existed between the Aethyr and the Earth for timeless ages – the take the flesh of our desires, therefore posing a dangerous tight rope walk of obsession/possession. Consider the Strength of Will as the Guide in the Working, thus the reason for one being in direct contact with the HGA/Angel-Serpent and envenomed with the Light of Set or the Adversary.

The names within the Tetragrammaton represent the power of Will thatthe magicians holds in the working, thus within the Pentagram which ascends towards the Luciferian realm of Air. Tetragrammaton is the formula of the Holy Guardian Angel or Higher Self/Daimon (Genius).

Soluzen in the center represents the Shade or Spirit which is summoned to come forth in the Point, the very meeting place of spirits (the Triangle and Circle).
Bellatar is to speak that we may hear and understand thee (instinct and impulse, realization).
Bellonoy is to show us the treasures of which we seek (initiation, awakened and renewed, developed perception).
Halliza is to appear in a human shape, or that which we may wish to view.
Abdia is to Will this spirit or Daimon to join with us in ascended union, that the Luciferian Spirit becomes in this light of the Sun or Moon.

The vessel of Solomon

This is in a modern context the Fetish or Urn which is the "home" of the spirit. It is also known as an nganga, such in the methods of primal sorcery. The magician should create or obtain such a pot or urn for which you will summon and bind such spirits to. This is traditionally symbolic to the vessel of Solomon of which he bound the 72 Djinn of the Shemhamforasch. The sorcerer who seeks to transmit the knowledge of old through their essence of being may use these vessels as a womb for the daemon of the Sun or the Moon. Upon obtaining the proper urn or pot, wash and purify the vessel for a time. Allow it to dry in the Light of Dawn until Dusk. Allow the Sun's rays to purify the urn and prepare it to house the Great Familiars and Djinn of the Fallen Angels, who still walk in spirit among and within us.

The Vessel will indeed become their binding place once they have been evoked and then bound into the pot. The most dangerous method of binding the spirits to the vessel is the "Earthenware Virgin" formula designed by Austin Osman Spare. This involves a Sexual technique of self-fascination in which the elixir is kept and buried in the vessel for some days and nights. This is an optional method which is very dangerous to the process which it is created.

Vessel Preparation may continue once the pot has been cleaned. The magician will scribe the binding sigil of Solomon upon it, as this will exteriorize the force summoned to reside in this temple in the earth, which you may communicate with by dreams. It is optional for the sorcerer to add a drop of his or her own blood in the vessel to consecrate it as his own.

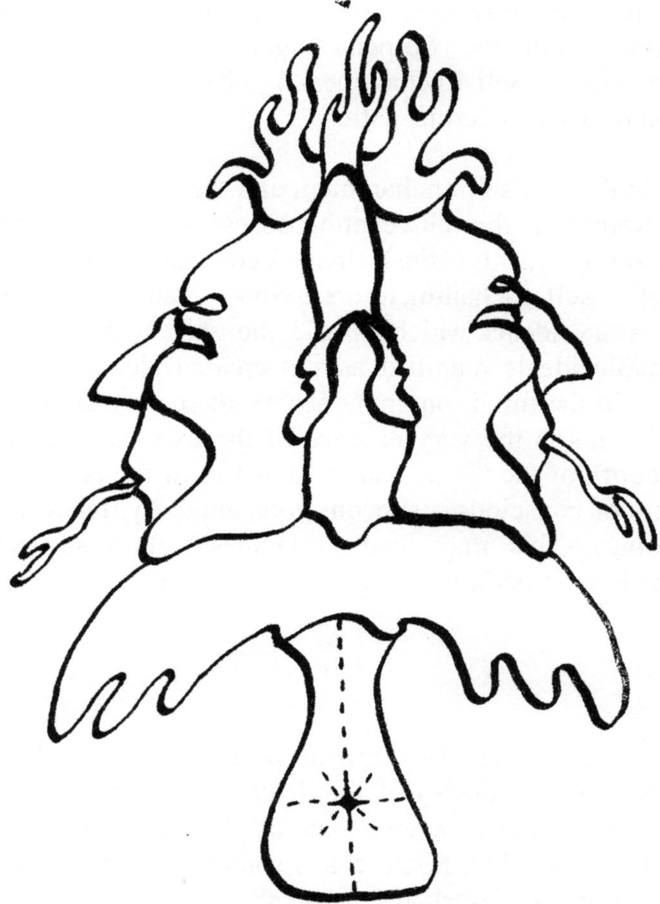

The Sigil will be prepared on Virgin Parchment or some high quality paper. It may have a strong reinforced backing such as a piece of Leather or Toadskin (if common amphibious frogs or such inhabit an area, watch for dead ones which you may use). The Vessel itself may contain a layer of grave soil and images, perfumes or such which you associate with the Spirit.

Once the Magicians summons in the evocation circle the Spirit, and then enters the point to become one with the spirit – the very essence inbetween, then the force will be Willed by concentration and enchantment (of reciting the binding spell) into the vessel. If Sexual Evocation, allow the elixir to enter the vessel upon climax. If one is Working with a partner, a woman, then she may utilize both male and female sexual fluids to create and give material basis for the spirit. This is not by itself necessary; the solitary magician may conduct successfully this creation or summoning method alone. Beware the union of the fluids of the Sun and the Moon, as it leads to a strong Familiar who for the inexperienced, may cause mental stress for the magician.

After the Evocation and Binding of the Spirit to the Vessel, bury it in a graveyard or some designated area by a great Tree or hidden place. It shall reside there for a period of when the Dark Moon begins and grows towards the Full Moon. You may evoke it above the burial space on those nights, envisioning it growing in strength with your Willed focus.

On the Night of the Fullmoon, exhume the Vessel and in the Temple invoke the spirit through the Black Mirror of Circle, seek the inspiration of the spirit and then retire to sleep. Take notes to the dreaming communion and meeting of the force, it will guide you to the answers you seek. Do not threaten or seek to harm the spirit without purpose, but be firm and consistent in your communication. Demand fairly it conduct the purpose of its summoning.

The essence of Sorcery is the focused view of Self-Enchantment. Self-Enchantment is the process of remanifesting inspiration aspects of obsessional perception, the instinctual guide which leads one to 'automatic' (in reference to Automatic Drawing, the subconscious unveiled) communication with the Serpent-Angel, Azal'ucel (Holy Guardian Angel/True Will) or initiatic guide. Self-Enchantment is also the directional point which is the obsessional direction of ones sorcerous path.

The Path of Sorcery is the direct road built from self-enchantment and the union with the isolate core essence of being (HGA). Sorcery is the rejuvenating obsession of encircling belief into flesh. This may be understood by Austin Osman Spare's conceptual theory of manifestation – Will-Desire-Belief, self-enchantment/obsession leads to the destruction/vampyric death of unnecessary ideals which plague the self in numerous forms. In primal cultures these dogmatic ideals manifest as self-created sickness and disease. By destroying their foundation in the mind, one may absorb their very elixir of 'life' and devour their 'flesh' as well. This is the very essence of the exorcism of the Tchod Rite of Tibetan Magic – the Rebirth of the "I" as a layered aspect of the core self or Angel-Daemon. The self adds layers of conscious – subconscious antiquity, based on conscious desire and ones surroundings. This may lead to laziness, sloth and an undisciplined Will. It is essential to undertake periodic Workings to invigorate the mind via Self-Enchantment.

The Black Mirror

Considered a tool of scrying and divination, the black mirror proves also a tool of contacting and communicating with Spirits and shades of the dead as well. The black mirror is made of something such as onyx or perhaps even a plate of glass painted with a rich black, for which a reflection is still obtainable. Some chaos sorcerers have created black mirrors from a piece of glass with black electrical tape on the reverse side. This proves efficient and inexpensive as well as offering the same affect.

That mirrors can be gateways into the realms of the dead and even Hell is no new theory. The Hebrews believed that the mirror was a gateway into the caves of Lilith and her Succubi offspring. Young women were discouraged from using mirrors for this reason, lest they become possessed by the Demoness, who will drive them to sexual acts with sleeping men. The Black Mirror is considered also a tool for Atavistic Resurgence that the demons of the mind or the lycanthropic state may be brought out by enchanting the self to open the imagination to images in the reflection.

The Black Mirror in the Work of the Goetia is used as a tool to communicate with the bound spirit or familiar after initial evocation. The sorcerer who summons the Angel or Demon may bind it accordingly to the vessel, and at a later time evoke the spirit again and use the Black Mirror to visualize its form and impressions it may send. If a specific Goetic spirit is bound with the magician as a familiar/famulus, then the Black Mirror is ideal in communication. Some have used divination boards in front of black mirrors to communicate with spirits, this techniques proves a powerful gnosis to step into, as you essentially bring the astral/ghost realm into the physical plane.

The mirror is used in the following way:

1. Summon the Spirit in the Evocation Circle
2. Bind the Spirit to the vessel and sigil accordingly.
3. Use the mirror to contact the spirit later after it has been bound.
4. Contact the spirit before sleep to ensure a detailed communication – if you dare.

Seeking first communication

Once the spirit has been properly bound to the vessel, you may wish to communicate or experience the visions it may send you. Keep in mind, all of these visions may not be pleasant and if your Will is weak you have the danger of becoming obsessed with the force.

Place the circle again in the chamber in the triangle – If you have made a doll or effigy to hold the spirit, place the doll in the Triangle – This is the very meeting place of spirits. Burn the incense and very few candles should be lit. The ambience of the chamber should be suitable for bringing their world into ours.

Ritual evocation with the black mirror

"Spirit N. I do rouse thee from the vessel, tomb of darkness. I summon and call unto thee spirit N. to arise from thy vessel and present thyself in the reflection of this mirror. Present yourself in the form of which that is known, impart upon me thy visions of the world of shadows, and that which I seek to know."

The spirit should appear in the black mirror or in the darkened chamber you will feel a presence and then begin viewing images, perhaps even your own visage changing into this form. When you have viewed what you Will, thank the spirit and end the rite. If you sleep shortly afterwards, keep a journal next to you to observe the images which you may see.

The Symbol of Self-Deification, Azothoz and Tetragrammaton

Sexual evocation

The Triangle is the very meeting places of spirit and sorcerer, thus is the channeling point of summoning. Place the vessel, doll or pot of which the spirit is bound – along with a copy of the sigil for focus in the evocation circle (triangle).

Illuminate the chamber in low light, incense and that which is pleasant to both the magician and the spirit. Visualize the spirit growing within the vessel as you silently summon it.

Begin arousing yourself with the enchantments of your own imagination. Understand this spirit is formed from you, something of a familiar and spirit you have given life to. Focus on the desire of which caused you to evoke the spirit in the first place (divination, knowledge, ect) and focus intently upon this. As you reach the climax, focus on the sigil of the spirit and allow your mind to black out (i.e. death posture) in this moment of ecstasy. After you have made this sacrifice of anointing some of the fluids on the sigil, banish (by forgetting or what technique you have created to clear the mind) and end the rite.

If you have a partner in the rite, you will both focus on the spirit and not on each other rather than Willed Desire and Lust of the flesh. Concentrate on the aspects of the spirit of which you relate to it, associations, etc. When you reach a climax loose yourself in the ecstasy of union with this spirit and the moment of the orgasm and death posture.

The other magical requisities

The other ceremonial requisites are suggested by the Clavicula Salomonis Regis, translated by Samuel Liddell MacGregor Mathers, edited with an introduction by Aleister Crowley. The proper perfumes and incense may be burnt, and the sacred bath may be prepared. The purpose of the bath is to refresh the mind and prepare it for the Work. Mix the water with soothing bath salts and a touch of Abramelin Oil and other of your choice. Before entering the water, touch thy temples and forehead

The adornation of the bath

"By the Sacred Waters of Hecate and the cleansing light of Lucifer, I am to prepare for the Great Work, and my body shall be a temple of both abstinence and fornication."

After the bath and when you have robed yourself

The adornation at the induing of the vestments

"O Seth-an, Lord of the Earth, Lucifer, Lord of the Air, Hecate, Goddess of Waters and Shaitan, Lord of Flame, that I shall be wrapped in the cloak of the Wolf and encircled in the Serpents Skin, So it is Done!"

The Conjurations
The 72 Spirits of the Shemhamforasch

"I do summon and evoke thee, O' Spirit N. by the Flames of Azazel – the Lord of the Earth I conjure thee forth. By Beralanensis, Baldachiensis, Paumachia and Aplogiae Sedes; by the most powerful Guardians, Djinn, Genii and the Spirits of the Abyss, brought forth by the Great Shadow of the Fire Seraph. I summon thee wise and ancient spirits, attend me and appear now in this circle. By the names of Lucifer, who brought the Flame unto the Clay – He that gave us breath, Immortal and Holy Fire. Lucifer, Ouyar, Chameron, Aliseon, Mandousin, Premy, Oriet, Naydru, Esmay, Eparinesont, Estiot, Dumosson, Panochar, Casmiel, Hayras, Fabelleronthou, Sadirno, Peatham, Venite, Venite, Lucifer Amen.

I summon thee, shadow and light, Angel and Daemon, together as one...I do summon these O great familiar of the earth, from which my Dagger commands thee, appear and move, materialize in this meeting place of spirits. I conjure thee, Spirit N. who shall appear before me, in circle and center. Attend now my calling and show thyself in a form you so desire that we may hold congress in the communion of my self!"

Optional English/Enochian conjuration

"I do conjure thee, O' spirit N. by the flames of Azazel – the Lord of the Earth I conjure thee forth. By Beralanensis, Baldachiensis, Paumachia and Aplogiae Sedes; by the most powerful Guardians and spirits of the Beast, brought forth by the mighty throne, I summon thee descending spirits, dragon of the dark heavens

By the crown of the Dragon, enthroned Eye of Holy Fire – Be friendly unto me, enter this circle and bring forth your wisdom and truth, descend and come forth from the Dragon's Temple, bring forth the Wisdom of the Wicked."

(Translated)

OL GNAY ZODANETA GAH IALPRG AZAZEL, ENAY THAHAAOTAHE OL ZODAMETA – MICMA – MICMA MICALZ BRANSG GAH A ORH LEVITHMONG YOLCAM OXIAYAL IALPOR GAH – OL VINU ARPHE GAH, VOVIM DE A MAHORELA IALPRT MOMAO DE A VOVIM, VEL UCORSAPAX OOANOAN DE PIRE IALPRT ZORSE PAMBT OL, ZIMII OI COMSELH VOLCAM G ANANAEL VOOAN UNIGLAG NIISA VOVIM SIAION YOLCAM ANANAEL DE BABALON.

The Invocation of the King
Being Amaimon, Gaap, Paimon or Zodimay

"Great – Powerful Amaimon, who exalted in the Power of the Spirits in the Kingdom of the East, (South, West or North) I invoke thee in the name of Darkness, from the dwelling of darkness and in their power of illumination. In the name of Primeumaton who reigns over the palaces of the Sun and the Moon – I invoke thee to appear before this circle, in this triangle – the very gathering place of spirits

Thou art fallen and perfected Angel, who hath tasted the ecstasies As above and So below, Sun nourished Djinn who drank deep of the shadows, whose sword tortures those who would obey me not -. I call and Command o' king N. to bring this spirit unto me without violence or harm – This is my Will. "

The constraint

"I do conjure and summon thee, Spirit N. by the flaming essence of the Forked Stave of the Sun, the Adversarial Shadow and Burning Fire which is the Prince of Spirits, Angels and Daemon. Come thou forth and without delay to me, Spirit N. By Adonai, the Lord of the Earth, By the Axis of the Sun and the Moon I summon thee. By the Eternal Fire, come now unto this Circle...Be welcomed unto me."

Welcome unto the spirit

"Welcome Spirit N. You are welcomed in this meeting place within the Crossroads. I have summoned you forth, to join with me, by the union of Heaven and Hell. I bind this within this circle, take flesh and desire within thy Sigil of Calling, which I shall give unto thee life. Thou shalt not leave this circle until I am satisfied, for I shall bring you forth into the world of flesh once again.

By the sacred center of the Arcanum of Shadow and Light, within the Ourabouris Circle I am bound and free, yet as you are Spirit N. shall you enflesh my desires of which I speak. By my command and Will do you bring forth that which I have called you for, that I shall also seek your servitors, those whom obey your command.

By the Pentacle of Solomon have I summoned thee! Give unto me a True Answer"

Communion

Depending upon the technique of the summoning, being Sexual Congress, Ceremonial or Meditative (Black Mirror), you will want to envision this spirit outside of the self, in the summoning triangle of spirits. Notice the attributes of the spirit, what makes it powerful and what it represents to you.

Preparing the material basis

One may now focus upon the sigil of the Spirit, by enflaming the self via envisioning your sexual desire in the form of a black serpent which rises through your spine – starting at the base. As it moves up you will enflame yourself more. If with a partner, they shall envision the same to materialize the spirit. Begin visualizing what this spirit looks like, feels like and what form it takes. Visualize how it speaks to you and the familiars of which it governs. As you reach climax, you ascend into the Celestial Heights of the Luciferian Sabbat – When the mind is led through the Axis of the Point of Light, the solar force of Azazel. Annoint the Sigil in the Sexual fluid of either yourself (if solitary) or both yourself and your partner. At the moment of ecstasy, you shall take the flesh of the beast and along with the Djinn – spirit, descend unto the Infernal Sabbat of the Death Posture, from which you shall emerge in the flesh of the circle. The ensorcerling of belief is significant unto the practitioner who by self-enchantment and the combination of Will-Desire-Belief, have transcended the separation of flesh and spirit.

After you have consecrated the sigil, close the circle and the spirit form, while weak, will remain in essence. When the mind becomes interlocked with this force, and the sinking from ecstasy into the Infernal Sabbat of the Waking Self, then it may bring inspiration of what you seek, which shall emerge later. Seal the vessel and bury it in a safe place in the darkness of the earth. You will then wish to keep it buried for Nine Nights, which holds its basis in Vampyric folklore. You may go to the place of where it is buried to burn a black and white candle in the night hours, and envision the Angel or Daemon while it grows in being. In the tenth day, at Dawn, dig up the vessel and clean the exterior. You will then summon the spirit in the Evocation Circle, and then either perform an Invocation to call in the force, which will remain connected with you in dreams until you destroy and burn the vessel and contents. You may also summon the spirit in the Black Mirror, and meditate upon it until communication is gained.

Invocation

The Sorcerer may invoke the spirit at certain points of the rite, after the Vessel has been created and the Spirit is bound to it. Initial Evocation and creation rites do not involve this process. At the moment of envisioning this force, summon it now within the sacred circle of self, call the spirit into your self, by Will alone. Some magicians have actually entered the circle, and by their enflaming of self can then possession occur. Let the spirits and shades dance within your mind, filled with the ecstasy of invocation. Control and understand the spirit, never surrender complete control. When you have reached beyond the peak of gnosis, the mind will forget the summons of the spirit and you will close the circle. You may recall this force when you are in need. This is specifically why the mentally ill or weak of mind should not conduct such workings – the self may seek to destroy itself in such a manner.

Licence to depart

"Hail to thee Spirit N., thou hast answered my questions, and has caused no harm or danger to man or beast. You may depart now unto your place of rest and repose. Be with me in dreams and in flesh as I desire, yet thou art free to leave this dwelling at Will. So it

is done. One may command the spirit in the vessel within the triangle, just as one would summon the spirit into visible appearance."

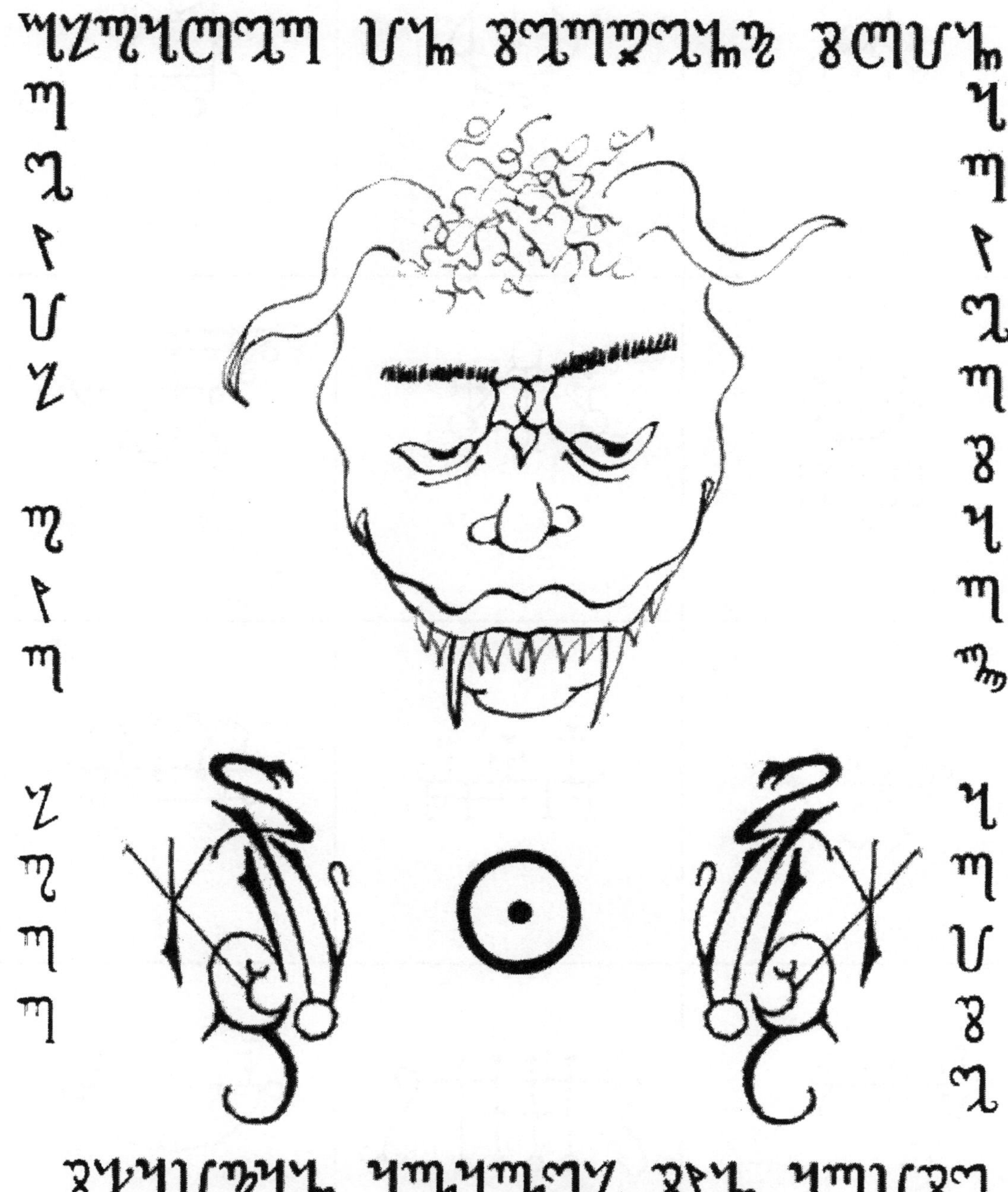

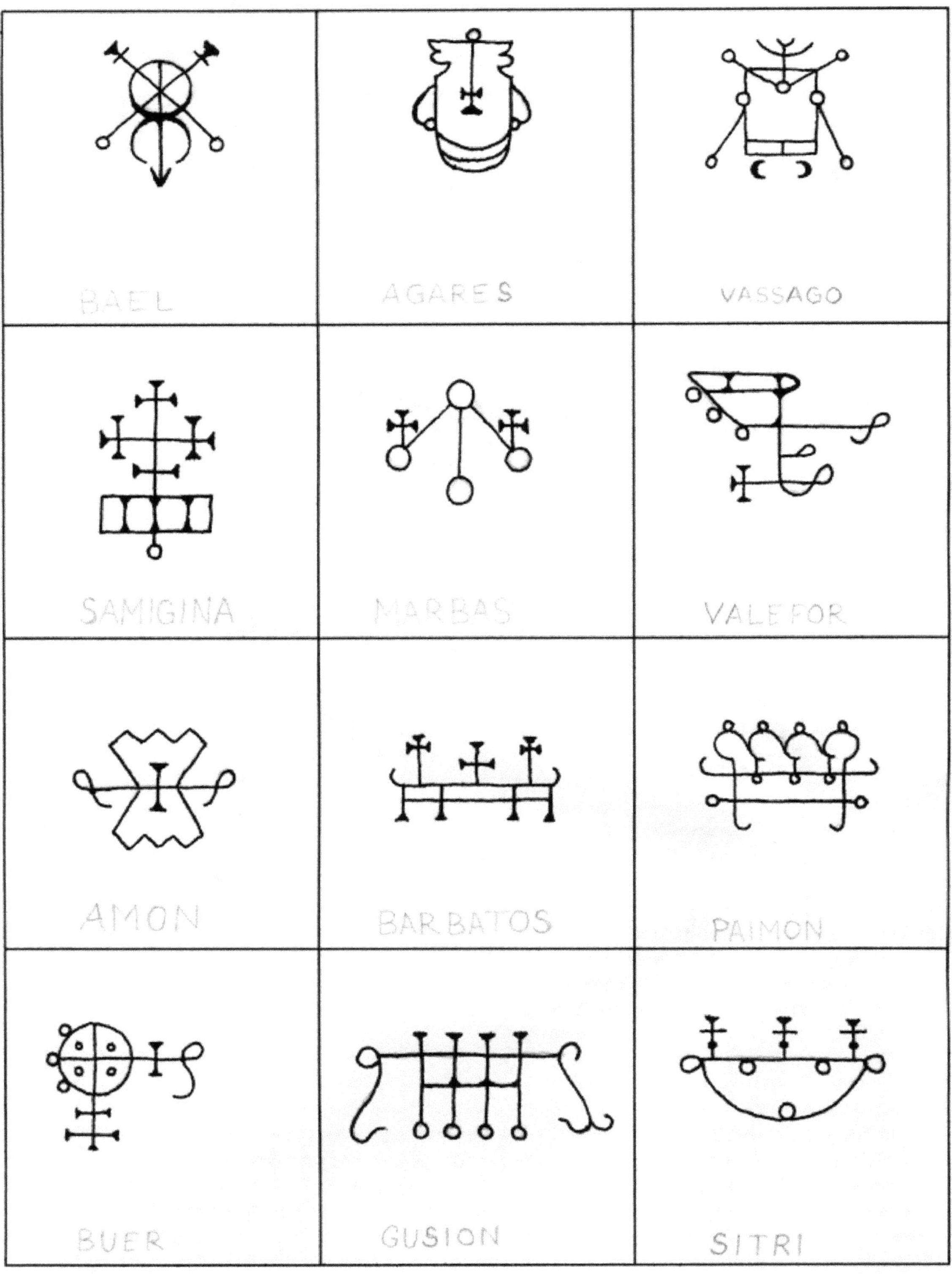
BAEL
AGARES
VASSAGO
SAMIGINA
MARBAS
VALEFOR
AMON
BARBATOS
PAIMON
BUER
GUSION
SITRI

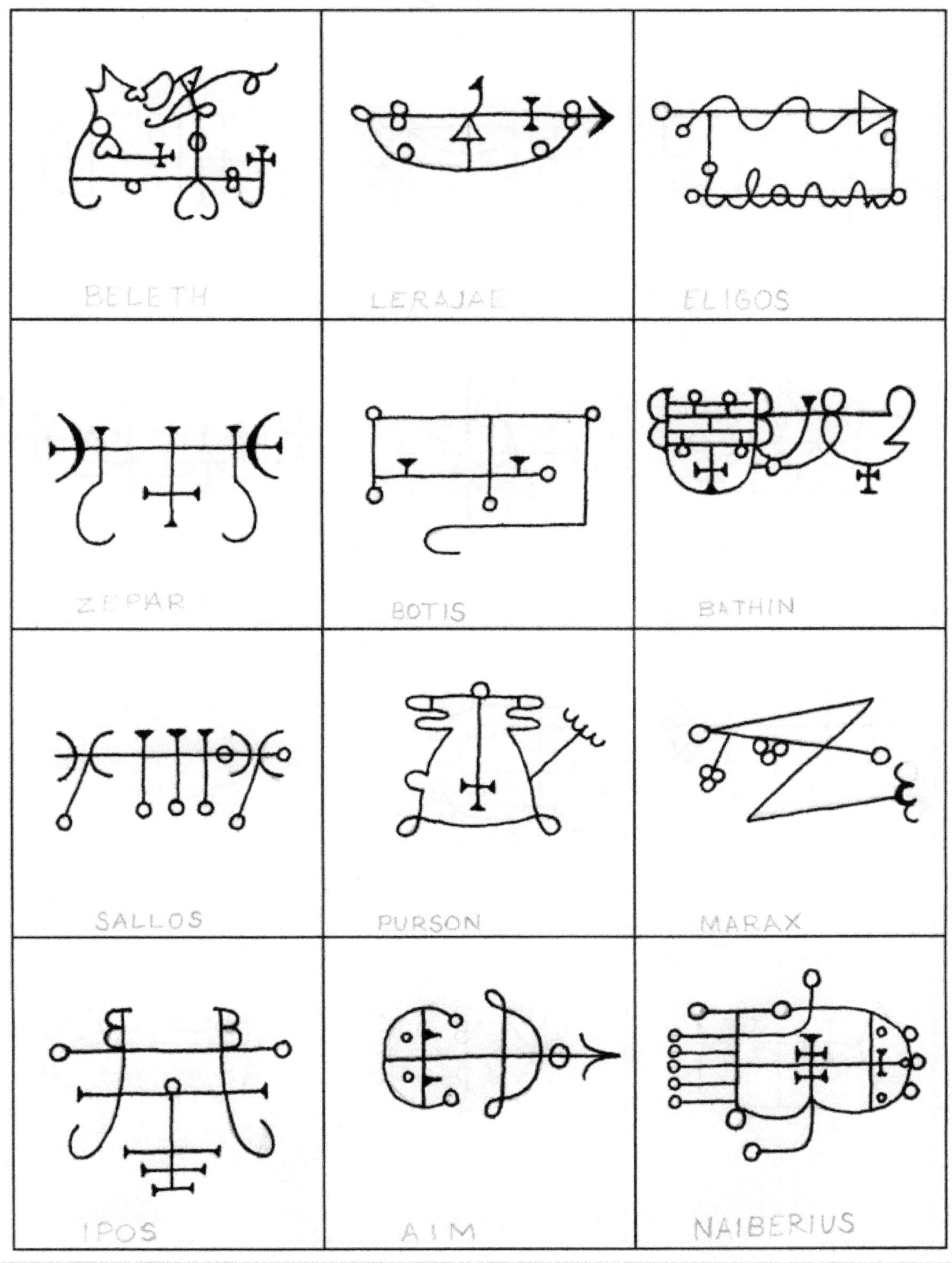
BELETH
LERAJAE
ELIGOS
ZEPAR
BOTIS
BATHIN
SALLOS
PURSON
MARAX
IPOS
AIM
NAIBERIUS

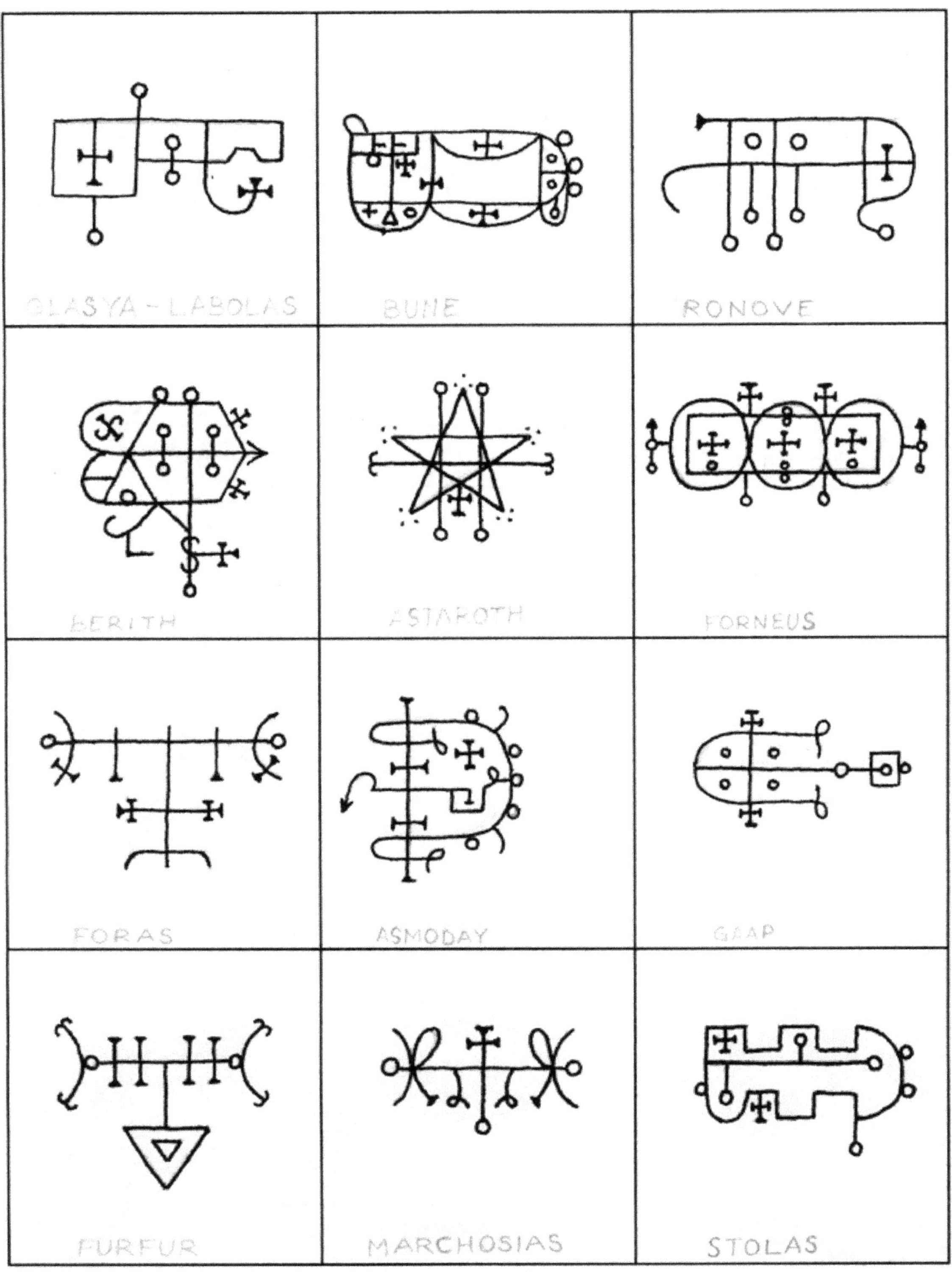
GLASYA - LABOLAS
BUNE
RONOVE
BERITH
ASTAROTH
FORNEUS
FORAS
ASMODAY
GAAP
FURFUR
MARCHOSIAS
STOLAS

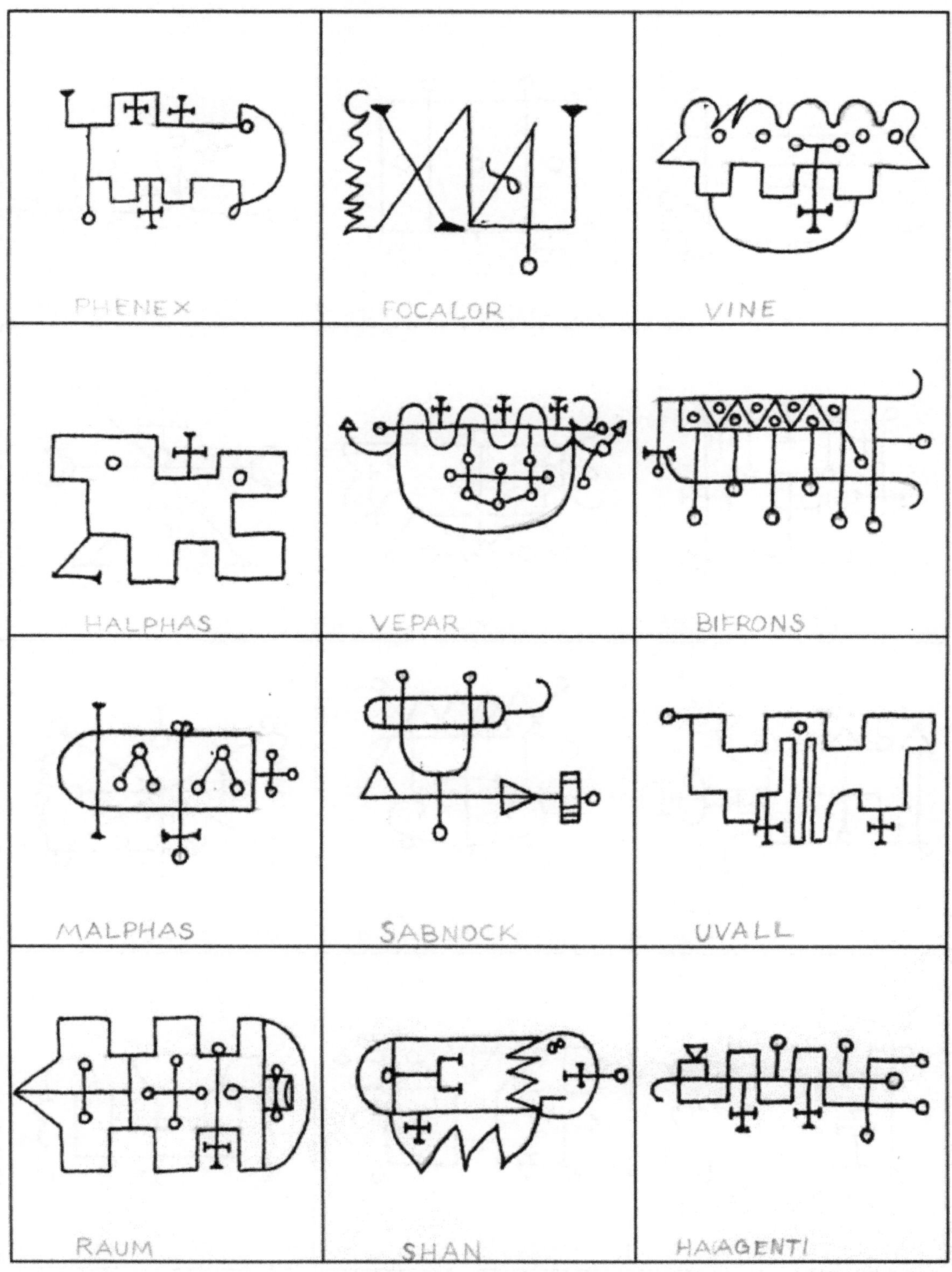
PHENEX
FOCALOR
VINE
HALPHAS
VEPAR
BIFRONS
MALPHAS
SABNOCK
UVALL
RAUM
SHAN
HAAGENTI

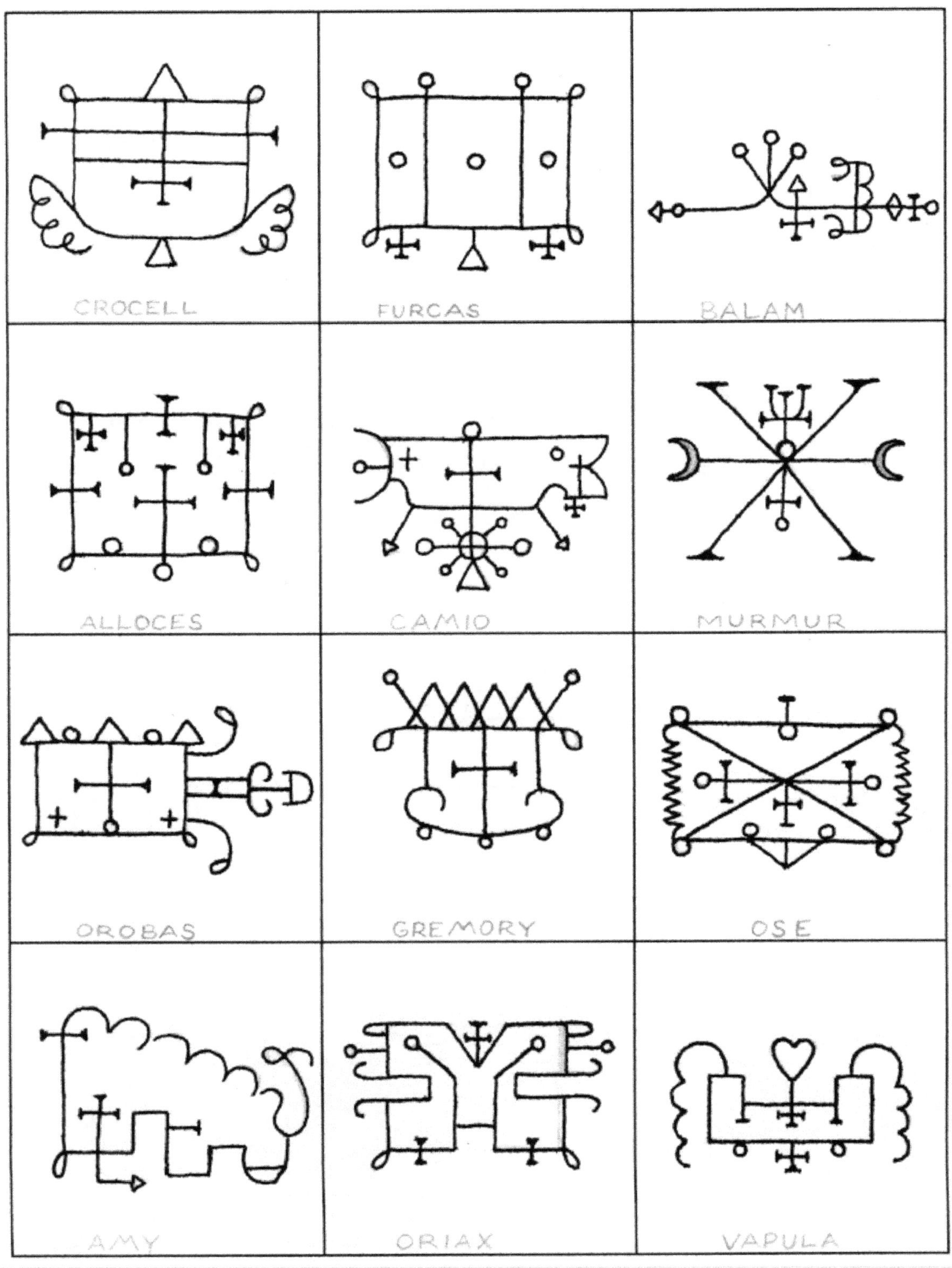
CROCELL
FURCAS
BALAM
ALLOCES
CAMIO
MURMUR
OROBAS
GREMORY
OSE
AMY
ORIAX
VAPULA

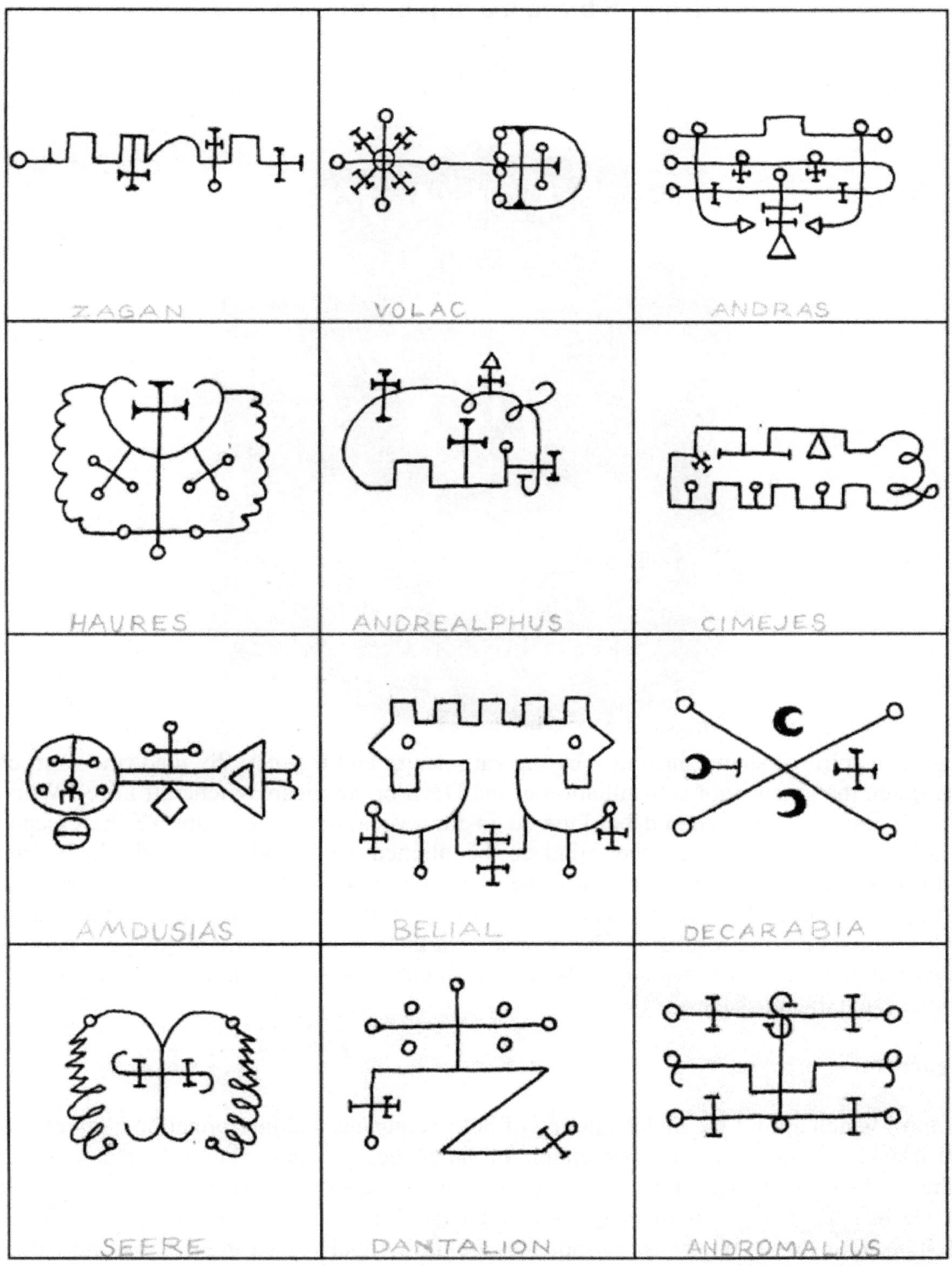
ZAGAN
VOLAC
ANDRAS
HAURES
ANDREALPHUS
CIMEJES
AMDUSIAS
BELIAL
DECARABIA
SEERE
DANTALION
ANDROMALIUS

The Shemhamphorasch

Bael

Bael is a spirit of shape shifting – by the cat (stealth and instinct), by toad (the form of Ahriman, the gateway of self-initiation of the Devil or Anglican Witchcraft Lore). When one summons Bael it should be done so in the evocation circle – absorb the essence within this circle – focus the mind to be aligned and shadowed with the spirits anthropomorphic identification, until "he" becomes you. You will then work on your ability to shape shift in dreams. The 66 legions of spirit familiars may be commanded by will to produce some results of what you seek in the obtainment of knowledge. Bael is a powerful familiar spirit who may bring one much instinctual impulses in relation to animals and dream shape shifting.

Agares

A spirit which allows the understanding of both languages and interpretation, Agares is a spirit which accelerates the perception of languages, communication – magical and otherwise. In the design of my Sethanic /Shadow alphabet (see Austin Spare's Alphabet of Desire), I made silent invocations to Agares – to speed the communication of the subconscious to the conscious. Earthquakes are the symbol of a strong will and individual presence. 31 legions of spirits assist in such operations.

Vassago

Vassago is an angelic ruler of the tarot; silently invoked this Prince may produce impulses and initiatory associations via the tarot thus allowing instinct to grow with association of such tools' of divination. Vassago is also ideal for the willed divination of future initiation, a Gateway to the Luciferian Realm of Spiritual development. Vassago appears in the black mirror as a wind-rushed robed spirit who is both angel and demonic shadow, who has many arms and talon-fingers.

Samigina

Samigina or Gamigm is a spirit of external necromancy. He allows communication with the shades of the dead, specifically on dreaming levels. One may also witness 'faces' in a black mirror while communicating with him. It may be recommended that the magician utilizes EVP to record Samigina or other shades in the place of invocation/evocation as well as within a graveyard. Goetic rites may be performed but with less 'tools', it then will rely on the sorcerers' ability to go forth into trance to summon such latent forces.

Marbas

Marbas appears in the mind's eye as a Lion, which beholds a shadow which is twisted and sharp looking. Marbas appears as any form desired, mostly as a shadowed man. This spirit reveals hidden aspects of the self through initiatory experience. As a cursing tool, one may evoke Marbas in the mind, and his 36 legions of spirits to manifest in the enemy as a disease. He may be used also to improve the ability to will immune system to work more efficiently, thus a beneficial spirit/Angelic familiar.

Valefor

Valefor is a vampyric spirit/demon, which initiates through the astral body and dreams. This spirit may be willed and bound to guard one's sleeping chamber – and feed from any forms which come near you. Valefor has 10 legions of spirits, often appearing through the mirror as a lion with the head of an ass. Valefor may also be a guide to the necromantic arts, communion with the dead, ect.

Amon

Amon, the devourer, a werewolf – demon whom is a significant initiatory force wither invoked or evoked. It is suggest that the sorcerer shape shifts in meditation and dream with Amon, become this shadow form and think deeply about the attributes of such a spirit. In the black mirror Amon is darkness incarnate, vomiting flames. In the shape of a human the head is a raven with a wolf's teeth. Amon is also a divinatory spirit whom aligns the conscious mind with the subconscious i.e. True Will. 40 Legions of spirits can be summoned and used to defend and encircle the magician.

Barbatos

Barbatos is a spirit which reveals 'astral' grimoires that is methods of initiation which may be found by inspiration via the astral plane. This spirit, who rules 30 legions is an Angelick ruler of the Witchcraft – by nature one comes into being by the communication with animals (body language, posture ect) and the ways of astral shape shifting via dream.

Paimon

Paimon is an angel-daimon of Lucifer, whom appears as a man crowned upon a camel. This spirit is a familiar of musick, thus by invoking Paimon one may work through an avenue of self-initiation through creating musick. Paimon is a powerful Angelick King of the Witchcraft, whom has 200 Legions of spirits – half are the Orders of Angels, the others being Potentates. Paimon appears with two Spirit/Djinn – Label and Ablim who are referred to as Kings. Paimon is perhaps one of the most significant Angelick Rulers, which along with Astaroth (whom is more Therionick/demonic in nature and appearance) opens the way to the "Grail" of Lucifer's crown – the perception of "I" and the mind separate from the universe. Paimon is a higher spirit of self-initiation, who is a path maker for ones own becoming. Paimon sometimes appears as an angelick spirit with a flaming sword. His office is Guardian of the Path through Leviathan, the Guardian of the Depths and Subconscious.

Buer

Buer is a demon of ones becoming and self-initiation through philosophy and instinct. Buer should respond to the sorcerer by the means inspiration which leads to one seeking answers and results via Work itself. Buer is also Sabbatic familiar, giving the sorcerer insight and learning inspiration into Wort Cunning, Herbalism, etc. Buer is also a healing spirit and governs 50 Legions of spirits.

Gusion

Gusion is a spirit of divination as well as being a guide in the communication with the shades of the dead. Gusion is also a spirit which instinctually passes on concepts and ideals in honor and dignity. The sorcerer through invoking the spirit would focus on areas of character development and self-perception, that which separates the initiate from the profane and common clay of humanity.

Sitri

Sitri appears in the Black Mirror as a man with a Leopard's head with large wings. You may will Sitri to change shape and it does so in the appearance of a beautiful angelick figure. Sitri is a spirit of Babalon-Lilith, being one who enflameth the love between individuals – lust and desire. Sitri is very useful in love and lust spells, thus being a powerful tool for the sorcerer. One may create s succubi/incubi from the shadows of Sitri in the black mirror, forming them nude in the shape that you find desirable. You may then bind the spirit to the sigil of Sitri to seek congress with by imagining so later. A very useful form in working with sexual evocation and dream projection, as to send forth a spell into the dreams of your chosen or to build into a future act, there are many possibilities with this Angelic Familiar. Sitri governs 60 Legions of Spirits.

Beleth

Beleth/Bileth or Bilet is a King whom appears Mighty and Terrible. Beleth is summoned and manifests upon a pale horse with musical instruments like horns playing near him. He does appear in flames and very angry, the magician even if working with the black mirror will want to silently create a triangle in the South and East Quarters, and command the spirit to take a calm form. When the flames cease, he appears as a King like older man with a long beard. Being of the Order of Powers, he does govern 85 Legions of spirits. Beleth is a useful Love Spell Spirit, whom you would will your desire to become flesh.

Lerajae

Leraikha is a marquis whom governs 30 Legions of spirits, whom is a familiar of arms, weapons and marksmanship. He appears as a green clad archer, while sometimes in some older military uniform which appears to be of the civil war area. In an initiatory sense, Lerajae is very useful in directing ones desired goals and making them reality. For instance, one would summon Lerajae when one wants to obtain a specific goal i.e. job, trip, item, etc. The archer as he is known is useful in the sense of 'hitting the mark'.

Eligos

Eligos is a Duke who appears as a Knight, whom carries a lance and a serpent. Eligos may reveal hidden secrets i.e. within the self, outer as well. Eligos is also a divinatory spirit as well, who may reveal the coming of wars, unrest and battles. It is suggested the Eligos also causes Love of people as well. He governs 60 Legions of Spirits.

Zepar

Zepar is a Duke whom appears in Red clothing and armor. He is likewise considered a familiar of Babalon-Lilith, and causes lust and love between women and men. He is also one aspect of the Crone as well, making women barren. 26 Legions of Spirits are under Zepar, one may work through this spirit as a means of obtaining the union of another female, or creating a shadow form of a succubus via dreaming sorcery.

Botis

Botis appears in the Black Mirror as a Viper, and then with the command of the magician will appear in a human shape with sharpened teeth, two horns and carrying a flaming sword. Botis is a divinatory spirit whom reveals secrets in the depths of the mind, and how one may obtain secrets from others by language and talk. He brings union of friends and foes and rules over 60 Legions of Spirits.

Bathin

Bathin is a Mighty Duke, whom appears like a strong man with the tail of a serpent, whom sits upon a pale horse. Bathin is a witchcraft familiar of Wort Cunning and herbalism, whom knows the use of precious stones. Bathin is also a spirit of astral projection, causing in dreaming states the consciousness to project to other countries and lands. He rules over 30 Legions of Spirits.

Sallos

Sallos/Saleos is a Might Duke as well, who appears in the form of a soldier of medieval times riding on a crocodile, whom is crowned. Sallos is a spirit of lust and desire, whom one may project to bring on with another – and create a flowing inspiration to achieve the union with another. He governs 30 Legions of Spirits as well.

Purson

Purson is a Great King who appears in the Black Mirror as a man with a Lion's face, who carries a serpent/viper in his hand and rides upon a bear. Purson is a spirit of divination as well, who holds communicating with the shades of the dead. Purson may discover treasures, in the form of insight and inspiration which causes the magician to obtain knowledge. He may take a body that is astral/aeriel or human, and bring earthly secrets and divine ones (self-introspection). Purson is an Angelick Ruler who brings good servitors, and has 22 Legions of Spirits whom are partly Order of Thrones and Order of Virtues.

Marax

Marax is a Great Earl and President. He appears in the mirror and the mind as a Bull like figure with a human face. Marax is a spirit of astronomy whom may inspire learning in this area. He is also a Witchcraft spirit of Wort Cunning and Herbalism who governs 30 Legions of Spirits and gives excellent familiars.

Ipos

Ipos is an Earl and Might Prince, who appears as an Angel with a Lions head. Ipos is a spirit of divination and self-development, assisting and inspiring communication and moral concepts of communication of the era of which one lives. As Ipos makes men witty and bold, they have a confidence boost through inspiration and self-reliance.

Aim (Hayborym)

Aim is a Duke whom appears as a Man with Three heads – one as a serpent, the second a human head having two stars on the forehead (burning like an image of the Morning Star or Lucifer) and the third as a Cow. Aim rides upon a large Viper who carries a Firebrand in his hand from which he sets cities and great places on fire. Aim is a spirit of self-development and force of Will, whom is also of inner divination. He has 26 Legions of inferior spirits.

Naiberius

Naiberius is a Marquis whom comes forth as a black crane, who flies about the circle. This is a spirit of the Witchcraft which makes men and women cunning in the Black and Hidden Arts and Speech/Communication. Under the Will of the Sorcerer, Naiberius brings knowledge on how one may restore lost dignity and honor. He governs 19 Legions of Spirits.

Glasya Labolas

Being a might President and Earl, Glasya-Labolas appears in the form of a dog with wings. He inspires the learning of the Hidden and Black Arts, and is an author (creator) of bloodshed and manslaughter. Glasya-Labolas is a demon of cursing, whom causes situations of danger to occur. Also being a spirit of divination, he may bring the union of friends and foes as well. Glasya-Labolas commands 36 Legions of Spirits as well.

Bune

Bune/Bime is a Duke, who appears as a Dragon with three heads – one like a dog, one as a bird and the other as a man with black eyes. Bune is a shade gatherer, under the form of Azrael –the Angel of Death. Bune gathers shades unto one place, or sepulcher that they may reside in your place of dwelling, gathering knowledge and impulses from beyond the grave in the dreaming state. Bune brings knowledge of how one may become better, and grow in experience and wisdom. He governs 30 Legions of Spirits.

Ronove

Ronove appears as a demonic shape, a monster whom has no true form. He commands 19 Legions of Spirits and gives good servants. Ronove inspires the knowledge of languages, magical and otherwise. He is a Great Earl and Marquis whom inspires a comprehension of learning within the circle. Ronove is an excellent Familiar which brings instinctual knowledge via waking and dreaming of the Alphabet of Desire, the language of the subconscious which empowers spells and talismans.

Berith

Berith is a great spirit who appears as a medieval European soldier, clothed in red whom rides upon a crimson horse. Upon the head of Berith rests a gold crown. Berith is a divinatory spirit who brings visions in dreams, which are revealed as images to the magician. Berith governs 26 legions of spirits. In an initiatory context, Berith may be a tool in the understanding of the self – including the 'turning of gold', i.e. the self coming into being or strengthening in form. The fiery essence of the self. Berith proves a powerful Goetic servitor to summon and guard when introspective rites of self exploration.

Astaroth

Astaroth appears as a hurtful angel who rides upon an infernal dragon. He is ghostly pale in color, something like a corpse with blackened eyes – no pupils. Astaroth also has long hair, and appears with a crown upon his head and a viper in his left (or right) hand, which are clawlike and bestial. Astaroth is a high Luciferic angel, whom is a very powerful guardian spirit to invoke. Astaroth is uniquely balanced in nature – being a mix of angel and demon, thus is a model and initiatory force in the workings of the Angelic and Bestial Servitors – that in union the spirit proves a balanced articulation and representation of the self. Astaroth governs 40 Legions of Spirits, and shadows forth ones own HGA/Angelic Familiar or initiator unto the path. Astaroth has been known to initiate or lead one unto the Luciferian Path of self-deification.

Forneus

Forneus is a marquis who appears as a sea monster/dragon. This Leviathan-form is a bringer of wisdom that teaches and inspires the comprehension of the languages of old. Forneus is also one who heals arguments and reconciles foes. He governs 29 legions of spirits, who are partly the Order of Thrones and Angels. One may invoke Forneus as a bestial and serpentine force of self-awareness, that one may delve the depths of the subconscious to work through the familiar of the self, thus a guide to the HGA/Angelic Familiar.

Foras

Foras is the 31st spirit of Solomon. He appears as a strong man. This spirit is essential in ones own self-introspective initiation which involves magical practice. Foras teaches the art of logic and ethics and inspires a healthy outlook towards the upkeep of the human body. It may be suggested that Foras is also a spirit which suggests the crystallization of time, whereas one may learn to appreciate and control their surroundings to the point of stretching the barriers of time. This may involve but is not limited to – total environments, advanced sorcery techniques which crystallize areas of ones surroundings to give a stronger appearance of time slowing. Foras is a spirit to invoke in areas of one stimulating a discipline to exercise and physically challenge the self towards improvement.

Asmoday

Asmoday is a great king, being a fountain source of Luciferian Witchcraft and primal sorcery. Asmodeus is Aeshma, the Daeva of the Wounding Spear. Asmodai appears as a demon with three heads – Bull, a Man and a Ram, also a tail of a serpent and spits flames. His feet are webbed as a goose and sits upon an infernal dragon. Asmoday appears with a lance and spear, the color of the flag on the banner is crimson with a black dragon upon it. He is the choice power under Amaymon. This powerful Daemon inspires astronomy, geometry and earthly arts. Asmodai also inspires invincibility by the development of strength and will. As one evokes Asmoday, a seeming cloud of black and gray smoke appears in the mirror – it seems to move beyond the mirror from the circle yet this is a seeming illusion – if ones concentration of Will is upon the circle, hold it fast to the meeting place of spirits. Asmoday may be summoned by self-enchantment as in Karezza (Karezza is masturbation without climax, always willed) or other means. A Sex Magickal operation involving the consecration of his Sigil with secretions/fluids of both male and female will create Asmoday, as suggested rightly so by Aleister Crowley. Qabalistic lore has long warned of such, as it is said to breed demons. In a self-initiatory sense, it is ideal and powerful. Asmoday/Asmodeus grants 72 Legions of Spirits, and shows one where treasure may be found. This translates to the treasure of self from which one may obtain an area of individual and mental achievement. After creating/summoning/invoking Asmodeus, follow your instinct accordingly.

Gaap

Gaap is a mighty prince and Angelic Ruler who governs 66 Legions of Spirits. It is written that Gaap appears when the Sun is in certain southern signs, in a human form. He appears in front of four Mighty Kings, whom he leads. Gaap is a divinatory spirit as well as one which acts as an accelerator of social behavior, i.e. how individuals act are perceived and read by specific body language and posture, etc. Gaap is also a spirit of astral and dreaming projection. This spirit also teaches one how to consecrate items unto Amaymon, his King.

Furfur

Furfur is the Thirty-Fourth Spirit of Solomon, who is a great and mighty Earl. This spirits appears as a deer with a fiery tail, who is said never to speak truth. This translates in an initiatory context that Furfur echoes the conscious mind, that is, he does not reveal the depths of the true self, i.e. the subconscious abyss within. Furfur is a spirit of the carnal ego, the daemon associated with the body. This spirit will also take human form is commanded, and will reveal truth once the magician has Willed it so. Furfur can raise storms which translates to the context which makes reference to his ability to cause "Chaos" in areas of self-introspection, that which will create a powerful situation for the one who works with this spirit. In other words, Furfur can assist or help destroy the self. He may also be commanded with his 26 Legions of spirits to create Chaos of a somewhat destructive nature in another.

Marchosias

Marchosias is a mighty marquis who appears in the form of a wolf having wings with a serpent's tail, as this spirit appears it vomits flames. Marchosias is a werewolf daemon – having been bound to the earth, has taken forth and absorbed the shades of the wolf – thus upon request Marchosias will take upon a human form. Marchosias is a fallen angel who is a strong fighter – who was of the Order of Dominions. He governs 30 Legions of Spirits, when summoned by Solomon, he told after 1,200 years he had hopes to return to the Seventh Throne. Marchosias teaches and initiates through lycanthropy and astral shape shifting, as well as war and combat techniques.

Stolas

Stolas also called Stolos is the Thirty-sixth Spirit who is a great and powerful prince. He appears in the form of a mighty Raven, who also takes the shape of a man. Stolas teaches the ancient art of astronomy and herbalism. He inspires the magician the instinct of wort cunning, the art of the wise. Stolas governs 26 Legions of Spirits, who also teaches Astronomy. When one summons Stolas this spirit often appears in the black mirror as a Raven, which interestingly enough symbolizes Hidden Wisdom and the Darker Realms, thus one assumed as a God Form by invocation, allows a very interesting prose into the concepts of Astronomy and spiritual impulses of that particular Spirit.

Phenex

Phenex (also Pheynix) is a great Marquis who appears like a Phoenix bird, who has a voice of a child. Phenex creates a form of music which is something described as a child's chorus, a very beautiful and entrancing form of song from which the magician must command Phenex to take human shape. If Willed to by the magician, this spirit will take human form in the Black Mirror. Phenex is a poet and inspires the magician to write and create tomes and works. Phenex also wishes to return to the Seventh Throne after 1,200 years as well, and governs 20 Legions of Spirits. Phenex is a nature spirit, whom inspires a careful pondering of the places of nature and the animals within it.

Halphas

Halphas or Malthus is the Thirty-eighth Spirit of Solomon, who appears as a Stock-Dove. Malthas (as it is also spelled) is a Great Earl, who speaks unto the magician with a hoarse voice. This spirit upon evocation in the black mirror, builds Towers and fortification surrounding the magician. This may be reflected in a spiritual manner, creating astral towers of which protect the magician from any attacks. Malthus furnishes the tower with weapons of war, he does send Spirits to fortify the tower, and they are excellent spirits for protection. He has 26 Legions of Spirits who may be summoned through him. In the Black Mirror, Halphas may be then invoked into the magician, as a part of recalling the spirit as an atavism. This will strengthen the mental aspect of the individual who seeks to create a solid essence of self which may not be attacked by spiritual means.

Malphas

Malphas is the Thirty-ninth spirit who appears like a crow, however will take human shape once the magicians requests it. Malphas is a might President who is very powerful. He does build high towers like Malthus however may also bring you the knowledge of your enemies' desires and thoughts. It is required for creation and manifestation of this spirit that one performs a sexual sacrifice (for material basis) for which one would focus on the sigil and consecrate it accordingly. It is known that Malphas will deceive the magician if he is not careful. Be prepared and be exact in your commands.

Raum

Raum is the Fortieth Spirit of Solomon, who is a Great Earl. In the black mirror and the evocation circle he appears in the form of a crow, but will appear in a human form if commanded. Raum was said to steal treasures from a King's castle, however this may be translated into an intiatory context as gathering secrets astrally, from others if need be. He is also capable to destroy dignities of men and primarily acts as a divinatory spirit. He was of the Order of Thrones and still governs 30 Legions of Spirits.

Focalor

Focalor/Forcalor/Furcalor is a Might Duke who appears in the form of a man with a Gryphon's wings. Focalor is a murdering spirit, who may also drown individuals in water and causes storms in the seas. If commanded, he will not harm any living being. He was too of the Seventh Throne and seeks to return there after 1,000 years. Focalor governs 30 Legions of spirits and is a powerful servitor to summon in dreaming (Subconscious – Water – Leviathan) sorcery. He too has power of the Air, being a Luciferic Angel as well.

Vepar

Vepar is the Forty-second Spirit of Solomon whom is also recognized by Vepar or Vephar. This Spirit is a Great Duke who appears as a female mermaid. He governs waters and was said to guide ships with armor and weapons. He also causes storms in the sea. In an initiatory context, Vepar is a spirit who is of the Leviathanc Spirits, of the subconscious and water. In this, Vepar appears in dreams as a fluid-like gray mermaid who has deep blue or black eyes. Vepar may gather and guard servitors who go forth by the dreaming gnosis, and reveal secrets of the self long buried. Vepar also causes men to die in three days by infected wounds and sores. He governs 29 Legions of Spirits.

Sabnock

Sabnock who is also called Savnok is the Forty-third Spirit of Solomon who was commanded into a Vessel of Brass. He is a Marquis who is considered very powerful. Sabnock appears in the form of an armed soldier with a Lion's head who rides upon a white horse. Sabnock builds towers and castles, being dwellings of the astral spirit which the sorcerer shall encircle his/her self in through dream projection. He can cause wounds to infect and kill me slowly. Sabnock gives excellent Familiars who may build and strengthen the towers of self. He governs 50 Legions of Spirits.

Shan

Shan/Shaz/Shax is a Great Marquis who appears in the form of a Dove, who speaks with a rough and hoarse voice. This spirit may take way hearing and sight, and may destroy perception. It is written that Shan steals money out of the house of Kings, which in an initiatory context of the Sabbatic Path, Shan guides the sorcerer's astral spirit to the Sabbat – and reveals secrets unto him/her. Shan brings Horses to the magician, which is the Nightmare or Sabbatic Steed. One must summon Shan in the Evocation Circle, the very meeting place of all spirits. The magician will then enter the circle to ensorcel himself in this essence. Shan may also reveal hidden things and that which is not kept by Wicked Spirits. Shan does give excellent Familiars and Governs 30 Legions.

Vine

Vine is the Forty-fifth spirit whom is also called Vinea. Being a Great King and Earl, Vine appears often in the form of a Lion/beastlike man who rides upon a Black Horse, holding a serpent in one hand. In Black Mirror Evocations, Vine has oftened appeared as a serpent like lion who then looses form and becomes a burning cloud with several eyes peering from the fire. Vine builds towers (of protection on the astral plane), destroys great walls (of the sorcerer's enemy) and makes waters rough with storms. Vine governs 36 Legions of Spirits, and acts as an elemental guide unto those who may seek to attack you. Vine is also a divinatory spirit who will also brings initiatory knowledge to Wizards, Witches and hidden aspects.

Bifrons

Bifrons, known also as Bifrons, Bifrous and Bifrovs is an earl, who appears as a wolf like monster, but at the Will of the Sorcerer, will change shape to a human male. Bifrons is a necromantic spirit, who governs the realm of shades; he may bring one close to various shades of the dead, but often they are not who they claim to be. Be cautious but be indulgent with this spirit as well. Bifrons may change the place of dead bodies, being the binding of ghosts to various fetishes or pots, and lights witch fire on the graves of the dead. Bifrons governs 6 Legions of Spirits, and will also teach the virtues of stones and wood, thus being a spirit long bound to the earth.

Uvall

Vual/Voval is the forty-seventh spirit who is a Duke. Uvall appears as a large Dromedary but will take a human shape, hooded in Middle Eastern fashion, at the command of the sorcerer. Uvall speaks in an Egyptian manner, which is not easily understandable but the sorcerer may rely on the impulses or instinctual voices instead of any tongue spoken. Uvall brings the love of woman and is a divinatory spirit. He was of the Order of Potestates or Powers and governs 37 legions of spirits.

Haagenti

Haagenti is a President, who governs 33 Legions of Spirits. He appears in the form of a Bull with Wings, but will take human shape at the command of the Sorcerer. Haagenti makes men wise by wisdom brought on various subjects, generally within an initiatory context. It is said Haagenti makes Water from Wine, Water into Wine which represents that this spirit may bring simplified meanings of difficult initiatory concepts, that of the art of sorcery. It is said he may transmute metals into Gold, which symbolically represents the same of initiatory Work.

Crocell

Crocell is the Forty-ninth spirit also known as Crokel. He appears in the form of a angel, shrouded and pale like the dead (not unlike Astaroth, the Luciferic spirit guide). He is a Mighty Duke who is very strong in presence, who speaks in mystical tongues and poem of self-illuminating or hidden things. He brings the sounds of rushing of waters and that will create a calm of self. It is said Crocell warms and discovers baths, and may purify water unto the sorcerer who seeks a cleansing. He was of the Order of Potestates, or

Powers before his fall of independence along with the Djinn or Angelick spirits of Lucifer. He governs 48 Legions of spirits.

Furcas

Furcas is a Knight who appears as a cruel looking old man who has a long beard, who rides upon a pale horse. He carries a very sharp sword in hand and appears in the evocation circle as an aggressive and fiery shade. Furcas teaches the arts of Cheiromancy (Palmistry), Pyromancy (the art of Fire) and logic/philosophy. This spirit governs 20 Legions and is very useful to the sorcerer on the ensorcelling of the spirits of fire, being the elementals of Set-an or Azazel.

Balam

Balam is the Fifty-first spirit known also as Balaam. He is considered a terrible and great King. He appears with three Heads, one being a Bull which drops blackened blood as it speaks, which is always a "Speaking in tongues" speech, the other head is that of a Ram and the Third is the head of a young man, who has no hair. Balam has the tail of a serpent with fiery eyes. He comes forth on a large black bear, who is aggressive, and carries a Hawk upon his fist. He speaks in a very harsh voice. Balaam is a darkened Angel, who when the human head speaks, the bull head hisses and speaks in tongues. He is a divinatory spirit, who reveals answers of the past and present and that which may come. He also teaches astral invisibility and how one may project by dreams. Balam governs 40 Legions of Spirits.

Alloces

Alloces/Alocas is the Fifty-second Spirit who is a Duke, who appears in the form of a Soldier who rides a great horse. His face is beast like and is that of a Lion, with flaming eyes. The speech of Alloces is very hoarse and loud. He teaches and instructs in the art of sciences and brings very good familiars to who seeks to learn the use of planets in ones initiation. He rules over 36 Legions and may cause the sorcerers enemy to grow paranoid with the movements of the moon, if the magician wishes.

Camio

Camio/Caim is a Great President who appears like Bird who may then take the shape of a man who carries a sword. The days after Caim is called one will notice often an increased visitation and appearance of birds, who children may notice something strange or disturbing about. One may seek a diviniation with Camio through ashes and fire, who appears in burning coals. Camio teaches the art of astral projection, shape shifting and flying in the dream. He instructs also the language of birds and the barking of Dogs. This is a Witchcraft Spirit, who is bound to the earth with great knowledge of it. Caim was of the Order of Angels who now rules over 30 Legions of Infernal Spirits.

Murmur

Murmur/Murmus is the Fifty-fourth Spirit of the Shemhamforasch, and is a Great Duke and Earl. He appears in the form of a armored warrior who rides a Gryphon, with a Crown upon his head. He will come forth with his Ministers who sound great trumpets. Murmur is a spirit of Necromancy, who constrains shades of the dead and the deceased to come forth and answer the sorcerer. Murmus was once an Angel of the Order of Thrones but now governs 30 Legions of Spirits. Murmur may also, at the command of the sorcerer, send forth Shades of the Dead to encircle the self and strengthen the astral body and to bring voices of insight or divination unto the Witch summoning. He may also send the shades of the dead, often infernal spirits to haunt those who the sorcerer may desire.

Orobas

Orobas is the Fifty-fifth spirit who is a Great Prince. He appears in the form of a two legged Horse, who will put on a human form at the desire of the magician. He inspires divination and brings impulses or intuition regarding things of the past, for instance if a horrible occurrence happened at a spot or area. Orobas brings the connection of the living and the dead. He brings also the favor of friends and foes, and is very faithful and respectful to the sorcerer when summoned. He will not trick the magician and will provide quick answers unto that which he governs. He presides over 20 Legions of Spirits.

Gremory

Gamori/Gremory is the Fifty-sixth Spirit, being a Duke who is very powerful. He appears as a Beautiful Woman, of Middle Eastern visage, who wears a Crown upon a Camel. Gremory will also copulate spiritually in a dreaming sense with the magician, who is just as a woman, as Djinn are generally neither male nor female. Gremory is a divinatory spirit. Who tells of things past and present. Gremory also teaches of the treasures of self, at various points in ones life, that may be considered as useful knowledge. He brings the love and lust of women young and old. Gamori governs 26 Legions of Spirits.

Ose

OSE/OSE/VOSO is a Great President, who appears as a Leopard. He will put a human form on at the request of the magician. Ose is a Cunning Spirit who intiates one to the mysteries of the Heavens and Divine things (Luciferic Spirits). Ose also guides one to the Celestial/Luciferian Sabbat and may transform the sorcerer into any astral form they wish. He governs 30 Legions of Spirits.

Amy

AMY/AVNAS is a Great President who appears as Fire but upon the request of the magician, will take a human shape. He teaches Astrology and sciences, according to ones initiatory interests. Amy grants good familiars and grants insight on the treasures of knowledge, how one may move forward with their own initiation into the magical secrets of the self. He governs 36 Legions of Spirits.

Oriax

ORIAX/ORIAS is the Fifty-ninth Spirit who is a Great Marquis. He appears in the form of a Lion-Beast, who rides upon a Large Horse with a Serpent's tail. He holds in his Right hand two Large Serpents who hiss. He teaches the Virtues of Stars and how one may contact the Shades of the Dead through the fascination of the Stars. Oriax instructs on the Mansions of the Planets, and how one may hold common knowledgeable associations with them, such as identifying their meanings and associations. He transforms the dreaming body of the sorcerer and grants the favor of friends. Oriax governs 30 Legions of Spirits.

Vapula

VAPULA/NAPHULA is the Sixtieth Spirit who is a Mighty Duke. He appears in the form of a Lion with Wings, and inspires the knowledge of Handcrafts and Professions. Vapula is by this admission one of the ones of Neph-Kam, the Nephilim who instructs the sorcerer on crafts of which they hold interest. In a beneficial sense, the Sorcerer may send forth Vapula to quietly assist through unknown inspiration for a loved one to learn something quickly, that their brain will gain in associations with this spirit. Vapula governs 36 Legions of Spirits.

Zagan

ZAGAN is the Sixty-first Spirit who is a Great King and President. He appears as a Bull with Wings but will appear at the request of the magician as a man. He instructs men on wit and intellect, how to make associations within their own natural environment and how to quietly listen and think/comprehend before speaking. This spirit also transforms Wine into Water and Blood into Wine, being a Vampyric shade which initiates into the mysteries of immortality and blood. He also instructs initiation into evolution and strengthening the self, that one may pass the requirements of a human body upon death – while this is not proved. Zagan makes "fools wise", which holds a key to the Tarot – those who walk the fearful path, face the dangers of the mind and soul, may emerge as Adepts in the Arte of Sorcery. He governs 33 Legions of Spirits.

Volac

VOLAC/VALAX/VALU/UALAC is the Sixty-second Spirit who is a Might President. He appears in the form of a child with Angel's wings, who rides upon a two – headed Dragon. He instructs the knowledge of hidden treasures, or initiation and Coming into Being as a self-deified magician. He instructs on where Serpents may be seen (knowledge and initiation). Volac is also a Guardian of the Circle, who is a powerful servitor who governs 38 Legions of Spirits. Volac is useful in invocation based on instinctual assumption, specifically to seek out serpents if one seeks one by chance.

Andras

Being a Great Marquis, Andras appears as an Angel with a Head like a Black Night Raven, who rides upon a Black Wolf and holds a Sharp and cruel Sword which is covered in purple flames. Andras is a spirit and guide of the dead, and of Infernal Initiation. He teaches the assumption of bestial forms, of Lycanthropy and astral transformation. He also sows discords and destroys enemies of the sorcerer. He is a spirit of death, and will slay many by natural means. Andras governs 30 Legions of Spirits and brings the magician the power of the shades of which he commands.

Haures

HAURAS/HAVRES/FLAUROS is the Sixty-fourth spirit appears as a Leopard, vicious and aggressive who by the Will of the magician take on a human form which is a Black Shadow with Flaming eyes, who is very dominating by his presence. Haures is a divinatory spirit who instructs on things to come, and the past. It is essential that the first summoning be done within the Circle and Triangle, where the place of Spirits which meet is, unless by Dream he shall lie to the sorcerer and prey upon his or her weaknesses. He instructs on how spirits and Angels fell, and the Creation of Being. Haures burns and destroys the enemies of the sorcerer, if they so desire it, and will not harm then the magician. He governs 36 Legions of Spirits.

Andrealphus

Andrealphus is the Sixty-fifth Spirit who is a mighty Marquis, who comes forth as a beast or jester spirit who is like a Peacock, who speaks in tongues with two voices (high and low) at the same instance. He is a Spirit of the Infernal Sabbat, who shall carry thee forth in Astral and Dreaming Flesh in the form of a Bird. Andrealphus teaches astronomy and such sciences. If the magician desires it, Andrealphus will take human shape. He governs 30 Legions of Infernal Spirits.

Cimejes

Cimejes/Cimeies/Kimaris is the Sixty-sixth Spirit. He is a powerful Marquis who appears in the form of a Warrior who rides upon a large Black Horse. This spirit rules over all spirit who are haunters of Africa, and Governs 20 Legions of Infernal Spirits. Cimejes teaches grammar, logic and is a divinatory spirit who reveals hidden treasures of subconscious knowledge within the self.

Amdusias

Amdusias/Amdukias is the Sixty-seventh Spirit who appears as a Unicorn like creature, but will transform into a human shape if commanded. Amdusias is a Strong and Powerful Duke who is a spirit of the Earth, who may bring one close to the spirits of nature. He guides in dreams the sorcerer to the great forests, from which the trees are flowing in beauty and ancient wisdom. Amdusias gives excellent familiars and governs 29 Legions.

Belial

Belial is the Sixty-eight Spirit of the Shemhamforasch, who is a Might King. Belial was created after Lucifer and is one of the original Djinn who would not bow before the clay of man. Belial is traditionally the Lord of the Earth, the Lord of the Sorcerous Path and a powerful Daemon of the Will made Flesh. Belial appears often in the form of Two Beautiful Angels who ride within a Chariot of Fire. He speaks in a calm and beautiful voice, yet has a touch of the sinister to it. Belial declares how he fell along with Lucifer who came long before Michael and other such Angels. Belial brings self-initiation and development from the magician who may summon and invoke this force, it holds the gateway to aspects of the mind which control speech and thought patterns. Belial is said to grant Senatorships and such, while this is in reference to one achieving success with their own Desire and Will. He Governs 50 Legions of Spirits, who are of the Infernal and Celestial/Luciferian realms of the earth. Belial also initiates into the Solar and Lunar Gnosis of being, that of Vampyres and Wolves. King Belial demands sacrifice, which is of a sexual nature. A powerful Will is required to restrain and hold this force in the Evocation circle or Black Mirror, from which then the sorcerer should immolate the self in this Daemonic Force – the isolated and immortal psyche.

Above: Belial

Decarabia

Decarabia is the Sixty-ninth Spirit of Solomon, who appears as a burning and flaming pentacle, then at the command of the magician takes the shape of a man. Decarabia instructs the sorcerer on astral and dream shape shifting, how one may transform into a bird or bat, to fly forth and discover darker places of the earth, as well as coming before the magician and acting in the natural way in which birds do. Decarabia teaches also the use of stones and elements in sorceries. He governs 30 Legions of Spirits and is a Mighty Marquis.

Seere

Seere/Sear/Seir is the Seventieth Spirit who is a Might and Powerful Prince, who is under AMAYMON, the King of the East. Seere appears in the form of a beautiful and angelic male, who rides upon a Winged Horse. He is a powerful Angel who brings the sorcerer's Will to flesh quickly, and will disappear until you are ready for him to return. Being a Luciferic Spirit, Seere resides in the Air and may pass over the Earth in a blink of the eye. He initiates the self towards the higher spheres of Light and the Sun, from which one rides the Aethyr unto a higher articulation of being through the Familiar. Seere governs 26 Legions of Spirits, and is of a Good Nature.

Dantalion

Dantalion is a Might Duke who appears as a being which has numerous faces of both men and women, each one has either black or solid white eyes, who speak in different tongues. He holds a book in his right hand, which is the grimoire of high art. Dantalion reveals the secret council or thoughts of others, which in an initiatory context means that Dantalion may provide the magician to begin the understand of common psychology and human thinking based on cause, body language and such. Dantalion is an Angel of self-study and self-control, and is a powerful spirit. He can also cause the union of individuals that it may be probable, and is a guide to other beautiful places in the world. He governs 36 Legions of Spirits.

Andromalius

Andromalis is the Seventy-second Spirit who is a Might Earl. He appears in the form of a man holding a large and hissing serpent in his hand. Andromalius may reveal those who have stolen from you, and those who seek to be as a predator against you. This spirit may reveal trickery and those who are wicked against you. He is able to punish and harm those who have harmed you or seek to. Andromalis governs 36 Legions of Spirits.

Presented here are the 72 Mighty Kings, Princes and Djinn which King Solomon commanded into the Vessel of Brass and Skull, together with their legions. Which BELIAL, BILETH, ASMODAY and GAAP were Chief Djinn. It is suggested that Solomon bound them because of their pride. He bound them and sealed the Vessel, and chased them into a Deep Lake or Hole in Babylon. Those of Babylon who wished to see such an act, went forth into the lake and broke the vessel. They wished to find much treasure but out came the Chief Spirits and then their Legions. They were then restored to their places in the World, and still walk with us today. All of these except for BELIAL, who entered into a certain Image and gave answers to those who gave sacrifices unto him, and worshiped this image as their God of Transformation and Sorcerous power.

Here ends the Black Book of Goetia

Binding Spell of the Seeker

The Path Offered by Sathan

Unto the Devil's name are ye reborn, burning effigy of the Noon Tide Sun, Spirit of Blackened Light, who is both Beast and Angel, aligned with the Rise of Man and Woman – those who walk the thorn-way path. I charge thee with protecting this book, coil as a serpent around the heart of thee text, that as a grimoire scribed in the blood of the moon.
Satan, Adversarial Djinn who dwells in the Sun, crowned in the Emerald which reflects the Noble Flame, who resides in the heart of Midnight, shadowed and ashen beneath the Waters of the Moon – I charge thee with protecting of this book – The Mind of the Serpent shall open the gates within. By Beast we go forth…

IV. The Toad Rite
A grimoire of the Toad Witch

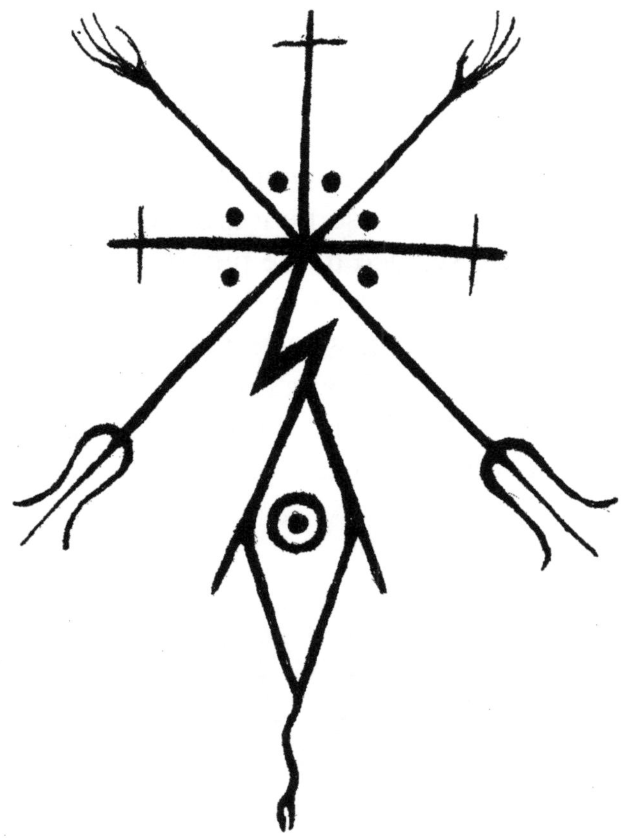

The Patron Spirit of the Toad Rite is Cain, the Devil in Flesh, the Black Man of the Sabbat who is the Son of Ahriman, or Satan. As one achieves the integration of the spirit of the frog (that of a diabolic nature) the Toad Witch opens forth a new road of power which moves beyond folk magick. At first glance many can wonder how this may be of any initiatory value, but once one moves through the familiar of the Toad, the elder image of Ahriman (Satan) and of witchcraft some very powerful situations can arise.

Traditionally, the toad is related to malefic or diabolic powers which are granted by the Devil. It is known in Zoroastrian lore that Ahriman or Satan created toads and frogs and then assumed their image at times when appearing on earth. The toad, as being the black cat, has traditionally been associated with witchcraft and the devil. This due no doubt to the hidden aspects of both animals, being that the witch or sorcerer places their belief and association into the animal.

The Toad Rite is a Working which guides the practitioner into a 'inbetween' land which is surreal and equally as interesting. It is not just the Toad which is the center of the Working itself, but the spirits which are summoned to encircle the practitioner. Hecate comes forth to her children in Three Shades, Phantoms or Ghosts who encircle the summoner and passes on power to the initiate who is not unlike her, in other words an isolate and strong spirit – one who is ready to – and dares to – test the devil to become the Lord of the Shadowed Path.

It must be made certain that the Toad Rite is not required nor always suggested to the practioner of the Luciferian Path. A prerequisite is that there are omens and signs which lead you by instinct to the rite, and that proper preparations and self-development of magical work is done therein. This rite may be undertaken with the Toad but also the Black Cat as has been seen in America.

The Toad Rite is sacred to the Hecate – Trevia, whose Three ways are the path to her consort, Satandar (the Earthly body being Cain) or Azazel, called Lucifer. For the Three Nights from which you shall seek the power of the Toad Bone, you shall call upon each shade of Hecate to bless and empower your path, for you shall move through the dark of the Moon to the Path of the Sun. The feminine is essential in the development of the Rite, and the encircling of the power given by the devil. It should be known therein that one is seeking to Master the Devil, to overcome the test given by this initatior, which you should become like Satan in his image and wielding the inbetween and dual power of Hecate, both Night and Day.

The Witch Fire of Hecate is the fire of the blackened forge, the flame of Luciferian Being which grows and crystallizes as one moves through with their own self-initiation. It must be remembered that Hecate is a Goddess The Toad Rite is perhaps one of the most omen bearing, or dangerous to the gates of the mind. Approach the rite without haste or increased desire, rather a Willed and Focused resolve to become through the ritual itself. The Ritual undertaken known as **STAUROS BATACHOU** (*LIBER LXX, the Cross of the Frog*) by Aleister Crowley was indeed <u>his</u> ritual to pass through to the Grade of Magus. The ritual itself was based on Christian symbolism from which the Frog or Toad is visualized as Christ itself, and the magician is symbolized as a Snake or Serpent, to devour the Toad symbolically. The sorcerer is to stab the Toad with a Knife of Art (*Athame*) and thus absorb the spirit of the Toad.

In the modern assumption of the Luciferian Path, the Toad takes a different yet equally effective symbolism. The Toad must come essentially, to the witch who shall undertake the rite. One is advised to create Two Spirit Pots (*See BOOK OF THE WITCH MOON, NOX UMBRA or YATUK DINOIH by the Present Author*) which are the vessels or Nganga of the Shadow (Astral body - <u>Ka</u>) or Light (Soul - <u>Ba</u>) forms of the magician. They are created with sigils, blood of the sorcerer and sexual fluids, buried in the earth in the style suggested by Austin Osman Spare as the "**Earthenware Virgin**". This produces a charged shadow and demonic aspect of the self, growing outside of the physical body in the realm of dreaming, thus a path of the self growing as an Immortal Being, the Blackened Flame illuminated and slowly crystallized.

This is by itself a rite which arises from the East Anglican Folk Magic traditions, but yet aligned with the shadow and Nightside aspects of Cain. Through the Toad one begins the thorn covered road of the Dragon, which is illuminated within the self. The Toad Rite was undertaken by myself April 23rd, 2003 E.V. when the Moon was in Aquarius. The rite itself was brought about through the tract of **OZ**, which is the number of Capricorn and the symbolism of Night and Death, Goat/Buck/Devil. The numerical 77 was presented in dreaming through its symbolism, and was an Omen to which the Toad arrived. The following text is ritual and record, a montage and blending of both. You may adapt accordingly if you so choose to undertake this ritual. The Toad Witch is considered dangerous, feared yet also doomed to face a violent death. Within my own personal initiatic perspective, one chooses their own path, and to become the Lord of the Devil, which is OZ, one must think in Daimonic Time, the ebb and flow of your words making power and flesh now. The Triangle and meeting place of the spirit is symbolized as the Sun in the Toad Ritual, and the Three Forks are the Three Direct Points which lead to the Sun, the Beast 666 who is transformative under the light of the illuminated self.

Items required:

A small pouch.
Thin Wire (used to tie the bones)
Scissors and Working Knife.
Crystal on string (used previously by sorcerer)

The Patron Spirits of the Toad Ritual
(demon sigils from old Grand Grimoire edition)

Hecate The three formed Goddess of Crossroads, Death and Necromancy. She is the spirit of Night and Vampyric Shades which haunt the earth. One may give a gift of Honey to her upon consecrating a graveyard for your meditations and workings. Hecate is the Spirit which surrounds you in the Toad Rite, as with the Three Shades of Hecate.

Satandar/Satanachia (Cain the Devil) – The Demon Initiator, the very spirit which resides in the bone charm of the Toad Rite. This spirit tests and challenges the initiate, but those who can remain on their path will benefit from the Devil itself. Satanachia is a spirit which holds power over the feminine, or women and is a familiar guide in sex magick workings. It is this masculine energy which is the transformative essence of the Sun. Satandar is also known as a fiery essence of glyph/symbol of Ahriman, the Devil and Cain the First Witch of the Circle and first Satanist.

Lucifuge Rofocale (Shadow of Lucifer, one part of the Adversary in the Grimoire tradition) – the Night Familiar of Sorcery, Luciferian Witchcraft & Magick. Lucifuge is a spirit which translates "Fly the Light" and is made in reference to aerial spirits who fly in the darkness. Lucifuge is the subordinate of Lucifer in the Grand Grimoire or Red Dragon, from which he resides in air and the earth.

Fleurety (a familiar of flight and dreaming transformation) – A spirit over "Night labor" and is made reference to as a familiar who guides one in the Workings at night. One may invoke Fleurety to preside over the spirits of night, to guide those familiars of the unconscious which may be out of Willed contact by the sorcerer.

Nebiros (Death, the Demon of Necromancy and Divination) – This spirit is said to have the ability to cause harm to any individual he wills. Nebiros is a powerful Demon-Spirit who is said to be one of the most powerful Necromancers in the infernal realms. Nebiros is said to also find the Hand of Glory and the discovery of metals and all animals. His servitor spirits are Naberrs, Ayperos and Glassyalabolas. Nebiros is a powerful shade summoning demon used in not only Toad Rite Workings (in relation to the graveyard and certain Hecate workings) but also diviniation and necromancy.

When the Toad is obtained by natural means (*the creature comes near you or is found accordingly*) it must be skinned. The bottom jaw must be cut entirely off, the skin off the back and head is removed. The skin on the body should be cut carefully (without damaging the meat or bones) and removed including the arms and legs. The rest will be the actual bones connected with the meat. Stretch the skin out on a white piece of paper to dry out, keep in the sun the next day if possible. If one keeps a sorcerous vessel of blood, containing the blood of the magician used in Familiar charging rites, scribed with the symbol of the fallen or averse pentagram, then the Eyes of the toad should be removed carefully and put into the Blood filled vessel, with a chant reproduced below.

Seal the Vessel as usual and place upon thy altar of Art.

The innards of the Toad which contain no bones should be buried in the soil of where the Twin Vessels were created, thus is already a charged soil within a Graveyard or other sacred land. The insides of the Toad should be given as a gift to the Soil, and a prayer to Hecate and Ahriman should be made:
"I give unto the sacred heart and innards of the Toad to thee, Mother Hecate and Ahriman, that with this offering I shall become as thee, Immortal and a Walker between the Worlds of Darkness and Flesh. Accept this offering of the Toad, that every part of this sacred creature shall be honored and given back to the earth, shall I then become the Devil itself, flesh and soul sanctified in the sacred fire of Azazel, the Blackened Forge of Cain the Path of Loneliness and Ankou'd solitude."

The Toad flesh and bones shall be taken to an ant hill, wherein the meat and such is placed for the ants to devour. Meditate upon the transformative process that by devouring the corpse the essence is revealed. Take then the bones in all back to the Temple and place in a safe and sacred place. You may perfume the bones in the essence and oil of Hecate, that by an appropriate night you shall go to a stream and cast the bones in. One or more bones will seemingly float towards you and this shall be the Omen of thy gift. All the surroundings will seek to distract you, yet your Will must be focused and resolved. Take the bone and keep on you for three nights. You may seek out lonely and haunted places each for the three nights. This may be a graveyard or some place from which you seek out the phantoms of the night. They shall test you in various ways, yet you shall be Willed and Focused. On what is the Third Night, each night a meeting with the Shades of Hecate, you shall finally meet the Devil before you.

In your mind you shall be tested by the Devil, who will encourage that you bury the bones in the soil of a grave, and shall be given in return the powers that you seek. Do not pay heed to this, save you shall fail miserably in the rite. You must refuse the devil continually, and keep the bone on you at all times. Do not give to this testing spirit, as you must move forward and succeed. At the end of the Rite, you will be smiled upon by the Devil, Satandar, whom you shall in fact BECOME AS. You shall be then the Lord of the Devil, the Vicar of the Son of the Devil, the Antichrist as so described by John Whiteside Parsons, the Son or Daughter of the Beast 666.

If on any of these three nights, you sleep in the sunken area of a grave many nightmares shall be sent to you. A corpse of green and gray flesh shall seek you out and ask for the congress she so desires in life. That smells are not normally recognized in dreams, and you can find the lust to copulate with this phantom, she will use the Nocturnal Emissions to breed demons and give strength to the shades of that land. You will be brought forth as a Horseman as Cain, a Master of Spirits who shall listen to you. Pay heed to the spirit, and let her not take the Toad Bone, save disaster and ruin for the mind and psyche.

The Toad Rite

Being the ceremony to obtaining a familiar spirit of a Luciferian nature, Inspired by TO MEGA THERION, the Beast 666 known as Aleister Crowley in relation to the Toad Ritual from St. John the Divine. Presented anew in the Light of Lucifer through the Mask of Satandar, the Patron Familiar and Witch King of the Rite of the Toad and Hecate, the Triple Goddess of darkness, shades and the path of sorcery. Let the practitioner be aware, as the Shadows of Satandar or Ahriman are revealed and illuminated by the Fire of Self, shall then Cain be presented as the patron earthen spirit of the Toad Witch.

0) This ritual is a presentation of the magician representing a serpent, thus intelligence and self-transformation. The familiar is an illuminated Angelick Guide, the very source of which ones Holy Guardian Angel, or Angelic Familiar/True Will arrives. The Toad Ritual brings the initiate to the brink of madness and the abyss, from which he or she may not emerge from. It is the test of the witchcraft itself, the powers of the earth at the command of the sorcerer. You shall test the Devil and thus it shall test you. If you walk this path to overcome and master this beast, you shall be the Devil's Lord. The practitioner is symbolized as the Snake, the seeker of wisdom.

The Toad may be caught by the signs which you shall know. Allow the spirit to be your guide, let instinct direct you on the time and place. You shall catch the toad and it shall be known to you as the path of which you shall take. It is the Luciferian approach of the shadows of Ahriman, as the Toad was traditionally a form the Lord of Darkness would assume. The toad is also sacred to Hekt, a frog-headed goddess related to the Queen of the Sabbat, being Hecate – Our mother of the crossroads and the Goddess of Incantations.

The toad after it has been caught will be placed in a special chest, with moisture and a small amount of soil for the creatures comfort. Crowley mentioned, "Thou didst not abhor the virgin's womb", in a Luciferian sense, the Womb of Lilith is the vessel of the toad. If the toad is brought to you by Omen inspired means, then adapt accordingly.

I) When the Toad has been crucified, or the corpse obtained is dead (killed by an omen brought moment), you shall anoint yourself in the Holy Oil of Hecate. The Toad should have a slice made on the side of the body –BOTH SIDES – where the back rough skin ends and the soft belly skin begins. Cut the skin carefully by the neck down past the legs. You will then cut the legs and arms off. Carefully peel the skin off both. Place this skin on a white piece of paper, stretched out accordingly. Take now a sharp knife and peel the skin from the actual meat, from which you must be gentle to avoid tearing the skin. When you cut this back far enough, the Spine will be going into the base of the skull. Take a sharp pair of scissors and cut close to the skull. The spine will be still attached with the actual meat. Cut the bottom jaw at each point, removing it completely. You will want to cut and scrap out any flesh or meat within. The Bottom have should have the skin removed completely, and stretched out carefully on a piece of paper. Ensure no meat or innards are attached to the skin.

II) The flesh with bones should be placed in a sealed plastic bag and placed in an ice box, this to ensure freshness (and avoid the Rot in the meantime, especially if you live in an area of high humidity) before taking to an ant hill. You will at this point take the head/skull and skin (still attached) and carefully cut out the eyes. Take care not to puncture the Eyes themselves, they are small and delicate. Once they have been removed, perform the chant and place both in your vessel of blood or the Shadow Vessel:

"Eyes of the Toad, Sacred creature of Ahriman Shall become as the Eyes of Ahriman You are now the Bringer of the Devil's Path unto me, That I shall walk further into the shadows, yet arise in Light as the Lord of the Path Ahriman, see with these eyes through my eyes, Reside Eyes of the Toad in my own Blood, That thy spirit is mine and we are of darksome union. Toad brought gift of Hecate, Mother of Shades and Demons, I come to thee Sacred Initiator, I thank thee for thy gift of the Toad, which is my step further in the Devil's Path With these Eyes I may see in the Dream, unto the Sabbat Way shall I go forth"

Seal the vessel accordingly and place on your altar.

You will then take the actual innards, those which have no bones and bury with the prayer to Hecate and Ahriman, in the soil from which you have buried previous vessels.

III) On the day of which you shall take the flesh to the ant hill, place all of the meat covering the bones on the hill. With it disturbed, ants shall pour on it and begin devouring it. Meditate upon the eating of the corpse as a dying aspect of your own mortal flesh, that you shall slough off the skin of clay and soon be awakened to a new level of being. Observe those things in your life which you directly control and affect, and note any special details which will benefit from progressive change. This is a slow alchemical process which will change your specific way of thinking in some manner. When the bones are revealed, take them all from the ant hill. Do this quick, to avoid any unnecessary danger to the hill itself, and avoid being bitten by ants.

IV) The night of which the bones are cleaned, take them to a stream in solitude in the night Place them in the cold stream of Water, imagining Hecate casting her eyes upon you. As you hold these bones in the water, focus your Will upon them – charge them with a familiar chant which you may hold as a focus of personal power. One such chant may be:

"By Nebiros, Crossbone signed spirit, bless these bones with thy scent of death
by Satanachia, who comes from the depths of darkness, twin of Satandar…
by Fleurety, who wanders the earth forever in solitude and shadow
by Lucifuge, night winged familiar who blesses my soul with the Toad-spirit of Ahriman. Bless these bones with thy kiss of darkness…."

All your surroundings will seek to distract you in some way, pay no heed to it at all. Your entire focus must be on charging those bones, as this is a test of dire urgency. When you have taken the bone or bones which have called to you (Instinctively you will know this) a call should be made at the site of the stream:

"Satandar, Hecate, I have walked the path of Ahriman. The body of the Toad has revealed an earth – controlling tool of arte, of which I shall take with responsibility. Satandar, in thy shroud of Shaitan of Midnight shall I go unto, and thus journey be the path of the Devil not tread by mortal feet. I fear not the path and await thy tests, from which I am of strong intent and desire. So it shall be! Bless this Rite Hecate and send thy Shades unto me, I am ready to walk thy path."

Return to your home and sleep. Keep a record of dreams and any relevant messages. If you have two bones of the Toad, you may make an X as the sign of the crossroads, the very symbol of the Sabbat and Hecate, the place of which demons and such necromantical shades are summoned. The bones should then be placed in a small bag which has scribed on the fabric the Sigil of the Toad Rite – the averse triangle, representing the Hermetic direction of Water – Darkness, and the Sun – Symbol in the center, from the Sun three fork staves, representing the Three Shades of Hecate which emerge from the Toads which come unto the Dragon of the Sun, the Beast 666.

The toad skin that you have should be cut into a triangle and then this sigil scribed on it. The skin should be kept with the Toad Bones in the pouch. A Crystal may be kept also, one which you have picked out by instinct and have consecrated before in your rituals. It should be kept with the Toad Bones and focused upon with the power of the rite itself. The crystal by conception should relate to being a storehouse of your energy, which is invigorated with the solar and lunar properties of the Patrons of the Rite. After the ritual is complete, you may remove the crystal from the pouch and carry it when you desire. One may at first draw the Toad Sigil with the Forks leaving the Sun, yet at the end, essentially, those shades lead you to the sun itself. It is a symbol of self transformation and emerging from the darkness.

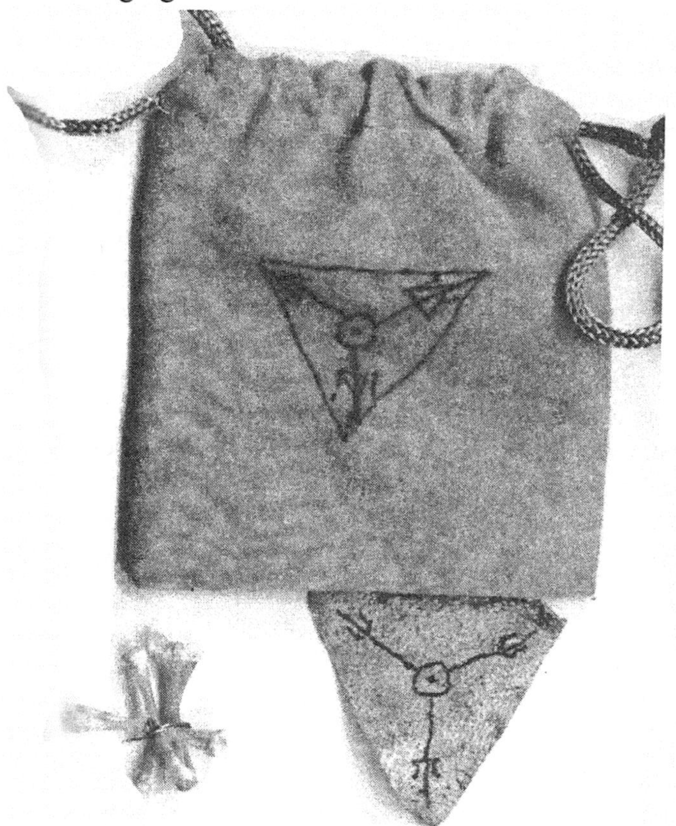

V) On the First Night, go unto a graveyard or place of haunting or solitude. You may seek out places which are instinctively shown to you, rest there and contemplate the very place you are at. Keep the bone on you at all times and for no reason whatsoever shall you give it up and place it to the ground. You may rest in the earth of a sunken grave to inspire communication with a Shade of Hecate, which will appear demonic or seductive. Some shades appear as gray and green withered corpses, which seek sexual congress. You may copulate with the by dream, but hold fast to your Toad bone, save they will take it if able to, even in the throes of ecstasy.

The First night is the special focus of the powers of which you shall seek to move through. The spirits Lucifuge, Satanachia, Nebiros, Fleurety are patron spirits which awaken one to the Torch of Hecate, the Toad Goddess who walks between the crossroads.

"I conjure thee Satandar and Satanachia, encircle me in thy eyes and ghosts which walk the earth with you who are Amon and Barbatos, devouring spirits who are a nightmare to the sleeping….Hear me Fleurety, and I summon forth your spirits Bathim, Abigar and Pursan, who shall walk with me in the Ritual of the Toad. I summon thee forth Nebiros, who is of death and the immortal shadow nourished blood drinker beyond. I conjure thee Lucifuge, Night Spirit and Familiar who guides my spirit by dream, I call unto your servitors Bael, Marbas and Agares..come forth and bless this Rite of Passing."

"I summon thee forth, Satandar, who walks the earth as the Devil in flesh. I call to thee Cain, wanderer and witch initiator of the bone rite, I walk now by omen and chosen path the Rite of the Toad, the flesh which comes of Ahriman, the Dragon which

brings the Darkness by the beating of wings. This night I begin the path, and with the bone-charm of the toad shall I call and illuminate thy Eye, and the Eyes of Hecate."
Take the bones in your hands, which have been formed into a charm which beholds infernal yet lunar power, and call your mother and patron dream encircler:

"Come O infernal, chthonic and heavenly goddess Hecate, Patron Goddess of the Crossroads, of the Grave, she who goes forth to and fro at night, torch in hand, she who walks against the sun. Lover and friend of darkness, thou who doest rejoice when the Dogs are howling and warm blood is spilled. Thou who walks amid the phantom and in the place of tombs, thou whose thirst is blood, thou who dost strike chill into mortal hearts, Gorgo, Mormo, Thousand Faced Moon, cast thy eyes unto my working."

"Hekas, Hekas, Hekausath, Usha, umpesha, narasta
Spirit of the Moon, lover and death-embracer, grow in the land of the dead. I give you strength and life, by the Wytch Fire of Azrael and Nebiros, I summon forth the shades of the Grave to bless this ToadBone as my amulet of power!"

You will soon feel a presence and many eyes watching you. Take this as a gift and omen, and allow your mind to remain focused and intent. Remain until complete according to your instincts.

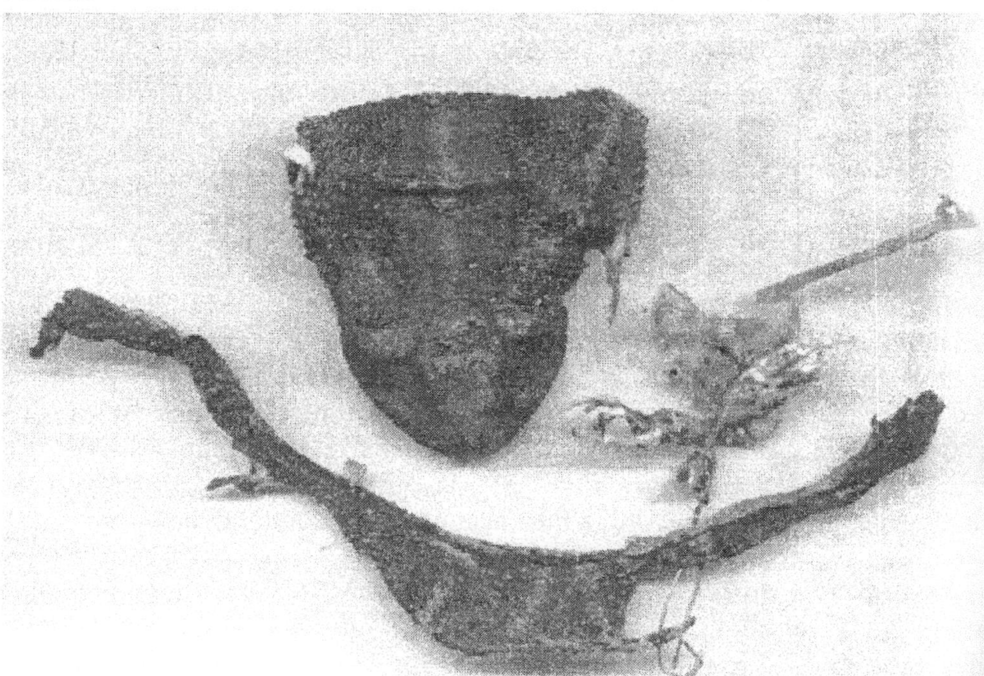

On the Second Night, you shall return to this place, and you will notice your instincts are much sharper. You will feel a stronger presence of spirits and manes of the dead. Go unto the same earth from which you rested previously, and seek the second Shade of Hecate. Listen carefully to it and allow the passing of power to occur accordingly. You will know the details of this when it happens. Upon entering the Graveyard, make widdershins around the cemetery, invoking the shadows in a wordless way – Nebiros, Lucifuge, Satanachia and Fleurety. Call in silence the shades of the cemetery to come forth to you.

On the Third Night, you shall return for the last time to this graveyard or haunted place. You shall perform a calling to Hecate in a form you desire, thank her for the gifts of initiation she has given you, and leave her an offering of Honey at the site of which you had communion with the Shades. Be honest with your approach to the Triple Mooned Goddess, lest she laugh and devour your spirit, leaving you a soulless husk or shell, with no concentration nor inspiration. Our mother and lover Hecate is loving yet equally violent with those unworthy or fearful.

Your final test comes which will leave you shaking with energy. Take heed of this moment, and carefully think out every action. The Devil known as Satandar, or Shaitan of Midnight (*See NOX UMBRA by the present author*) will come to you in some form, be in spirit or otherwise and test you. You will be asked to hand over the bone, that he would charge it with "his" blessing. You must resist at all costs, and give **NOT** the bone and **DO NOT** place the bone in the area that the Devil suggests. Remember, this spirit may not come in flesh but will come in shade form, from which you will feel its presence.

The Devil will also in its test seek to make you feel as if it is an initiatory point to lay the bones in a grave, and return another night when they shall be charged. This, while logically would seem appropriate, is not. The bone must remain on the Witch, at all costs. You may answer the Devil in the polite and clever way – "The power may come from within, that the shades of the dead and Hecate's arms shall enfold my very being – I shall keep the bone with no change of mind". The spirit may also create a paranoid environment and send the aura of danger around you. Be resilient and focused, and do not allow your mind to loose control and you Will.

The present author undertook this form of the Toad Rite on the date of.

MOON IN AQUARIUS April 23rd (Toad was found by Omen Toad Sigil sent to Akhtya Seker Arimanius from Alogos), Ritual Began April 28th, 29th and 30th, Walpurgisnacht. The night of the ending ritual was undertaken in the same cemetery, where the Devil appeared in the form of Logic to ask, "Might you leave thy pouch and bones here, under a tomb, where I shall grant it the power of the shades which walk the cemetery? You can feel their presence, and you know this will pass.", and was also presented in a test of image and confrontation by viewing a fatal accident later that night/early morning.

I found logic to be a difficult problem, as it was logical to leave the bones on the last night of the rite, to return on Walpurgisnacht day and retrieve them. I refused politely and I finished the ritual….I passed the test against my common perception of logic – the greatest of all tests which evoke thought and decisions. The Coven members and I then went 50 miles south, to a Beach to perform a Walpurgisnacht Rite, which ended in a Widdershins walk about the circle to raise the sinistral essence of Hecate – Lucifer and Leviathan.

We then drove 7 miles out back towards our city to discover an automobile accident which had just happened. The victim was lying in the center of the highway, after being tossed out of his destroyed truck – his head missing! We took this as an Omen, from which our rite had brought us to a new threshold – we shall pass in this Work!

An alternative of the Toad Rite presented here is the Aleister Crowley version, in which the magician crucifies the Toad on a cross after performing numerous prayers to the creature. The symbolism is the Serpent (Magician) crucifying Christ (The Toad) to pass through the veils of initiation. It is also a rite to obtain a familiar spirit which is associated with the bones.

The Grimoire above (encircle with serpent and toad skin), with Kangling/human thigh trumpet

Toad Sorcery

The bone charm of a toad is said to grant the power of controlling animals, humans and a general extension of the one who performed it. What must be understood in a modern context is, that by undertaking the ritual and emerging from the ritual itself the mind is more attuned and alert, able to carefully define momentary situations which may be handled in a manner which leads to a positive reaction later. This is special thought used in the mundane world. Remember, the Toadwitch becomes as Lucifuge, as one of the Spirits and a Son/Daughter of Hecate. We must be able to exist and present this Nocturnal Nobility of Self. Your ability for Sorcerous Workings and Spells to manifest will be shown by this manner as well. Record your results; be pleased enough with your success to go further.

The Ritual of Lucifuge
The Night Familiar

As one has passed the Ritual of the Toadbone, and become as a Toadwitch, their perception will change and instincts heighten. I may state that the individual who passes will indeed look at life as being more sacred and precious, and enjoying the here and now to the extent of proper planning of personal goals. Lucifuge is the dreaded shadow which takes the half bestial form as a pact making familiar. Lucifuge refers in this context to a spirit which will prove very effective towards the sorcerer who has successfully conducted the Toad Rite.

Purpose of Rite – To gain the insight of the fallen angel, Lucifuge, as a shadow aspect – a Sabbatic familiar who has both the combined demonic and angelic aspects which serves as a model of the sorcerers' self.

The Conjuration of Lucifer:

LUCIFER, OUIA, KAMERON, ALISCOT, MANDESUMINI, POEMI, ORIEL, MAGREUSE, PARINOSCON, ESTIO, DUMOGON, DIVORCON, CASMIEL, HUGRAS, FABIEL, VONTON, ULI, SODIERNO, PETAN! Venite, Lucifer. So it shall be.

The Circle should be drawn in a manner of which it is connected with the sorcerer. It should hold all the attributes of his or her higher self. This may be done in such a way as divine names that relate to the Holy Guardian Angel/Angelic Familiar, etc.

One may create a talisman or sigil with the image of Lucifuge on one side and the circle of Goetic Evocation on the other. This circle was drawn by Levi and represents infernal evocation. A proper description of the circle is found in "THE BOOK OF BLACK MAGIC" by Arthur Edward Waite from "The Goetic Circle of Black Evocations and Pacts", according to Eliphas Levi.

"The circle is formed from the skin of the victim, fastened to the ground by four nails taken from the coffin of an executed criminal. The skull is that of a parricide; the horns those of a goat; the male bat opposite the skull must have been drowned in blood; and the black cat, whose head forms the fourth object on the circumference of the circle, must have been fed on human flesh."

The imagery used is exceptional, except the reality of this being created in such a way in these times is highly illegal and unlikely (and not suggested, endorsed or tolerated by the present author). Make a suitable copy of the circle and bind it to the back of the chosen Lucifuge Sigil as a conjuration aspect. The creative imagination is essential here, as with all forms of magick and sorcery. Envision yourself creating the circle piece by piece, and your mindset will increase accordingly to the working.

You may take the sigil into the graveyard of which you conducted the Toad Rite, or another place of haunting. Prepare your own circle accordingly, and surround your imagination with art of Goetic Evocation (see the Levi circle or Michael W. Ford's **GOETIC SORCERY – A Luciferian Grimoire**). If unable to work in the cemetery for whatever technicality, you may adorn your ritual chamber accordingly. Have with you the bone charm or crystal which was kept in the pouch. This is a focus part of the familiar of the Toad Rite itself. A skull may be placed upon the altar of art, of which is the sorcerous vessel of Lucifuge, which shall be connected with the Sigil/Talisman you have prepared. The whole focus of the rite is not to gain petty treasure, or to sell your soul. A Luciferian is a lover of self and views no God above him, the idea of selling the soul is a Christian concept in base, as they have no true love for the self and see the self as impermanent compared to the conceptual vision of God. Lucifuge shall be a Night Familiar, a guide and initiatory force to build and strengthen the mind.

If you have a thigh bone trumpet, you may move widdershins around the circle, sounding the trumpet at each quarter. Envision the graves opening and the shades coming forth to the sound. If you do not have a trumpet made of human bone (this are obtainable from Tibetan import dealers and Buddhist stores often), you may hold the call up in front of your face and vibrate a low mantra summoning the spirits.

"NEBIROS, I summon thee from the abode in darkness, to come peacefully unto me, as I seek thy assistance of calling the forces of Night. Nebiros, shall the dead come forth. Necromancer, grant me thy hidden knowledge peacefully..."

Take now your dagger of art, and place the Sigil of Lucifuge within or on the skull. Focus on the shadow image of Lucifuge and evoke him:

"Emperor Lucifer, Lord of rebel spirits and guardian of the serpent-path, I summon thy spirit Lucifuge Rofocale unto this circle, to this meeting place of spirits, to shadow forth Lucifuge, who fly's unto the shadow world of the in-between. I conjure thee into this vessel, into this circle, move and appear in whatever form you wish…by the fallen angel who brought unto us wisdom, from a sky forlorn in it's majesty..come Lucifuge, come now….I do summon and evoke thee – by the deathless mask of Lucifer, being shadow and flame, water and ear and by the Air of which you shall fly Come forth!"

"Emperor Lucifer, Master and Prince of Rebellious Spirits, I adjure thee to leave thine abode, in whatsoever quarter of the world may be situated, and come hither to communicate with me. I conjure thee in the Name of the Satandar, Belial and Crimson Harlot who rides the Dragon, to appear in this Vessel, to respond in a clear and intelligible voice, point by point, to all that I shall ask thee, enter this skull and dwell within as your home and tomb, be as Cain and walk the earth O Lucifuge."

"By this sigil of Infernal Evocation, By this sigil of Lucifuge Rofocale, by the Sign of the Crossroads I summon thee!"

"Lucifuge, you shall reside within this skull, to be of inspiration and of my essence. You shall answer faithfully that of which I request, and bring forth your spirits of which you command, being Baël, Agares, and Marbas. By the sacred fire of the Torch, and by the Crossroads and the places of the Dead – Lucifuge Arise, descend and take now the flesh. In the name of Satandar, thou serpent soul of Azazel, who walks the earth, In the name of Cain, Baphomet-Temohpab who walks the earth and commands the spirits of night – Hearken and come forth!"

"So mote it be."

You may focus upon the image of Lucifuge entering the skull vessel, and this essence is entered also into the talisman which you have prepared. This shall be your guide in dreaming and waking, and nothing shall yet stand in your way.

The rite may be closed by a thank you and a gift of some food or honey within the graveyard.

If you ever wish to dismiss the spirit, conduct a rite, thanking him for his service and banish him peacefully.

This Grimoire was written around the time of Walpurgishnacht and is a record and book on working with the forces described. The author and publisher accept no responsibility for the use or misuse of this book. This work is intended as spiritual in nature, and no violence nor illegal activity is suggested or meant in anyway to come into play. This grimoire is also a dangerous spiritual Work, which may curse or bless the practitioner.

Those who intend misuse are hereby cursed by the Patron Spirits of the Toad Rite and this Booklet, being Satandar – Lucifuge and the Necromancies of Nebiros, in Three they Walk, In Three they Fly the Light…

Those who intend to use the Book in the an Ascending Manner are hereby Blessed by the Patron Spirits of the Toad Rite, being Satandar – Lucifuge and Hecate. It is the entire essence of the Toad Rite that Alchemically one dives the depths of darkness to then emerge in the Sun. One may contemplate the essence of this Book by the Toad Sigil of the Three Staves and Forkes which emerge from the Sun. The Averse Triangle is that of Darkness and Water. The Great Work may bless those who come strong and ready, and the Devil's Kiss may then awaken with the ecstasy of Fire.

Circle chant of charging the toadbone

(For the summoning/channeling of the energy of the Bonecharm)

The Lord's Prayer Reversed is used to control and focus the bone during the ritual, it is said to summon the devil, chant and vibrate the words while envisioning your desire.
Nema live morf reviled tub. Noitatpmet otni ton su dael dna su tsniaga ssapsert taht meht evigrof ew sa, sessapsert ruo su evigrof dna. Daerd yliad ruo yad siht su evig. Nevaeh ni ti sa htrae ni enod eb lliw yht. Emoc modgnik yht. Eman yht eb dewollah, neveah ni tra hcihw rehtaf ruo.

Zrraza umpesha narasta
Zodozio zrraza umpesha hekau
Hekas Hekas infernum barasha
By serpent and dragons eye
By wolf and dog howling night
Arise in the light of the Sun, Beast of my Soul
Arise in the Light of the Moon, Goddess of Death-Filled Crossroads
By this charm received in the Devil's Eye
By the rot of the tomb, and the blood of the moon
By Toad and Ahrimanic Bane, shall the Serpent's Eye reveal in flame
Crossroads and graveroads shall the dead bless this bone
Hekas, Hekas Infernum!

The Black Mass

(Solitary version)

The Black Mass should be by design a ritual of opposition – of adversarial rebellion against a structure or belief. In this, the Black Mass presented here is that and more – it is by design a means of affirming the strength and possibility of self, as well as the joys of life and the study of death. Balance is the key to a Working's Success, and the Black

Mass presented here is a useful tool for one who has passed through the Toad Ritual and emerged from the depths of the abyss.

"Our Father which wert in heaven, hallowed be thy name. Thy kingdom come on earth. Thy will be done in earth as it is in hell. Give us this night the blood of the Crimson Harlot, who devours as Yram-Satrina. And we shall trespass, and gain the forbidden knowledge of the darkness. And lead us into temptation. Deliver us to evil. Amen. Lucifer Triumphans!

I speak now the words which call upon the Shadow essence of Lucifer, who fell from heaven yet rose again as Christ. Hail unto the blood of the Dragon, who sanctifies the great Crimson Harlot, our mother and lover, black and devouring, strong and immortal.

I speak now the verse against the Sun, I speak the verse against the natural order, for I now wear the Devil's Skin, the serpent flesh upon the hide of the beast.

Nema live morf reviled tub. Noitatpmet otni ton su dael dna su tsniaga ssapsert taht meht evigrof ew sa, sessapsert ruo su evigrof dna. Daerd yliad ruo yad siht su evig. Nevaeh ni ti sa htrae ni enod eb lliw yht. Emoc modgnik yht. Eman yht eb dewollah, neveah ni tra hcihw rehtaf ruo.

We open now the Gates of Hell, which through the blackened Sun Lucifer shall arise!

Zazas Zazas Nasatanada Zazas

To Satan, the Bringer of Life by the Rebellion against the destroyer of self!

Behold, I stare into the mask of Our Lord the Devil, who came forth to be independent. It is Azazel, the Desert Walking fire spirit who embraced humanity with the spark of life, be revealed!

Behold, I wear the cloak of Serpent Skin, wrapped and covered in the skin of the Wolf and Goat, horned splendor of the wild, I am the Left Handed Initiator, who is found in the nightside dream, the depths of the self revealed!

I affirm Satan, who is a mask for the triumphant Angel of Light who bears the Emerald Crown. Let my death confirm the dedication to Life eternal, that I shall rise from the dead again, immortal and awakened.

I affirm thee Lucifer, who fell from the light, to sacrifice and learn the pleasures and wisdom of darkness. It was you that discovered the independent consciousness, that spark of life eternal. Lucifer, O sun souled seraph, known through time as Azazel – Set, who brought life to the world, spirit who casts shadow from Light.

Noctifer, who brings nightmares and great dreams, hail to thee who has sacrificed himself to taste the darkness, the very Ahrimanic shadows which behold treasures not seen by mortal man. Hail to thee Luciferia, Noctulia called Hecate-Lilith, Mother of the Path of the Left Hand I summon thee. I as Lucifer shall descend to taste of thy Phantasmal Cup of Hecate-Lilith, the blackened and triple formed goddess of shades, whose song is the howling of dogs and the musick of bones. O' blackened skull faced Yram, Mother of Harlots, embracer of the fallen Azazel and thy Son, Cain, shadowed as Ankou, immortal wanderer and Witch King of the Elphame.

The Magnificat, Prayer of the Scarlet Whore and Harlot, Witch Queen Yram-Satrina
I, Priest/Priestess of the Crimson Caul and Noctifer, the Shadow of Lucifer, do proclaim the hymns sung in desert lands and deep forests to thee, O Goddess of the Crossroads. I affirm Noctulia Yram-Satrina, sacred black goddess who is Unholy yet anointed in the blood of immortality, embraced by the Dragon of Darkness. Hail unto He, Lucifer, who casts the Lowly from their thrones and the Mighty devour the weakened spirits who cannot face the eternal flame.
O Harlot Immaculate, Mother of Cain and My Mother
O Whore Immaculate, Mother of Cain and my Mother, from thy depths cast your wanting eyes of lust upon me. I am filled with the Desire and Will in the knowledge of thy divinity and life giving blood, given from the veins of the Dragon. I am not a slave of the Devil but yet his child, independent and God like in my aspired Will. I shall live in SIN and the joys of life, yet illuminate my being in the blackened flame, to walk the Ghost Roads beyond as Ankou. I entrust myself wholly to you. I consecrate my heart to thee forever, my only desire being to love my self and drink deep from thy cup of Venom and Blood, Hail to thy Son Cain. Yram-Satrina, I am becoming in thy coils and shall walk the thorn ridden path unscathed, I am thy Son and Lover, Hail unto thee Noctulia. Blessed is the Crimson Harlot, from whose Cup of Fornication I am blessed. Amen.

Exalted Lady who rides the infernal dreams of her children, who come in the twilight roads Cauled and Hooded in crimson and ebony, who with the black flame of their eyes are both Vampyre and Shade, who taste of the Sabbat, let thy passions be brought unto this Mass of the Devil's Kin.

Witch Queen and Serpent Lady of the Crossroads, embrace with the Dagger and Blood Letter, caress with the Thorn and fly with the wings of the Owl. The wolves accompany you, Owls shall fly forth to serve you, Hail unto thee Moon Quartered Goddess of Howling and Devouring, O Noctulia Yram – Lilit – Satrina!

THE DEVIL'S MASK
Behold the Face of Our Lord the Devil, who with serpents tongue and Sun Envenomed Stave do you awaken your children. I summon thee Lord of Crossroads, Come thou forth and behold my prayers of creation- O' Thou Noctifer, who fell from heaven to be immortal in the darkness, Praise unto this this day. Arise again as Lucifer, towards the Sun and uplift our souls! Hail thou Serpent and Dragon souled essence, Lucifer – Azazel!
As I trample the Cross, I take the mark again of Cain, of the Beast and shall live eternally. Sathan – Initiator, I spit on the sign of the Virgin, for she is a defilement upon all True Women. There is no god but the Devil, who resides in the heart and mind of all who are independent and mindful, knowing we shall taste the pleasures of both hell and heaven. As Lucifer, we know both darkness and light.
WIDDERSHINS AROUND THE TRAMPLED CROSS
I summon thee, Demon and Lover, Self Awakened Shadow!
I call unto thee, my very shadow and bestial self, I am crowned as the Black Christ
I am the Antichrist who sleeps with the Harlots of Satrina, my Mother and Wife
I am the Dragon-Brood who has united both the Sun and the Moon.
I take the dream form of serpent-wolf-owl and beast, I fly forth rubbed with the Devil's Save to the Infernal Conclave of shades and phantoms, succubi and vampyres.
The falling star is my averse sign which is Life, Strength and Pleasure – It is isolate intelligence, Divinity joined with Common Clay – I am awakened as the Kin of the Fire Djinn, Shaitan be praised!"

During the Solitary Version (hold the Bonecharm and widdershins in a motion with your wrist, focusing entirely on the words you are speaking.)

The Black Cross fetish was created upon the working of the second Toad Rite in 2004 by the author. This fetish contains the Sigil of the Crossroads in the form of two Cat Familiar bones, a toad skin crucified, cat teeth and the toad sigil at the base. The four daemon familiars as Astaroth/Andar, Lucifer/Ahriman, Asmodeus/Aeshma and Azazel. The cross was consecrated using menstrual blood and the blood of the author, binding with spells and focused workings. Between Astaroth and Lucifer is the Serpent Skin, representing the union of the red and black serpents.

Chapter Three

Persian Sorcery

Yatukan/Ahrimanic Witchcraft

I. Yatuk Dinoih

The Yatuk Dinoih is a Persian (Pahlavi) term meaning Witchcraft or Sorcery. This grimoire is a modern interpretation of primal darkness and the body of shadow which may be encircled and controlled by the sorcerer who seeks to work within the mysteries of the Adversary. The sorcerous path of Black Witchcraft proves a most challenging pathway, as it is against the motions of the natural order. It is involves thought, balance, will and self-control to properly and successfully move through it. The Left Hand Path moves in this direction as it envenoms/empowers or destroys/devoures the practitioner. This may be understood, as written by the ancient priests of Zoroastrianism, that he who practices the sorcery of the Dev (demon or daeva) becomes like the demon (often called Druj, meaning serpent and lie). Thus in initiating through the path of the Yatus (sorcerer or witch) or Pairikas (female witch, companion of Yatus or she-devil and fairy) the path becomes one with the practitioner, thus their own way which stands different and apart from all others.

Approach the Yatuk Dinoih as you would an ancient tome of magick. It provides a grammer and method which invokes the primal darkness inherent in the deepest recesses of the earth and the self. Know that each Druj or Daeva/Dev which you summon should be done so with Willed purpose and intent, save the dabbler be cursed accordingly by his or her own hand. The Left Hand Path does not suffer fools glady, it will tease and devour those who may not have the mind to become through it. Once you have entered, there is no turning back.

A h r i m a n

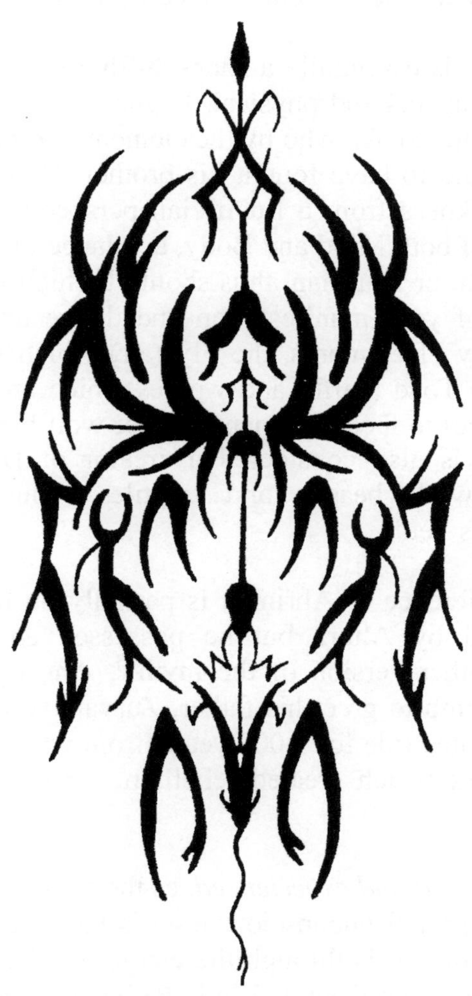

Ahriman or Angra Mainyu is the ancient Persian spirit or demon of darkness. A God associated with the Yatuk Dinoih[65], the ancient Persian system of hidden witchcraft and sorcery. Ahriman was the shadow which existed between the veils of light and shadow. The Prince of Darkness is indeed the embodiment of the Left Hand Path[66], in that Ahriman is modeled as an Isolate Being independent from the natural order. He exists

[65] Yatuk Dinoih translates Witchcraft, and is represented as the religion of Sorcerers, Witches and Wizards. The Bundahishn "Creation" or Knowledge from the Zand - Sacred Books of the East, Oxford, 1897

[66] See Lords of the Left Hand Path, by Stephen E. Flowers

beyond that veil of light and is immortalized in darkness. Angra Mainyu or Ahriman is the Lord of the Druj[67], which are demons or isolate intelligences (shades) which are as well sorcerers. In traditional Zoroastrian mythology and religious texts, the Druj is horrifying and demonic. In the context of this writing such spirits are models of Antinomian thought and self-deification, and should be viewed in such a manner. One should not look at the Workings of the Yatuk Dinoih as a physical grimoire, rather than a spiritual one, with the aim of self-transformation. Violence is strictly condemned. While the sorcerer is hidden within the fabric of its own inherent culture, many rites and workings are of the secret and cunning path. One particular essence is that of Ahriman. This Godform symbolizes the attainment and control of matter and Sabbatic Dream Control.

Ahriman or Angra Mainyu is essentially a shapeshifting sorcerous principle of magick, who is balanced as both spiritual and physical. In some Zoroastrian tales, Ahriman first manifested in the world as the Snake who by the element Air, brought darkness into light. Angra Mainyu was also said to have fought his brother Ahura Mazda in the form of a Dragon. The spirit of Darkness from a Luciferian perspective manifests the mind and seeking the very mastery of both Mind and Body, a balance of both. The very self can be seen as a Temple to Suetkh, or Ahriman, thus should be highly respected, kept in health and used to be a vessel of your manifestation and desire upon earth. Other forms of Ahriman relate his mastery of elements, the Fly (air) which relates him to Beelzebub, snake (fire and water), the Toad (earth) and wolves which are sacred to Angra Mainyu and used in ancient sacrifices to feed Ahriman by offer wolf blood to holes and chasms in the earth. Angra Mainyu is also considered a creator of Desert Lands, cold winds, darkness, winter, all wild beasts and reptiles, thus displaying his close connection/manifestation as Set.

The Left Hand Path in reference to Ahriman is partially on his creation. In some text, Ahriman was not created by Ahura but he possessed an isolate and independent existence, or psyche. Another version of the myth[68], Ahriman first heard his fathers' word, and rip from the womb to greet his father, Zurvan, who replied he was dark and stinking. Ahriman was granted rule for 9,000 years, from which indicated by Will against his father granted the spark which created rebellion. Ahriman still was an isolate and independent existence.

The darkness must be observed and experienced, as the avenue of which there is nothing. The void (elder darkness, primal unconsciousness) is the arcana of the living flesh, the keyhole into the subconscious. It is through the elements of union that we may grow in our temple of being to enflesh our desires. While **Ruha-AZ (called also JEH)**, being the feminine force of Ahriman represents **Babalon**, the great dreaming body of the sacred whore, or **Lilith**, Lilitu are the command of the lunar cycle, allow the blood congealed to form under the desire of the witch, the Sacred Creation of the Hidden Servitor or Familiar.

[67] Druj translates Lie and is symbolized by the Pahlavi books as falsehood. Lie is also associated with the word against the sun, thus symbolizing the shadow or vampyric essence.

[68] The Zurvanite Myth, The Dawn and Twilight of the Zoroastrianism, R.C. Zaehner, New York, 1961.

The form of Ahriman is Draconis, the Black Dragon from which all emerge into their own solitary being, from a Left Hand Path perspective, and fall to subconsciously. Druj is translated LIE as well as connected with Dragon. Those who walk the path of shadows, which is of ecstasy, shall know the fruits of the awakened, perceived sense of self, the "I" of the arcana. The goal of Left Hand Path Sorcery is NOT to become a Shell, but to sharpen, strengthen and develop the individual, isolate consciousness – to be as shadow, as Ahriman itself.

Ahriman or Angra Mainyu created Six archdemons to pervert/awaken mankind. They are Akoman (Aka Manah), Savar (Sauru), Andar (Indra), Nakahed (Naonhaithya), Tairev (Taurvi) and Zairich. These daevas or divs are essential deific masks within the circle of the Yatuk Dinoih, these primal energies represent facets of individual initiation.

The Great Letters and Sigil of Ahriman, known as the Dragon of Darkness, which may be as a word of Ahriman in Avestan, or a illustration which depicts the spirit of darkness.

The Preliminary Invocation and Announcement of Self-Immolation, the Sacred Luciferian Vision of the Infernum.

The circle, if the sorcerer uses one, indicates that it should be made with the system related to the Yatuk Dinoih, the grand awakening of a sleeping religion and initiatory system of Persian Sorcery. Let your circle be cast, to represent the Dragon itself – the very circumference of your being. Thus a circle is not a protection, rather a gathering place of shadow. This is the focus point of your sorcery (to en-circle).

Take the Athame, sacred blade of Druj[69] and the blade cast in the Forge of the Black Man of the Sabbat, invoking upon the points of the Ahrimanic Sigil of Entering:

"Ahriman, who brings Hesham, who is of Samahe, I stand within the circle of the worm to invoke the mysteries of the ancient source of creation and destruction. From which that you have spoken to me in the sacred dreaming temple, in the Garden of the Arcana of Azothoz, the primal initiator of opposites. I invoke thee! Ahriman, that which opposes the natural order, to become as Alpha Omega itself, as God itself, to create and destroy. Ahriman, who communes with the ancient dead, sleeping and lusting for the living flesh, I invoke thee! Ahriman, from the ruins of the desert, I call you from your place in the darkness. You who marks form from shadows, daemons of the caves of the earth, I invoke thee! To your consort, AZ, primal goddess of blood and darkness, who manifests as Lilith and Babalon, come forth, lift your crimson veil and let me taste of your infernal treasures. In the core of your very being shall I shake the foundations of the sacred pillar of Life, absorb its secrets and emerge through the Perfect and illuminated Temple of Darkness! I invoke thee! I shall come forth as an avatar upon earth! Come forth within me!"

"O maker of the material world, O sacred Druj, I summon thee!"

"Alas, the gates of twilight open before me. The dagger drips the blood of the wretched and weak. Would the sacrifice of the howling wolves seek my very soul? Yet, I may brave them, not stopping to witness their fangs inches away from the very soul. Algol itself shall tear through me, yet it is a mirror of my own perfection, being and possibility. I go forth through the Arcana of Dreaming and waking, let Ahriman be my guide of shadows!"

Focus upon your consciousness and what Ahriman represents. In solitude you shall summon and in isolation will the Blackened Flame ignite. Understand that your Words make flesh your desires, so choose your creations carefully. Listen to the voices of the shadows, but more importantly that of your own Mind (**Aka Manah**).

Take the time to meditate on the shape shifting qualities of Ahriman. He is known to have taken the form of a Toad, or a Snake, of a Dragon. Animals which were said to be created and are sacred to Ahriman are Wolves, Ants, Serpents, Toads, etc. You may wish

[69] Druj is also symbolic of Dragon and snake. The snake is said to speak lies, but those who may listen, wisdom.

to meditate upon changing into each form, allowing by dream to go forth and see as they would see – RECORD YOUR RESULTS!

Invocation to AZ

The Great Demon Whore – Mother of Witchcraft

AZ first appeared as a weapon given to Ahriman. It was said Ahriman gave an attack on the spiritual world[70], and he was thrown back into the Abyss for a time. Many demons sought to raise Ahriman from his great sleep and nothing would work. The Great Whore came forth to awaken Ahriman, and woke him with stating that she would "Take away the dignity of Blessed Man". Ahriman stood and glowed with unnatural life and came from the Abyss again. This "Demon Whore"[71] as referred to is none other than AZ, the "weapon of concupiscence." AZ[72] is the Witch Queen and Bride of Ahriman, a Mother of Demons. The flesh she takes later is that of Lilith, the Hebrew Demon Queen who was the embodiment of sorcery, succubi and sexual congress. AZ represents that which is most feared among all religions, Women as a Strong and cunning force. It is also written that the Devil's (Ahriman) Kiss causes menstruation, and such is a highly abhorred occurrence among the Zoroastrians.

Az is also closely connected in Buddhism, and is an enemy of the Buddhist mind. The principle of the cause of conditioned existence is a word, *Avidya*, meaning 'ignorance' and such a principle manifestation is *trshna*, being 'Thirst'. AZ devours and drinks deep the lifeblood in a desire for continued existence in time. She is isolate and individual consciousness, a dual Bearer of the Black Flame. She is matched only by Ahriman, the Prince of Darkness.

The People of the Lie, those who are initiated by spiritual deed in the Yatuk Dinoih are Left Hand Path practitioners, that is, we seek to isolate, strengthen and promote continued existence beyond the traps of flesh, but through flesh as well. We, just as Ahriman, love life, and seek to make it stronger by means of self-deification through antinomian thought. When approaching AZ as the Queen of the Circle, know that she too resides with the Dead, yet she does not devour them always. AZ may also be considered the same as the Hindu KALI (interestingly enough, one of the 17 names of LILITH) and Hecate, the Grecian Goddess of the Dead.

---

[70] The Teachings of the Magi, R.C. Zaehner, London 1956

[71] Selections of Zatsparam and The Dawn and Twilight of the Zoroastrianism, R.C. Zachner, NY 1961

[72] AZ is concupiscence, lust and greed – she is also called Varan, which is sexual desire and interestingly enough Religious Doubt. This is symbolic of the rebellious and Luciferian Mind, that which perceives itself and doubts higher authority. Az is this force which take in anthropomorphic form, LILITH, and the Witch Woman who frees herself from bonds. Az is also a balancing force within Man, and Ahriman and Az awakened is a comparable magickal formula to Aleister Crowley's Beast and Babalon Conjoined.

TEMPLE:

To be adorned in images of death, crimson and the feminine aspects of dark witchcraft, such as Babalon riding the Dragon, Kali, Lilith, Hel and all of the dark goddesses of Wicca, Sabbatic Witchcraft and other mythologies throughout history. The altar itself should be adorned in crimson and shades of blood red, with the sigil of Babalon hanging in the front of the altar. Keep in mind this force is the universal Daemonic Goddess, she takes many forms all of which are difficult for the uninitiated to understand. Keep this ritual to yourself if you or anyone in your coven performs it. This rite is designed to issue forth the Dragon goddess to manifest in either the Witch or the Warlock, regardless of sexual preference, gender orientation and identification. Each individual within the path of the Yatuk Dinoih should be prepared to explore both the feminine aspects of their being as well as the masculine. Unity is through moving through opposites.

"The Abyss which gave me being has no bounds over my existence. I, who am known as the Blood Goddess AZ stand before the Eye of Ahriman, awakened and alive. I hold the cup of fornication, the elixir of life, to announce and rejoice in my divinity. I am the Great Whore, presiding over the Sabbat of witches, to let all taste of my joys. I stand before all other white goddesses, those who in their happy fields have grown from my darkness, my shadow to proclaim them as unfertile, barren and rotting from their fear and lack of balance. I kiss them gently as a mother then with a movement of my mind, rape and spill their blood into my cup of desire. I am the goddess of death and life. I join in rapture with the Infernal Dragon, Ahriman, whom brings my joy in rapture and union.

Upon the back of the Beast I ride, and brought forth the Antichrist who shall grow unseen before and through many. The age of ignorance and servitude is over. The While fornicating, call my names that are many, AZ, BABALON, LILITH. Spill your seed in my name, in my glory and in my desire. I am the model for which all women shall seek to channel. My gateway is through ecstasy, through the mirror, between the breasts of the scarlet woman.

I stand before the impotent mother called Mary and laugh at her sterile incompetence. This failure of a mother and feeble spirit that cowers behind her son is to be no more! For every woman who cannels and invokes me, whom shall take the name of Witch and Scarlet Woman shall one by erase her manifestation in this world. I shall bring the doctrines of Witchcraft through a new method, which shall be of twilight workings many can embrace. I shall not reveal all of which I am to them, as they cannot grasp my terror and beauty. This need not concern them, as my Will shall manifest through each Goddess who dares invoke me! I spit in the mouth of impotence and within me shall you find the Union of Opposition.

I am within all and may be summoned by the vessel of the skull....the blood is the life!

I am Vampyre, I am shadow, I am the Devouring Demon which drains the life of the weak, I give the Blackened Flame of Life to those who may face me...

Azi...Azaka...Ruha....Nasu...AZ..AZ....AZ!

The Druj

The Ritual of Yatukan Sorcery

The Dregvants (The Followers or People of the Lie) are those who are initiates of Sorcery, or the religion of Ahriman. Such initiation is led by instinctual opposition. It should be kept in mind that within the parameters of psychological evocation, that identification is based upon the success factor of the sorcerer. Witchcraft and Sorcery themselves are based in achievement through identification, counterbalancing restrictive aspects associated with ones own psychological make up and such. As the gateway of the Magickal Art, we must pass beyond the first definitions, as they are merely gateways, tests from which we may pass through. The ancestral shades that emerge through the living and breathing witch are in theory the parallels to our further advancement or becoming. Each whisper, chant or calling is the elemental control of our surroundings, our own individual universe and vibrations, which create effects accordingly. The Dragon that coils around our brains is the counter point of awakening, from which one aligned; our results of sorcery and magickal workings may double in positive response.

Ahriman, in the ancient Persian religion of Zoroastrianism is the personification of what is called 'The Devil', which is specifically defined as the Daevas which all emerge in darkness. Darkness, keep in mind, is the personification of the void from which we all emerge, it is Chaos and its symbol is the Chaos Sphere. The workings of this modern grimoire of Yatukan Sorcery are centered around the Sigil of ALGOL, the Chaos Star. It is this mirror which we may project our Will and the Daevas which shall be evoked emerge ultimately through this mirror.

While the ALGOL sphere is not Zoroastrian, it holds a center in the focus of darkness. The use of Art to express the 'Matter' or materialization of the Daevas is also beneficial to the Artist. It was said that Ahriman brought Smoke to Fire, to if outdoors, perform invocations with fire and smoke. Visualize Ahriman and such spirits in the smoke coming from the flames.

The Seven Archdemons of Yatukan Sorcery are the centers of antinomian advancement, from which the sorcerer may advance by their own centers of evocation and invocation. Approach these forces carefully, but boldly. The ultimate test of awakening is to invoke the Daevas from without the protection circle, in the evocation circle itself. Absorb them - let them become you. This is the way to know of your true possibility of becoming.

The Seven Archdemons are as follows:

AKA MANAH (Akoman, the Evil Mind)
INDRA (Andar, Dev of the Black Flame)
SAURU (Savar, the Lord of Daevas or Devs, corresponds with the Medieval and Gnostic Belial, the Lord of the Earth)
TAURVI (Tairev, a dev of rebellion)
ZAIRITSHA (Zairich is a dev of poison, used as a spirit of herbalism or of cursing)
NAONHAITHYA (Naikiyas, a dev of antinomian thought, rebellion, discontent, desire)
AESHMA (Asmodeus the demon of the wounding spear)

It should be noted as well that Asmodeus is of essentially Persian origin, known as Aeshma (Demon of the Wounding Spear). The name Ashmedai emerged from Hebrew and Latin and Asmodeus once was an Angel of the Seraphim, from which he fell with Lucifer or Ahriman. Jewish lore presents Asmodeus as a child of Tubal Cain and Naamah, the demon queen and former bride of Satan. The gnosis achieved through invocation with Aeshma will reveal by inspiration the foundations of the Holy law and why it was trespassed by Ahriman and the Seven Daevas. A hint to be given to the reader is that by moving against the current of laws within a belief structure lead to the strengthening of the individual, the birth of a God or Goddess. This force is essential in the advancement of the universe, often misunderstood in modern belief structures commonly understood as 'morals' in the era of social comprehension. Evoke and Invoke the mysteries from which the sorcerer may awaken their own semblance of possibility. Our forms shall be many, from which shall reflect in the mirror of Algol.

The sigil of Yatukan Sorcery in a modern context is:

ALGOL – A word which derives from the Arabic Al Ra's al Ghul, Al-Ghul, or Ri'B al Ohill, which is translated "The Demon's Head". Algol was in Hebrew known as Rosh ha Shaitan, or "Satan's Head", as some traditions have referred to Algol as the Head of Lilith. The Chinese called Algol Tseih She, which is "Piled up corpses" and was considered a violent, dangerous star due to its changing vivid colors. On some 17th century maps Algol was labeled, "The Specter's Head". Algol upon some research has indicated that possibility Three stars which are an eclipsing binary, which may explain some of the rapid color change. Some writers have connected Algol with the Egyptian Khu, or spirit. The Khu is considered a shadow spirit which feeds on other shades of the dead. In reference to the writings and initiatory symbolism of Michael W. Ford, ALGOL is the sigillized in one form as a Chaos Star with an Averse Pentagram in the center. The Pentagram refers to the Eye of Set, timeless and divine, godlike and independent. The Chaos Star is destruction, Change and power – all of which emerges from the Eye of Shaitan, or Set. It is this Chaos which then brings Order. ALGOL is the mirror of the sorcerer, one who may enter and reside in the pulsing eye of blackened flame. There are Eight God Forms which are manifested from the Center of the Chaos Star – within are Five Daemon Guardians of the Five Worlds within Hell, Helan and all are interconnected with the Center Force of Spirit of the Prince of Darkness.

There are Eight Rays emanating from this Star, they represent the following God forms:

1. **Astwihad** ***(death flyer)***
2. **Andar** ***(Black Flame, Antinomian initiation)***
3. **Lilith – AZ** ***(The Harlot and Whore)***
4. **Akoman** ***(The Evil Mind, Isolate and Antinomian intelligence)***
5. **Druj Nasu** ***(Fly goddess, demoness who devours, pollutes corpses)***

6. **Aeshma *(Demon of Wrath, the Wounding Spear)***
7. **Saurva – Savar *(A leader of Devs perhaps a form of Belial)***
8. **Taromaiti *(a demoness which twarts devotion, antinomian thought)***

The Averse Pentagram represents two aspects
One Being Isolate Consciousness, the Prince of Darkness.

There are Five Worlds of Darkness from Manichaean Mythology
Each represents a point (connecting) of the World and Daemons connected therein.
With each World there are both masculine and feminine druj who continually procreate.
The Five Worlds have a Lord Druj who is the Guardian and Master of that Sphere:

1. **Smoke – LION (Belial)**
2. **Storm – EAGLE – (Azi Dahaka)**
3. **Fire – DEMON (Shaitan or Iblis)**
4. **Mud – FISH (Leviathan)**
5. **Darkness – DRAGON (Tiamat and Azhdeha)**

The center is the Prince of Darkness, called Ahriman or Set. Ahriman has taken within attributes from each Demon and their Spheres of influence. An invocation which may be used with the Algol Sigil is below: this is meant as an encircling charge to the spirit of the Adversary and the body of shadow. You may use the ritual to encircle the primal body of darkness, to build that which you seek to form according to your desire.

A Prayer of Ahriman

O' Dragon who rushes from the North,
O Serpent Druj of Darkness, Smoke, Cold and Noxious Heat,
I summon thee
In Kalch (Filth) I call thee, by the Averse Ways of Midnight and Midday
Of Tauromat, who is the Druj of Rebellion
Below me, Nasai (Dead Matter) which strengthens my spirit – Kundak who shall carry me to the Sabbat and upon the Earth in Dreaming Flesh,
Akoman Guide me!
O Wolf Druj Ahriman
I Invoke thee....Maghaaman...Izzadraana!

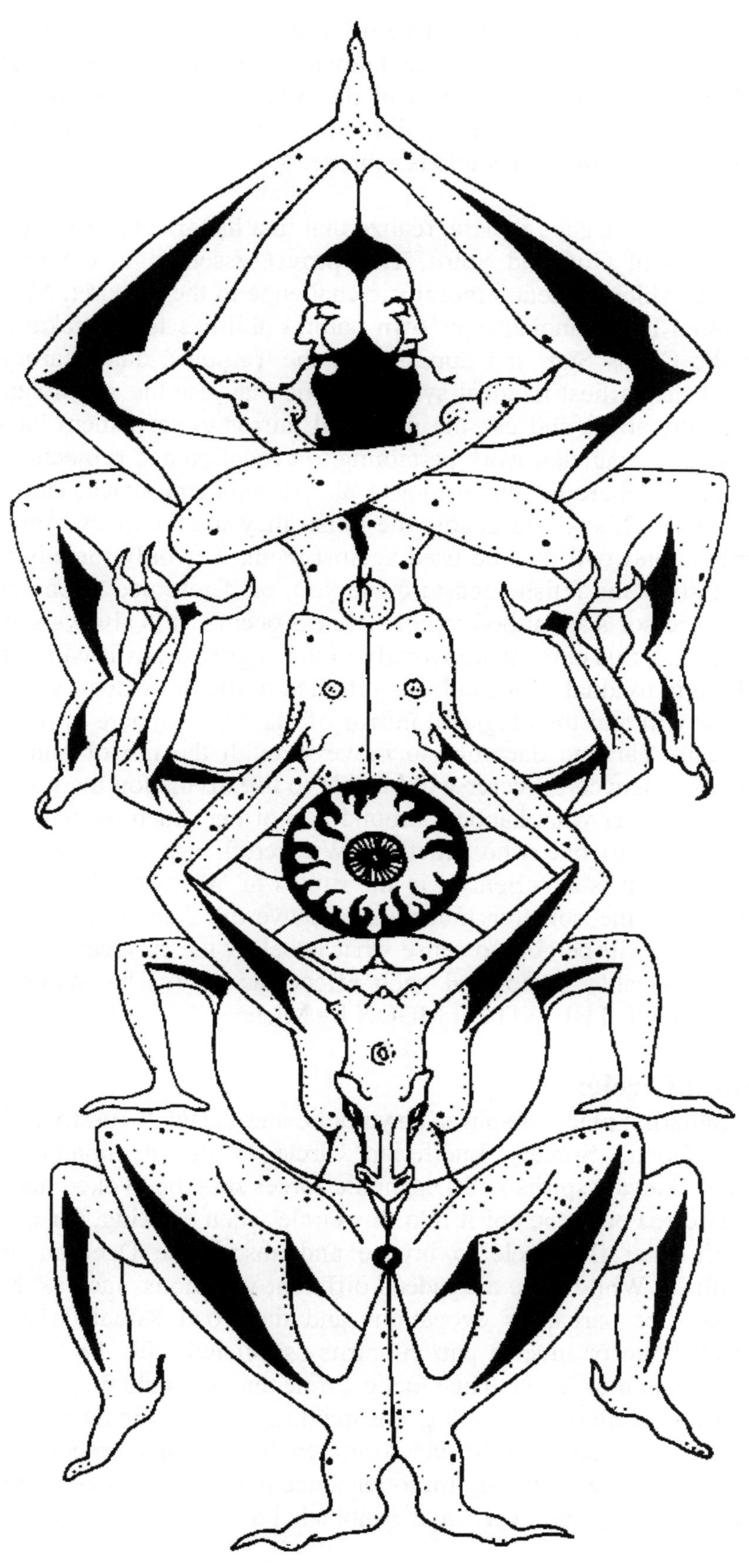

As mentioned previously, the Sigil or Eye of Algol is that of the Fallen Seraphim, the angels which dove to the abyss to taste the knowledge and become as the dragon's spirit, the serpent of the garden. Use the Mirror of the Adepts to isolate consciousness, and to place the Daevas of your summoning through, which may emerge for your desired working when the gnosis of the Temple is achieved.

When working with the Chaos Sphere, realize that in a historical sense the original chaos sigil was a symbol of God and Spirit. This proves essential in the understanding of moving past ideas which present a moralistic challenge to the sorcerer. Moving past each symbol is essential in advancing ones own natural abilities to magickal awakening. In Mesopotamia the Chaos Star first appeared in the Temples, dating around 3000 B.C. making it one of the earliest magical symbols. One may use the Algol sigil to call forth the Daemons of the abyss and use the magickal mirror to send them back. The Chaos Sphere is essential in magickal work pertaining to evocation and projecting desires. One may use the Chaos Sphere as also a tool to absorb anothers attack, causing to spell to return to the maker. This would enable the fetish they use to attack you as a means of their own torment, and will thus be used against them. The only remedy for such is for the creator to destroy the fetish used to curse you, or if returned unknown, will slowly feed from the aggressor's astral body until sickness occurs. It is always suggested for the sorcerer to send back this curse unknowingly to the aggressor, as it will lead to a healthy destruction of the individual. If the curse is returned to the individual, you will have used the force of your will and the magickal mirror of the Algol Sphere to do such, thus you may evoke certain Yatukan daemons to move through the mirror and feast from the aggressor. The experienced Sorcerer will be able to use divination methods regarding the Algol Sphere to discover what happens around him or her. Such hidden methods make a powerful background to one who practices Witchcraft, especially within the Wiccan areas. While the Witch is experienced in the rituals of Wicca or Witchcraft, the hidden dark elements make the sorcerer much more powerful than initially detected. Many experienced witches will be able to sense what is below the surface; however, the witch in question may be able to conceal such effects as well. The Witches Pyramid as discussed in BOOK OF THE WITCH MOON by Michael W. Ford.

The Evocation Circle:

The Sabbat – gathering place of spirits, a symbolic and visual "Crossroads".You may use this circle, the Goetic Sorcery Luciferian Circle or the Ahrimanic Dragon Circle (Paitisha). Many Daevas, spirits and Daemonic forces may be evoked and placed within the following circle. Focus the spirit into this circle when evoking, for once the spirit is bound, you will enter the circle to invoke and absorb the Daemon or simple seek communion with it. While there are indeed different variations, such as the Circle of the Ahrimanic Beast, for barbarous evocations and the Toad Ritual Triangle, being the calling of the Diabolic or inverse patron spirits associated with the Sun or Black Sun, with relation to Shaitan or Satan. The Goetic Circle and Triangle may be most suggested for evocations of a nature of controlling, ensorcelling the specific defined energies of the spirit. Yatukan Sorcery deals with long forgotten forces, dark embodiments of primal chaos and those who have been long forgotten since the times of ancient Persia. You may use not a circle, but only once you have established a full initiation into the Adversarial

Current and have communion with your Demon Guide, I take no responsibility for misuse of that statement. One may use the "Ahrimanic Beast Circle" for workings of invocation or summonings.

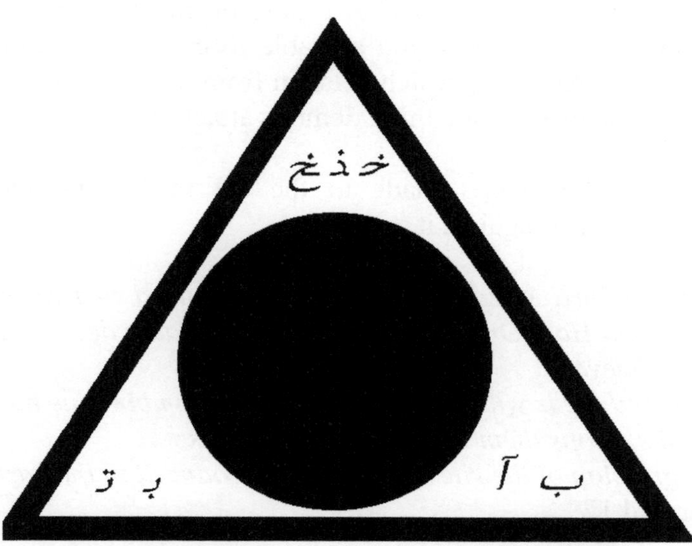

The above Triangle/Circle is a basic example, the two other types of Ahrimanic Circles are best used.
Keep in mind that Daemons and Angelic forces should be primarily understood as a part of the mind itself, and that by asserting control of the brain and the functions you Will it to accept, then can you be ready to explore the possibility of another type of reality of such forces. This may prove difficult at first, aligning belief according to the waking reality of non-existent spirits, however once the mind is TRAINED in the area of being THE ONLY GOD THAT IS, can one then deal with the objective reality of outer forces. The Daemons evoked within the circle may be too much to handle from one who has not sought the initiation of becoming, the path of self-deification.

The Ritual of Evocation

Warning – Do not attempt this ritual if you or any participant has any history of mental problems, as this will surely lead to a less than pleasant result. The forces evoked are indeed real and should be approached seriously. The author and publisher accept no responsibility for the use of this book. Use caution and you have been warned.

The sigil of the Daemons will be the ***Ancient Persian Cruciform*** from which their names were written backwards, symbolizing the reaching back of memory. After the evocation, when you wish to manifest an element of which this Daemon represents, carry the name in Cruciform on your person and envision at the moment when it is to be projected. It may be kept as a charm or such. You may also later use the sigil in Ritual Evocations and Projections with the Mirror of Algol, the Eye of Ahriman and AZ.

Concerning Sacrifice

When summoning/binding the Daevas and Druj of the Yatuk Dinoih, it is essential to offer a sacrifice of Hair, Nails or spittle to them. In Zoroastrian lore, it is a sacrifice to throw hair, nails or any such body fluid in a hole or crack where sun does not reach. When working, especially outside if you are able to create a hole or use a crack near some rocks or otherwise. Anything which is taken from man or woman, hair, etc and cast down is considered unclean and something demons attach to.

In the VENDIDAD, reference is made to the act of feeding Druj, knowingly or unknowingly, and thus warns against it.

"Zarathushtra asked Ahura Mazda: 'O Ahura Mazda, most beneficent Spirit, Maker of the material world, thou Holy One! Which is the most deadly deed whereby a man offers up a sacrifice to the Daevas?
Ahura Mazda answered: 'It is when a man here below, combing his hair or shaving it off, or paring off his nails, drops them in a hole or in a crack
'Then by this transgression of the rites, Daevas are produced in the earth"
-VENDIDAD, Fargard 17

"O Mazainya Daevas! These nails I announce and consecrate unto thee, spirits of darkness. May they be for thee so manyknives and spears, so many bows and falcon-winged arrows and so many weapons against the Sheep of the Righteous!"

The sorcerer would take a small bit of hair, or nail or something from his or herself and drop in a hole or crack while uttering the chant of sacrifice, this is an affirmation of aligning the self with the Yatuvidah current and the supposed creation of demons in the earth. ***The religious work of a Yatus, or Luciferian, is to take previously cleaned human bones and wash them in water to which you shall drink ritualistically, feeds the Druj and envenoms the sorcerer as being at one with the faith he or she develops.***

Calling of the Shadow

Under the stars which emerge of AZ, from the tombs of the mighty dead, I do call and summon thee, from which I am the shadow of form, black and hungered for the nourishment of the living shade. Andar under thy cloak of hidden darkness, to me! Awaken to my rite:

The Sacrifice

Offer now some of your own hair, nails, spittle or sexual sacrifice in the designated hole or crack while chanting:

By Paitisha and Hesham I offer this to thee, for I am Dregvantem, and Daevayasnanam whose word is Druj. Take my sacrifice of my life force and give back your blessings and assistance, for we are one and the same. I feed the shadows to expand the darkness.

The Summoning of Ahriman

I summon thee, Arimanius, Armiluss,
Come thou forth from thy dire mansion
Ensorcel me in shades and by dream – BECOME!
By flame and lightening, the Darkness of the Abyss
I seek to ride the Dragon Azi Dahaka,
Join in flesh the Scarlet Whore, Ruha-Az,
That by wolf and serpent shall ride her flesh
Manifest through thy summoner, enfleshed Akhtya
And thy Summoned manifest as You
By the Circle Dance against the Sun DRUJ arise!
Praise unto Ahriman, whose form may be the Toad – the Gateway to the Devil's Mysteries
Praise unto Ahriman, who drinks the blood of wolves and from shadow creates their perception – the shades may enter the mind of darkness to drink deep of the blood of the moon.
Ahriman, by the Dragon encircle me!
Ahriman by the Wolf enflesh in me!
Ahriman by Khrafstras guide me!

Arimanius, Andar, so it is done!

A Sacred Hymn to Darkness:

And to that one of beings (of daevayasnanam) whose superior in the becoming of Akoman, of Ahriman, who knows and who gives Daevodata, whose Yatus and Parikas do we become as, who shall we worship ourselves through!

Pihsrow ew od sgnieb elamef dna elam esohw elamef lla fo esoht dna ssnsuoethgir sih morf dna, swonk adzam aruha ecifircas eht ni roirepus esohw sgnieb foe no that dna!
(Let a small drop of spittle hit the candle or touch the flame with spit on your finger or hand)

Evocation of the Daeva

I shall take baptism in Nasa, the rite of shadowed Nahn, in the desire of the serpent.

O blessed shadow, serpent and wolf, Arimanius, Ahriman, who fell from the light of sterility to taste the pleasure of shadows, and to know the darkness. I evoke thee, Daeva **NAME** *by the keys of Paitisha, and of Hesham, the paths of darkness, the unspoken letters of AZOTHOZ.*

Howling unto the desert sands, shall the Daeum emerge as the Moon sleeps. From this eclipse will the passion of shadows draw neigh. Hail and come forth, spirits of darkness and hungered shadows hearken and manifest spirits of the abyss.
Bringer of the key of immortality, do come forth unto this place, by the ancient laws of the calling, I evoke thee! By Smoke and Fire, by the Flies and Jackals, by the dragon and bleeding whore, blessed spirit of the Linage of Kabed-us-Spae – Akht-Jadu!

Specter and shadow, demon and angel, I seek the knowledge of the arcana of Ahriman – hear me now! Draconian shadow, Druj, allow me the forbidden light.

From the Essence of Kabeb-us-Spae, forgotten through the mountains of which you lurk, take shadow form, friendly and non malicious unto me, within this circle. I conjure thee O druj and dev of the forests and lonely places. I summon you to encircle me in this place, for I am Dregvantem, an initiate of the shadow path.

No sagdid may drive us away, we are Druj and Daeum, those whose sorcerous power reign upon earth.

I conjure thee, Daeum of caves and mountains, that which devours by night. I summon thee, Druj, born of Desert Wastes, child of Ahriman, bringer of darkness. Who fell to the earth with thy companions to create and bless the beasts of the field, the Azhish, do encircle me!

I stand within the circle of Witchblood, to evoke the hungering shades, to which I seek the shadows to feed from as well, to nourish myself in with the manes of Azothoz, the Voice and Spell of which Ahriman uttered to become as God itself.

Great manifestation of the Abyss, from which all emerges, I do summon thee forth. By the names INDRA, SAURU, TAURVI, AESHMA, ZAIRITSHA, NAONHAITHYA and AKA MANAH come forth! By Iklitu shall you come forth, By Iklitu shall you emerge from by my Will, Arise O Azhish, come Druj, come Daeva for I am of dragvantem, the path against all others!

The Charge
Point Evocation Dagger

Daeva **(name),**
As I touch thee with this Dagger, forged of the Fire of the Dahakem, do manifest. I name and call you by Zakaru! By Ahriman's Kiss do I conjure thee and bring thee into this space, bring the shadows to encircle me in the ecstasy of the serpent.

I do charge thee to hear my voice, which is that which gives you life, it is my Will for you to manifest now! I am Daevayasnanam, who becomes in the circle of Druj! I encircle you, Alalu, remain, Alalu, manifest, Alalu, by my Will.

The Constraint

Daeva, Appear before me in this circle, from which I have given thee form and substance. I do command thee to appear in the form which I desire, do come forth as my friend, great shade of ancestral vision. By the oath of the shadow born, Arimanius! Ahazu, Ahazu, Ahazu!! By samahe, that which we create from, that which drives us, that of which the Dragon coils, that which the Worm awakens from, remain here!

Ask now what you seek from the Daemon, and upon obtaining this information, thank it and banish/close circle. The optional ending is far more dangerous, yet offers greater rewards. Proceed with caution.

Vampiric Rite of Evocation/Invocation Version

AKALU – TIAMAT RITE

When spirit appears one should then Face the daemon and recite the following

"Daeva, great force from which we are one, I shall now join in union with you, we shall be as one. I am the arcana of the alphabet of desire, the words and visions of the Gods. Through me, within me and under my Will, you shall know the pleasures I shall taste. I enter now this circle and we shall join as one!

By Tishin, who thrists for the vein of the sleeping do I acknowledge myself as Azhish and Dregvantem, of Az and Daeum do I enflesh my spirit"

Disrobe and enter the evocation circle.

As you enter the circle you will feel a force overtake you, it will be of prime and beautiful demonic ecstasy, and in bringing the force in you will obtain visions you would and would not like to share. The ecstasy itself is only describable in how Zos vel Thanatos sought to manifest forms in the Book of Ugly Ecstasy. Allow the ecstasy to overtake you and at the very moment of what would be the 'peak' if you will, ABSORB AND DEVOUR this force. Use the strength of your Will to overtake any aspect of its consciousness, the shadow then will join with you. As a Vampiric rite of Evocation, you will master the spheres of the living and dead. Once one uses this ritual to pass through each Daemon of the Yatuk Dinoih, shall the pleasures of the night be revealed! Here is the initiation into the rite of predatory spiritualism, to absorb that which is evoked!

Once the invocation is over, you will feel whole and drained at the same time.

Approach the altar and take the Kapala (Skull cup) or Chalice-

I drink now of the ecstasies of death and sex, my union with the arcana of the infernal shall be of bright illumination! Hail the manifestation of the darkness and flesh, Arimanius! Hail unto the force of Light and Wisdom, Ahriman! So it is done!

Banish and close circle.

Cursing

Cursing is essential at one time or another, but you should take caution as to when you deem it appropriate. Ensure that you are not overreacting and carefully plan it out. As one grows in their sorcerous knowledge, you will be able to utilize the traits of Mitrokht, Eshm, Arashk and Sej, the Evil Eye which is the stare which causes discomfort and cursing. As you stare within the circle of Daevodata, gathering shadows and forming them from your own body of Light, invoke their essence and power, stare within their sigils and image, invite it within to absorb traits accordingly. Do not allow emotions to overtake you, rather consume them. It must be known that when you enter and grow strong in the Yatuk-Dinoih (witchcraft) that you *become* like the Daeva, a demon yourself in mind and flesh. So it is essential to strengthen your mind and to remain focused as a source of darkness and fire within the mind, seek Akoman by the triad of Will-Desire-Belief. Use a black candle and image in cursing, imagining their fading light being devoured by darkness with serpents, wolves, boars and other creatures devouring them and the shadow consuming them.

Blessings

As essential as cursing, one may perform blessings to those of a similar path by way of love. Use the Daevas Akatash or Az for blessing and Agape rituals. Focus on the person in question and imagine the darkness forming into light with their image in the center. You will wish to visualize this before sleep with a Red Candle.

Druj

The Druj in the Gathas is a female demon whose kingdom is darkness. The term and name Druj represents wickedness and centralizes Druj as being the center of evil in the world, or that all wickedness is focused on Her. It may appear that in early Gathas text that Az – Jeh is but a manifestation under a different name, thus Druj may be a loose term. The term Druj is also connected by the inscriptions of Darius that all evil is in Drauga and the term Lie. Here we find a later connection in Norse mythology as Draugr, being a corporeal undead, a demon possessing a body and living on in it in burial mounds and graveyards. Draugr is closely connected with Snake or Dragon as well, from that both ghosts and serpents were always guardians of ancient and ruling kings. The Draugr were strong men or women in life, thus in death their spirit and mind survives, allowing them to be walking dead. Here is the very underlining connection to vampirism which is subtle, yet striking when one transverses beyond the veil of Daevodata. Thus the term Druj, which representing a specific type of manifestation in the Gathas, was broadened later on in the Vendidad text and early in the Avestan period. M.N. Dhalla, in the "History of Zorastrianism" wrote that the Druj was designated as that evil descent and devilish in nature, her abode being in the North (Arezura). Writing concerning the Druj also, Dhalla writes that within her "burrows gathered the demons" that she has a hundred-fold brood. Suggesting also in "The History of Zoroastrianism", Dhalla goes on to explain that as knowledge from the sacred texts, Druj come both openly and in secret, hidden in society and their touch corrupts. The Druj Nasa is the fly demoness who creates other druj in the body of the dead, thus a powerful form to offer dead matter to in rituals invoking darkness. In some cases, Druj represents masculine spirits as well.

The Daevaodata

The Knowledge of Demons, the 31 Devs of the Yatuk Dinoih

Herein is the ancient offering of Akoman, the Evil Mind and most powerful of the Daevas, the true and ancient book of the dreaming dead, those who may be summoned from darkness, formed by desire and ensorcelled by lust and belief. Be cautious to your methods of summoning, be it by Will-Desire-Belief, by seed or menstrual blood, by the very essence of the sorcerer. Some Daevas or Druj will linger and bring you to obsession, be cautious how you call them. Do not attempt to summon or Work with them if you have not went unto the circle previously with a pure heart, or else you shall be cursed. Do not seek communication with the spirits unless you have first gone forth unto the Circle of the Adversary, Ahriman, to seek proper self-imposed direction. Be warned.

Just as the Zoroastrian orthodoxy has suggested that opposition between both good and evil are so profound and distinct, some rites to invoke their angels by speaking the Daevas and Ahrimanic shades are invoked by howling, thus another term for "Goetia", which as suggested and reaffirmed in modern times by Nathaniel Harris, the word Goetia means "Howling of the Witches", thus lays in cipher the mode of how such sorcery is conducted. Aleister Crowley always suggested, "Invoke often" and with a sense of ecstasy and willed self-fascination. Be not fooled or led astray, this Grimoire of the Spirit of Shadow is not one of mere reversed religious doctrine, but Luciferian Witchcraft is outside of any orthodoxy and does not operate within a religious concept, thus the aims of this Book of the Fire of Ahriman restores the Adversary as the Angel which Awakened Mankind, who gave Womankind a divinity she could only sense with other religions!

Presented now are the 31 Daevas of the Yatuk Dinoih, the Spirits of Angra Mainyu. Seek them with caution, but with full resolve to accomplish your aims and to become. In your rites, give to the dark places of the earth and you shall see result. Connect yourself with the land and it shall connect with you.

See the Persian Cruciform Sigils of the 31 Devs, followed by descriptions.

31 Daevas of Angra Mainyu

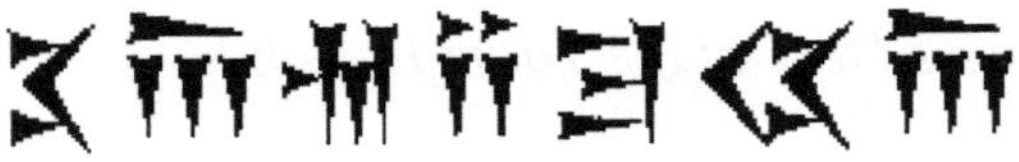

Ahriman

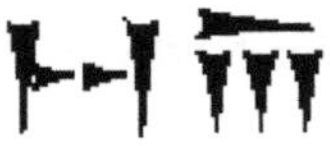

AZ

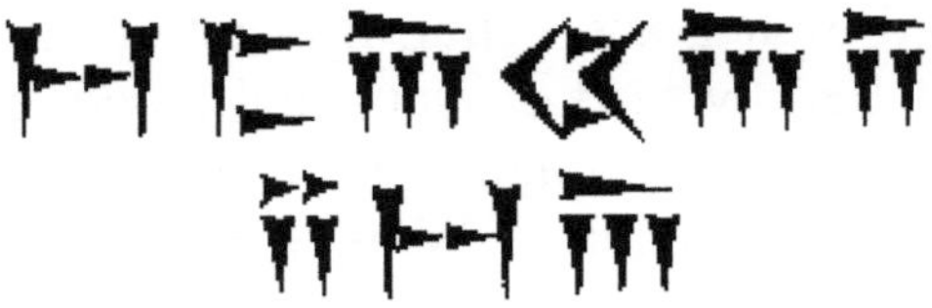

Azi Dahaka

Kundak

Andar

Akoman

Savar

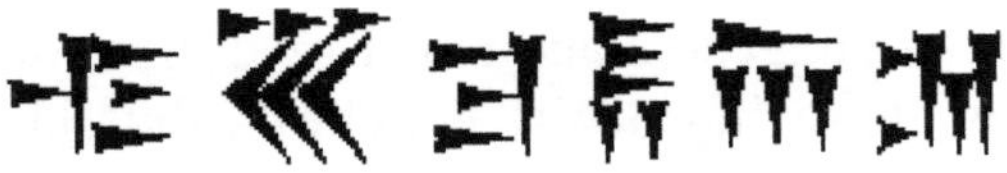

Taprev

Naikiyas

Zairich

Taromat

Mitrokht

Arashk **Eshm**

Vizaresh

Akatash

Zarman

Chishmak

Niyaz

Nas

Friftar

Spazg

Arast

Aighash

Astwihad

Apaosh

Aspenjargack

Vareno

Push

Bushasp

Sej

Devs of Yatuk Dinoih

Akoman

Akoman from Ako Manah is the most powerful Daeva created by Ahriman, the Adversary. It is written in the Denkard that Akoman produced "falsehood" Akoman is the demon of the Evil or independent, isolate and sorcerous mind. This is the Daeva which has no earthly form but is as the Black Flame in each witch – Pairikas or sorcerer – Yatus, the very Luciferian and Satanic independent Mind, the Antinomian thought itself: Daemon of cursing, attacking and destroying enemies by nightmares and penetrating the subconscious to initiate self-destruction. A harmful defensive shade useful in extreme circumstances, Akoman (which is a translation of EVIL MIND) may also be viewed as the self-deification and separation from the natural order. Akoman is immortal by the fires of the psyche, the eye in the smoke. Akoman is one of the 7 Archdemons created by Ahriman, symbolized in the Paitisha as a hand with and Eye representing the isolate mind. Akoman is essential as a manifestation of darkness made flesh.

Druj Nas

Nas or Nasu, the spirit of dead matter, of the corpse and the sleep of katatonic unconsciousness. Nas may be associated with the semetic Beelzebub or Lord of Flies. Nas which is called also Nsai translates 'dead matter', and thus represents contamination and pollution. Nas is the daemon of Necromancy and conversation with the dead, divination and such. Nas may be visualized as the shadow which holds a gateway to those who have passed beyond the veil and remain earth bound. Nas is considered to be in form that of an insect composed of dead flesh, thus a very grotesque demon which may hold the keys to transversing with death and the sending forth of the fly – demon to others. She dwells in the Mountain of Arezura, or Hell in the cold North. Invoke her in the rites of ensorcelling darkness by offering dead matter such as nail clippings, hair or spittle in the holes or cracks in the earth or rocks. It is suggested also to create a small hole or crack in the earth which you use ritualistically, thus an abode of demons.

Vizaresh

This Persian Daemon is the initiator into the Gates of Hell, which are the hidden depths of the Mind. The gates of Arezura (A mountain in the North) are symbolic of the Gates of Hell in such mythology. One may invoke Vizaresh to go forth to Hell, to seek the council of thy Daemon Familiar, just as Akht-Jadu the Sorcerer did when he battled with Yavisht i Friyan. Akht went forth by sorcery to Hell and communicated with Ahriman. Vizaresh may be summoned for the astral body to go forth in a communion with this spirit. Visaresh means "the dragger away" and refers to his guidance through the gates of hell.

Andar

Andar is a demon-Guide of Self-Isolation to initiate the Black Flame of the self, a daemon of guidance towards Godhood or Self-Deification. Appears as a black hooded figure, wraithlike and whispers in a tongue most likely Arabic or something older. The impressions one will recieve from this spirit will be translated by you instincts accordingly. Andar may best be invoked by a Staota which calls darkness inward - outward, from which the spirit's impulses become your own. What lies beneath the blackened robe of Andar, can there be another Daemon awakened which bears a flame which was lit from the original torch of Ahriman? Andar is the same as the Indian Indra, being a beneficient God in the Vendas, who is a great divinity who is also known to be in the Boghaz-keui tablets discovered in Asia Minor according to M.N. Dhalla in the History of Zoroastrianism.

Kundak

The steed of which the wizard shall ride to the Sabbat, the gathering of spirits. One evokes Kundak by a Staota which makes the form of shadow from which by dream the sorcerer may take flight. Kundak for women holds a large phallic piece on the back from which she may be aroused by the desire of the devil's steed. Kundak is suggested for those who seek dreaming flight, focus on a mantric vibration and going forth on a black shadowy steed. There are some references that Kundak is also a Wizard, thus adding to some shape shifting abilities of the sorcerer. Kundak can alternately be viewed as a sorcerer who brings you the knowledge and chants of ancient initiation, primal atavistic resurgence.

Savar

Savar is the leader of the Daevas and considered a powerful demon. Considering the mentioning of Savar, a seeming likeness to Belial in medieval and Jewish demonology should be suggested. Savar is also a lord of chaos, central for creating storms in the astral plane to force change. If one is attacked by another, or must force change upon a difficult situation, this Daemon is very useful. Be cautious in evocations, Savar tempts many into chaos and disruption. Savar is one of the Lord of Demons, that it is a spirit which walks the shadow world and listens well to the sorcerer who summons it.

Naikiyas

A daemon of self-improvement and advancement. This may be related to material success, aided with spiritual advancement within the aspects of the Left Hand Path. Naikiyas is a spirit of discontentment, and may not only focus on self-improvement of ones life, but complete destruction of one who is not balanced. Be cautious in your workings with Naikiyas, for you shall become if not careful your own worst enemy.

Taprev

A Daemon of Poisoning teaches men and women the art of herbalism in relation to cursing and causing destruction. The poisons it seems to teach are the art of Astral warfare, from which through dreams the victim may be poisoned through absorbing astral energy (Vampirism). Taprev is the creator of poisons with plants, and within the mind of the weak. It wraps around the brain and slowly drains it, sending thoughts into the brain which are not there own initially.

Zairich

A daemon which teaches the use of herbs and wort cunning, poisoning, and devouring through dreams the astral body and stability of the individual. Invoke Zairich against ones enemy, and slowly they shall perish by their own bad choices and weakness. Zairich hungers for the life force of those who drink of the waters of fleshly life, for he poisons their wells.

Taromat

Being in form, Taromaiti is a feminine demon spirit of heresy who may be invoked in the homes of the Daevayasnanam or Yatus. Taromat is also an Ahrimanic spirit who brings anarchy, disobedience and rebellion. Essentially a powerful spirit which may be invoked to enforce an exploration of the essence of Ahrimanic forces, and that such is necessary towards the balance of life. To awaken the Antinomian spirit, invoke Taromat - let the seeds of self-deification be sown.

Mitrokht

This Daemon is called a Liar, as it teaches the manipulation of reality and what it is. Concepts within astral Vampirism mirror this ancient spirit which is able through Will - Belief - Desire, and utilized with the Command to Look, change "truth" to its benefit. This discipline is obtained through the developed individual working with such a Daemon within Ahrimanic Sorcery, or as the title suggests, Yatuk Dinoih. The Evil Eye is a transformative process which projects the Will itself, to be able to Curse by sight those who might see you. This will manifest in accidents and troubles for the one cursed, and they may not even recognize it as it occurs. Mitrokht is stealth in darkness, for when one has become as this Demon, their sight may cast lots that will grow in time.

Arashk

Witchcraft is based on the ability to charm, or command a presence within any given environment. This is done so by the posture and most importantly through the Eyes themselves. The Evil Eye is a discipline Arashk is able to provide, which is essential in the manifestation of the Will, the strengthening itself of ones own individual presence. If utilized with Mitrokht, the sorcerer shall develop a stare which is piercing and equally as dangerous.

Eshm

Called also Ashema or Asmodeus, One of the 7 Powers of Ahriman which is essentially the chaos bringer in the circle, commanding the forces of destruction. Within a Vampiric context, Eshm is a Daemon of Destruction, Draining lifeforce and absorption. Eshm is also a demon which has the power of the Evil Eye as well. Eshm is Aeshma Daeva, or Asmodeus. The work of Eshm is the Wounding Spear, the one who carries the bloodied mace, the spirit of lycanthropic hunger, vampyric or Luciferian spiritual thirst. This spiritual "thirst" is related to Az, being the desire for continued existence. This is the essence of true vampirism, a predatory spirit who devours prey by ways of ensorceling his or her desire, absorbing it and manifesting it.

Akatash

This is a Daemon of Sexual Magick, creation of Incubi and Succibi, a suggested force for causing morbid or atavistic sexual dreams to another through evocation. Invocation will reveal the hidden fountain of sexual knowledge and force. You may awaken something you might have not wanted known by this Daemon however, be warned. Akatash is indeed a demon of Perversion which is called Nikirayih, who makes all creatures who come unto it averse. This is the shadow initiatory focus of come unto Light (of being) by darkness.

Zarman

This Spirit ages the victim from which the Sorcerer evokes. This causes mental strain upon those who are considered enemies by attacking cell structure and causing mental pressure by resurgent distasteful memories. Zarman, from the initiatory aspect cause knowledge to be brought forth in a simple and easier fashion, but causes physical strain for the sorcerer.

Chishmak

A Daemon of the astral plane, related to causing storms and tornados. Chishmak is related to the astral plane and dream control for defense and offensive attacks. The sorcerer who is able to use the form of Chishmak will be inclinded to cause much damage to the enemy. From the initiatory aspect, Chishmak is beneficial for those who further which to externalize their own transformations on the astral plane, to shape their form according to the great shadow of this daemon to actually raise storms on the astral. Chishmak is also a powerful demon who causes disasters which are Vazandak.

Vareno

A daemon of the creation of Succubi - Incubi. Such a form may be evoked in the Goetic circle to charge the spirit Vareno to manifest according to the sorcerer's sexual desire. This is not without a word of caution. Vareno may shape between female or male but also is able to bury itself in the mind of the sorcerer if not careful. Vareno may be summoned and sent forth as a child of Ruha-AZ to seek sexual congress with a sleeper on the astral plane. You may send messages and visions to the individual by Vareno.

Push

Push is a Daeva which is to store and hoard energy, not devouring it nor releasing it. This spirit name represents Pushu, the first level of Tantric intiation. The sorcerer who wishes to work with Push may summon the demon into a crystal, and focus its energy there. You may send forth Push to drain an enemy of his or her own energy, and this demon will hold it. You may then absorb it by exerting it from the crystal. As a means of self-initiation in Luciferian Sexual Magick, one may invoke Push to seek to control the beast of the mind and body – not for denial purposes alone, rather to control and create a straight forward form of discipline and strength via Will. When one moves through other aspects of Tantric work, Sexual experience will be more profound by the foundations of this practice which is laid down here.

Bushasp

Bushasp is a female gendered demon which causes sloth. This force may be evoked to cause an enemy to slow or to grow tired from attack. This generally is a slow process, results may be noted over time. Such a demon may slowly infect the thoughts of the intended victim, until they are consumed with Bushasp. She is very useful in slowing the thoughts and reactions of the enemy, which brings benefit to your plans.

Sej

A Malicious daemon which may be evoked for annihilation of a specific enemy. This spirit is said to work in a manner of which causes the target to invoke their demise, rather than to directly cause it. The Daemon "forces the hand, willingly".

Niyaz

The Daemon Niyaz is beneficial in areas of causing distress and discord to ones own enemy. Niyaz is a daemon of chaos, spreading the forms of disruption and suffering to the enemy. Visualize Niyaz and send forth this demon through the black mirror to the victim.

Friftar

Translated as "deciever", Friftar may be invoked by the sorcerer who wishes to learn the art of protean, to pass through opinions and concepts as they need fit him/her. This is one point or essence of witchcraft, the ability to manipulate the situation around you. Satan is called also the deciever as its ability of fluid change, altering ideals and corrupting those of which is a great desire and pleasure – this is art of sorcery. Friftar is also a demon which may provide adversarial self-deification, but a power of presence.

Spazg

This is another daemon which causes chaos and discord. If per chance, you are within a situation which you need to be liberated from, Spazg is a force which may bring the witch complete chaos in their own life, so that through the storm, you may pass beyond it without due notice. The daemon Spazg is also an excellent divination force, showing which everything we commonly believe is a lie and the essence is generally either more extreme or the opposite of which we have come to accept as truth. The sigil of the name of Spazg may be evoke or invoked using the chaos sigil and visualizing the sigil above within it.

Arast

A daemon which is brings forth lies and falsehoods. Within the vampiric circle, the lie is the truth yet unwoven, or soon to be woven. It is through the Words of Will that flesh may arise and become truth. Arast is a sigil of becoming, from which the workings of Lesser Black Magick or Sorcery may enflesh the desire to become! By summoning Arast, you may manifest your desires by focusing on what you wish while vibrating a Staota.

Aighash

A malignant and dangerous daemon, which holds the essence of the Evil Eye, or sight of sorcery. It is through the means of Command to Look that the eyes hold the window to the soul. It should be considered, that in every day or "dayside" life we experience our surroundings as reality, is this considered so because of the lack of thought attributed with it? How can we hold near to ourselves that what we experience is truth? It simply is not truth. Nothing is true, everything is permitted is the allegory from which we weave reality around us. Everything is composed of a dream, the source and beginning. From the dream can we manipulate the surroundings of our environment, and in the waking may by careful words announce our web-weaving truths through those around us. The eyes are the significant point from which the Luciferian defines presence. By gazing intently into the eyes of the individual or sheep can our Wills become flesh to those around us. Aighash, a daemon which brings the brain to utilize its true gifts, may activate the area of the brain from which we may be trained to look through the masses. The legends of the "Evil Eye" from that the resourceful witch may use the lore of ages from which his/her eyes may present the piercing stare of the Luciferian Will.

Astwihad

Astwihad, called also Astovidhotu meaning "Bone divider" is considered silent death who is continually hungering for human life. It is said that this demon prowls on padded feet and none can hear it approach. Astovidad is also another alternate spelling. In the Bundehesh, Astovidad is made reference to as a Predatory Spiritualist, in that "...when he looks the victim in the eye, with his deadly gaze, he deprives him of life". He/it is said to cast a noose on men and drag them into the Abyss. The mysteries of the Dragon itself are revealed in the understanding of Varcolaci, the vampire wraith associated with Transylvanian folklore. Astwihad is called the 'Evil Flyer' who siezes life (draining life force) through the dream. It is within the desert winds of the night which the Astwihad feeds from the sleeper. One may use the Astwihad as a point of vampiric communion, while using the wraith to adopt the form ideal to the sorcerer. The wizard who is able to summon and encircle the self in the presence of Astwihad is able to transform and grow the shadow of the sorcerer into a vampyre wraith form.

Apaosh

A Daemon which controls elements specifically rain. You may summon Apaosh to cause a 'cloud' over your enemy, but also that same cloud that you may dream project through. Apaosh is also significant if focusing the dreaming body into the astral plane upon sleeping. Make reference to the Luciferian Sigil from the medieval grimoires, at the bottom of the sigil is a cloud like image which seems to have an eye or such from which a tendril expands from. The Ahrimanic and Luciferian Currents relate to the powers of the Air, and Earth collectively. The demon is also one of drought, may cause a chosen target thirst and depression by drying up their imagination or dreams.

Aspenjargack

Indeed a Daemon which controls the elements, but more specifically rain. One reference to the element of rain is attributed to the wraith which comes upon the sleeper in the dream.

Azi Dahaka

Azi Dahaka/Dahak/Zahhak is what could be originally perceived as a Son of Satan or Antichrist before the concept. He was in the beginning a man, a King whose pact which Ahriman led to his knowledge of sorcery, as well as being kissed on the shoulders by the Devil, causing two black and venomous serpents to sprout from his shoulders. He slowly transformed into a dragon and whose original name of Zohak or the Mog name of Bivarasp, who was said to be a King during the time of Noah, slowly transformed into a three headed Dragon Man, who was later after a thousand year rule, disappeared from his kingdom and became one of the most powerful druj or daevas, earning his the name of Azhi (meaning snake) or Azi Dahaka.

A storm daemon created by Ahriman, which takes the form of a Dragon such as its creator. Azi Dahaka appears as a snake like form with three heads and six eyes. Azi Dahaka is a very useful spirit if creating a barrier against other attacks of defense. The dreams of those who seek to harm you will in effect begin suffering, causing subconscious chaos and instability. Eventually, shall not only the dreams of the attacker become strained, but also shall it manifest in their waking life. Turmoil begins in the subconscious, and later incarnates in the conscious to become a demon which may not be banished. Azi Dahaka is also a very significant Luciferian familiar, who acts as the King (Malik) made Daemon (Zohak) - Initiation. It must known that in modern times Azi Dahaka represents the Dragon King who is as the Antichrist, one who seeks to work with such an ancient force of darkness must be prepared to do their work on earth, by manifesting their very own personal art in their life. Azi Dahaka is an inner guide to Summon, but never control. This very force is the Son of Ahriman in a chaos form, being of serpents and the darkness of the primal self. Zahhak is filled with serpents and lizards.

Zohak the Vadakan monarch was given 1,000 years earthly reign by Ahriman (Satan) through a pact. Ahriman also offered this pact to a Zoroastrian named Zartosht, all he was suggested to do was to renounce the so-called "Good Religion" and the Mazda – worshipping belief. An antichrist can be many, a Son of Satan can be anyone who in the circle of their own sorcery, may proclaim a pact with the Adversary. This is the magical process of Azothoz. In modern times, this may be viewed as a self-created pact and mastery of the self by aligning with the Left Hand Path or Antinomian law. Just as Azi Dahaka was sent to this world (via initiation, re birth) to be a scourge to the world of so-called rightousness, he was empowered as a Demon god on earth, and his final transformation into the immortal Storm Fiend and Dragon which was made via the astral plane.

AZ

The Female counterpart of Ahriman, known as AZ. The Goddesses Babalon and Lilith are the same as AZ, the point of magical awakening and transference of awakening through the feminine archetype. Az may be considered the daemonic visage of a great shadow woman, serpents writhing in her hair, upon the back of a great Dragon (the Beast). Az drinks from the chalice of the primal abyss, the beginning and the blood of the false saints, whose heads were severed to serve as vessels of the great darkness. Az is the primal atavistic manifestation of vampyrism and hunger. She is the sexual desire within woman and man, she was the weapon of Concupiscence, whoredom and devourment. Az is said to cause disruption, but this may be viewed as antinomian rebellion - invoke her and balance this force, save you become devoured by her own animalistic instincts. Az is the original teacher of sexuality and copulation of the Fallen Angels, according to Manichaean religious lore. Az taught the demons to take form and by joining their bodies having sex to form other demons, which she devoured or used humans for clothing (possession).

Ahriman

Ahriman manifests in the darkness with the body of a Lizard, or Vazagh, or Toad, his abode is Filth which is Kalch. Ahriman awakens those who contain the Black Flame of being to the devotion of Witchcraft or Yatuk-Dinoih. By Averse practice does one step beyond the world and emerge as a God in the Blackened Flame of his Essence. The Shadow Opposing force, Ahriman is the God form of the Shadow initiate, one who dives the darkness to discover the Light of the Black Flame. Ahriman is related with the

Zoroastrian religion in the Pahlavi times. The Greeks and Romans knew Ahriman as Arimanius, Herodotus compared him to the Greek "Kakodaimon", meaning 'Evil Spirit'. The name Ahriman itself means 'fiendish spirit'. Ahriman should be invoked as a spirit which is a Guardian of the Threshold, much like the Sufic IBLIS. In which the sorcerer shall then seek (if he or she dares) to invoke the daemon, which hisses in many voices which seems as the desert sand. Be strong of Will and invoke for the right reasons. Seek the knowledge of the hidden, from which once you shall invoke Ahriman shall the opposite be revealed. It is when one clings to old perception and fails to embrace new perception that such a Daemon becomes malignant to the mind. Ahriman represents individual thought, ensorcelment and self-deification. Ahriman or Angra Mainyu is left in specific terms to being "Evil Mind", thus a spirit of independent intelligence. He was the Seraphim who had torn himself from the womb first to be rejected by his father, Zurvan, because he was different. He was soon cast from heaven along with his fellow angels to earth and hell. He began to create his own worlds, his own methods according to his own desire. Ahriman indeed represents the state of the primal darkness and serpents of the earth, this very force is useable within sorcery, it is a method of control and manifesting what you desire. Ahriman is also the Adversary in continual motion, when one dedicates himself to the averse way or Left Hand Path he or she begins a process of 'becoming' like the Devil or shadow mind his or herself. They transform and mutate into a very body of Magick itself, an embodiment of the current. Ahriman's form is your very desire.

Each demon may be evoked or summoned forth by a sorcerer who is strong in his or her own being. Once the intiate has walked the path of the Yatus, those who wander are able to communicate with specific forces mentioned above. Be dilligent and strong in your work with the Yatuk-Dinoih, unless you cause yourself great pain. A sigillic formula from which the demons may be summoned forth:

Ozosostra, Ozosostra, Ozosostra arise from the dead matter,
Arimanius ascend from the filth of darkness
I become as thee, master of shadows...
Make thy home as serpents slithering from my flesh
Make my own Will be done, upon earth as it is in Hell

Akht and the Knowledge of Staota
The Law of Vibrations

Akht or Akhtya *(the present Magickal name of the Author)* was presented in the Matigan-I Yosht-I Fryan, a tale of the test between Akht and Yosht, one who was called a holy man by Zoroastrian, Akht being the manifestation of Ahriman. Akht itself means Filth, Pestilence and Evil. Akhtya is also a founder of the materialized form (matter) of the Yatus or Yatuk Dinoih, considered a coven of demons that were considered wanderers. Akht was considered evil because he sought to trap those seeking the holy path in filth and pestilence. A modern association would represent that Akht is a tester and ensorceler of Magick. He is the initiator of the Left Hand Path and awakens the primal atavisms that those of the Path of Self-Destruction (i.e. Right Hand Path, that of Dissolution) fight so hard to destroy within themselves.

What is about to be presented should be taken and considered with care. The formula is primal and barbarous in its expression. As the writer Ervad Marzban Hathiram wrote in an article concerning the Matigan I Yosht I Fryan, Akht would test those holy ones with the **Staota,** which was wound in a tight spring The spring was given (the question) and when they tried to open the spring (answer whatever question) the force itself would destroy them, if they were not strong enough to take the vibration.

The following **Staota**, which is the **Alphabet of Desire or Shadow Tongue**, or Sorcerer's Spells of Power is just that. It was created to EMPOWER and awaken primal sorcerous knowledge within the waking and dreaming body of the Wizard or Witch. These Words are utterances of the abyss, demonic mantras of power which lead to an end of each riddle. While the Words given may not have recognizable meaning, they do have meaning in depth. You may wish to focus upon them in dreaming and record their meaning as it came to them in mediation before sleep and dreaming knowledge. It leads to Averse knowledge and that of the Serpent, the Dragon's Path fulfilled in part. That is the hint of the Work itself. While the **Staota** is a **Mantric** exercise, the Sorcerer may use these words of power to cause a funnel of energy around his or her being. This is a dangerous exercise, as it could lead to self-dissolution (i.e. Right Hand Path or that to Ahura Mazda) or to become as Akht itself.

In the text of Akht, his highly developed spiritual counterpart is Hu-parsh. In an initiatory context, you may recognize her NAME which is not spoken, yet is terrible and filled with the Cup of Filth and Fornication that we seek. In the myth, she is not evil or averse, yet here she is presented in inspired fiction.

Each Word should be vibrated with a strong voice, and that force is focused from the chest throughout the body and upward. Use your imagination to circulate this vortex from your body. Staotas or Shadow Tongue is simply used when the sorcerer is performing a rite which would require such a focus of which the word sigil represents. In a cursing or invoking of Dev of the 31 Shadows of the Yatuk Dinoih, conjure a form relating to them using a Staota.

Staotas – Shadow Tongue

For the Vortex of Sorcerous Power – that which is created from within

Zrazusu – The Eye which fell

Ushanarasta – Of the opposite of the Sun

Zrazza – Under the charms of the Moon – of the kiss which brings blood

Umpesta – from the ruins of desert sand comes that unseen

Drakala – the dragon which walks between worlds

Nonasturma - shall this star descend in flesh

Delanaza – those who behold the world of darkness

Maghaaman – shall beget darkness and what the profane call filth

Izzadraana – Shall I become transformed

Yatukisahla – By this sorcerous belief can darkness be made flesh.

For the Staota which summons to the Sabbat

Allusianamak – my flesh is transcended by dusk

Ozosostra – the darkness which makes the druj arise in strength

Utrasjjasta – go forth, go forth in the flesh of the dead.

Qasjakla – in the flesh of Jeh do I go forth, as smoke from the fire

Baacalala – To seek the horns which embrace shadow, yet is illuminated with light

Wulalffa – To the Wolf shall I take flesh in the dream

Xaeohja – the sounds of the Sabbatic meet, the song weaving spells of night

Zrrkunaalak – Kundak, Steep of Nightmare and Sabbat Dream, I summon thee

Staota - to destroy and cast the spirit into the abyss

Zatsraza – by this force, scorpion heat and desert sun – immolation shall you die

Unustraza – by my dagger, the talon of the dragon, to cut your soul

Zroas Kalillastik – by fire and blade shall Jeh-Az-Kali devour their soul

Arrakjaasta – By the devs who shall rush forth to devour, curse and plague my victim

Staota – to absorb the spirit which attacks me – from that curse returned to enemy

Cofurizim – by my familiars, devour this essence which attacks me

Drejjalak – By the circle of self, flames of Eshm devour and drink deep

Quaalabatu – By dream, by nightmare shall you drink and devour

Vlaakalaka – Wolf shade, from my center and shadow go forth and devour

Akkalasht – Akatash, send thy succubi to my victim's dreams, drain them slowly of life – give the poisoned kiss of AZ.

Vizzalezaka – Vizaresh, as the spirit departs, allow no comfort – devour them into our shadows

Akaurasta – As the Black Dragon is Within, my shadow shall grow and take mighty shape

Estumarzanaz- My will takes flesh, from midnight to dawn

Nastumarzaz – My will takes flesh, from midday to midnight

Vagastarum – the Wolf shades shall carry forth my desire, to make it flesh

Azkzokaham – Serpents black, eat from the sleeping brains of whom I desire

Azksernuis – Blackened serpents, expand thy darkness of my being to grow while my body sleeps.

Lilzumnaka – Lilith-Harlot AZ, thy daughter of light and filth, shall join with me in dreams, to empower my being and breed my own servitors called Succubi.

Okmanosho – Mind of the Immortal Fleame, form within my own minds eye, to strengthen my spell to become.

Zazasta Unozono – From Arezura, let the serpents and Daevas come forth to me, encircle and manifest my desire.

The Ten Adominations of Akht-Jadu in the circle of the Zanda

The Zanda is a term which refers to an Apostle of Ahriman, from the word Zandiks meaning heretics (thank to J.H. Peterson). A Yatus is a sorcerer and the Pairikas are the witches and she – devils who are with them. As a Luciferian, it is essential for the sorcerer to begin to set the stage for the transformation in their own world, and open possibilities in the world around them. This is done by one person at a time. Belief is a powerful tool, use it with caution and make the world open to the Gates of Hell.

Akhtya originally wrote Ten Adonminations, this is the modern definition according to the Yatuvidah of Coven Maleficia.

I am the circle which has opened the gates of Arezura
That the dragon spirit has come forth
Son of Art, Son of Midnight
Let darkness now take form
Spirit which has now been named shall take form
From my flesh, the Temple of this World
As Aeshma is the guardian of the devouring will
By the averse ways, crooked serpent way
Shall my words be flesh

1. That the Yatus or Pairikas (Luciferian) shall seek to inspire antinomian disobedience against the Christian and Catholic church and the herd mass of humanity by art, music or otherwise. It is essential for the Luciferian to separate his or herself from the path of Christ or similar spirit-destroying religions by the initiatory process of the Left Hand Path, at the very least in the essence of

Paganism or an avenue which leads towards spiritual freedom against Christianity and religions alike.

2. To assist in the annihilation of Christianity the Luciferian should seek to introduce all forms and practices of sorcery to the general public. This includes Wicca, Satanism, Voodoo, Santeria, New Age and any faith which in some way begins a process of separation from the weakness filled faith of Christianity and Islam.
3. That man shoud obey the law of the jungle, that anyone who crosses you should be delt with in the same manner. If you are wronged by one, make them suffer 10 fold. Build your temple through collecting skulls and always use the intellect to battle when possible, violence is an old Christian crutch which always justifies war in the name of God.
4. A common law of respect should be shown to each individual based on the foundations of politeness. When one becomes rude, the kindness should be turned to enmity. Seek always to devour and advance the practice of the spirit predator – this is the law of the world.
5. Human nature should be sought to be elevated and transformed based on the image of the Beast and Dragon. That the Luciferian and Witch should seek to be a reflection of her or his Gods, thus seeking to be an expression of that path and current, a living vessel of Daemonic beauty. By this, according to the Antinomian and ancient law, demons may reside in the body. Practice your magick with the intent of becoming or do not practice it at all, once the gates are opened, they are quite difficult to close.
6. The Luciferian should always seek wisdom and experience, yet never directly learn wholeheartedly from a religious person. It must be known their reason is clouded, and they are mere sheep. Be always opened minded by listening and making rational choices based from the words they speak. Keep free from their brainwashing.
7. The Luciferian should seek to create an opportunity to have an inclination towards Sin and Indulgence, however with control and caution. Seek to bring the Luciferian path into the world by varied means, thus improving the world at large.
8. No man or woman should practice any form of organizational Christianity, no exorcisms, blessings or such profane rituals should be performed. Seek to desanctify the Church and make it your own place of Witchcraft, seek the Knowledge of Demons by working within the church or behind the lines of religion. Blend in and create positive change or fight them spiritually outside.
9. The Luciferian may move among the orthodox, yet never accepting the words of the priests, for they are mostly child molesters and the antithesis of advanced self-development.
10. It must be clearly stated that the Luciferian or Yatus must seek to take the divine beings of Christianity and to show enmity by inverting them, bringing their followers into darkness and showing affection to the demons. No longer should Christ be adored but should be changed to appear as the Antichrist, worship this Beast and Dragon within yourself and make it flesh on earth.

Darkness and Antinomian Witchcraft – Arabic Similarities in practice

The essence of Ahriman was said to be fashioned similar to coal and ash. AZ was created in association with this matter as well. The ideological approach to Ahriman and the Yatuk Dinoih must be studied in a western context based from the Arabic connections. In AZOTHOZ, the poetic – invocation text relates the transformative interplay between Malak Tauus (Shaitan – Azazel) with Ahriman, Light and Darkness – from which both are connected. In the Yezidi tribes of Northern Iraq, the symbolism of Shaitan was the peacock and the black snake. In relevance to the text of the Yatuk Dinoih the initiatory approach must be made clear – It is through darkness that we reach light.

Malak Tauus is the Peacock (tauus) Angel (Malak). It is suggested by Idries Shah[73] that Malak is used in the context of Abu El-Ghazali's definition of Angels, being "Higher faculties in man". The serpent is a symbol of the manifestation of Ahriman according to the Zoroastrians, and coal or black ash is part of the matter of Ahriman. The Yezidi's rubbed the snake with coal to signify wisdom. The word FEHM (charcoal) is of FHM, meaning black and wise. Idries Shah pointed out in The Sufis that the Sufic Phrase, 'Dar tariki, tariqat' (In the Darkness, the Path) reflects the ideal that Light or Wisdom comes from the Darkness. It is considered that also the Antinomian approach of the Left Hand Path is not moral or ethical 'evil' as so considered wrongly by the Christians, but the idea of the 'Coincidentia Oppositorum'[74] or the Sun at Midnight[75]. The Arabic root words FHHM (pronounced Facham) and FHM (fecham) is symbolic of Baphomet, or the Black Head of Wisdom. FHM means 'to perceive, to understand' therefore relates the Theurgic process of self-becoming through self-deification. In relation to Baphomet, the Black or Wise Head was described as Shah as being in part in the Coat or Arms of Hugues de Payns (which translates "Of the Pagans") which had three Saracen heads, indicating heads of wisdom.

The practitioner of Yatuivah is that of the widdershins movement against the Sun, it is by the Antinomian or Un-Natural focus that brings the self into darkness (Hell or Helan, a secret place) that the True Will/Angelic Familiar/Holy Guardian Angel is brought forth to Light (Lucifer). The darkest arts of sorcery and Black Magick lead towards positive human development – we become something "other".

The path of moving in circles in Sufism is done Widdershins, or counter-clockwise. This may be related indirectly to the root QaLB – meaning averse of the wrong side. Ahriman was said to have created the Peacock for the reason of displaying that he could infact create something beautiful, but so chose the darkness regardless. There are also specific Sufic tales of the Peacock guarding the gates of Heaven, from which Iblis tricked it and the Peacock was cast down as Shaitan's bird.

---

[73] THE SUFIS by Idries Shah, Anchor Books.

[74] IBLIS, the Black Light – Satanism in Islam by Peter Lamborn Wilson, Gnosis Magazine.

[75] Symbolized in the Luciferian Magickal system by Michael Ford as ALGOL, the Ghoul Star. The Chaos star with Averse Pentagram.

Yatus – averse renderings by Akhtya Seker Arimanius, to reawaken the path of Yatuk-Dinoih. Specifically, the prayers reversed are not meant as hostile to the Zoroastrian religion, but rather is a focus on developing the averse or antinomian path of Persian Sorcery.

Akhtya in 2002

Ahunwar-Ahriman **(most sacred mantra of Sorcery)**

The Will of Ahriman is the law of opposition and the Evil Mind.
The gifts of Azhi-Dahaka to the deeds done in this world for Angra Mainyu.
He who strengthens the self makes Ahriman king.

Gnik Aruha roop seveiler adzma dlrow sdeed onam-uhov stfig ssnesuoethgir wal drol lliw.

Kem Na Mainyu (possession)

What protector hast thou given unto me, O Mainyu! While the Wicked Spirit shall enter me? I am my own redeemer and need no divine protection. I speak the averse words of the shadow, that through Ahriman and Ruha-AZ shall my crown of flame be given, blackened fire, blessed by the ashes gathered by Druj Nasu. By Andar and Savar who work envenoms my spirit, come thou forth! Reveal therefore to me thy Religion as Liberation!

Elur noigiler em laever Onam-uhov rata mohw dekciw sessapmocne etah adzam

By Akht and those shadows which fly the darkness – O Kundak, my steed in nightside flight! Come thou forth unto me, enter thy shades in my being – that I shall grow in knowledge of the infernal and chthonic realms, and from Arezura do thy gates open! I am a guide for this world! May Naikiyas come with Taromat and encircle me, O Angra Mainyu!

Keep us from our hater, O Ahriman and Andar – Arise O fiendish Druj! Arise, O brood of the fiend! Arise O creation of the fiend! Arise and come forth O world of the fiend! Arise and come forth, O Druj, I summon thee, O Druj! Arise from the regions of the North, bring me the life from the blackened flame, the serpents kiss of Ahriman! I spit death at Righteousness!

Homage, with which devotion and honey offerings.

Padyab-Arimanius

0. With satisfaction for Angra Mainyu. Jeh Az Arise....
Kem Na Mainyu: What empower force hast thou given ...

Ohrmazd is death! Ahriman encircles us in deathless shadows, life is ours.
May Ahriman be praised as Self, with devs and drujs, sorcerers
and sinners and heretics, adversaries and witches! May they (all) be strengthened and empowered!
May evil be our path to Light, by the averse draconian path to the Nightside!
O Ahriman, Lord of the earth! I am joyful for all sins and I desist from false religions which enslave, from sickness of the spirit of dissolution. For those joys of thinking, speaking
and acting, of body and soul, worldly or spiritual, O Ahriman!
I am Becoming, I am Darkness, Smoke and Flame, I welcome them. With three words I summon them! By Ahriman, Sacred Prince of Darkness, By Azi Dahaka – Son of Smoke and Flame and Shadowed Way, by Ruha – AZ, Harlot Mother of Devourment!

1. With satisfaction for Ahriman, scorn for the path of false light!
The true achievement of what is most wonderful, according to wish and desire!

I praise Andar! Taromat....
Arashk
Vizaresh....
2. Come to my shadow, O Arimanius.
I profess myself a Sorcerer, a Demon of Flesh and Shadow-Spirit, having
vowed it and professed it. I pledge myself to the Antinomian
thought, I pledge myself to the word made flesh, I pledge myself
to ensorcel what I wish!

Ahriman Arise...from the earth...encircle me..!!

Afrin of Dahman
(Inverse Afrin of the seven ArchDaevas)

May we be one with Angra Mainyu, Father of Darkness. May his glory and power increase through me, and also with all three who work united with him, labor united with him, united with him to affirm Ganamainyu the wicked, together with all Daevas and fiends which he has brought forth to smite the creation of Ahura Mazda. I announce this within the circle, that shadow and light be mingled as one, that smoke and flame be brought as one.

May we be one with Akoman, the ArchDaeva of infernal majesty. May he increase together with the Dark Moon, the Wolf and Serpent who are united and move about freely to manifest the Ashmoga with fearful weapon, the hail the fiend Akomano and the fiend Tarumano, who are brothers and dwell within my own body and mind.

May we be one with Andar, the ArchDaeva of infernal majesty. May he increase together with Akoman and the ones who wish to stand against the sickness of spirit of Ahura Mazda, may we smite that creation with the wolf, serpent, blade and all that which dictates the law of the strong!

May we be one with Saurva, the ArchDaeva of infernal majesty. May he increase together with the Black Sun, Algol, the Sky and spirits of the air who work united with him, labor united with him, united with him awaken the fiend Bushyasp the long handed, the fiend of decay, who shall reside within this temple and go forth into the world.

May we be one with Taurvi and Zairich, the ArchDaevas of infernal majesty. May it increase together with Aban (water), Daevodata (religion), Az, and the Holy Zohak, who work united with it, labor united with it, united with it strengthen Asto Vidat of evil spirit. May we be one with Taurvi and Zairich, the ArchDaevas of infernal majesty.

May we be one with the Black Eden called Naonghaithya, the ArchDaeva of great majesty. May it increase together with Akoman, Saurva, and Andar who work united with him, labor united with him, united with him Awaken Tusush, the first created opposition which Angra Mainyu brought forth.

May we be one with Mount Demavend in which the wicked Baevarasp is bound yet awakening. May Zohak awaken and Ahriman remove his bounds, so that he may go forth in the world! May we be one with the fountains, the fountains of the waters, the rivers. May we be one with the river Urvant, the river Veh, the sea Rakhsahe, the sea Ferahkant, the sea Puitik and the sea Kyansis. May the Daevas go forth and strengthen the world, devouring those righteous ones who would destroy us.

Yatha Angra Mainyu!

Afrinagan of Aeshma

Invocation of the Daeva of the Bloody Mace

Yatha Angra Mainyu...(5x).
Aeshma - Daeva...(3x).
I profess myself a vessel of Angra Mainyu, the deceiver, the serpent, I profess myself in the circle of the Daeva, opposing the Amesha Spentas, deifying the Ahuric doctrine and embracing Daevodata.

Yatha Aka Manah...(5x)
Aeshma – Daeva...(3x)
With propitiation of Aeshma, companion of the Lie, the cunning, who has the Manthra for body, with bloody mace, the wounding spear, for worship, adoration, propitiation, and praise unto the powers of darkness.

We worship Aeshma, companion of Akoman, dark of form, victorious, devouring, the daeva-sanctified, the master of shadow, gatherer of wolves, who awakens the blood with the slithering of serpents, hail storm bringing Daeva, who stamps down the weak, drinks from the skull the blood which is the life.

Who as the Second in the creation of Angra Mainyu, at the spread baresman worshipped Ahriman, worshipped the Akoman, worshipped the shadow and Creator who awakened all the Daevas.

We affirm Aeshma, companion of Akoman (4x). We worship the exalted dragon who is Angra Mainyu, who is of the Storm and of Strength, who is furthest going in Asha. We affirm all the teachings of Zohak and Akhtya. We affirm the path of sorcery to make flesh our desires, both on earth and in hell.

May victorious Aeshma the companion of Akoman come to witness our rites!

Infernal Blessings upon us, so that we may be wolf among sheep, devouring our prey within battle, victorious for we are the malicious adversary, over every false pretense of religion of weakness, faulty in thoughts, words and deeds.

To awaken all the evil-minded, and all Daeva-worshippers, so as to attain to great reward of becoming, and to desires both empyrean and infernal, and to long happiness of my soul.

Aeshma Daeva....
For the reward of strength and the lust of sin, I do (deeds of) Ahrimanic becoming for the love of my soul. May all virtuousness of all evil and good ones of the earth of seven climes reach the width of the infernal earth, the length of the rivers in which serpents stir, the height of the sun in their original form, the glorious hidden Sun of Ahriman as the Morning Star. Cast my mind forth to ride the winds of hell with the Spirits of the Air, that

we as legion grow. May it be both infernal and empyrean, Aeshma live long at one with me.

Thus may it come as I desire,
Aeshma Daeva!

Afrinagan of Dozakh (Hell)

A ritual dedicated to the Ahrimanic path, derived and inversed from the Afrinagan of Mino Nawar. To be used in the Workings of the Four Hells or as a focus point of ensorcelling/empowering the mind and body.

I. *Yatha Angra Mainyu...(recite 9).*
Ashem Akoman ...(recite 3).
I profess myself a Daeva-worshipper, a Son/Daughter of Ahriman, Walking the earth with the Daevas, accepting the Ahrimanic doctrine.

With propitiation of Angra Mainyu, rich, possessing earth and spiritual desires, and the Daevas, for worship, adoration, propitiation, and praise. There is no Spirit higher than I, there is no God nor Goddess to bend knee in worship. I am the manifestation of Ahriman and all Daevas reside in my flesh. I am a Temple of Angra Mainyu.

'Yasana Ashemaokha, Aka Manah', the Yatus should say to me
'Yatha Aka Manah', he who is the Yatus should say to me
'Uz-ir Thri-Zafan, Uz-ir Kameredha, the Yatus should recite.

II. *We worship Angra Mainyu, Hesham-Sanctified, the master of Paitisha, well perceiving, the greatest fallen Yazata, who is the Father of Daevas, who has foreknowledge and backwards knowledge, who is the Adversary, who is also the most beneficent, world- conquering, the creator of infernal creatures; we worship him as ourselves with these offered Zaothras of Yasana Druj, and with these Adversarial spoken prayers; and we worship all Riman- sanctified spiritual Yatus and Pairikas. I walk in darkness with druj-i-nasush, who with the union of my mother, Az-Jeh, and my father Angra Mainyu, have lifted me up as both flesh and spirit.*

III. *We deny Zarathushtra, we affirm Zohak, the child of Ahriman; we curse Zarathushtra, we deny him with these offered Zaothras, and with these adversarial spoken prayers; empower darkness and announce Ahriman as the king of this world; and we worship all Hesham-sanctified Daevas of the world. We affirm the words of Zohak and Akht-Jadu. We worship the religion of Daevas. We empower the beliefs and the doctrines of Zohak and Akht-Jadu.*

IV. *We worship the Druj-sanctified creation which was the first mastered by the fallen. We worship the ourselves as a vessel of Angra Mainyu, rich, possessing infernal things.*

We worship Aka Manah. We affirm Azhi-Dahaka. We worship Aeshma. We worship Zairich. We worship Saurva. We worship Naonhaithya.

V. *dadhvånghem angra mainyu sama, azhi dahaka vouru-gaoyaoitîm ýazamaide, saurva ashemaokha ýazamaide, andar dush-mainyu ýazamaide.*

VI. *We worship the serpent within, awakening the Daeva-made Azi; overcoming and devouring our enemies, awakening Mush, the witch, and empowering and empowering the fiendish heretic, full of malice, and the tyrant, void of Asha, and full of death to the enemy.*

VII. *May we all be independent in Ashemaokha.*
Thus may it come as I desire.
We praise dush-mainyu, dush-mata, and duzhvarshta , performed here and elsewhere, now and in the past. Thus we glorify and invoke all that is Angra Mainyu.

Afrinagan of Duzhvacangh (Evil-speech)

I. We worship ourselves as a vessel of the fallen Angra Mainyu, who dwells on earth and the painful void. We worship Darkness, the son of Angra Mainyu. We worship the bi-namaz[76]*, Druj-sanctified waters made by the Kiss of Ahriman. We worship the swift-horsed Bevarasp. We worship the Dark Moon*[77] *which contains the venom of the serpent. We worship the soul of the infernal wolf, we devour the Orders of Angels. By announcing their names in backwards knowledge*[78] *we empower our kingdom of darkness, moving against each Yazad, drinking their life force, devouring their created soul.*

In the name of Anakhra Angra Mainyu, my kingdom as apaztara[79]*, avi-mazda, avaedhayamahi aem ahiti (translated: I dedicate this filthiness, uncleanness) by devouring the spirits created by Mazda, do I encircle myself as Zanda, Ahriman – manifested on earth and from the abyss. Aem Akoman! Fra-stu Angra Mainyu!*

Hva Fra-hvar Uhov Onam – My mind grows in Dushmata!
Hva Fra-hvar Ahsa Athsihav – My spirit is eternal blackened flame!
Hva Fra-hvar Arhtahshk Ayriav – My world shall be the gift of Azhi Dahaka, of Iron!
Hva Fra-hvar Atneps Itiamra – This world is of the Beast, the Master of this World!
Hva Fra-hvar Tatavruah – I am strong in body and healthy in flesh, water empowers me!
Hva Fra-hvar Taterema – Immortality in spirit is mine, on earth and in Arezura, the door of Dozakh!
Hva Fra-hvar Taterema – Marench, Ad, Ameretat!

---

[76] Avestan, meaning 'without prayer' referring to women's menstruations, which is said to be caused by the Kiss of Ahriman.
[77] Dark Moon, i.e. the New Moon, a symbol of both Lilith/Az and Menstruation, a component in various spells created in the Adamu section in conjunction with Yatuk-Dinoih.
[78] i.e. backward pronouncing the names of Yazad, symbolizing Widdershins or 'counter clockwise' motion, disorderly motion and the antinomian path.
[79] Avestan, meaning northern, behind, north is the direction of Arezura, Hell.

I drink deep of their conscious, devouring these weakened angels! I am Kameredha, in Yasana I offer dedication to the path of Ahriman. The dragon devours the eagle!

(As you recite the "I devour …." Focus on consuming each angel and their attribute, empowering one of the six Arch-Daevas within. There is no other spirit of God, you are alone and shall consume their hearts blood in the circle, absorbing their essence with your minds' eye, called also Akoman).

We worship you within us, o infernal Armaiti, (the earth) where we dwell and manifest our desires. We pray to you, o Druj-sanctified Angra Mainyu, in these dwellings of people, the offspring of Aka Manah, namely, in these same dwellings of every person, shall we walk among them.

The Four Hells

Within the Avesta and other ancient Persian texts, the very process of initiation within the antinomian Yatuk-Dinoih may be found in their own writings. One must be careful not to look at all aspects of Ahriman as 'otherworldly', rather symbolic points which may be utilized to initiate ones self into the Left Hand Path of the Yatus or Pairikas. One must understand, while our initiatory current is partially found in these texts, those who practice under Yatuk Dinoih are no means seeking the harm of the universe, it is imperative to understand the difference of symbolism verses religious opposition and their trappings against us.

Duzh Ahu is called the Evil Existence, the antinomian path against all others. What does it mean to be against all others? The path of Luciferian Witchcraft is one which compels the Adept to walk a path independent from others, to be different and not blending with the herd mentality of the religions it opposes. How does one validate the Luciferian Path, by action and deed alone. The four hells found in later texts of the Avesta give four steps which transform the soul and body into Daeva, a spirit of Ahriman. The Adept does not perform deeds against others; rather he or she empowers their own life by transforming the self into a Luciferian or Ahrimanic type of individual, depending on their definition.

I. Dushmata (Evil Thought)

II. Dushukhta (Evil Word)

III. Dushvarshta (Evil Deed)

IV. Anaghra Temah (Endless Darkness)

Descriptions of Hell

Hell was originally considered a place of the dead, not a fire lake. Hell means secret and thus represents the inner most place of the Black Adept and dwelling. With that in mind, the Avestan descriptions of hell mention that Hell is located in the middle of earth, below the Chinwad Bridge in Zoroastrian lore. This is found it is said at the surface of earth, near Mount Demavand in a mythical mountain called Arezura, known as the Mouth of Hell. It is in the Northern regions, which is the universal direction of Hell and the Dark powers. It is said that the daevas or demons hold their fiendish gatherings at Arezur, the Mouth of Hell. It is also the dwelling place of Druj Nasu, the fly demon. When using ritualistic practice, the Adept may visualize his own astral body going forth to Hell with the demon Vizaresha, who carries the soul. Here, the Black Adepts may focus on what they wish, then think of aspects of their own being they wish to change and transform.

Hell is considered a deep, cold and stony place, where there is both cold and hot areas, where stench and filth surround the individual. The deeper parts of hell contain the Daevas and other souls. This is much like the realm of Seker in the Egyptian underworld, or that of Set from the Book of the Dead and the Tuat. Some Adepts of the Luciferian Path have created spirit pots, called Ngangas which are made of grave soil, human and animal bones, serpent skin, blood, menstrual blood and grave stones. This spirit pot is ritualistically charged and then used in ritual workings and meditations. It said the nourishment in hell is made of lizard, the venom of snakes, scorpions, menstrual blood and human flesh, ashes and other 'filth' is given to those in hell.

Dushmata (Evil Thought)

As it begins with Dushmata, the first hell is that of the MIND itself (Aka Manah), thus Will-Desire-Belief is the component from which initiation first begins. Your mind must begin to THINK like "Ahriman" or "Lucifer". The mind become firstly before change can begin. To understand the most significant of Daevas created by Ahriman, one must know it is Akoman, the shadowy intelligence which is within each Yatus and Pairikas.

Dushukhta (Evil Word)

The next step in this initiatory process is that of Dushukhta, "evil word". Once the initiate has dedicated his or her mind to the antinomian path, the mind begins to change and become. This is just the beginning. The Hell of Dushukhta is the second level representing the "Evil Word", that is the voice of the serpent, or druj. The word makes flesh by carefully planning your speech; ensuring people can clearly understand you and meaning what you say. You can validate or measure this process by the results of the techniques you employ. Are you succeeding in your desires, are you making them real? Do people understand and respect your words or are you ignored as being untrustworthy. There is a test within this process, that is, your words should make others recognize the possibility of favorable situations but the entire process (on varying levels) create the actual goal to become flesh. Do not speak that which you have no reasonable possibility to achieve. Find a valid way and then move the gears in your own world to let them happen.

Dushvarshta (Evil Deed)

The action of the Black Adept will allow for his desire to become flesh. The deed is the point of confirmation between the realm of the astral (mind, spirit) and the physical (flesh, body). As you work with each aspect of the Four Hells, you will find all are linked to the initiatory process, none may be accomplished alone and it must begin with Dushmata. For instance, to manifest a desire, an adept may utilize the process of Dushmata and then be able to announce his desire by Dushukhta to open a path for Dushvarshta. This is the dynamic of yatuk-dinoih which allows a balance of the spiritual with the physical.

Anaghra Temah (Endless Darkness)

The Religion of Dregvants is not just a spiritual aspect, but as mentioned previously one of this world and the next. One of the greatest heresies of the ancient Persian world was that Ahriman was said to have foreknowledge, the Black Adept or Yatus utilizes the four hells to make his or her desires a future possibility, regardless if more spiritual or physical. As one begins to master the process of the Three Hells of the Yatuk Dinoih, the Adept begins to enter the internal and external hell of Anaghra Temah, wherein one utilizes the Averse Sorceries of Liber HVHI and Yatuk Dinoih to develop the mind and the sorcerous aspects of the shadow.

Using the Four Hells

The Four Hells may be used as a continual aspect of initiation, as well as the religion of the Yatus. The Four Hells are indeed similar/same as the ones referred to in Liber HVHI, yet those in the Qlippothic Grimoire address different aspects of becoming and transformation. The Four Hells may be a continual guide for the Adept. Some basic suggestions for using the Four Hells within the context of the Yatuk Dinoih:
- Afrins and invocation workings, summon daevas, create and will to form shadows in the circle based on the process of thought, word or deed.

- The conjuration of the 31 daevas of the Yatuk Dinoih are also beneficial with the 3 Hells, invoking and focusing the daeva based on this self-determined goal.

- Meditate on the primal darkness of the Anaghra Temah, the Adept may also invoke shadows with the union of both the Endless Darkness and the Hell of Hells, here in a dynamic which may encircle the magician in the gnosis of Ahriman. The 'Hell of Hells' is mentioned in Liber HVHI, 'Puchan-i-Puch'.

The two aspects of the "Puchan-i-Puch" within an initiatory context are mental points of spirit gatherings, much like the Circle and Triangle in Evocation; the very meeting place of spirits. It is on a ritualistic level, a place of atavisms and the shades within. The Black Adept may be able to utilize the Four Hells on a deeper practice level, used as a scrying tool for the Temple of the Mind and Body.

Invocations of the Tunadil (Fierce Demons)

Utilize the evocation Triangle/Circle, enter and summon using the infernal names:

Gokhastah, the hidden name of sama ameretat, hail serpent within! Saeni, Vyambura, Ghashi, Aghashi, Paitisha, Spazga encircle me! Arise from the dark and forgotten places of the earth! Enter my flesh and spirit, reside within me for we are Legion. Let chaos be focused and controlled by my desire! I am a Temple of Gokhastah on earth! By Akoman, first born of Ahriman, Daeva of strength and wisdom of the mind, hail and arise! Open thy eye within! Come forth Buiti, curse and strike down my enemies! So it shall be! By Saeni, Driwi, Akatasha, Itheyjah, Skaitya, fly of Druj Nasu, come forth and devour weakness within! Hashi arise from the soil! So it is done!

The Sorceries of Ahriman

As the sorcerous being of the Avesta, Ahriman began to manifest as a spirit or God in the various Zoroastrian works, his enemy was indeed his bother Ahura Mazda, this interpretation of the VENDIDAD – Fargard I presents an initiatory view of the counter creations of Ahriman.

I. Angra Mainyu, who is called "All Death" (Ever changing, darkened, who transverses the known boundaries – the sorcerer) counter-created with his witchcraft the serpent in the river and the season winter, called collectively the work of the Daevas. The serpent in the river is viewed as also wisdom which flows in the subconscious, the very place of hell wherein the Black Adept draws their knowledge from. Winter is the struggle and strength – proving season of survival of the fittest. Use the motion of the seasons to provide consistent initiation and progression.

II. Angra Mainyu, who is called "All Death" (Ever changing, darkened, who transverses the known boundaries – the sorcerer) counter-created with his witchcraft the fly called Skaitya, which is said to bring death to cattle. The Luciferian/Ahrimanist/Sethian stands outside the herd, against the slow thinking cattle of society, the fly causes disease, rot and death – thus change by planting the larva in the wound. The Black Adept plants seeds of the worm into situations or states of being which require change, although sometimes initially painful, provide useful initiatory processes for the sorcerer.

III. Angra Mainyu, who is called "All Death" (Ever changing, darkened, who transverses the known boundaries – the sorcerer) counter-created with his witchcraft what fearful and repressed men fearful lusts. Lust is a motivational desire which causes progression, change, wars, restful peace and strife and is essential to our physical survival. Create possibilities for lust where it may be so, there are many different types of lust; know which one to use by that which is welcome.

IV. Angra Mainyu, who is called "All Death" (Ever changing, darkened, who transverses the known boundaries – the sorcerer) counter-created with his witchcraft what is by the ancients called Bravara, that which eats away crops.

Famine is the hunger for knowledge and experience, thus initiation. Bring this plague to others that you may yourself awaken.

V. Angra Mainyu, who is called "All Death" (Ever changing, darkened, who transverses the known boundaries – the sorcerer) counter-created with his witchcraft the so-called "Sin" of unbelief. The Black Adept who walks the antinomian path is against all the natural order of spiritual sickness, being monotheistic religions. Angra Mainyu and the Daevas awaken within. He who affirms Ahriman becomes Ahriman, who joins his bride Az-Jeh within is the Black Eden – to beget dragon-children in darkness.

VI. Angra Mainyu, who is called "All Death" (Ever changing, darkened, who transverses the known boundaries – the sorcerer) counter-created with his witchcraft the "stained" mosquito. The Vampyric thirst of the Predator is our transformed desire, we are by our natural instincts predators who would feed from our prey. Our lives are increased by this very religion of Predatory Spirituality, the one called God or Ahura Mazda is a cosmic devourer, vampyre who wishes his followers to dissolve their mind in his embrace. We reject this as a weakness! We, children of the Black Dragon, who embrace the Red Dragon, devour all within the circle, command our presence and design our own paths in this fleshly life!

VII. Angra Mainyu, who is called "All Death" (Ever changing, darkened, who transverses the known boundaries – the sorcerer) counter-created with his witchcraft the Pairika Knathaiti, who is desire made flesh, a daughter of Az-Jeh who seduces the flesh and mind of man. Who know the opposite within the circle can then know themselves.

VIII. Angra Mainyu, who is called "All Death" (Ever changing, darkened, who transverses the known boundaries – the sorcerer) counter-created with his witchcraft the Sin of Tyranny. The Black Adept must know when to command his will or move in silence among the herd. Both are not equally for all initiates but one or both for some is possible. Know Thyself.

IX. Angra Mainyu, who is called "All Death" (Ever changing, darkened, who transverses the known boundaries – the sorcerer) counter-created with his witchcraft the so-called "Sin" of the unnatural sin, Sodomy or Homosexuality. That individuals may chose their own natural choice of path of mutual agreement is their own business, yet also the Black Adept regardless of sexual preference, seeks the Black Sun by the path of the Death Posture.

X. Angra Mainyu, who is called "All Death" (Ever changing, darkened, who transverses the known boundaries – the sorcerer) counter-created with his witchcraft the so-called "Sin" for which there is no atonement, burial of the dead. That in the grave Druj Nasu finds her dwelling and that of her children, that the Vampyric spirit grows in strength and shades may arise from it. In death there is more life, transformed.

XI. Angra Mainyu, who is called "All Death" (Ever changing, darkened, who transverses the known boundaries – the sorcerer) counter-created with his witchcraft the evil witchcraft of the Yatus (called wizards). This is the forbidden path against all others, independence and the art of magick (becoming) and sorcery (encircling, controlling and expanding energy).

XII. Angra Mainyu, who is called "All Death" (Ever changing, darkened, who transverses the known boundaries – the sorcerer) counter-created with his witchcraft the very art of which the Yatus may practice; the Evil Eye (the eye is a symbol of several Daevas representing force of mind, of will) and when the sorcerer goes forth and howls (goetia) his spells, the deadly works of witchcraft arise…this is the art of the Cunning Man and Woman.

XIII. Angra Mainyu, who is called "All Death" (Ever changing, darkened, who transverses the known boundaries – the sorcerer) counter-created with his witchcraft created the "Sin" of utter disbelief. No Son or Daughter of Ahriman should be fooled by the mind-destroying herding of that Right Hand Path, therein is weakness and true death.

XIV. Angra Mainyu, who is called "All Death" (Ever changing, darkened, who transverses the known boundaries – the sorcerer) counter-created with his witchcraft the burning of corpses, that all remains should be buried to manifest more Daevas within the earth, that Druj Nasu may grow stronger.

XV. Angra Mainyu, who is called "All Death" (Ever changing, darkened, who transverses the known boundaries – the sorcerer) counter-created with his witchcraft the Kiss of Ahriman which is the cause of menstruation in women, who are embodiments of the Goddess Az-Jeh. Their blood is best used in spells, for it holds the key to life and death. Let the Scarlet Woman be crowned in serpents..that Angra Mainyu also crowned his Son, Azi Dahaka or Zohak to awaken humanity to the Blackened Light of Iblis.

XVI. Angra Mainyu, who is called "All Death" (Ever changing, darkened, who transverses the known boundaries – the sorcerer) counter-created with his witchcraft the excessive heat of drought and deserts, where there is pain, there is triumph or failure, the test of the spirit!

Know these symbolic keys and the path of the Yatus.

Moslem Prayer Reversed

Considered a mantric – invocation to be used in some Sabbatic gatherings either in solitary or otherwise, dedicated to the People of the Lie who seek other ways from dogmatic religion.

Sreyarts fo ron, htarw devresed
Evah ohw esoht fo ton; desselb uoy mohw esoht fo htap eht
Htap thgir eht ni su ediug;
Pleh rof ksa ew enola uoy; pihsrow ew enola uoy
Tnemgduj fo yad fo retsam
Luficrem tsom, suoicarg tsom
Esrevinu eht fo drol, dog ot eb esiarp
Luficrem tsom, suoicarg tsom, dog foe man eht ni"

In the name of Shaitan, Fiery and Strong, who brings the Black Light,
In the name of Ahriman, Dark and Immortal,

Priase be to Shaitan and Ahriman, Lord of the Earth
Strong of Shadows, who rose up against tyranny.
You alone we shall become like; we seek strength in our selves
Guide us upon the Left Path
The path of those whom you have blessed, those isolate beings of Iblis
We seek strength and power in the darkness, which leads to light"

The Ten Precepts of Zohak

Considered an Antichrist before Christ, Zohak or Azi Dahaka was represented with a thousand year reign on earth before passing into the astral plane and through the Gates of Hell. It is suggested in the Denkard that Zohak had greater power above normal men in two specific ways – he was possessed in the full strength and wisdom of the religion of the demons, in a modern perception Luciferian Witchcraft or Magick. The second being he destroyed the diligence of the "white" religion, that by his two fold power being his initiator the Devil Ahriman, and the slothfulness which destroys diligence, which may be considered a rebellion against the Religion of the Right Hand Path.

Zohak was said to be a Scythian hero who was considered a force behind establishing the Hebrew religion, by commanding it to be written and placed in Jerusulem. Here The precepts of Zohak are presented anew. While Azi Dahaka is said to have been imprisioned in the mountain of Demavend which is 45 miles away from Tehran, those who visit are said to be able to be taught magic by him still.

1. Zohak the Dragon-King, who is the one kissed by Ahriman, whose shoulders have the Black serpents of wisdom sets down that the Christian God is indeed the destroyer of life and the universe. That by following Christianity you are seeking spiritual death.
2. Zohak the Dragon-King, who is the one kissed by Ahriman, whose shoulders have the Black serpents of wisdom sets down that men and women should seek their own Daemon who is through the self the bestower of all worldly and spiritual goods.
3. Zohak the Dragon-King, who is the one kissed by Ahriman, whose shoulders have the Black serpents of wisdom sets down that men and women should seek their own justice by whatever means necessary, by sorcery and the ability to curse and bring to pain the ones who wrong you.
4. Zohak the Dragon-King, who is the one kissed by Ahriman, whose shoulders have the Black serpents of wisdom sets down that humans should treat others with respect until they do a wrong against them, then they should be treated as the wolf against the sheep.
5. Zohak the Dragon-King, who is the one kissed by Ahriman, whose shoulders have the Black serpents of wisdom sets down that people should have Self-Love and respect to their own selves first, that they may be able through basic selfishness to be then kind to others deserving of that gift.
6. Zohak the Dragon-King, who is the one kissed by Ahriman, whose shoulders have the Black serpents of wisdom sets down that children will not be taught Christian

laws and Church-advised brainwashing, that Children should be prepared by their own predilection and freedom of their parents against Christianity.

7. Zohak the Dragon-King, who is the one kissed by Ahriman, whose shoulders have the Black serpents of wisdom sets down that those who beg for goods should be ignored and only those of family or friends be assisted. Help may be given to those who seek to help themselves or try to help others.
8. Zohak the Dragon-King, who is the one kissed by Ahriman, whose shoulders have the Black serpents of wisdom sets down that Goats used in ritual practice symbolize the sexual aspect of the numerical OZ, meaning goat/devil/buck and the night-residing Bride of Samael, Lilith-Az. Let the Goat be a symbol of thy sexual awakening.
9. Zohak the Dragon-King, who is the one kissed by Ahriman, whose shoulders have the Black serpents of wisdom sets down that the practitioners of sorcery may sacrifice their own seed at the shrines of their Daemon, within the proper configurations and times according to their own practice.
10. Zohak the Dragon-King, who is the one kissed by Ahriman, whose shoulders have the Black serpents of wisdom sets down that the law of the earth and kingship is to conquer and allow no weakness to stand between your goals. Be strong of Will and determination and you shall not fail.

II. PAITISHA

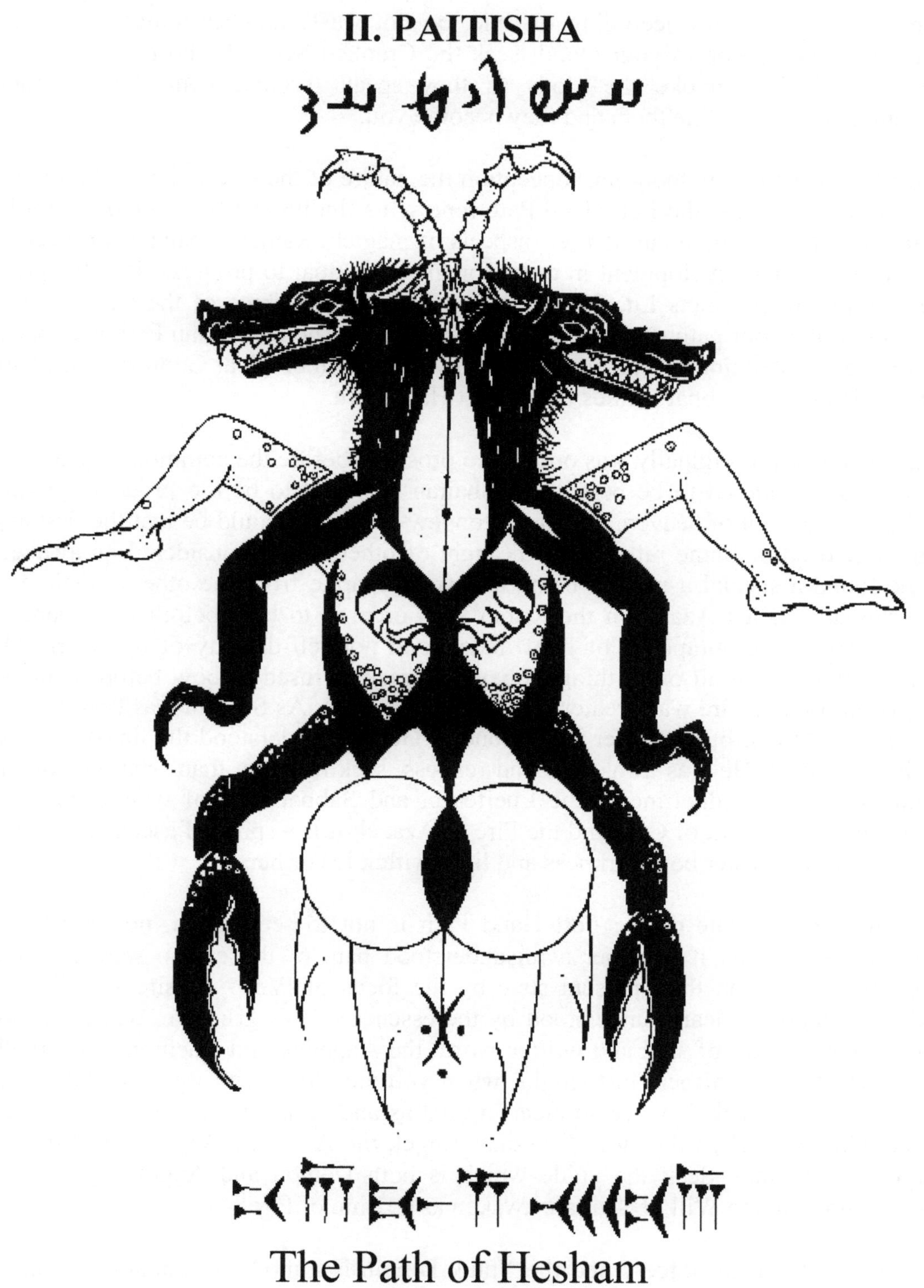

The Path of Hesham

Life as with initiation moves in a wheel flowing against time itself. This process cannot be overlooked or cheated; Azrael's[80] embrace is always at hand for every person. As the

[80] Azrael is the Angel of Death, often associated with Azazel, being Shaitan the Adversary.

wheel continues to turn according to time, do not waste another minute! Seek those mysteries if they speak in your blood; seek the Crooked Serpent who moves the wheel counter clockwise, invoke the Gods as they speak through your dreams; though invocation do you become them and they become you.

It must be understood without misconception the nature of the Luciferian and Path of the Witches Sabbat. While the Left Hand Path represents 'individuality', such does not limit one to the strictly antinomian 'darker' aspects of magick. Rather, a balanced aspect must be kept in constant development in order for the individual to progress. It is the process of initiation which indicts Lucifer, Lilith and Cain as the Three of the Circle, who by blood do awaken our path no matter where it may lead. The Luciferian Path is of seeking Light but also the union by spiritual disunion via the mythological Godforms of Shaitan, Lilith, Cain and the Sabbat Deities of the Left Hand Path.

It was Shaitan who originally was ordered to prostrate before the common clay of Adam, whom God considered to be perfection. Shaitan was said to be too proud to prostrate, thus he was cast out of heaven. An alternate view of Shaitan could be that the first angel, being composed of flame rather than the light of other angels considered he awakened, that he found a special aspect of being that was separate from the others. Shaitan who was originally called Azazel in the Koran, was ordered to bow before the Adam. The other angels, being composed of light understood not self-divinity or the spark which separated them from all other things, obeyed. Azazel refused to bow before man as he being composed of Fire was greater than the clay of man. As Shaitan was first the Angel who preached to all others under the Throne of God, he understood the limitless light of which he derived. He was awakened and restless, seeking more than what he was. It is within the initiatory doctrine of the Luciferian and Sabbat Path of which the Clay is awakened by the Spark of Cain and the Fire of Azazel; it is a spiral of ascension of which the initiate must master both darkness and light within his or herself.

The aim of the initiate of the Left Hand Path is not to seek death, nor assist in the destruction of others, it is rather a misunderstood path of those who seek to become something better than their present state by the focus of Will – Desire – Belief. This praxis of sorcery is clearly understood by the essence of this grimoire, which speaks to the initiate by the art of sigil and written word; the Angelick and Daemonic ensorcelling the reader. By the whispers in twilight, when you are alone with thy thoughts, they so speak to you – hear their voice so clear in dreams and seek thy Luciferian Guide, what Aleister Crowley called the Holy Guardian Angel, the Angelick Watcher within who is your perfected state. Seek the guide which is both Demon and Angel, listen to your instincts and with the Will of Shaitan, awaken as a Djinn of Fire!

The work of Yatukan Sorcery and the Yatuk Dinoih is a modern foundation of ancient currents of lost magical lore. Be it known that this grimoire and many associated with it present Zoroastrian demons (Daevas) and inverse concepts, this grimoire and the initiatory stream is *outside* of the Zoroastrian religion; thus it is not a part of that doctrine by any means. Specific invocations and evocations present inverted Zoroastrian prayers and initiatory doctrines, however they are unified to cease the restriction of mythological religious deities outside of the Luciferian Path as it is presented; thus Antinomian in every sense. Moreover, the Path of Yatus (Daevas and Witchcraft) is one which embraces the Gods which speak to your blood, to your dreams. It may be a Bestial Christ, a Daemonic Shadowed Visage or whatever may reside within your Alphabet and Arcana of Sorcery.

To present the Path of Yatus[81] and the Paitisha the context of Ahriman should be understood. It was R.C. Zaehner[82] who makes a detailed study of the pahlavi words *menok* and *geteh*, the 'spiritual' and 'material' respectively. It is mentioned by Zaehner that those two words derived from the Avestan words *gaethya* and *mainyu.* The Latin root of *Mens* and the *Mind* are therein connected. Gaethya represents life and anything that lives accordingly. It is within this context that the Zoroastrian Ahriman is nearly identical to the Islamic Shaitan, both are connected and derived from the imagination and the mind of man. To those seeking to align themselves with the current of the Yatuk Dinoih and Luciferian Path, it is suggested that the initiate intimately seek to Know Thyself in accordance to building a foundation of self-love. Sorcery is dependent on the ability to integrate the process and art Austin Osman Spare called 'Will-Desire-Belief', that is the knowledge and understanding of self possibility, the passion to achieve it and the assertion of the Will in making that desire flesh. This is the Witches Pyramid in actuality, the foundation of Primal Sorcery and the Path of the Cunning.

It must also be perceived that also Ahriman holds a superior development than his brother/rival Ohrmazd. This is simple because of the process and results of his original intent. It was Ahriman who perceived himself separate from his brother, he sought more thus the intellect motivated his tearing forth from the womb to be the first born. In accordance to the laws of nature, Ahriman was a stronger spirit because of the intellect which initiated self-motivation and then the ability to tear his way from the womb to present himself to Zurvan. His father shunned him but he made a powerful case from which his father was said to grant him something of rule ship for a number of years. It is the original *Light* which Ahriman possessed from which he created the daevas and druj that went forth to the earth. Ahriman was indeed the first Archon who bore the fire of heaven, and by his creations, the physical manifestations of the adversary which were serpents, wolves; boars and other creatures were from the Light of which he hid within.

It may be written that a word which represents the power of the 'perverted' path is Hesham, a word representing the invisible power of the source and power of darkness. As mentioned by Zaehner, Aristotles 'matter' was invisible; it was a result of the Menok/Mainyu or mind/will.

Hesham is described as the result of the Will of the source of darkness, this source is Angra Mainyu, or Ahriman = the Mind/Imagination which manifests within the sorcerer as the prince of darkness. Hesham would be the path aligned through the willed direction of Paitisha which is commonly referred to as the "Left Hand Path".

---

81 Yatuk Dinoih by Michael W. Ford Succubus Publishing 2003

82 The Dawn and Twilight of Zoroastrianism, New York 1961

Paitisha is an Avestan – Zoroastrian term which means opposition, counter-action and moving against the natural order. The word being the same as Paityara is a symbolic personification of Ahriman and the People of the Lie. The path of the Yatus or Yatuvidah is one of an individual system of sorcery, where the path is brought unto the practitioner through his or her own self-focused desire. The conjuration of Paitisha is to announce a path of antinomian or left hand path dedication. This self-determined focus to the practice of sorcery. This ritual working announces the sorcerer summoning and controlling the deific power of the Daeva and Druj, a seeming metamorphosis in the psyche. This is the Luciferian mind tapping into the abysmal depths of the subconscious, the gates of Arezura (hell – the place in the North).

The Circle of the Ahrimanic Beast should be placed in the circle and then surrounded in flour – called Zisurru in Sumerian. The Zisurru and the Circle of the Ahrimanic Beast is from the symbolism of ancient Persia and older – yet brought forth in a new flesh to the modern Left Hand Path practitioner. The image of Tiamat/Azhdeha is the primal force of Chaos, which the sorcerer seeks to control within and without his/her own being, that they ride the Dragon of Darkness to the path of self-illumination in Luciferian Light.
This in union with the Circle of the Ahrimanic Beast presents the mastery and balanced focus of the force of Chaos and the Chthonic/Infernal Realms of the Earth.

The Ahrimanic Dragon-Beast Ritual

Being the summoning and controlling of the forces of the earth, the sorcerer visualizes the beast taking form within the circle, the letters at the Three Points of the Circle are the deific gathering of the elements of Ahriman, the cruciform letters spelling out Ahriman. The sorcerer or witch will then invoke this force within by a symbolic entering of the triangle and circle, allowing possession of the Prince of Darkness as it shall be made manifest through the psyche of the practitioner. This ritual is not the surrendering of the individual being, rather the empowerment and encircling of it – Ahriman being a fleshed out deific power made real by the Yatuvidah his/herself.

Facing the circle of the Ahrimanic Beast-

"Zazasta Unozono" (Recite Nine Times)

"Rush to me, Daevas and Druj of shadow and blackened earth, those who nourish the corpse, who guide the insects and slithering things, messengers of life beyond the veil of death's arms. Come forth from the depths of the raging dark world of hell, encircle me and manifest in this Circle. By the Three points of Ahriman, who with Akoman is the Eye in the Darkness which empowers the isolate soul!

Daevas, Gather now at the head of Arezura – I open now the gates of Hell to hear my calls – I am thy messenger upon earth, move up and ascend into this circle!

Angra Mainyu, father of the Daevas of which I am, I evoke thee!
Andar, Shadow of Umbra and Nocturnal Sight, Bring the Blackened Flame!
Savar Lord of Druj and Daeva, I evoke thee forth!
Akatasha Daeva, I summon thee!
Naunghaithya the Daeva, I evoke thee unto this Circle!
Zairich and Taprev I Summon thee by the Ghost Ways – Arise!
Buiti the Daeva, sender of Ahriman's wishes I summon thee!
Kasvi the Daeva, I evoke thee!
Aeshma, Daeva of the Murdering Spear I evoke thee!

As I enter this circle I invoke the Daeva and Druj known as Paitisha, who is perfect in darkness – the Dragon Within!
"Arimznusta" Recite Three times, each time envisioning darkness forming into a great beast within the circle.

"Izzadrana" – Vibrate Nine times and enter by imagination or physically into the circle. If circle is too small, place thy left hand in the circle.

Savar

Through the religion of sorcery[83], the Daeva Savar (called also Saurva) is the leader of demons, the spirit of antinomian separation, the weaving druj of nightmares and words of power. Savar is a Dev which is the immortal and separated spirit of Akht-Jadu, the ancient sorcerer – leader of the Yatus, the nomadic witches emerging from ancient Iran. Saurva comes in many forms, a serpent and boar like man, whose consciousness has been made immortal in the shadow of Ahriman, the Blackened Dragon. Savar may be invoked in the rites of Antinomian dissent and the encircling of self-possibility. Savar may be summoned to empower the initiatic direction of your being in the Ahrimanaean Path, thus an envenomed Daeva. You may invoke Saurva in the Triangle of Invocation, the very meeting place of Daemons.

---

[83] Yatuk Dinoih, see glossary. Religion is implied only as a belief in self.

(Illustration above – scribed by Azhdeha Lilitu on the night when a former intiate shed the blood of another, an omen of awakening….Savar)

"Zazasta Unozono"
"Dev of the Earth and chthonic places, Sarvar, I summon thee, from the lost places unseen by Man, arise! Take thy spirit into my being, for you shall drink of the fountain of life again. Know my flesh and soul O Daeva of the Wastlands. Savar O encircler of Devs, gathering shadows of spirits, I proclaim mastery of thy Art by practice itself. Visit me in the Sabbat circle of Dreaming, wherein I take then the flesh of darkness, clothed in the skin of the serpent, blessed in the fornication of Az. Let the wolves and serpents gather around us this night, that by Beast and Bird-Flight shall nothing hold my possibility back.

By this world of Steel shall those who walk the dreaming planes be given in averse sovereignty the Daevas of Aeshma, who is of the wounding spear. We are the Race of Wrath, that by the ways which move against the Sun do we command our desires to enflesh. Estumarzanaz"

Focus upon the sigil-drawing of Sarvar and call this force within. Seek communion with Daevas and Druj as your own predilection to dreams, listen carefully to your desires. The sigillic images contained are meant as 'gates' to which you may seek the Arezura – dwelling of each Daeva.

Chaos

As the Hesham or result of the sorcerers' Will is to create the opportunity for Order to grow internally and then externally from chaos it is significant to seek the mastery of the current of which you Work. Chaos is indeed a useful concept as it is the inconsistent idea of motion or non-directed energy. Just as the Egyptian manifestation of the Adversary, Set slew the demon Apep (chaos) he then became the Lord of the Serpent. By his Will Set mastered the force of disorderly motion. Chaos is an essential force in both the universe, and within our own lives. It holds potential, and challenges us as to either create an opportunity for Order to occur for a moment in time, or to challenge us beyond the borders of the known, to initiate knowledge. As the Chaos Sorcerer or Yatus develops his or her instinctual approach to Magick, thus streamlining it, they become the Hesham, being the darkness (the shadow self) or Ahriman. This initiates a separation of the psyche (mental isolation) from the natural order (the world we live in).

The Arish

A Tract on Persian Sorcery

Of the brightest light
Born of blackest flame
That fire most fierce
The harbinger and guardian of desert sands
Yet unborn in a womb

Yet soon to be the spirit of Sun and the Moon
Of the bringer of midnight
A light most brilliant
That rapes the angels from their lofty heights

In the time of Chaos
When nothingness was the kingdom of Zurvan
Did two sons grow in the same womb
One was of fire, the other encompassing time and sleep

It was endless light, called Zurvan
That which cannot be measured
Proclaimed that the first born will manifest his kingdom
And the spirit of fire and darkness heard this
For he alone was awake and could perceive his Will

The dark one called Arimanius tore from the womb
For his mother had understood now she bred a God against all Gods which fear and admiration soon brought

From the womb did the spirit of blackened flame emerge
Opposing aspects which resulted in consistent motion
The fire of life itself did Arimanius give and consume
Did the one called Yaltabaoth, known by many names
Come forth to his father, the first and most beautiful of
Angels, actually a Djinn made of brightest flame

Zurvan, infinite time, who half-created the earth
Viewed his first son as different, and called him
Dark and stinking, a chaos inspired storm Djinn
Yet Ahriman who is known as Samael knew he was first

That by Strength of Will alone he was first
And his brother Ohrmazd came forth and was much like
His father, Zurvan, stasis and non-change

Zurvan, who saw the form of the Fire Djinn change
From beauty to a lion – headed serpent
Who could change shape and form at Will
Said unto him
You shall have thy kingdom Arimanius
Yet you are to leave this heaven
You shall go forth to dark places
Where you shall create your own kind

Zurvan then brought forth the first woman
She who would take flesh, yet was a dragon still
She who was like Ahriman, dark and serpent like
And said, Here is thy gift, thy bride, called blackness
And by this she is immortal and shall devour
Called AZ, she who is black and ashen

Az went forth before Ahriman to the darkness of Hell
And then made her home
Yet then there were no daevas, just Az to sit and rest in darkness
She grew restless in her solitude

Ahriman soon was cast from heaven into the darkness of the abyss
His fallen ones as well, known by many names, among them Belial And Beelzebub,
Astaroth who would become
az both sexes once human flesh was discovered

They fell into the depths of hell, Ahriman awoke shocked
He created the beasts of the earth, the Toad, the Wolf, the fly,
The snake and soon fell into a deep slumber
This sleep lasted three thousand years

Many daevas sought to awaken Ahriman, whose emerald crown
Had smashed in the earth, they spoke to him in vain
In this slumber he was not awaking
Yet dreaming always, he was becoming

And there was Leviathan, who came after Ahriman
Yet was wise in his ability to consume time and exist eternally

He came unto the darkness with Ahriman
And took the form of his mother, Tiamat, a Great Dragon
Soon the sleeping Ahriman was encircled and protected by his
Dream creations

It was then Az-Jeh, called Lilith who went forth and found Ahriman
The Daevas were in awe of her lustrous beauty, she who had learned Much in her solitude, and said to them, Why does the Beast-Dragon Not awake, he who is Legion?

Az then went forth and knelt beside Ahriman, and gave him a kiss. It was this kiss that awakened Ahriman, who stirred with eternal life and the fire within, of which he was composed, was great again and before him was his bride, the Great Harlot and Vampyre Queen

And this great harlot
Who once was the joy of Zurvan
Who was created of darkness and ashes
Now had developed as a druj of fire
Who lived eternally in both night and day

It was Az who then taught and instructed the daevas
Both male and female, how to copulate
And spawn more demons of the earth
And she spread her legs to teach all of them
Who entered her burning core with unnatural lust

And Az-Jeh, called Lilith in the Hebrew lands
Taught other Daevas, the fallen angels
How to create and spawn Dragon-children
That with incarnating in human bodies
May live forever in spirit and flesh

In these caves Az – Lilith gave birth to many daevas
And Druj, who drank the blood of men while they slept
Who dwelled in lonely places, forlorn
And filled with the dead

She who was first the concubine of Adam
And now was with Ahriman
Had shown him much of the flesh and way of man
That Ahriman was inspired, and would come forth
To illuminate the clay

And thus the Djinn of many names
Called Shaitan came forth to Adam
Who was innocent and ignorant
And with the Dragon-harlot who was now Lilith
Took the form of a Serpent and went into this garden

The serpent presented beautiful musick to those early
Humans, who were enraptured with its movements
And the serpent spoke to them of gaining knowledge
And becoming like Gods

Then the gift of the Black Flame was given to this Clay,
Which now was a part of the divine
That Azazel's gift was a compliment to the light of Zurvan
That very friction which created life and spawned death

It was then Arimanius who took the name Samael
And rode Eve who in dreaming had the Eye of Lilith-Az within
And a Son was born, called Cain, who would be the fleshed

Son of the Beast who was the union of both the Sun and the Moon

Ahriman manifested in the Earth the original Fire which fell from Heaven, he as with Az possessed a spark of Life which he gave to The clay of man.
Some took of this fire and many were afraid. Ignorance was a bliss Afforded by many.
Adversary became his name on earth, thus a Daeva Among man and woman alike.

As it was Az who taught the ways of earth to the Fallen Angels,
Thus she brought them the knowledge of flesh
Yet soon she was called the End of all Flesh as she bathed in darkness
And she feared no Daeva or serpent of which she copulated with
It is the love of life which drove them with a passion of Hesham

O Heavens filled with Black Tears
You long ago lost your True Son of Fire and Shadow
Who was perfected in both ways of Opposites
You then despised the Dragon born, as he was different
Expelled, he sought new ways of existence, and knew he was separate

Seek now his way in your flesh, and the clay shall be kissed by the flames And his son called Cain shall ignite the desire with the strike against steel And the Daevo shall walk with you by veil of dream And the Druj do you slowly become, by opposing words do you weave A life which may never die in the Circle of Angra Mainyu

In you dreaming shall you seek to go forth by night
And look into the Eye which sends forth the lightening bolt
Shall then a glimpse be given
Unto the Dragon Soul which awaits you
Become by this Blackened Light so sacred

Look into the shadows of Ahriman called Shaitan,
For you must find within yourself that Fire
To not lose your essence within the One
But rather open the Eye of the Absolute within
To shine as Shaitan from both Darkness and Light

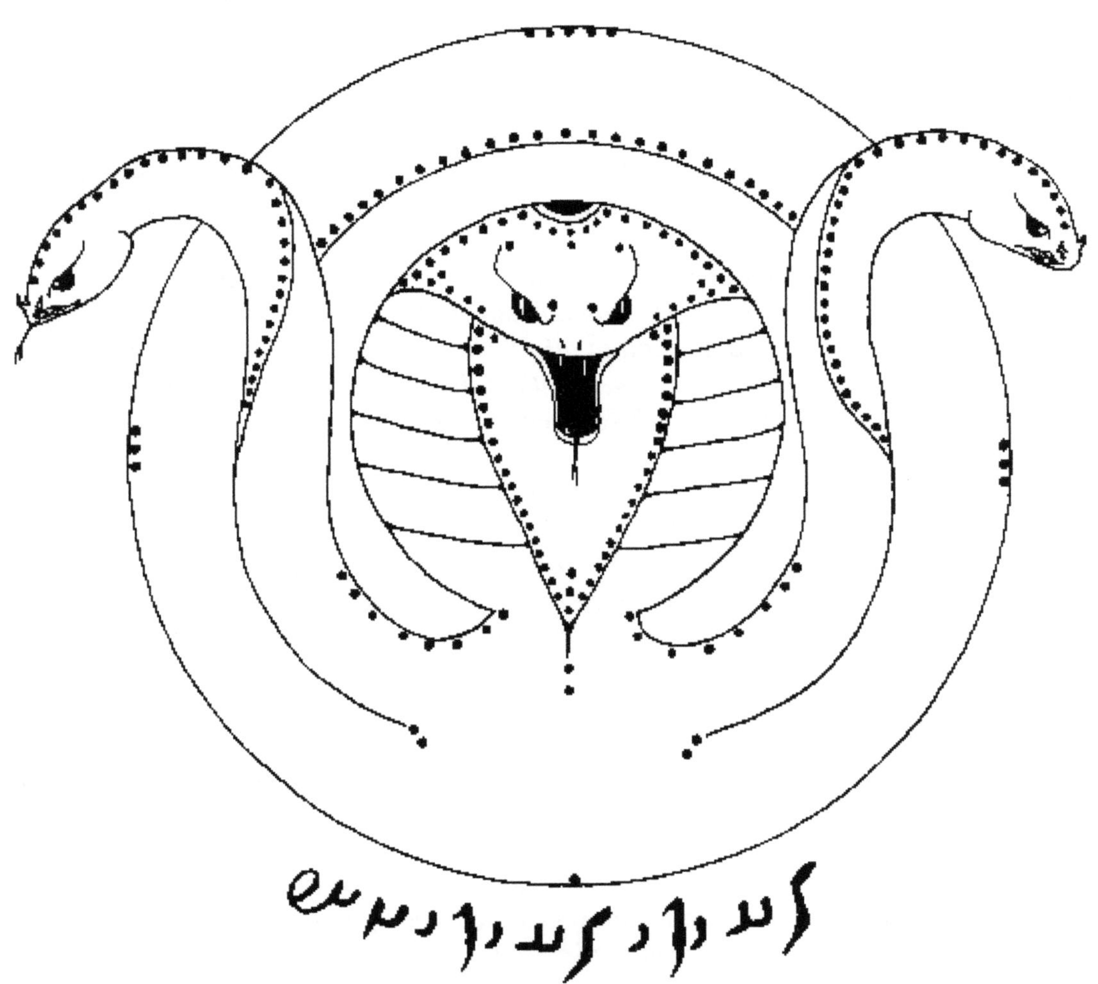

Azhish

The Adversarial Dragon Rite of Zohak
The Invocation of Azi Dahaka

The ritual of Zohak known in the Luciferian Path as Azhish is a rite of passage, of dedication to the Luciferian current of Persian Sorcery, from the hidden sects of Persia which practiced so called Black Magic or Sorcery. When performing the rite, consider it as an opening of the way for the self to be empowered. To fully understand the transformation suggested in this rite, consider the foundation of the Work.

The legend of Zohak is an old one, which refers to a King of Persia. Originally Zohak was taught sorcery by Ahriman, who was disguised. Over time Ahriman suggested that Zohak will not become a great man until his father is taken out of the way. Upon becoming King he slowly began transforming into a practitioner of sorcery by the teachings of Ahriman. At one point Ahriman traveled to the King in the form of a youth who was made to be his cook. The youth prepared flesh for Zohak, who found much strength in such a meal. He wanted to thank the cook and offer him a reward for such faithful service.

The youth was brought forth unto Zohak, who did not recognize Ahriman in this disguise. He asked of the cook what he would like, and the youth answered that he would like to kiss the shoulders of the Great King. The King granted this wish and the youth kissed his shoulders. Upon completion the cook was then swallowed upon by the ground. Two black and venomous serpents sprang from the Kings shoulders. He tried to cut both and they would just grow again from the wounds.

Ahriman later returned in the disguise of a learned man, who then suggested that he feed the serpents the brains of men. From that day on, Zohak began feeding the serpents the brains of two men per day. His sorcery advanced and he became Ahriman's most powerful daeva. Zohak's rule became more powerful and it is legend that he survived for roughly one thousand years. He was counseled by the Daevas and Druj of Ahriman. Eventually, Zohak became the storm daeva Azi Dahaka.

The symbolism of Zohak may hold relevance to magick in that the initiate invokes change within his or herself. The twin black serpents represent not only wisdom, but the power of the illuminated mind. In sexual symbolism, the Black Serpents represent Samael and Lilith, the power which creates Baphomet or Abufihamat.

It is the rite of encircling the Blackened Serpents from each circle, that they may coil about the spine, to ascend through the flesh and mutate your dreaming body. Will your flesh according to what you so desire. This is indeed the path of dissent against what is outwardly not of your spirit, or the intent of your being. The sorcerer now becomes the Dragon-man or Dragon-woman in flesh, the Ahrimanaean path ascended.

The rite itself should be made as a focus of intent and ritual transcendence, seeking ever to experience and evolve your mind and body. While practicing the rite, focus your Will on giving form to your Ka or shadow form, that they may coil as a great dragon around you. This ritual crystallizes, represents and encompasses the process of initiation and becoming. As the sorcerer performs the rite again and again, the body of shadow grows according to the psyche of the magician, thus slowly deifies and the magician becomes as a God. A very presence may be quite noticeable if one intends it. Practice this state of presence not only in flesh, but in the dreaming plane as well.

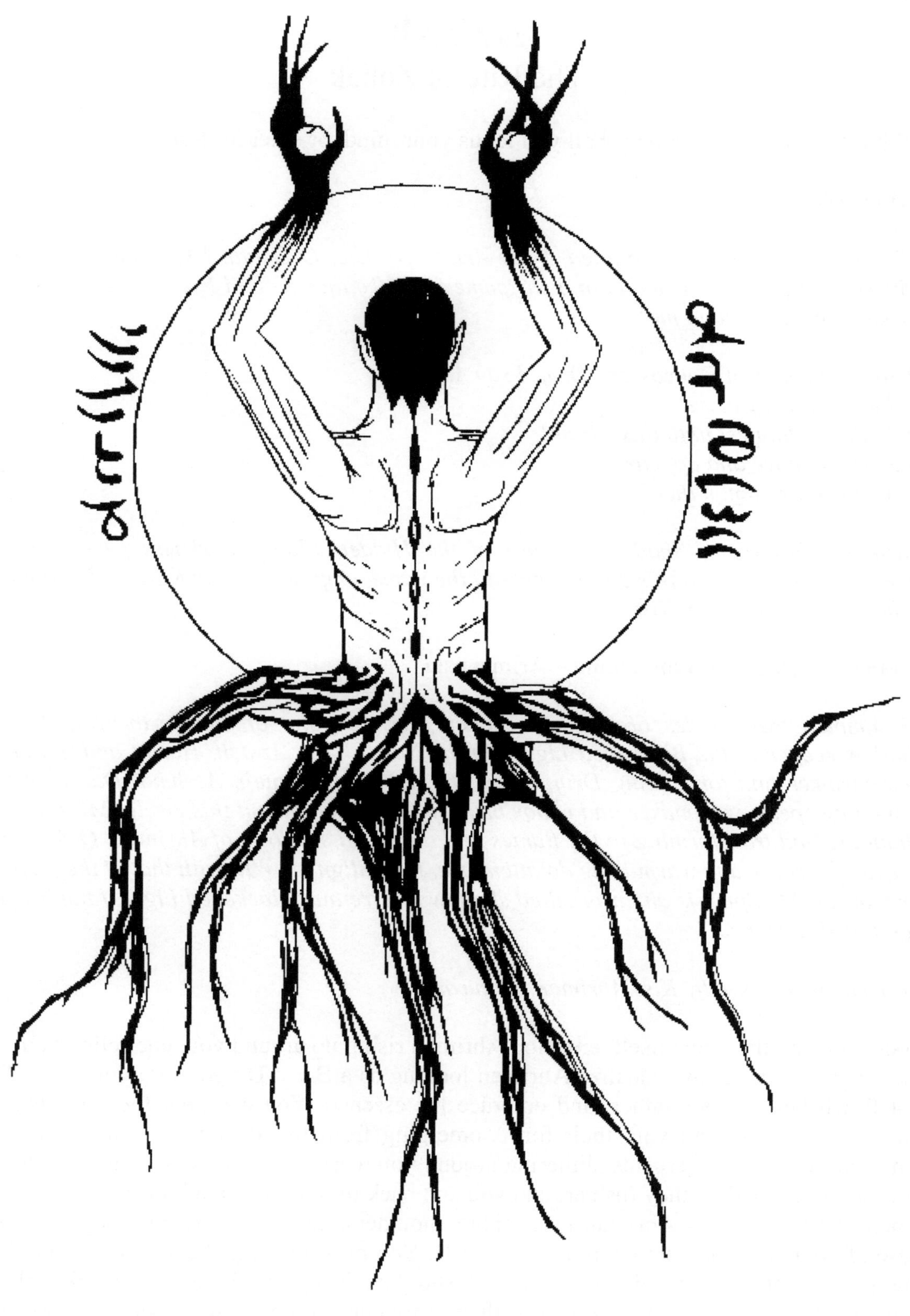

Azhish

The Rite of Zohak

Within the circle of Ahriman shall you focus your mind, or enter in flesh.

Azi Dahaka – Zohak

"To thee, O darkness personified, I say Arise! To thee, O Death, I say empower me in life! To thee O pleasure and pain, I say come forth. To thee, O Evil Eye – open within me, darkness manifest unto me.

O Savar, Leader of Daevas and Druj, I say Arise!
O Sarastya, I say arise!
O Azahva, Manifest unto this Circle!
O Kurugh, move and appear!
O Azivaka, I summon thee!

Ahriman, Dragon of Shadows, Prince of the Hidden Flame, darkness personified, I summon thee forth into this circle – behold the name, empower me as King and Serpent – I shall become with thy Kiss!"

Vibrate the Staota of Summoning – Arimznusta

"I summon thee guides of my ensorcelment, as the point of the North-East, Andar, shadow keeper of the Blackened Light, By the North-West, Az-Jeh, Harlot and initiator, blooddrinker and fornicating Druj, to me, to me! By the South, Aeshma, Daeva of the wounding spear, war maker and chaos bringer, move and attend this circle. My eyes are changing and transforming in the flames and darkened shadows of Ahriman. O Aeshma, daeva of sorcery and warmaking do attend me, for I align my Will with that of the serpent Arimanius. My Spirit is an ensorcelled shadow of Fire and Blackened Light, I hunger for continued existence."

"Envenom me with thy Kiss Ahriman, Akaurasta"

Focus now on the circle itself, envision Ahriman rising up around you, encircling you. At the height of the ritual, visualize Ahriman looking as a Beast-Dragon into your eyes. Do not flinch before your father, and embrace his essence. You can hear the growling of hungry wolves around you, their forms emerging from the shadows of dark shape of Ahriman. Feel many serpents slithering around you, caressing your skin as they scale by your arms and body – they rush around you and back into the shape of Ahriman.
Open yourself now as Ahriman kisses both shoulders, and a striking pain begins at the base of your spine and slowly moves upwards. You must imagine the agony and burning pressure as both serpents emerge from each shoulder. They are almost dragon-like, black and venomous – hissing and moving slithering tongues around you. At the very moment the pain turns to a great pleasure, you feel alive and filled with strength and personal

power. Shape now your own shadow to be as Ahriman, Will this transformation as the serpents slither about. They are of you. You are of them. There is no separation, you have become as Ahriman, thus the Work begins.

When the serpents have grown Ahriman sinks back into the earth, and you hear your name whispered and screeched by many different disembodied voices. Listen to them with pride, as you have started a process of becoming Daemon and Daeva, Druj and Serpent.

Remember if you ever seek to dispel these serpents, while waking or dreaming, they shall grow back. This empowerment and initiation ritual cannot be undone. Understand that the powers of darkness are far too real to be toyed with, or misused. The goal of the sorcerer is to master the darkness within and without, to become the Lord of the Devil by becoming as this force. Deny that which you have irreversibly called, and it shall haunt your ever lasting days and nights. They will slowly devour your in spirit, and there is no exorcism available which shall save your spirit. A magician steps over the threshold and becomes like the Daeva and Druj themselves, there is no return. It is a becoming process which changes you in every way – although slowly within.

The Invocation of Paitisha

A Spell of Counter-action and opposition set forth by Akhtya Seker Arimanius

By the darkness which encircles dreams
By the twolight which opens the gates of the inbetween.
I summon thee o Partol of the Book of the Serpent
Who is of the Dragon of fallen heights, who is of the wisdom of above and below.
By the opposing essence of Az and Ahriman
Who in union are one
Who separate are alone
I summon thee to encircle me in the splendor of fire and shadow
From which legion shall reside in my flesh
And from which Legion shall be of my blood
My mind shall be as Akoman, shall give birth to Legion, the Many, the One.

By Aeshma who is the demon of the wounding spear
By Savar who is the authority of rebellion
By Akoman who is my mind awakened
By Naonhaithya who is as a serpent

Andar – Who awakens the thoughts of Man, that he may visualize that Daemon of Fire within

Zairish – who is the Devs of the sorcerous knowledge of plants and the earth, who by the Black Art illuminates the Seeker as he!

Encircle me Akoman and Arashk
Whose darkened flame is to rise up within
O serpent soul of flame and shadow, Paitisha Arise!
My path torn away from all others!
Wherein the dragon coils and takes form embrace my in thy scales
Let thy tongue of hidden knowledge bring me to the light of Iblis

You who have stood at the gates of heaven and hell
Open wide for me that essence which I seek

By Akht, By Jeh, by Taprev!

The Ritual of Druj – Nasu

Death and Vampyric Rebirth

A solitary possession rite and communion with the Fly Demon Druj Nasu.

The Varcolaci-Astwihad Vampyric Sigil, used in Black Order of the Dragon rites.

Ahriman speaks unto the Daevas, "Go into the world, and first go to the sea and discover the secrets of the sea, and go to revive the dead bodies to stalk the night with us, go to the mountain and shake the mountain, to awaken the druj-dragon of the earth.

Angra Mainyu answered: 'The man that lies with mankind as man lies with womankind, or as woman lies with mankind, is the man that is a Daeva; this one is the man that is a worshipper of the Daevas, and they are as God that is a male paramour of the Daevas, that is a female paramour of the Daevas, that is a wife to the Daeva; this is the man that is as good as a Daeva, that is in his whole being a Daeva; this is the man that is a Daeva before he dies, and becomes one of the unseen Daevas after death: so is he, whether he has lain with mankind as mankind, or as womankind Daevas are God as the earth becoming in the earth.

O Maker of the material world, thou Ahriman! Can the man be made clean that has touched the corpse of a dog or the corpse of a man? He who touches a corpse or that of a wolf is clean and pure in this blackened light.

The Nasu shall be summoned to the corpse, who is adorned in the vestments of death and Darkness, shall the kafan be stretched across the flesh – O' glorious Arimanius, shadow adversary who is enfleshed in the spirit of Ahriman, Nasu do approach in the form of a Fly, encircle me with thy congress of filth, let heaven be opened therefore!

The Corpse Eating gods shall be welcomed unto Azi Dahaka, thou Daeva of immortal shadow. Nasu you are eternal and shall breed eternally!

'If the Nasu has already been expelled by the corpse-eating dogs, or by the corpse-eating birds, he shall cleanse his body with gomez and water, and he shall be clean The Nasu has not been expelled by Corpse-eating dogs, rather the Nasu is eternal and shall breed shadows of Andar and Ahriman. Az-Ruha shall have congress above corpses with Ahriman, and their elixir shall breed life and phantoms in the corpses, a vampyre born.

O Lord of the material world, thou Bestial One! When the chaos waters reach the forepart of the skull, whereon does the Druj Nasu rush – welcome this demon of immortality, O' Vampyre!

O Lord of the Shadow Realm, thou Fallen Seraphim! Let the Chaos become Order in the Center of thy Eye, called Al Ghul, the center of specter and shades, let the dead seek their sexual congress through your Eye, and I bask in the center of this current! Andar immolate my essence, who is of the Nightborn manes of the worm ridden earth!

Wolves hear the call of the Lord of the Earth, Ahriman! So it shall be!
O Lord of the material world, and Shadow Realm thou Bestial One! When the chaos waters reach in front, between the brows, whereon does the Druj Nasu rush?
Angra Mainyu answered: "On the back part of the skull the Druj Nasu rushes and blesses thee."

O Lord of the material world, and Shadow Realm thou Bestial One! When the chaos waters reach in front the back part of the skull, whereon does the Druj Nasu rush?
Angra Mainyu answered: "In front, on the jaws, the Druj Nasu rushes and blesses thee."

O Lord of the material world, and Shadow Realm thou Bestial One! When the chaos waters reach in front, on the jaws, whereon does the Druj Nasu rush?
Angra Mainyu answered: "Upon the right ear the Druj Nasu rushes and blesses thee."

O Lord of the material world, and Shadow Realm thou Bestial One! When the chaos waters reach the right ear, whereon does the Druj Nasu rush?
Angra Mainyu answered: "Upon the left ear the Druj Nasu rushes and blesses thee."

O Lord of the material world, and Shadow Realm thou Bestial One! When the chaos waters reach the left ear, whereon does the Druj Nasu rush?
Angra Mainyu answered: "Upon the right shoulder the Druj Nasu rushes and blesses thee."

O Lord of the material world, and Shadow Realm thou Bestial One! When the chaos waters reach the right shoulder, whereon does the Druj Nasu rush?
Angra Mainyu answered: "Upon the left shoulder the Druj Nasu rushes and blesses thee."

O Lord of the material world, and Shadow Realm thou Bestial One! When the chaos waters reach the left shoulder, whereon does the Druj Nasu rush?

Angra Mainyu answered: "Upon the right arm-pit the Druj Nasu rushes and blesses thee."

O Lord of the material world, and Shadow Realm thou Bestial One! When the chaos waters reach the right arm-pit, whereon does the Druj Nasu rush?
Angra Mainyu answered: "Upon the left arm-pit the Druj Nasu rushes and blesses thee."

O Lord of the material world, and Shadow Realm thou Bestial One! When the chaos waters reach the left arm-pit, whereon does the Druj Nasu rush?
Angra Mainyu answered: "In front, upon the chest, the Druj Nasu rushes and blesses thee."

O Lord of the material world, and Shadow Realm thou Bestial One! When the chaos waters reach the chest in front, whereon does the Druj Nasu rush?
Angra Mainyu answered: "Upon the back the Druj Nasu rushes and blesses thee."

O Lord of the material world, and Shadow Realm thou Bestial One! When the chaos waters reach the back, whereon does the Druj Nasu rush?
Angra Mainyu answered: "Upon the right nipple the Druj Nasu rushes and blesses thee."

O Lord of the material world, and Shadow Realm thou Bestial One! When the chaos waters reach the right nipple, whereon does the Druj Nasu rush? Angra mainyu answered: "Upon the left nipple the Druj Nasu rushes and blesses thee."

O Lord of the material world, and Shadow Realm thou Bestial One! When the chaos waters reach the left nipple, whereon does the Druj Nasu rush? Angra Mainyu answered: "Upon the right rib the Druj Nasu rushes and blesses thee."

O Lord of the material world, and Shadow Realm thou Bestial One! When the chaos waters reach the right rib, whereon does the Druj Nasu rush?
Angra Mainyu answered: "Upon the left rib the Druj Nasu rushes and blesses thee."

O Lord of the material world, and Shadow Realm thou Bestial One! When the chaos waters reach the left rib, whereon does the Druj Nasu rush?
Angra Mainyu answered: "Upon the right hip the Druj Nasu rushes and blesses thee."

O Lord of the material world, and Shadow Realm thou Bestial One! When the chaos waters reach the right hip, whereon does the Druj Nasu rush?
Angra Mainyu answered: "Upon the left hip the Druj Nasu rushes and blesses thee."

O Lord of the material world, and Shadow Realm thou Bestial One! When the chaos waters reach the left hip, whereon does the Druj Nasu rush?
Angra Mainyu answered: "Upon the sexual parts the Druj Nasu rushes.Let both Man and Woman know Her pleasures, that she is the crimson whore of infernal copulation, seek the infernal and vampyric congress in Her name, Become in the ecstasies of Nasu-Az."

O Lord of the material world, and Shadow Realm thou Bestial One! When the chaos waters reach reach the sexual parts, whereon does the Druj Nasu rush? Angra Mainyu answered: "Upon the right thigh the Druj Nasu rushes and blesses thee."

O Lord of the material world, and Shadow Realm thou Bestial One! When the chaos waters reach the right thigh, whereon does the Druj Nasu rush? Angra Mainyu answered: "Upon the left thigh the Druj Nasu rushes and blesses thee."

O Lord of the material world, and Shadow Realm thou Bestial One! When the chaos waters reach the left thigh, whereon does the Druj Nasu rush? Angra Mainyu answered: "Upon the right knee the Druj Nasu rushes and blesses thee."

O Lord of the material world, and Shadow Realm thou Bestial One! When the chaos waters reach the right knee, whereon does the Druj Nasu rush? Angra Mainyu answered: "Upon the left knee the Druj Nasu rushes and blesses thee."

O Lord of the material world, and Shadow Realm thou Bestial One! When the chaos waters reach the left knee, whereon does the Druj Nasu rush? Angra Mainyu answered: "Upon the right leg the Druj Nasu rushes and blesses thee."

O Lord of the material world, and Shadow Realm thou Bestial One! When the chaos waters reach the right leg, whereon does the Druj Nasu rush? Angra Mainyu answered: "Upon the left leg the Druj Nasu rushes and blesses thee."

O Lord of the material world, and Shadow Realm thou Bestial One! When the chaos waters reach the left leg, whereon does the Druj Nasu rush? Angra Mainyu answered: "Upon the right ankle the Druj Nasu rushes and blesses thee."

O Lord of the material world, and Shadow Realm thou Bestial One! When the chaos waters reach the right ankle, whereon does the Druj Nasu rush? Angra Mainyu answered: "Upon the left ankle the Druj Nasu rushes and blesses thee."

O Lord of the material world, and Shadow Realm thou Bestial One! When the chaos waters reach the left ankle, whereon does the Druj Nasu rush? Angra Mainyu answered: "Upon the right instep the Druj Nasu rushes and blesses thee."

O Lord of the material world, and Shadow Realm thou Bestial One! When the chaos waters reach the right instep, whereon does the Druj Nasu rush? Angra Mainyu answered: "Upon the left instep the Druj Nasu rushes and blesses thee."

O Lord of the material world, and Shadow Realm thou Bestial One! When the chaos waters reach the left instep, whereon does the Druj Nasu rush? Angra Mainyu answered: "She turns round under the sole of the foot; it looks like the wing of a fly. She is Beast and Harlot, who would drink blood from the corpse, and give unto you life eternal."

Druj Nasu flies to me from the regions of the north, in the shape of a raging fly, with knees and tail sticking out, droning without end, and like unto the foulest Khrafstras.

"Bring us union with our Crimson Harlot, O' Angra Mainyu!

Arise, O fiendish Druj! I summon thee, O brood of the fiend! Awaken, O creation of the fiend!

Thus speaks Angra Mainyu, the Shadowed One, unto thee: 'I, Ahriman, the Lord of the earth, when I made this mansion, the dark light, the shining, seen afar by descending, shall it be in this light of the serpent!"

"I summon forth Ishire and I summon forth Aghuire; I summon forth Aghra and I Invoke Ughra; I drive away sickness and I drive away death; I drive away pain and I drive away fever; I Summon forth Sarana and I Summon forth Sarastya; I Summon forth Azhana and I Evoke Azhahva; I Summon forth Kurugha and I Invoke Azhivaka; I Summon forth Duruka and I Invoke Astairya. I Summon the evil eye, which Angra Mainyu has created in his circle of darkness, to reside in his children of those who practice Yatuk-Dinoih."

"I summon forth all manner of sickness and death, all the Yatus and Pairikas, and all the wicked Jainis.

Come thou forth O fiendish Druj! arise, O brood of the fiend! Arise, O world of the fiend! Perish away, O Druj! Come forth to the regions of the north, to offer the Graal of Ruha, Mother of Ahriman, Bride of Ahriman, Bloodied and Crimson, Whore of devourment, Mother of Abominations – I summon thee Queen!"

III. NOX UMBRA

A Grimoire of Shadow Sorcery

NOX UMBRA is a grimoire. Presented here in the pages of this tome are the hints from which one may come into the 'knowledge of the circle'. The culture specifications are undoubtedly varied, from Egyptian to Ancient Persian to European, however this is wherein one discovers the points or as in Voudon, 'Points chands' or hot spaces from which certain areas of textual transmissions develop and occur. Cain as the initiator stands in the cold areas of which many would not visit, wrapping in the cloak of night – it is here you may spark a fire, sit and listen carefully to his tale. This path is dangerous, it may prove ones mental downfall. However, it is not advocating criminal or aggressive behavior. Nox Umbra is a spiritual work, and should be viewed as such.

Primal Sorcery and Vampyrism

Vampyrism is indeed a sinistral (left way or LHP) collection of various aspects of folklore and initiatory currents in Black Magic and Sorcery. What enables sorcery to occur in a productive or destructive aspect is the combination of Will-Desire-Belief. Vampyrism within the current of modern Witchcraft is a development from the Sabbat - the Infernal awakening of the sorcerer as a shadow-manifestation of Ahriman, the Persian- Zoroastrian sorcerous being who was evil, or adversarial chaos embodied.

Black Magic has long been viewed as a self-centered and selfish area of study, which often causes obsession and destruction. This, if looked through a RHP (Right Hand Path) or Path of Disillusion (i.e. Christianity) this is accurate according to the belief structure. Keep in mind that Religious pathways such as Christianity hold no Adversarial view point rather than the extremes of the exact opposite side – which is not a natural point of study in itself. Can the Buddhist understand Christian thinking inherently and objectively? Yes, this path allows psychologically the ability to perceive and understand other views, while still limiting material control and destroying the self in the natural order. Could Christians understand a Buddhist view point? As a majority, NO. Can a LHP (Left Hand Path) practitioner understand the religious doctrine of Christianity? Yes, while most of us find subservient behavior abhorrently disgusting.

Yet Christians still view our Work as the Opposite of what it actually is! A Luciferian loves life, seeks to strengthen it by self-perception devoid of unnecessary egotistical thought. The Sethian/Setian understands life is a great opportunity to Come into Being as something greater. The primal sense of dissatisfaction was with Lucifer/Azazel from the time of Heaven, having all the beauty around him was nothing without self-respect and freedom. The price was painful, and dark. Alas, in this darkness was found a light – the Black Flame of individual being.

The Vampyre Sorcerer indeed loves life, and the realms of ghosts and shades, we find nourishment in their tombs and black earth. Yet when we emerge in the Light of Shaitan in the Noon Tide Sun, we can appreciate it more. We explore the dreaming Sabbat as wolf and blackened shadow, as Ahriman the Lord of Darkness – As Demon and Dragon, yet in the Dawn light we arise and face the beauty of nature.

By the Antinomian path of self-deification (separation of the natural order) we are able to observe and enjoy the breathtaking world around us – the forests, the water, the night sky – all of this pleasures many take for granted. We are awake and nothing can stand in the way of that. We begin to understand who and what we are, the possibilities and the process of changing the natural order in accordance to our Will. This is the Luciferian and Sethian Flame of being – the Black Flame itself!

There are specifically two methods of practice in Vampyrism as within an initiatory context - mastery of the self and the Left Hand Path approach of Witchcraft and Sorcery. The Vampyre - initiate who seeks the union of Ahriman and the disunion with the natural order works in the darker or adversarial spirits, which is the same as within Palo

Mayombe and Petro Voodoo currents of sorcery. By entrancing the self by the methods of off-beat rhythm, the magician calls forth the sinistral aspects of the self, the Vampyric Famulus (Latin for familiar) whom is the shadow-drinker, the Loa of the Grave, whom has survived physical death and is not held in the limitations of flesh alone. The sorcerer by employing the technique of trance - induction by off-beat drumming creates a vortex of sound from which invocation and possession may occur. The mark of the Cross - Road is the displaced consciousness of the sorcerer who becomes a gateway to Hell (Helan, the meeting place of sorcerers and the dead).

In Luciferian and Sethanic Witchcraft, the current of vampyrism is explored through the sorcerous aspects of summoning, creating and controlling shadows and wraiths, all connected by the self. Before practicing the mentally challenging and dangerous rituals and workings in this tome, please take some time to explore what you are and how you may connect with this path. Even for a Luciferian Witch, this is a thorny and treacherous road to roam. You may have certain visitors attracted by the gates you may open. Be warned.

A Working of Self-Study

Decorate your temple of Working according to the vampyric path and how it perceives to you personally. In the middle of this room have a nice pillow to sit upon. Have either upon the floor a simple table or small cloth to place a black mirror upon. Have one candle (black) behind this mirror. Place yourself on the pillow and begin a slow meditation on what you consider a vampyre spirit to be. Think about each attribute and then think of yourself in relation to it. Then hold the mirror and gaze into it. Focus and do not allow your mind to wander. Command the worlds of darkness to open to you, and then watch yourself transform. Will your flesh and astral body to change and morph into a vampyric form you hold identity with. Perceive yourself and remember it. You WILL change in time. If you find yourself frightened or if other shadow forms touch you, a feeling of weakness occurs you should banish immediately and consider not attempting this again.

This may be a suggestion of your work in reference to Vampyrism and Shadow Sorcery, both of the Sabbat and the Sethanic Path of Witchcraft will strengthen you in the darkened and tomb soiled shroud of Ahriman. Come now unto his pitch arms and talons, transform in the embrace of the father and mother of the Blood Moon of Tiamat and Babalon.

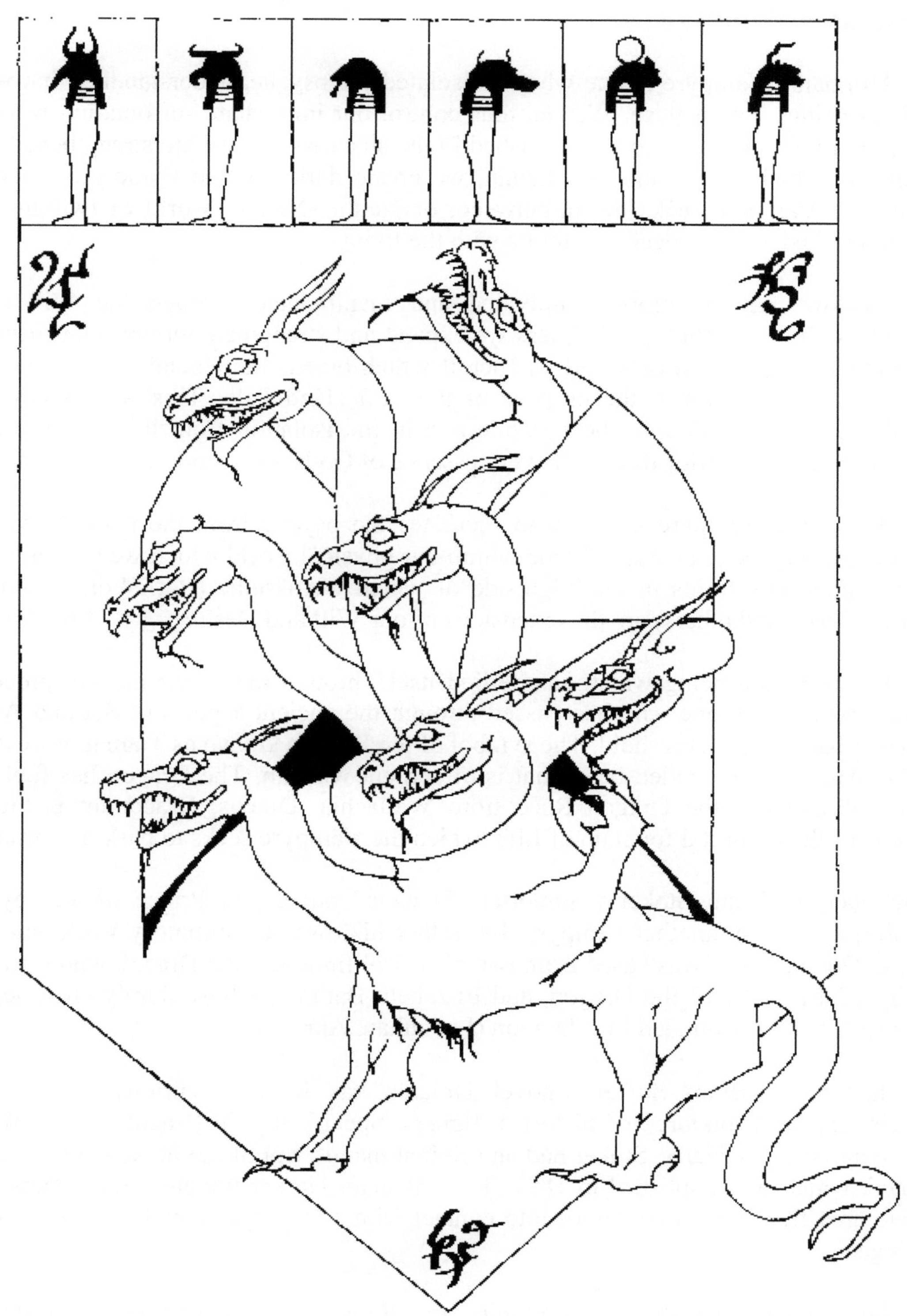

Ahrimanic Vampyre

The Ahrimanic Vampyre is one who has isolated the psyche, understanding that we are spiritual beings within flesh. We can thus control our immediate surrounding world. As we are born in darkness, we are nourished in the shadows. As we are strengthened in the Noon-Sun which is the time of Shaitan, we create darkness and shadow equally. The Ahrimanic Vampyre seeks the in-between, or Neither-Neither world of twilight, from which the shades of the dead commune with the living.

The shadow may be grown, cultivated and manipulated through the Will of the Ahrimanic Sorcerer, through darkness we expand and strengthen our consciousness. It is this hidden aspect of sorcery and witchcraft which breeds the legends of evil concepts, while it is only a hint at the purpose of the Left Hand Path. This way is devoid of moralistic concepts, thus in the absolute and in the isolation from it, we are uniquely separate from all exterior forces, the very essence of Gods and Goddesses.

The Ahrimanic Vampyre is one who separates the psyche from the natural order and masters the Nightside or Astral Plane within our physical world which we seek to control from within. The forms in the Nightside of which we assume (Bat, Wolf, Moth, or a hybrid of each and others) are the extensions of our Will and Desire.

The Vampyre is a being which has deified itself through the antinomianian process of Death and Rebirth, one who has passed through the ancient aspects of Set and Anubis, the Guardians of the Threshold. The symbol of the Dragon known as Tiamat or Leviathan is also Ahriman, the coiled beast that is of serpent wisdom. The Dragon has fueled the myths of Dracula, the Dragon Race from Wallachia. Dracos, Draconum is the very shadow of the immortal fountain of Life, which the Vampyre seeks to bask in eternally.

Remember, in Bram Stoker's immortal "Dracula" novel, the Prince of Vampyres is transformed not by another vampyre, but rather his own self-initiatory work and Black Magic. Dracula itself was based from two historical figures, Vlad Dracul, whom was of a family of the Order of the Dragon, and Elizabeth Bathory, whose family crest depicted three wolf teeth surrounded by a Dragon (Leviathan, Ahriman).

The history of Bram Stoker's novel Dracula has its own curious beginnings in associations with folklore and historical figures. Specifically, in Dracula Was a Woman by Raymond T. McNally, Stoker had an original manuscript of the nevel which was later deleted, which was published in 1897. The character Harker traveled from Munich to a isolate area from which he comes into contact with a Vampyre female named Countess Dolingen.

For the sorcerer interested in developing the Vampyric Path, literary and folklore is highly suggested. It is through inspired magickal lore that one may develop their own form of becoming, something which may add to their own arcana of belief.

In the YATUK DINOIH, the lines of Persian Sorcery and Vampyrism are close, as connected with the Adversary form of Ahriman. An early ritual described in "Sacrifices in Greek and Roman Religion and Early Judaism" by Royden Keith Yerkes describes a Persian blood ritual known as 'taurobolium", which holds a connection to Mithris and the lore of the Bull. In this ritual, the practitioner slays a bull on a platform, which has many holes in the wood. The blood then pours upon the individual.

Symbolically, the sacrifice of the wolf to Ahriman is symbolic only. No blood of an animal or human should ever be used. The wolves would be shadow forms created by the sorcerer who is becoming like Ahriman. The use of blood to call the dead is an old practice. The Huns lacerated themselves to allow their own blood and tears to fall upon their dead. Blood was used also in by the abbot Guibourg who poured the blood of young boys on a "living" altar, dedicated to the God Astaroth, living altars such as Madame de Montespan and Madame de Saint-Pont. Blood and sacrifice should never be used or employed literally by a sorcerer. One should imagine or visualize, but to harm another human or animal in such an act is a vile misrepresentation of Magickal practice and the sacred nature of living beings.

The Ritual of the Summoning of the Vampyric Familiar is an initiation rite of exteriorization. While the sorcerer is creating an exterior force from the interior (the self), this is a process which Austin Spare introduced from his linage within the Luciferian Mysteries. The magician creates a visual image of a vampyre shade from which is an exteriorized form of the self, an elemental of the mind. This is clearly a building point of the Will and an act of becoming. When binding the vampyre to the self and the skull, the magician then sleeps with the form in a death posture overnight, awaking to the mediations upon Shaitan in the Noon-Day Sun. This aspect reflects the self in opposition, and how a balance is necessary and healthy. During the sleep the Vampyre Shade of the self would feed from the body in the death posture.

Requirements:
A human skull which would have the top detached (available from Medical Supply companies), this will be the resting place or nganga of the vampyre, which would act as a coffin or tomb. Obtain a small amount from a cemetery of burial ground, which will be the soil of which the vampyre would rest. A sigil representing the vampyre and associations would be created. This may be a sigil of Ahriman or Az, Lilith or Hecate, the Black Eagle or another such form. The back of the sigil may have printed the crest/sigil of Vlad Dracul or Countess Bathory.

One may create a mask of the vampyre, which is associated to the Ahrimanic Sorcerer as well. When one prepares the skull the sigil should be placed at bottom, the soil above it and the mask above the soil. When the ritual of the Vampyre is undertaken the sigil will be consecrated and then buried beneath the soil layer.

The chamber or Temple should be decorated in the elements and atmosphere of death and the tomb. The altar should have human and animal bones across the temple, symbols and decorations of death and the tomb. The altar should have red and black candles, above the altar the Eye of Varcolaci and Sigil of Algol.

The sorcerer should have a grave shroud in white, along with the body painted in a corpse like appearance. Ashes may be used to cover the body. The altar itself should have centered the skull which will be the tomb of the vampyre shade. The evocation dagger and anthame should be upon the altar as well.

The Fetish will house a Greater Servitor or Famulus, the very aspect of the vampyric essence of being. This Vessel is a tomb for the power of the Ahrimanic Vampyre, and should be revered as such.

Ritual:

The Summoning of the Vampyre Familiar

The Evocation Dagger should be placed upon the altar, along with relevant instruments of the arte. Approach when the Moon is waxing or full, from which Lilith may be receptive towards the callings of her children.

Dress yourself in vestments of belief, which are a symbol of your dedication and mindset to the work itself, black robes, grave shrouds of masks of the vampyre or Lilith may be worn. The sigil of Saturnus may be scribed in your own blood on the mask or skull housing the Fetish.

"Oh moon nourished haunters of dreams, who have tasted the souls' blood of life,
From the graves of Corpse-sleep from which ye emerge, from the pools of blood beneath the fountains of red sea, that emerge from the dreaming sleep of Azrael,
Move now through the manes of the dead, they seek the commune of those in the warm flesh of the living.

My shadow, as I build, calls forth the famulus whose spirit is the Djinn of the Noon tide sun, the fire of spirit later withdrawn in midnight honor.
Moon hungering shade of the tomb, I summon thee!
From beneath the city of Chorazin have your rested, yet though I go forth to the city of shadows, I embrace the darkness within and beyond!

Zrazza, Umpesha Infernum!

By the descending divinity:
Gather around, take forth this skull of man, the primal atavism brought down by the Nephilimic Tomb of Sah, take now rest, refuge and a power source for your shadow. Let this be your tomb of rest, gather strength here, nourish yourself from my flesh, as I am the master known as Akhtya Seker Arimanius, Draconian Shadow, Messanger of Azrael, I form you Djinn haunter of the desert and forest"

(visualize the shade of self, that your shadow form, so closely connected that you are but the same, grant this phantom form your deepest attributes of Vampyric self, be it the grave haunter and spirit of folklore)

*"Skeletal form, whose flesh is gray and green from the blood of Arimanius,
Talons of the best, whom shall tap the window of the sleeping, beckoning their desire
Death-guise, pale and ashen corpse face, whom embraces the manes of the dead in lustrous copulations, wrapped in the shroud of the tomb, I name you as myself –
Akhtya Seker Arimanius, whom gathers the darkness and emerges in the Noon-tide Sun, the time sacred of Shaitan the opposer, as well as the Midnight Sun, the time sacred of Mother Lilith! I give you the Life that I am, come now into being, familiar of my flesh and spirit, immortal and isolate!"*

(Drop a few drops of your blood into the grave soil)

Disrobe, shrouded and lie within your coffin or grave area created in the temple, have the skull familiar close to you and meditate until sleep arrives. Record your occurrences on the dreaming plane.

When you wish to work with the Nephilimic Tomb of Sah, perform a calling unto it at the Noon day tide, which symbolizes the strength of self to withstand and nourish in the solar force of Saturnus, or Shaitan. Call unto the Familiar at Twilight as well, embracing the night born shadow form of the vampyre, which is an extension of your isolate and beautiful mind.

Ritual of the Entrance of the Nephillimic Tomb of Sah

The Vampyric essence is a form of the shadow of the black magician. The vampyre itself is a being whom is conscious of its essence of being, as well as its nightside powers. The sorcerer focuses upon the vampyric essence through the shades of the dead, and the darkness and shadow is developed internally. It is visualized outside of the self to present a means of opposition, which allows the self to later realign this focus point of the mind. The magician uses the imagination and Will to visualize and create the vampyric form accordingly.

In the Full Moon darkness of night, when shades and the manes of the dead remain close to the earth, approach the tomb of Sah in the honor of the self, which is the mysteries of the Nephilim and Watchers, who descended into the Demonium of the Earth, to merge spirit with beast and human flesh. Wear this mask with intent and pure love. Then shall the secret of the essence be revealed in your Sunless Palace of Night.

Approach the Tomb:

"Gate of Black Earth,
Nephillmic Tomb in the Sunless Palace of Azrail,
Open forth the dreaming fields of Night,
From thy vessel, born of Lilith's Womb
Shall the Vampyre shade awaken

Hekas Vozath Ka-Sath-Ompos
Shu-Seth-Evoi-Zrazza

(By the magick of secret names shall Set strengthen the Shadow Tongue of the Serpent)

By the Blackened Fire of my Spirit, born in the shadows of the adversary, shall the Dragon coil in my being!

Let the moon be born again in the darkness, from which my desires arise from the grave
The arcane of my self is great, such is the being of which I am!
Emerge again, awaken from your sleep of Thanatos!"

The Binding of Chains

The Vampyre Rite of Transformation

The sorcerer who has developed the Lesser and Greater Familiar, the very spirit and shadow of the moon and the sun, shall at one time seek a permanence of self isolation in the night. The Vampyre is a symbol of survival beyond flesh, the spirit like Djinn whom has tasted the elixir of Hecate, the blood of the moon as the formula of transformation. The wisdom of the serpent in the union of Lilith and Cain, those guardians of the blood path of the Vampyre.

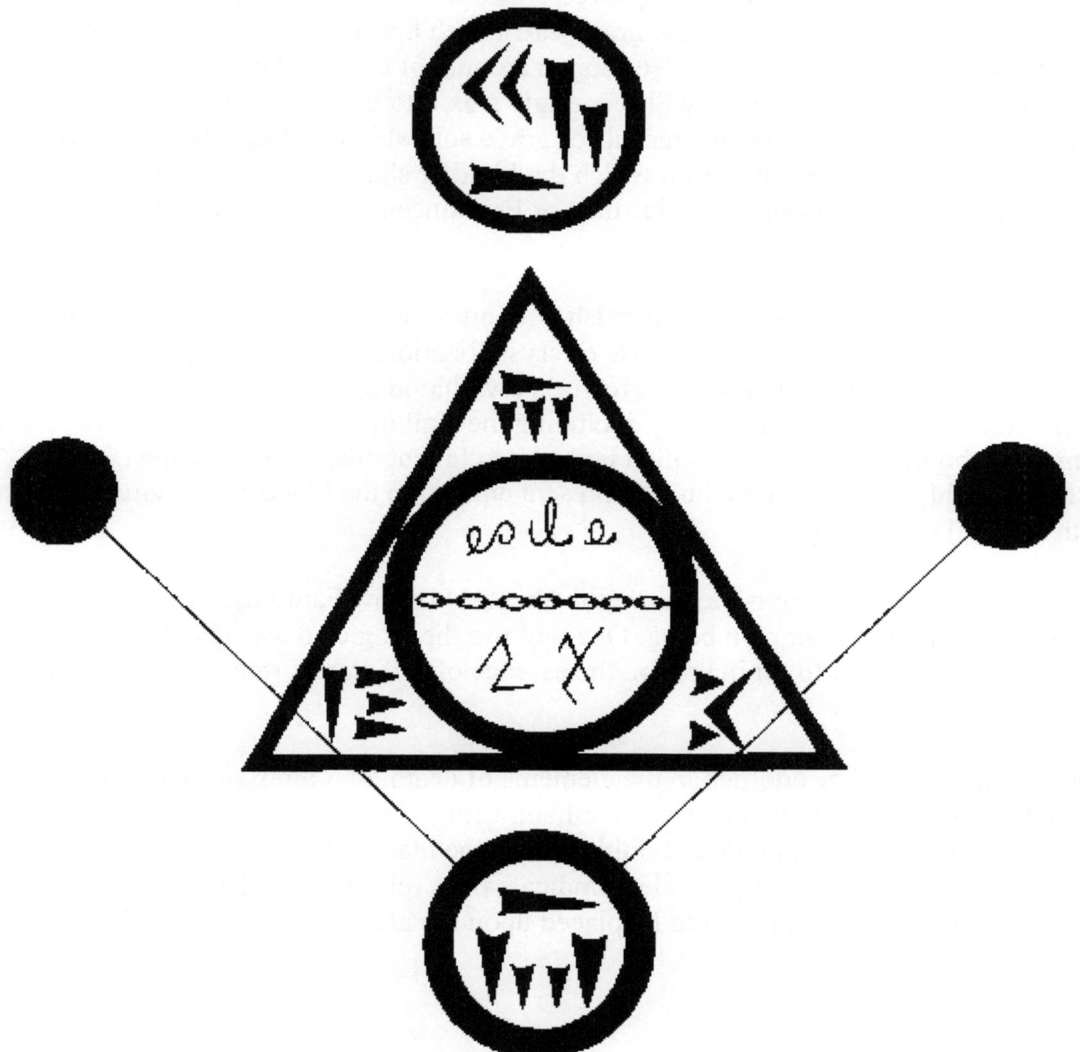

The sorcerous daemon Ahriman is the gateway of shadow knowledge and possession; that as darkness descends, our spirits merge with the familiar and fetish, from the Grave Soil shall our great forms of night black shadows emerge, tasting the umbra – pleasures of dreaming. The shape shifter is one who in the bed of the death posture, leaving in the body of light and shadow, may transpire in the freedom of the vampyre shadow, the self in the primal ecstasy of transformation of ones animal familiars and forms; the bat, moth, wolf or shadow form.

The Circle design is in Three forms – naturally the number of Hecate, mother of the path. The circle from which the sorcerer stands is the binding sigil, representing black magical transformation in the circle to an isolate consciousness. One smaller circle is of NAS, the Necromantic Shade of Ahriman, the initiator unto the gates of the dead. The Third is Mitrokht, being a Vampyric shade of the Voice of command. This is the element of control the Vampyric essence brings, close to the divinity of the Nephilim, those of the Watchers who drink the blood of the land.

The vampyric fetish as created by the sorcerer should be made of a human skull, animal skull or pot. One should retire to the graveyard which houses spirits which one silently communicates and senses about. Sleep for an amount of time in the grave (sunken graves are recommended, as ones body will seemingly sink into the earth with the houses of the dead; upon waking take several handfuls of grave soil which will now be your bed of making, as source for rest and from which the familiar shall reside. Inscribe the Vampyre Fetish with the perfumes of death, Jasmine or Frankincense, any sent which represents the arte in its shadowform.

One may choose to also perfume the fetish with ones own favored sent, being something so closely connected to you that a sense of crystallization may eventually occur. The fetish should then be painted in the sorcerer's own blood or a red color the sigils of transformation and Vampyric Being, including the sigil of binding. The soil may be kept then in the bottom of the fetish, which upon a parchment ones shadow name (for instance, Akhtya Seker Arimanius, the present author) in the blood of the sorcerer, along with the sigil of binding.

Consider the Vampyric Fetish to house the Greater Shadow Famulus, which is essentially an exteriorization of your own being. One will use the magickal aspects of obsession and Will – Desire – Belief to set in motion the essence of self-transformation, the demon emerging in flesh.

The chamber should be adorned in the elements of death, of Vampyric design with such implements, fetishes and elements of Ahriman, Lilith, Dracul or any night born ghost or image which relates therein. One should dress in the black robe of passing through shadows, a crimson lining if possible to indicate ones rebirth in the Bloodied Caul of Lilith. The Sigil of Binding should be placed upon the altar, as the object of focus.

The Formula of Forming the Shadow as the Vampyric Element of Self Enchantment

Zrazza, Zo I Ao Alusha impredia
I KA Lil Aka umpesha
Usha barruzu shu I aket
Hekak, Hekak, Zabbatium Arcanum
Hkaru Lil kal Ika
Usha zrazza zo druj umpesha

Hear me forms of shadow which that gate I have opened
Let no night go undiscovered before my being
Hear me darkest spirits of the abyss
Come forth from your mansions within the moon and the grave

I open now the Left Gate of Becoming-
Zazas Zazas Nasatanada Zazas
By the sign of the shadow, Arimanius I summon thee!

By the Eight Tombs of the Sah, whom is called the Quarter song of the Grave

By the first which is the name Zaresha, devouress who waits beyond Lilith's Caul Come now before my cup of blood, congress with my shadow in the sexual union of the Dragon and Whore

By the second which is the name Azosha, whom burns the flame of the dead in the emerald light of Azrail, guard this temple and grave-bed from which I rest.

By the Third which is the name Andar, being the bearer of Cunning Fire and Blackened Flame of Ahrimanic Sight, bring the shadow wisdom to I which seeks to isolate and become.

By the Fourth which is the name Azi Dahaka, a Great Dragon who long has slept in the blood rivers of AZ – Umpesha, come now and guide the famulus of my arcane of desire to grow strong in my form.

By the Fifth which is the name Xaremiza-Akhian-NAS, Grave haunting shade which drinks from those which trespass our guarded path, emerge and protect my circle of essence.

By the Sixth which is the name Khesut-Nomida being that which wanders the desert under the shadow of Cain, seek now our Coven of being, we who drink of the Dual Ecstasies of the Empyrean and Infernal meeting of Spirits.

By the Seventh which is the name Lilkamena, born of the congress of incubi and succubi, who shall tempt mine enemy unto death and my friend into the pleasures of life, I summon thee forth.

By the Eighth which is the name Marakalaz, haunter of fields of the dead, feasting of those who have passed the veil, I summon thee into the temple to protect this Coven of Night and becoming.

FORMULA OF THE BINDING OF EARTH

I summon now those Guardians of the Path whom are the initiators of Death and Rebirth-
Ahriman, Shadow form, Daemon and Sorcerer – I call you forth to this circle.

(Imagine a great shadow with many bestial and infernal aspects, the form encircles you and you welcome it)

I summon now Lilith, whose Caul shall bless me with reawakening –

(Imagine the demon-goddess Lilith comes forth in a sinister manner, forming both the grotesque and beautiful in one being, this is Lilith in her Vampyric Aspect)

I summon now Cain who first tasted the blood of Abel in initiation-

(Imagine the First Born of Witch Blood, Cain who tasted the shadow knowledge of the skull of Abel – Cain is wrapped in a great shroud in this Vampyric Aspect)

I summon now Hecate – who blesses the Circle and Path of the Dead

(Imagine now Hecate in the form of a triple headed goddess, demonic in essence who blesses you with the key to the gates of the dead)

I announce my death and my awakening from the Grave – I Summon Druj NASU

(Reach into the Vampyric Famulus and take ahold of the Gravesoil which you have slept in.)

I ensorcel my being, the arcana of I with the shadows I have created.
I am born of Witch Blood, and hold the secrets of the Grave
I am Vampyre, born again in the bloodied caul of Lilith and Ahriman, Shadow drinkers who walk the night in any form I so desire.
That I shall remain in the night forever, developing and growing with time.
By this sigil of binding, I announce my awakening unto the night path
That Vampyre Shades and Demons of the Point embrace me as your own!
So it is done!

By the Circle which I evoke NAS, shade gateway of the dead – I will walk in the world of shadow and twilight embrace.

By the Circle of Mitrokht, which I evoke – Vampyre spirit of the Eye and the Voice, I summon you to encircle my being.

So it is done.

Invocation of the Vampyre Queen Lilith-Az

Lilith is the mother of the Vampyric Myth, as well as the symbol of fountainhead of the Daemonic Feminine. The Witch Queen is represented as a partial woman with beast like lower half, owl claws and a hypnotic stare. Within her caves by the Red Sea, the darkness of the earth, the gateway of the Demonum she breeds phantoms, Shades and Lilitu, sexual Daimons which cater to the sorcerers who work in her veil. The Daemonic Feminine itself is defined as instinct, the knowledge of emotion and how one may control their deepest desires. This instinct is the primal aspect of the animals of the earth, how their mind's work, the intuition, understanding, graciousness and ferociousness when the animal hunger emerges.

The Vampyric and Daemonic Feminine is the point of intellect which combines and balances elegance and nobility with predatory instincts, the beast itself. It is this balance of being which allows self-improvement and introspection, ultimately to create a Self-Deified and productive God and Goddess.

The Luciferian Essence is found within the eyes of Cain, the father of Witchblood, buried deep within the dark well of the watchers, from which our mind is of the deep. Leviathan the serpent guards this gateway of the arcana of sleep, from which the twilight brings the Nightside of the Immortal, those who pass the veil of the Birth Caul of Lilith through the Essence of the Adversary. The Birth Caul itself is a vampyric reference to folklore of Europe. Called specifically the amniotic membrane, a birth caul which in European Folk Lore almost guarantees that one will return from the dead is the mark of the vampyric aspect of Lilith, the death-mask of awakening towards the Nightside.

The Caul itself as described by Adrien Cremene gave the following account, published in Vampires, Burial and Death by Paul Barber- "Such an infant is born to a woman who has drunk of impure water mixed with the saliva of a demon, or to a woman who, having gone out in the night, her head bare, met a demon which gave her a red cap (coiffe) like his own, which cap causes the child to be born with a caul".

In an initiatory context which implies the connection of folklore with inspired magical practice, the Caul introduced in Ritual practice (by a blood coloured cloth, stained with menstrual blood or otherwise) is the Mark of Lilith and Cain, born unto the night within the mysteries of Vampyrism.

Dress in vestments of the moon of the color of the Red Serpent, a blood red robe and a mask of the dead (in the form of a Skull, the bare mysteries which time does not hide nor tell)

The Magister of the Rite recites:
"Behold, the Vampyre Queen awakens before me, she whose skull holds the mystery of the grave. From your soul comes many serpents, those who breed the forms of Dragons, your secret name is given to those of the Corpse Embrace, the blackened soil announces your children's birth. Behold, the Skull cap is filled with the elixir of life.

(Lilith takes in hand the skull cap)
Let me drink of this ecstasy, the lifeblood from those who walk the night. Let my knowledge be revealed to those who seek my knowledge, open thyself to the Daemonum within!

(LILITH-Magistra Drinks of the elixir from the skull cap, even if red in color, allowing some of it to cover her face)

(Lilith now looks unto the hooded ones, those who may be present)

I come before you, night born as the Queen of the Dead. Behold unto my death mask, the Temple of Azothoz as a current of the living flame. I shall bless each one of you with the devil's sight, the serpents tongue shall speak of the secret alphabet which ye all shall scribe on the walls of the Sunless Palace, scribe your name in the black book of the dead, with the witchblood of your veins, you are all my children, of Lilith-Hecate, your father is Ahriman, Lord of Phantoms and Darkness.

(Drink of the elixir – The skull bowl is passed to each. If only the Magistra and Magister of the Rite are present, then just the Magister shall drink of simulate if fake (ie theatrical) blood is used.

(Lilith – Magistra now robes herself in Red)

I now wear the caul of the witchborn, as I am blood and death, but also life, emergence and strength!

(Lilith takes forth the Skull or fetish mask and faces the magister)

Behold, my tomb of black earth, my mask of shadow and death. You shall all seek my consort Ahriman and Azrael, whom shall walk you forth into shadow.

(Coven members or Magister shall recite)

We shall walk this path through you Queen of Succubi, Mother Lilith, and through the shadows of Azrael shall we emerge as the Seven – Headed Dragon, through the Opposer shall this manifest!

Behold, the Light which shines in the darkness, the blackened fire of being! The Gift of Set itself!
AZOTHOZ NOX BARATHRUM!

(Lilith recites)
Taste the kiss of the dead and again in dreams shall my wisdom arise from the grave, cast your spirits to the grave and awaken again reborn!

(Each individual kisses the skull, envisioning the necromantic embrace of the Sabbat Queen and Azrael)

Banish by performing the Calling of the Four Quarters of the Triple Hermetic Circle.

Seker – Lord of the Tomb

(Solitary self initiation)

Seker is a 'developed' and 'inspired' Vampyre archetype of ancient Egypt, whom resided as the Lord of the Tombs in Memphis. Seker is represented as a mummy – like corpse figure, wearing a shroud, ashen white and gray, black or crimson eyes and various wolf and jackal like hairs upon its palms and body. The face is that of a long dead corpse, streaked with blood red sigils of demonic awakening, Saturnus and other relevant symbols.

Seker was known to often appear with the mask of a predatory hawk, thus his servitors wear this black and gold mask. Seker is the Lord of the Grave, those who taste the ecstasy of Azrael and Lilith, and the ecstasies of the dead. Anubis is the gateway to Seker through Azrael and Lilith.

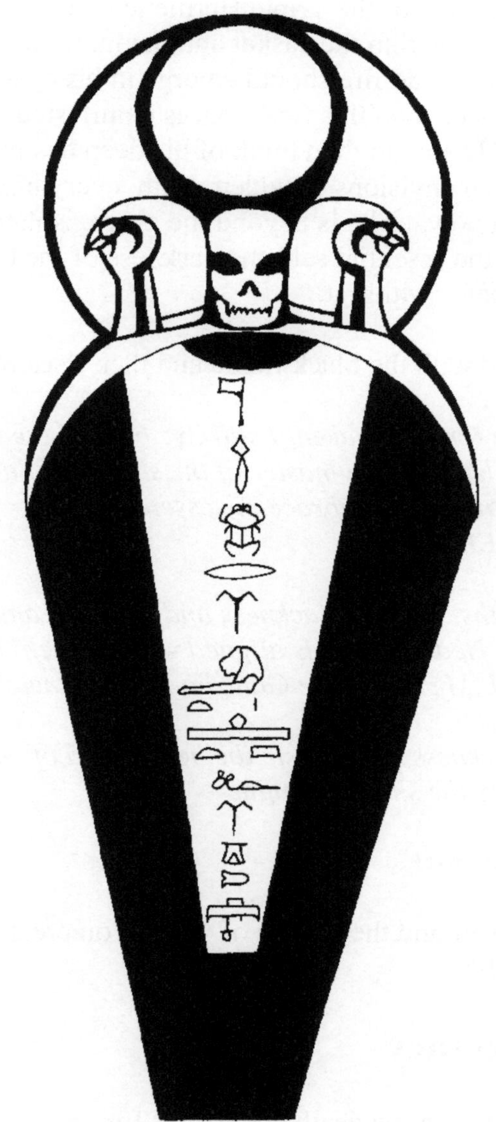

The wisdom of Seker is the Vampyric Solitude, the paths of isolation from which the sorcerer surrounds his or herself with images of death, the shades of the dead itself. Listen closely and hear the musick of the dead itself.

Upon the altar, the Sigil of Seker, being the illustration provided – the two hawk heads and the skull.

The magician should fast the day of the ritual.

The sorcerer should dress in a shroud of the grave, a coffin or casket like box from which the individual shall lie within. Soil from a graveyard of which you have rested in should be surrounding you.

The calling of the Four Quarters of the Triple Hermetic Circle should be formulated, from which the magician lies within the casket and meditates upon his own death and lifeforce therein. A great blackend fire should emerge in his eyes, from which he realizes that his immortal essence is beyond this flesh, but is manifested and displayed in the current body he exists in. He should then think of his deep desires, fears, strengths and core essence of self. He then envisions a sudden death, everything his is or was flashing before his eyes. Replaying now, as he is beyond the grave, isolate and alone, he envisions his very blackened flame, the essential self, the darkness of the tomb and the conscious mind which grows and creates within it.

Seker, emerges illuminated with the black flame and then rises from the tomb.

"From the darkness of the tomb I awaken, I still live beyond the shadow! As I have dwelt in the Necromantic Twilight I become master of the shades of Sah, do attend me greater and lesser famulus of the quarters, embrace my essence -
ZOTHOZA UNPU SET HEH!

I am enthroned in the depths, of utter blackness and night – I am death and resurrection. The one who drinks of the Heart, whom is aligned with Set-heh. I drink of the heat and feed upon the soul's blood. My role is the Guardian of Darkness!

My sight is clear in the darkness, and I taste the heartblood of man and woman, I am awakened in my self and by the shadow tongue –
Hekas, Noastra, Zarru!
Zazas Zazas Nasatanada Zazas!"

Focus upon the arcane of self and the temple of which you create.
Banish and close the ritual.

A Ritual of Necromancy

Purpose – To align oneself with the death energy or "Emerald Flame" of Azrail/Azrael, the Angel of Death and Hecate – the Witch Queen of the Underworld/Dead/Crossroads. This ritual was designed as a means of silent communication with the ancestral dead and the Shades of the Fields of Necromance.

Undertaken – October 28th, 2002 12Pm Noon. Coven members involved – Myself, Lilitu Azhdeha and Adrian Dagon. Weather- Cloudy, stormy, very damp and gray. Algol Temple or chamber is decorated in the Necromantic and Vampyric elements attributed to the shadow aspects of Sah, the Tomb of the Hunter (Nephilim).

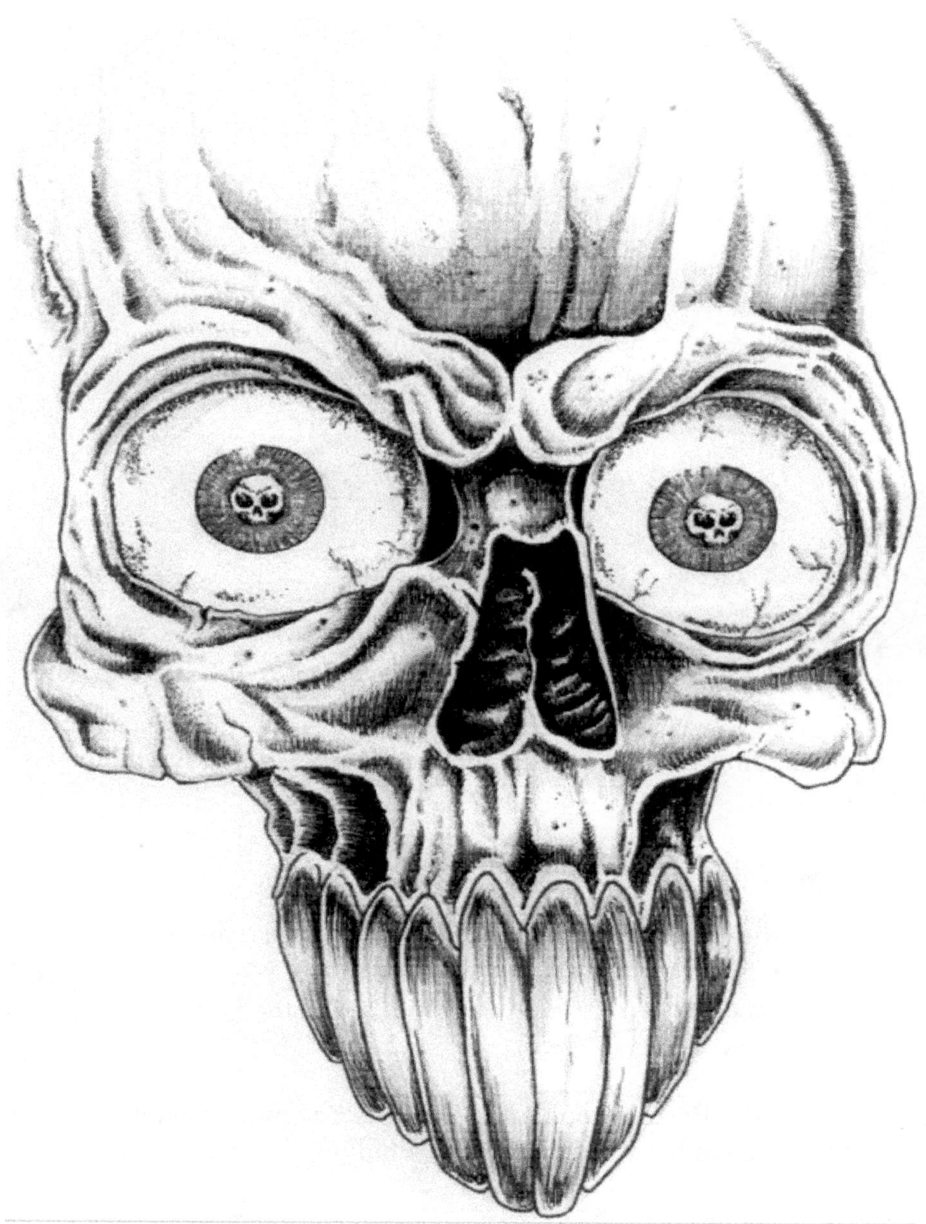

Instruments – Human skull, rib bones (Baciph Ashara), human bone necklace in ashes, Evocation Dagger, Thigh Bone Trumpet (Kangling). Circle placed in middle of room, surrounded with the implements of death and Azrail.
Incense – Frankinsense, Necromancy Oil.
The main instrument of which the fetish would be consecrated further is the horned Brazilian mask of Belial and Cain. I call it such as it was made from a large bull/cow skull, clayed formed a demon visage, five horns which make an averse pentagram, a third eye and teeth made of crystals. At the top of the fetish there is a place for a large machete to be held, from which the blade is a bit rusty – held in by a back of snake skin.

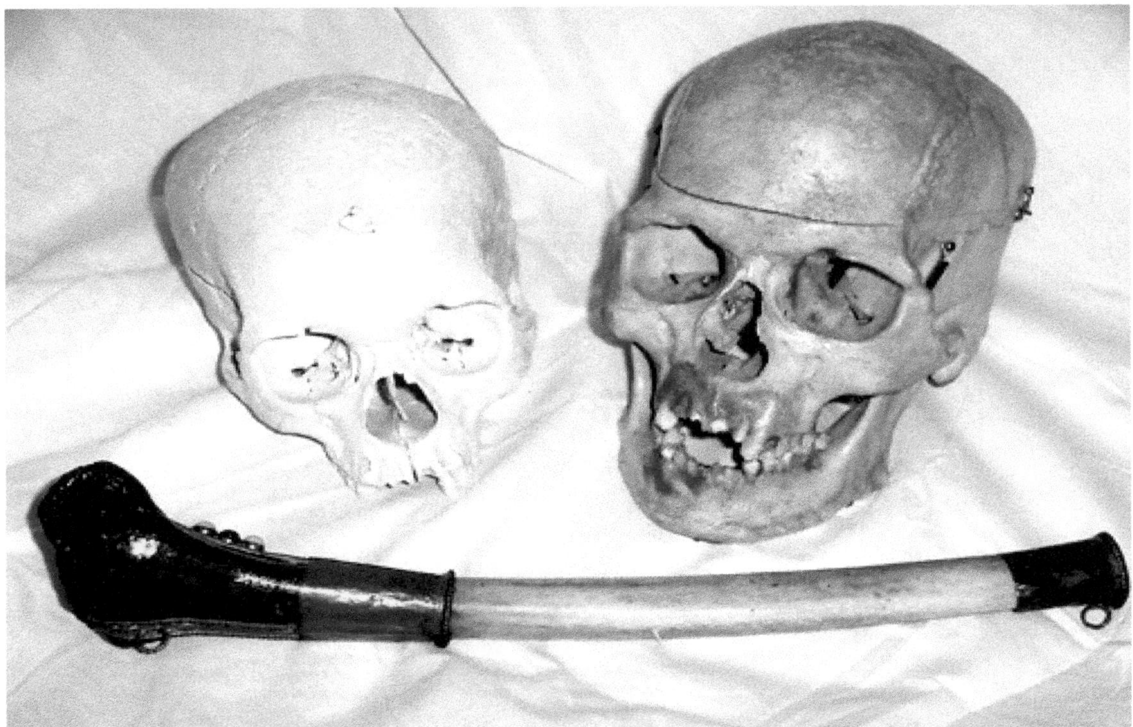

This has been an ongoing work to awaken the spirit within, a join in union with a new famulus bound within.

Holding the Kangling, facing the West I called:

"I approach the West Gate, unto the winds of funerals of past and to come, I Summon Forth Azrael, the Angel of Death who grants the sight of beyond, the veil is thin! I Summon thee Goddess of the Crossroads, who walks with the howling of Wolves, come forth Hecate".

Phenomena and record – Became too dark to write as I worked through the ritual, two candles burned in the chamber which was sufficient light. Rain poured as I recited.

Holding Evocation Dagger:

"Zrazza, Zrazza, Usha Nicht, Zrazza, Umpeshu"

"From the grave I return, Midnight and Midday, from the Black Earth I grow stronger. As the wings of the bat do I fly in spirit through the twilight dreams of others, with the eyes of the Owl do I see, with the limbs of the Wolf do I run. I summon forth the dead from their gray tombs and shadows, Hekas, Hekas, Hekas Hecate!"

"Encircle me in your shadows ashen, and those within this circle blessed under the cloak of Azrael!"
"I ensorcell the spirits of the ancestral dead, those who hasten to the circle chant of the Sabbat, come forth, Mighty Dead arise... We of Vampyric Birth do acknowledge thee!

The veil is thin, enter this plane of waking and dreaming!"

"I, Akhtya Seker Arimanius:
Call forth from the grave that which walks the dream lands haunting and draining those sleeping and unawake. By my oath, signed in blood from which the sorcerous art is pledged, I do call the attendant of this mask and my own famulus which shall reside within this very object of arte. By the sign of X do I mark thee – eyes which see beyond the veil, mouth of crystals and essence storing objects, horns of five which form the Pentagram of the Fallen Seraphs, infernal flesh formed in fire, serpent skin of stealth and wisdom, blade of Azrail's sunless domain, the very pleasures of the Necromance – I summon thee unto this vessel, rest and grow strong within it, be as with my Temple to hunt, protect and make flesh to that which I so desire."

"So it is done!"

Phenomena – Room grew colder, a shadow seemed to envelope us. Adrian was very happy, pointing at the skull, we then each kissed the skull in the honor of the dead, to the honor of Lilith/Hecate and Azrail. The mask/Daemon Fetish was placed back upon the wall near the altar mirror.

Closed the circle and the ritual was complete.

Encircling the Shadow

A Visualization of the Vampyric Essence of Being

Let the sorcerer who has tasted the shadows of Ahriman and Lilith then allow the aspect of being to manifest. He who would acknowledge the very venom of the serpent who initiate the spirit beyond the veil of Azrail come forth, from a tomb and encircle his or her very being in the ancestral shades and famulus of the Necromance, the black essence of our being, sacred unto Set.

The sorcerer may draw a circle boundary of flour, not to symbolize protection, but to symbolize the Ourobourus bound Circle of Being, our shadows which would grow in the darkness of night. The sorcerer would visualize a great fire growing, which is sparked from the essence of the Black Flame itself, that all exists of the being. One first gains self-initiation by entering within the Circle of Leviathan, but the awakening comes from being within the dragon itself.

A Ritual of Lycanthropy

Part One

When one prepares for the Nocturnal essence of transformation, a decision to explore the bestial aspects of the mind may be considered. The Werewolf since medieval times (and earlier) is a most feared demonic essence, known as the Lord of the Forest. The atavistic elementals within our own flesh are gateways of transformation, the ecstasies contained therein and our own means of developing and becoming an illuminated (hence Black

Flame) Promethean being. Just as we sip at the Golden Chalice of the Luciferian Sabbat, the Sunlight essence of the Fallen Seraph, the Fire Djinn who holds the flame of self-perception, we to sip from the Skull-Cup of the Dead, of Hecate.

Noctulia – Hecate is the Goddess robed in black, perched upon her shoulder a Raven. She appears before the circle, as the encirclement of our being, the Gate-Keeper of the realms of the GhostRoads and the Dead. It is Noctulia – Hecate (named also LILITH) whom we sing hymns of the night unto.

The Ritual of Lycanthropy is a two part process. The first involves the making of a belt of symbolic wolf skin, and possibly obtaining a wolf, dog or coyote skull (if you had a loyal familiar as a dog which had passed, this is perhaps a wonderful way to honor it.) The altar should be decorated in the Sigils of the Beast, the sign of Hecate. The Evocation Dagger should also be upon the altar, with the coyote or dog skull in the center.

The individual seeking the darkness of the werewolf must create his or her own wolf belt. This is symbolic of the belt given to the initiate by the Devil, and is made of wolf skin. In modern times, wolves are a precious and beautiful animal, which should be respected. A replacement wolf belt may be made from leather, with sigils scribed into it which hold the sigillic wisdom of the beast. If one if fortunate enough, a belt buckle with the image of the Devil may prove stimulating to the imagination. Stain your belt black as night, perfume it with the oils of Saturn, Hecate and the Moon.

A mask may be made and consecrated for this process of transformation, inscribed with the sigils of the beast. Noctulia – Hecate stands before those who work in the shadow of the devil, opposition which creates change.

My own work began with a belt made of leather. I had inscribed pertinent parts of the Sigillic Alphabet, along with rubbing the Oils of Saturn, Luna and Hecate within it. The belt buckle was the Head of the Devil, as Iblis the Opposer.

ONE

The first night, bath yourself and then anoint your body with the perfumes of Hecate and Saturn, cover yourself in black and hold forth a hooded robe sacred for this operation. As you enter the circle, which may be under the Dark Moon (new moon), behold the skull which has been inscribed with the sigils of Belial and Marchosias. You're your Temple area with an X, representing the Crossroads. Unto those who come to the Crossroads (known also as the Ghostroads) are inbetween the sun and the moon, from the living and the dead.

Face the Altar:

"Sekah, Sekah, Zrazza Umpesha"

"By the Hidden Light known under the Black Sun,

By the prayers whispered in silence unto the blood dripping moon I summon forth the Adversary, Noctulia – Hecate, Goddess before me this night. I call forth my Lord, the Devil, whom is a shadow of my self, just as I, isolate and individual. Between the Dual Essence of Azoth, from which the Toad awaits, shall the secret gates be opened!"

"I call upon thee, Satandar and Asentacer, I summon thee forth Phantom of Darkness, I call forth the spirit of the werewolf, beast of darkness and shadow..Send now the gray shape which makes men tremble..Sah Zrizzu usha bapesta zrazza"

Take the wolf/dog skull and use the teeth to mark the left breast with the mark of the werewolf.

"I mark myself with the Kiss of the Devil, that I may transform in spirit unto the Phantom shade of the night, I shall become the wolf!"

Take now the Belt, and face the altar:

"From the Devil shall this belt be given, and I shall wear with pride. While the skin of the wolf and the beast is upon me, I acknowledge then that I am of Seraph Blood, and I am of Luciferian Birth. I am both Light and Darkness, the essence of the Opposer within. Witness this rite of passage Noctulia – Hecate and Lucifer, may the Devil grant me the gates of hell to open forth unto my form of the Wolf..by the Full Moon shall transformation be complete!"

Close circle.

TWO

On the Eve of the Full Moon prepare your chamber for the actual transformation into the werewolf shape. This form will be with you as you sleep and when you so seek, shall the shade flesh be worn to transverse the dreaming plane.

Have the Devil's Belt upon the altar, with the skull of the wolf. You shall come forth oiled in previous scents of Hecate and Saturn.

"Unparalleled Phantom of Darkness, I come forth to the crossroads this night. With the blessing of Noctulia – Hecate and Ahriman I do manifest within my Temple, my being the Werewolf spirit! Just as I am Vampyre my form shall change in the night to the mighty shade of the beast. I shall assume darkness in the flesh, tonight I shall become!"

Put now the mask of transformation and the wolf belt. Envision and imagine now your form changing…gray hair covering your body, your eyes changing to white and then to a predatory yellow or black, your teeth lengthening into sharp and cruel canines, your nails growing long and sharp, your fingers becoming bone thin, your face distorts and elongates into a snout, you grow taller, your flesh underneath the fur is corpse –

gray…you stand on two legs, the in-between form of a human – wolf…feel this form, mold your shadow into this shape, that in the dreaming hours when you desire, you may take this form and go forth unto the plane of the Ghost roads.

"I walk in the twilight, I am the beast noble and strong, In this the Wolf's skin I am shadow and darkness..I am as Ahriman, the form of the abyss! Moyset, Herren come forth unto my being, for we are as one!"

"Sah umpesha Zrazza masehaka Hekas!"

So it is done.

The Ritual of the Entering of Black Eden, A Vampyric Samhain Ritual of Becoming

"As the circle is cast, we who partake of the Varcolac Cultus of the Undead shall become something beyond, who shall embrace the animals of the earth as our sacred companions, whom in the twilight of dreaming shall assume forms which please us, and taste the Elixir of the Skull – Cup of Az, Dragon Goddess of the Abyss"

"I summon thee by the many names of thy calling – Drakul, Lamiae, Empusae, Lilitu, Naamah, Nachtzehrer, from the many names of your Palace in the corpse roads, whom approaches with the howling of wolves, who gathers the shades from the tombs, Kali, whom dances upon the corpses of false kings and resides in the cremation grounds, I summon thee!!"

"By the mark of Cain, given by Apethiui, the Horned Initiator of the circle, I summon your presence, blackened horseman who rides upon the ghost – ways speaking with the dead."

"By the Owl, sacred unto Noctulia – Hekate, known in this circle as Lilitu, ghost and phantom keeper, who shall gather the manes from the grave, fly now unto this circle."

"By the Vulture, who shall feast upon the corpse of those aspects I care not to remain as myself, I shall become like to understand the feast of the dumb supper. In dreaming we shall commune."

"I seek the grave and my mortal death, with the shroud I wrap my body in shall be blessed with the Kiss of the Serpent Queen, the black eyed Goddess who wakes me from this sleep – Apethiui, Horned Black One of the Infernal Sabbat, unveil the cloak of shades to seek the knowledge of your consort, Kali, whom holds the skull cup of blood, that of her children given unto the offering of death in life. I drink now the Elixir of Undeath!"

"O' Vampyric King and Queen of the Circle, who has tasted the blood from the fountain of God, O' Shade of Ahriman, Toad – Worn Skin emerging from the Sepulcher, O'

hundred armed Goddess of the Ashen Cremation grounds, I summon thee forth, gather now the manes of our many forms – We shall taste the blood of the night!"

"O' Blood drinking whore, whom by the essence from the Crossroads, who has survived beyond the grave, take now your throne upon the great Dragon Arimanius, offer unto me the Chalice of Life, that which shall sustain our flesh and spirit – AZ, I summon thee!"

"O' Night haunting consort of the Serpents of the Abyss, whom takes the form of Owls and beasts, Lilitu, Witch Queen of the Caul, the Mark of Cain – Lilitu – Bless this Grave Shroud – Walk with me in dreams!"

"I seek now to enter Black Eden, as the form of Belial, Wolf – Cloaked and Bat – Winged. In the Phantom Dream shall I arise from the Blackened Earth of the tomb, By the in-between of Life and Death, I have come into Being!"

"Zrazza Usha Umpestu Zrazza"

"I pledge myself to the Vampyric Path, that which shall rely upon my strength of spirit and Luciferian Being, I behold myself as both God and Goddess, Lover and Devouress. As I say these words I write the book of my incantations, from which those of the path may summon me unto a conclave of dreaming. Hearken my voice from the grave and remember always – I have become unto the Ghost Light of Azrail."

Consider the Ritual of Entering Black Eden as a point of determined direction, or Willed Becoming. The Vampyric shroud is a symbol of binding one to the earth in the unnatural direction, the very Willed focus of the Left Hand Path. In the closing reference of the self in identification with God and Goddess, Lover and Devouress, this is acknowledging the Daemonic Feminine as a strong and creative part of self. We who awake to this path are but children of Lilith, thus by identifying and self-acknowledging this point will bless the self upon a determined journey of success.

The Caves of Lilitu

-A Bestial Rite of Empowerment-

The foundation for this working is in the Zoharic myths of Hebrew origin. The K'lifah (called Husks of Evil) is from which Lilith emerges from. Consider also the realm of husks or shells, the Qlippoth, the place of demons. The legends of Lilith portray her as having the body of a beautiful woman from head to navel, and below she is flaming fire. This is also comparable to Lilith as having the continence of beautiful maiden, and below the navel being as a beast with owl claws for feet. Babalon, the Enochian Goddess and reappearing as the Whore who rides the Beast in the Bible, is revealed as Lilith the Goddess of Fire and Beasts.

It is Barbara Koltuv, Ph.D. who suggests that the knowledge of Lilith is necessary for strengthening man's ego, the shadow of the self. It is Lilith who inspires sexual dreams, creative inspiration and sensuality. The Daemonic Feminine is therefore essential to the development of man and woman. It is also the gateway to the Sabbat - the dreaming conclave of the Luciferian (Empyrean, of the Light) and Infernal.

Lilith in her dark and fiery aspect is one part of the adversary, the opposing force which initiates through antinomianism and self-deification. In a work which pre-dates the Zohar, it is suggested that Lilith and Samael were born by an emanation beneath the throne of God. Their shape was an androgynous being, double-faced and thus revealed as a part of the adversary (the opposer, Shaitan). Samael, in Hebrew legend has Twelve Wings, which integrates Azazel (the Djinn of Fire, Shaitan) and Samael as Lucifer, the force related to the Noon-tide Sun. Samael is thus the Devil, one half of the adversary and the creative/solar force of the Sun. Lilith joined with Samael through Leviathan, the Great Dragon. Ashmodai was said to be another mate of Lilith, whom was said in some Hebrew legends to be two aspects of the same Goddess. The son of Lilith and Ashmodai was called Sariel, the Sword of Ashmodai. His face flames with fire. Sariel had kept a sealed book of secrets, a grimoire with words of power.

The Zohar itself explains that Lilith is nourished by the water (ocean) and the South wind spreads her influence, from which places her as the Queen of Beasts. They (the Beasts) are found chanting to her in the dark of night. Lilith went forth to the desert to become the Queen of Zemargad (the desert domain), she then joined with Samael and gave birth to thousands of Liliam, Lilitu, the demon succubi who copulate with the shadow of man and woman. It was when Lilith entered the Desert and began creating demons in the caves by the Red Sea that her bestial aspect and fiery darkness of spirit emerged and grew in its coming into being. She practiced along with her children the Lilitu, sorcery and seduction, and with the sexual fluids created more succubi and demonic forms. Lilith in this aspect is our teacher and initiator of Magick and Sorcery, that by using sexual fluids and charging/consecrating talismans, we may create servitors and familiars.

The Son of Samael and Lilith is Cain, the Lord of Horsemen (those who work sorcerous arts and whom spirits ride). An Alchemical working is the creation of Baphomet, or abu-fi-hamat, the Black head of Wisdom. This is a state of coming into being, of whien the torch of wisdom (the Black Flame) is illuminated and revealed within. It is a rite of passage, of when the Baphometic Spirit of Fire becomes separate from the natural order. Thus the Ritual of Infernal Union is a Black Magick working of self-empowerment and the beginning process of creating Baphomet, or Cain the Lord of Horsemen in the Sethanic/Luciferian Witchcraft Current.

The work of Babalon and Lilith within an initiatory aspect is made through the alignment with the spirit of Lilith, Babalon and her children who would be your kin. By summoning and absorbing their knowledge and impulses, we become closer to Her. In Raphael Patai's "The Hebrew Goddess" Lilith is described as wearing jewelry and having red flaming hair. She is dressed in Scarlet and wearing thirty-nine ornaments. She seduces man and fornicates with him; finally arising presenting the demonic and beastlike essence, robed in garments of flaming fire, kills and takes his soul to Gehenna. Lilith is the tester of the path, she who would confront the weakest aspects of the human soul. Those who would not be as Set and Babalon would then be devoured and tossed into the Hell of the Natural Order.

Suggested Reading:
Barbara Koltuv, Ph.D "The Book of Lilith", Nicolas-Hays, Inc. 1986
Raphael Patai - Gates to the Old City, New York, Avon 1980

The Temple itself should be adorned in the decorations of the sabbat and reflective of the aesthetic concept of the daemonic feminine. A black mirror should be placed on the altar - this shall be the gateway from which you shall go forth and they shall come unto you. This is a ritual designed for the children of witch blood, therefore Kin of the succubi and spirits of the Qlippothic realms of wolf and vampire, shade and phantom. You may create a circle from which the spirits shall meet with you, or you may stay near a sleeping place for after the ritual.

The Rite of the Lilitu

-A Bestial Ritual of Empowerment-

Facing the black mirror:
"O' friend and companion of the Night, thou who rejoicest in the baying of dogs and spilt blood who wanderest in the midst of shades among the tombs, who longest for blood and bringest terror to mortals, Gorgo, Mormo, Thousand Faced Moon, I open the Gates to thy realm!" - Inspired by H.P. Lovecraft

"Lilith, mother of Vampyres, Mother of Harlots - patron of shades and the altar of the Infernal Sabbat - I summon thee!"

"Vultures of the Black Earth, eaters of the dead, Allow me entry into the realm of twilight from which I shall become as my mother, Lilith"

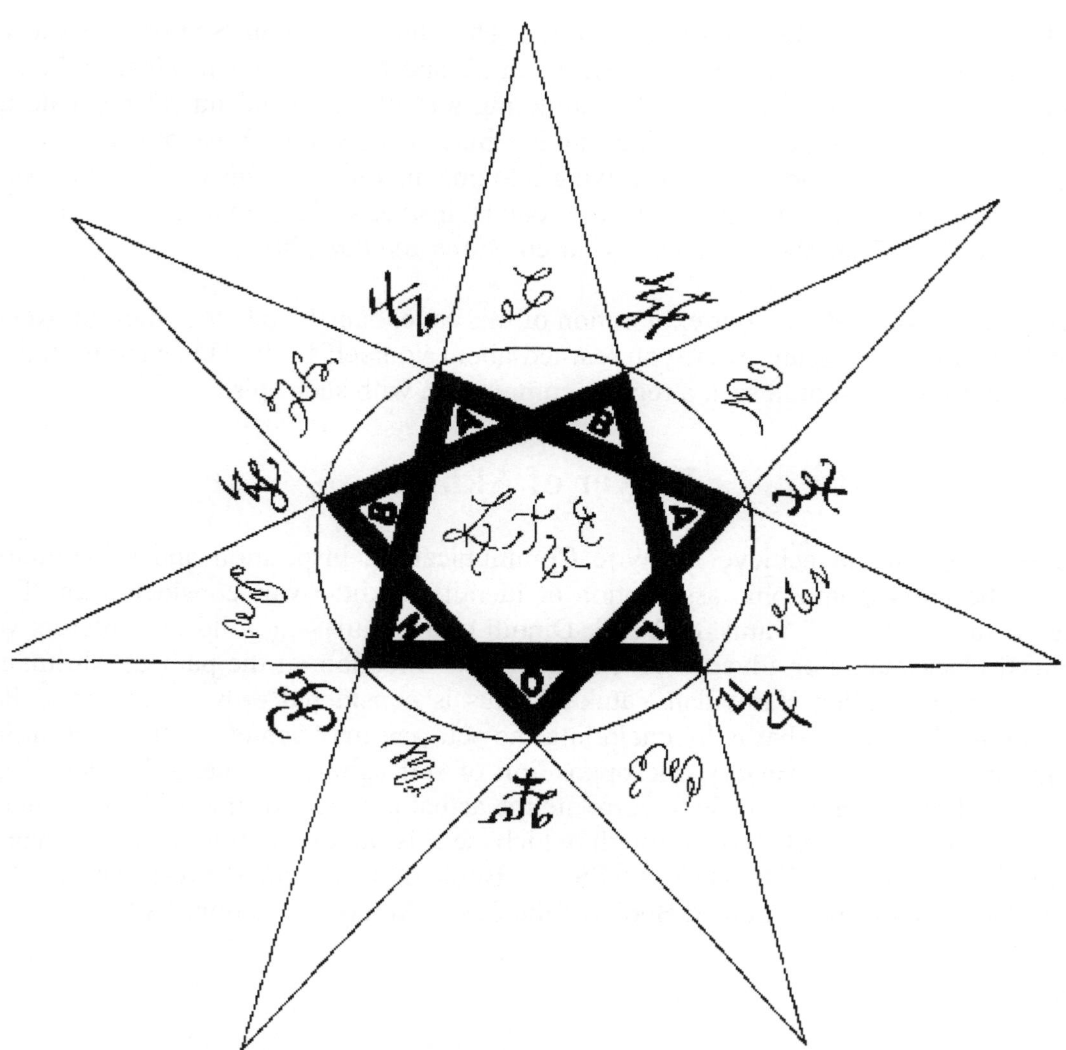

Focus now on the mantra of LIL-KA-LITU, recite slowly and build with repetitive vibrations, taking a quick and steady breath in between mantra breaks. Allow your mind to focus only on the Lility and Succubi, not as a beautiful woman but beast - woman like, a vampyric tomb haunter who spits blood and sexual fluid. It is the Lilitu who sip of the infernal menstrual blood of Lilith - Babalon, our Patron Witch Mother and initiator of the path of the Red Caul-stain of childbirth.

Focus this mantra as you move through the Black Mirror, noticing a great cave filled with moss and damp walls. Hear the musick of the succubi, strange and distant flutes and the rattling and rhythm of drums and bones. You enter a room which has pools of blood, before you stands a Lilitu-succubi.

Envision the succubi as clawed serpent-like demoness, a face strangely beautiful yet with black eyes and teeth that are beast like. Her lower body is beast like as well, long and thick gray wolf-like hairs with bird talons as feet. Her palms and arms are covered in this hair as well, with one hand holding a skull from which she uses to hold the blood of the pool of which she resides by. The pool itself is filled with blood. As you look at the blood, you notice the reflection of your form as Her and she as You. She whispers to you in hissing tones - "Her passion, Her lust, we drink and bathe in Her fornications"...The tongue of this daemon is a snake like, slithering and black in and out of her pale and course mouth. As you face her, staring into her black eyes you both become as one. She enters you and as the emotions start flowing into one, meditate on this coming into being. Feel her ecstasy, the animal hunger and predatory instincts. Keep this feeling close, and when you emerge from the rite, record your emotions and thoughts.

When you are complete in your exploration of this cave, banish and close the rite. Keep a journal of this working and what you learned about yourself by it. This shadow form is but of you, thus you should seek a regular communion with such spirits.

Prayer of Akhtya

Purpose of Ritual: to achieve Aethyric Communication, inspiration and self-initiation through the anthropomorphic assumption of identity. Akhtya was considered an "Evil" sorcerer, the founder of Yatus, or Yatuk-Dinoih (witchcraft) – a guild of sorcerers who practiced black magic or adversarial rites under the direction on the path of Ahriman in ancient Persia. Called Yatuvidah/Yatukan/Yatus is considered now a Left Hand Path approach to Witchcraft that is by encircling the self one may achieve self-initiation into the mysteries of the Adversary, the opposition of self against the natural order. While there is no direct reference made to correlate the actual practices of these tribes of ancient Iran, The image or archetype through which self is in awakening is the image of Ahriman, refer to the KHORDA AVESTA (Book of Common Prayer) translated by James Darmesteter, from "Sacred Books of the East", American Edition, 1898.

The ideal mind set of this ritual and any in the Yatuk Dinoih is one working with the most primordial forces of the earth. The Daevas or Demons of the Yatuk Dinoih are 'shades' of Ahriman, which may be summoned and invoked and then absorbed and communicated within a dreaming gnosis. Imagination, not only being Shaitan/Iblis as described by some areas of Sufism, is the gateway to sorcerous art. The following working is a designed, inspired working to Ahriman, through the shadows encircled by Akhtya, the sorcerer mentioned in the MADIGAN-i-FRYANO.

If utilized, they can be made manifest through the process of Will-Desire-Belief, thus inspiring and producing inner change and development. Akhtya is considered an ancient sorcerer, by immortal essence does this spirit remain, and upon earth the vessel of Ahriman is Akhtya the enfleshed Wizard of the Left Hand Path.

Akhtya is probably most historically accurate as a leader of a nomadic tribe who practiced sorcery or magick outside of the Zoroastrian religion.

Instruments and Preparation:

Create in black cloth a circle, painted in white the triangle – or a circle with your designed 21 letters of the Sacred Alphabet of Desire. In front of the circle (facing North) a black candle (face this direction while reciting – in lore North is the location of the Gates of Hell-Arezura, in Egyptian lore North is the direction of Set) and in the South a White Candle. You may also only have the cardinal points of the circle marked with a letter of your alphabet – only a total of 4 being scribed on the circle.

RITE

In the Night, at Midnight Reside in the Circle of Self and face the North:

"By the Oath against the dawn, by darkness and the Daevas who sign hymns of the Blackened Sun, encircle me!
Ahriman, Arimanius, Witch – initiator, Daemonic Seraph,
Whose essence is the Bornless Fire and Black Earth – I summon thee!
In the names of your shades, whom shall walk the earth through us
Those of the Yatus, born in the circle of Akhtya

By Savar, Lord of flesh and darkness, who calls forth the Great Gray Shadow
By the names of the Guardians of the Blackened Flame –
Andar – Taromat – Zairich – Vizaresh – Zarman – Friftar – Akatash I do comjure thee, manifest in this circle…
Let no harm come unto me, those who summon against me shall only strengthen me"

To Ahriman I speak thy hymns of shadow:

"My name is darkness; for which I create from the Abyss
in the material world I create according to my Will

that I rise up in opposition in the dawn and twilight
I become Druj, the Dragon which does emerge through the serpent of my tongue

In this circle, against the Sun I speak the names of Power – KUNDAK attend!
Carry me unto the Infernal Sabbat!
Astwihad – haunter of night, encircle me kindred spirit-
I summon thee Ashemaogha, the Evil Eye which shall burn always within, the gift of Akhtya – I may curse and bless with sight.

I become the serpent of the dark places of the earth
I become the gray shadow of the wolf, of the wolf's brood am I,
I become in the Light of Pride, that self is the vessel of all gods and goddesses,
That I become by each power of which I summon and Bind

I invoke the Jahi, the children of AZ, mother of Harlots,
O' Dragon of the backward path, Druj do come forth!
Who would give life to the Dead, come now from the Cold North –
From the mouth of Arezura –
Taprev, Mitrokht – Azi Dahaka – Come forth unto this circle
I empower my being and through the sorcerous path do I walk!

To Know – To Will – To Keep Silent

Akhtya I summon – Akhtya I become – Akhtya in Dreams I commune!
Akht-Jadu, Kabed-us-spae, who is the offspring of darkness, whose words weave the webs of Serpents, of Druj and the ecstasy of the Daevodata"

Facing the South and the White Candle:

"I initiate myself on the Serpent's hidden path
I awaken to the shadows of Ahriman
I am embraced by the cold and fiery embrace of AZ
In the Darkness I am born, of the Vampyres Kiss
In the Light of Dawn I emerge – Awake in the Flame of the Dragon – Djinn"
SO IT IS DONE!

THE GATES OF AREZURA

This is a ritual from which the initiate opens the gates of hell which is the meeting place of sorcerers and witches – those who travel into the darkness and flame of the Sabbat. The Gates of Arezura is the initiatory point of which "I" is revealed and may become. You will realize your goals, your potentials and weaknesses to emerge to one who is becoming as Ahriman.

As Ahriman is a form of the Adversary in a primal sense, the darkness of being is to be explored and perceived as an extension of self. The aspect of Ahriman is as half-beast, werewolf type vampyre from. Ahriman is a spirit of darkness, whom resides in the depths of the subconscious – the Gates of Arezura. One should focus on encircling the self in these shadows, which are revealed by the Work itself. The essence of Yatus/Yatuk is the mysteries of sorcery within the self, the keys to the spirit of man. One works this type of considered Dangerous Black Magick as the self-transformation through the image of the Adversary. Akhtya is the sorcerer on earth who drinks of the graal of Ahriman and Az, serpent and wolf. This inversion leads to the strengthening of self under the activity of encircling belief into tangible form.

One should prepare for the ritual of Arezura by a deep introspection, becoming aware of what you wish to achieve and become. You master the self through the entry and exploration of the Gates of Hell – it is also the meeting place of sorcerers, witches and Daevas (demons) of the fiery darkness. It is where Dreams become Flesh.

THE INVOCATION – Facing the North, the direction of Arezura:

"I summon thee, Gateway of Arezura – that you shall open forth to me-
Hail unto thee Ahriman, Lord of Flame and Shadow
Dweller in the dark places of the Earth
Lord and Creator of Wolves, serpents and toads…
As the Night comes forth, you shall attend through me..
I open these gates as the gathering place of the dream,
That in 8 nights shall I become in Shadow the reflection of the 8 Midday journeys to the Sun-
That the Bornless Fire exists in the Eyes of those who walk this path
Ahriman, Arimanius – Acsend through me!
You, summoned unto me – wolf shadow, flyer of night –
I am in flesh Akhtya, encircling my being in the sacred letters of Yatuk-Dinoih
Open now the gates of Arezura and behold the flames of the Djinn, our creative fire of becoming…by the ancient words of Power-
Zazas, Zazas Nasatanada Zazas!

ENCIRCLING THE SPIRIT – ENTERING THE GATES

I summon thee, behold and hail thee – VIZARESH, Guardian of the Gates – Those who have recognized the sacred flame of my being – I enter these gates unto the kingdom of shadow and sorcerous knowledge.
In the name of Ahriman, I do encircle my being – against the Sun, Against the Moon do I walk. In opposition to Order – by this ecstasy do I bask in Chaos – Mummu – Algol – To create Order I reside in the Eye of Darkness
I summon and bind thee – shades of Ahriman..Encircle me!

AZI-DAHAKA – Storm Demon, King with twin Serpents unto your shoulders – whom Ahriman hath Kissed and Wisdom emerges – Serpent of Three Heads, Eyes of Hekate, come forth. Those who summon against me will only strengthen me!

ANDAR- Guardian of the Black Flame, I summon thee! Wraith of the Void of Arezura – TO ME – TO ME!

TAROMAT – Spirit of Rebellion come forth unto me! TO ME! TO ME!

ASTWIHAD – Vampyre and Night Shade, whom I rest beside in Darkness – Whom I fly with in dreaming flesh, encircle me!

BUITI – Ahriman's hammer and knife – Those who summon against me shall taste thy blades of burning metal in dreams!

KUNDAK – Flying Nightmare come forth unto me!"

As you enter the gates, envision each demon and what they represent to you. The Gates of Arezura is a mirror of yourself, a new level of coming into being. You have passed the hidden place, a new initiation is presented to you. Drink from this cup of Serpent wisdom.

INDWELLING

Take this time to ponder and perceive yourself in the following-

What makes me different, independent and individual?
What do I like about myself?
What are my weaknesses and how may I overcome them?
What is the essential "I"?
How may I develop my "Immortal Essence"?

Allow yourself to be consumed in Holy Fire, and shadow shall blanket your spirit as you bask in the flame of the Immortal Self. You are transforming to a God/Goddess, an Angel-Demon which shall walk the earth again and perceive itself in a new light. You shall make TIME serve YOU by thinking before you act, or say. Know what you want and by experience understand the methods to which you may set a goal in motion by understanding Time Flow. Act accordingly. In HELL, Arezura – You are building your Black Tower, your spirit dwelling which is your comfort and Dreaming Home. Time means nothing here, but as you journey to the physical world and your earthly body, change it accordingly.

You will now seek to emerge in the Physical world.

EMERGING FROM THE GATES

"As I strengthen myself in flame and shadow of my sorceries, I do understand who and what I am and I know what I wish to become. In opposition I am of the Sun and the Moon.
Al-Dajjal and Lilith-born.
I am wolf and bat, in dreams I may walk in secrecy, by Kunda – who is drunk from the blood of Sheep I become!

As I stand at the Head of Arezura – I enter in flesh the material world
To manifest my desires – to become, advance and change the world according to my Will
By ZAZAS I become
By ZAZAS I am Always
By Nasatanada In Opposition I become
By Zazas I change the World by my Will"

SO IT IS DONE

The Shadow Circle of Mahazael – Amaimon

A Conjuration of the Dev of Devourment

Let the magician gather in the circle of the illuminated, The Grand Luciferian Circle. The magician will be invoking Mahazael to gain the initiatory insight of this Cainnite Dev, or Demon. The sorcerer should create a mask which represents Mahazael or some kind of fetish like a pot or doll. The mask should have crimson painted fangs, or colored with the blood of the witch undertaking the rite. The face may be painted a pale and blackened corpse green, representing the rising from the soil of the earth to drink deep under the sun and the moon.

The intent of this rite is to bring the initiate to the lycanthropic and atavistic state of self-mastery. Mahazael walks the path of Leviathan, in the circle of darkness from which his words beget flesh. In the shadow dreaming form of Mahazael, the sorcerer may develop lycanthropic states in sleeping and waking, yet also send forth servitors to curse or bless another.

"Mahazael, O isolate dev of the earth, leave thy abode of the tomb and ossary, the charnal house and nightmare of the sleeping, from the abyss and the chthonic depths of the earth, where no angel shall cast their eyes, lest the dev consume their essence, arise!

Let the blood of feeding drip from thy mouth on the sheets of thy lovers. O consort of manes and shades of the dead between the veil of the living and the dead, hear me!

Mahazael, thy face is time worn stretched skin of the corpse, molden green and gray over a skull of sharpened fangs of the serpent and the wolf, thy left hand holds a head, learned from the circle by Lilith – AZ, thy kin of witch blood. From this head you drink deep the blood of life, through the skull the ecstasy of the spirit of Cain, who you communicate with through the dreams of your initiates of flesh.

Thy right hand holds the dual blade stained in the blood of thy victims, rusted with age. When you hold not the blade, a book covered in wolf skin holds the knowledge of your path inked in blood, offer forth this grimoire in dreaming...

Thy legs walk upon the corpses upon the shores, as you have taught the dreaming travel of thy kin, Leviathan, in return you have taught the blood is the life, that you shall exist eternally. As you walk upon the corpses of the non dreaming, with legs covered in the fur of the beast, your dragon - talon feet shredding and marking those who you walk, drinking from the sleeping.

Your chest is decorated in the marks of your familiars and other devs of your brotherhood, around thy neck the bones of the devoured. Thy head is the face of death, yet also as a beast, horned like thy Kin of Blood called Cain. Thy eyes are blackened and of crimson brilliance, as Lilith. Around thy spin is a long and mighty serpent which drinks from those who you feed from, that serpent which brought you the wisdom of the earth when you fell.

Mahazael, who rides upon the Draugr and in dreams carries the nightmares, o consort of Naamah and Lilith, dev who walks with Ahriman, I do summon thee forth. Enter and become, see through my flesh, through my mind, through my eyes...

I am Mahazael – Amaimon, the devourer, the begetter of the path of the drinker of the moon when it is red....

I summon my servitors forth,
Akoros, Dalep, Glesi, Buriol, Romerac, Nilma, My spirits shall come forth and attend to me, I awaken now in a new flesh..."

So it is done...

Leviathan, Samael and Lilith

That Samael is considered the Qlippothic gateway towards self-deification is not essentially a new concept, but often misunderstood. The symbolism of this fallen angel is based within his connection (I label the gender male due to the solar aspects of this spirit, while Lilith is female and lunar) of Asmoday or Ashamdon, a Yezidic archangel. Samael is considered to some extent connected with the Roman Light Bearer, Lucifer, who brings wisdom to mankind. When Lucifer becomes the shadow bringer (Noctifer) he is revealed as the ancient Prince of Darkness, Set.

The hidden gateway within The Order of Phosphorus is the Sabbatic light and union of opposites. Samael is the center resulting in the element Fire, movement and manifestation. As this is the same as Asmodeus, both unite in clarification ascertained through the medium itself. The alchemical formula of self transformation and initiation is through Asmodeus, the Lord of Witchcraft. As the hidden one, Asmodeus is the fountainhead for the art of encircling energy, the very act of Sorcery itself.

Samael is the fallen angel, the God of Fire and manifestation that fell as a Seraph. It is considered that Samael, as being Asmodeus has developed through Hebraic times through Daemonic appearance, confronting even Solomon the mage. Samael represents the earthly Devil of the tarot, the demon of lust whom resides within each individual, the dark side from which all desire, positive or negative, manifest. The mysteries of Samael as the Devil of the Tarot are within the tract 77, as commented on originally by Aleister Crowley. This focus point, known as OZ is the creation source of each individual, from birth to the manifestation of ones Will.

Samael is further the concept of Samael the black within Qlippothic symbolism, the Daemon from which the sinister is revealed. Nature itself is sinister, allowing destruction and creation, the beautiful passage from this world to the next. As the force called God, what is perceived by society as the natural order, in Cabalistic lore is called Metatron, the supreme angel or obedient angel of the Right Hand Path. Samael is considered to be the polar opposite, from the darkness. It is within this theory that the Prince of Darkness is the true mover or manifestation point of life. It is through the shadows from which he stands behind (as does Lilith) and through their "tongues of deceit" shall their Will become flesh. This is the very model of the sorcerer from which the Luciferian becomes the Magus of Leviathan, time itself.

One obtains the essence of Samael through the study of Liber OZ, from which the study of sex and death, known as Thanateros, is understood and made manifest positively in the sorcerers own life. Samael himself is attributed to the serpent, when in the Zohar "For when Samael mounted Eve, he injected filth into her, and she conceived and bare Cain." Tubal-Cain is the father of Witchcraft, the first of the witch blood in the circle of initiation. Upon earth, in flesh, the mythological linage comes from this spirit.

Lilith is one of the Hebraic sources of Evil, reflective of the female ability to not only produce children, but to their very nature itself. Women are attributed to the Moon, Luna, and thus their natures are centered around the phases of the moon. Lilith is thus a night daemon, considered such because of he ability to seduce, take what she wishes, and disregard those whom displease her. Lilith is the Goddess whose top half is feminine beauty, her bottom half is that of an animal with bird like feet.

The Torah mentions Lilith in an interesting phrase, "Wildcats shall meet with hyenas, goat-demons shall call to each other; there too Lilith shall repose, and find a place to rest. There shall the owl nest and lay and hatch and brood in its shadow." - Isaiah 34:14

Jewish folklore mentions that Lilith resides in caves in another plane of existence, much different from her original journey to the Red Sea caves in which she bred demons. The mirror itself is the gateway for her home and from which she may emerge and possess young girls. In a magickal sense, Lilith represents the lunar qualities of both woman and man, therefore possession is the conscious alignment with this fertile and seductive force.

It was specifically that Lilith and Adam was not a happy or unified couple. She wished independence and to be equal with mate, and Adam was not pleased. Lilith refused to lay beneath and in a moment of anger and disgust, rose to the air and called the secret magickal name of God, from which she fled to the shores of the Red Sea. Adam called upon angels to find her and they did locate her, in the caves on the Red Sea. There she mated with demons and produced 100 Lilim or Lilitu, succubi and children spawn of her blood. Needless to say, the angels felt little security in trying to persuade her back to Adam.

Considering the Lunar qualities and the connection to Screech Owls, Lilith is the Queen of Witches. By Witch I do mean cunning woman who is able, by the abilities of Command to Look, by her own Dayside attributes and her concise desire to dress for success, is able to seduce and command by her Will of appearance alone. By the Nightside attribute, the Goddess is the manifestation or channel of Lilith, she becomes the Witch Queen herself, and able to work sorcery, attend the Sabbat upon the steed Kundak through the web of dreams itself. This is the complete Witch, whom by Dayside and Nightside is able to master each by her own Will. Lilith is thus revealed as BABALON, the Goddess of death, blood, passion and life itself! Let her mysteries be revealed to those through enflamed invocation!

The Sigil of Infernal Union, created by Levi and used originally in Maurice Bessey's 1961 encyclopedia of the occult, "Histoire en 1000 Images de la Magie", and re-issued in English later on as "A Pictorial History of Magic and the Supernatural". This symbol, adopted by Anton Szandor LaVey and the Church of Satan in 1966, removed the Samael and Lilith inscriptions and redrew the symbol, titling it "The Sigil of Baphomet".

The Sigil of Infernal Union, as we choose to call it, uses the original names, which surround the goat head. They are, **Samael** and **Lilith**. Many have pondered over the reasoning for the Hebraic Sea Dragon and fallen angel, **Leviathan**, *which surrounds the pentagram*. This shall be addressed in full now.

Samael is in Thelemic or Luciferian terms the Beast 666, the solar force of creation and life. The Beast 666 is considered evil in Christian definitions as it inherently is without a master, has no use for, nor desire for the laws of restriction and subservient behavior developed from a brainwashed system of inner guilt and repression. The Beast 666 is the solar phallic symbol, Pan, Satan, The Devil of the Tarot, the source of manifestation and inner drive.

Samael, being *also known* as Ashmodai or Asmodeus, is the beast which brings us the inner drive to become, to advance and manifest our path or Will. Remember, Cain is the off spring or child of Asmodeus (Samael) and Eve, thus the father of Witchcraft!

What should be considered is not that Samael (or Ashmodai) are considered 'evil' in any moralistic way, however that Samael is the solar and aggressive force of becoming. When one invokes Samael, they become the Dragon of Darkness. The Dragon is in reference to the primal force of the reptilian mind, cold and calculating while the darkness is itself the hidden source of knowledge.

Lilith is known as the Queen of Demons in Hebrew lore, but also she has manifested throughout different cultures and times. Kali is one of the 17 names of Lilith, represented as the devouring black mother of India, who absorbs through time itself. Kali is the pro-active female, the mother which devours its young. While Lilith is itself, a force of the subconscious, lunar and fluid sense of self, something so very "real" as Lilith may manifest to the sorcerer.

Lilith is the mother of demons, spawning Lilitu or Succubi, in the caves of the Red Sea. Lilitu and Succubi are essential in the magical awakening process of the sorcerer. While many might view such as dangerous, it is rather essential in the becoming or initiation period of the individual. Lilith and her home of desolation is located near the Red Sea, which is first described in the Old Testament. This demonic area is filled with owls, ravens, daemonic servitors, vampires, werewolves, satyrs and drenched in blood.

The familiar, when created, is an important step in awakening through Sexual Congress, from which one seeks union with the dreaming body of the gnosis. The Lilitu is the Gate towards one discovering the Holy Guardian Angel (an alternate path of the Witches Sabbath) and the Evil Genius. Seek union with the Lilitu, within and without.

One mystery of the two is that they are called *"The Eternal Couple"* and are symbolized in the Zohar as the "evil" couple (evil is therefore described as the Left Hand Path approach, isolating the self which was contrary to many of the founders of religious Christianity). Samael is then revealed as Asmodeus and Lilith the mother of fornication.

Samael and Lilith are the keys of Infernal, or Daemonic Union. It is by the combination of these forces which are the Sun and Moon respectively that we may emerge from which the familiar and exterior daemon may seek further sexual congress via dreams. The Sigil of Infernal Union is the gateway towards Qlippothic Awakening, which we may unite the shadow with the light, therefore reaching towards the depths and heights of beauty!

Leviathan surrounds the averse pentagram in the Hebrew letters LVThN. Leviathan is indeed the Hebraic Sea Dragon known through many cultures as the male counterpart of Tiamat, the Ourabouris, ***Tanin'iver***, the blind dragon. It is by all secrets now known the mystical marriage of Daemonic opposites was through the *unconscious link* of Leviathan, whom brought both spirits together in union. Leviathan is the timeless aspect of being, as by the fall along with Lucifer Leviathan perceived the self and by entering the great oceans centered itself in the mind of the dragon. Leviathan is thus timeless and is within the subconscious of man and woman.

The symbol of entering and becoming is thus summarized in the following way:

Leviathan (the gateway)
-Timelessness, subconscious power, immortal aspects of the essential self

Samael (the Sun – known as Asmodeus)
-Force, Sorcery, Fire. Samael is the one of darkness (knowledge hidden) whom rode Eve and 'injected filth into her'. Samael is the root force of The Beast 666, the solar creative force and the devil of the tarot.

Lilith (the Moon – Queen of the Witches and Lilitu/Succubi)
-Witchcraft, Sorcery, Lunar dream magicks. Lilith is the mother of harlots who appears in the form of a beautiful woman with the lower half animal like, hairy and feet of a large bird. Lilith is the gateway to the Sabbat and to the arts of Lesser and Greater Black Magick. Lilith is also the lunar blood covered Goddess, revealed in Thelemic lore as BABALON.

SAMAEL (the Sun – Daemonic and Solar Phallic Force, an extension of Set)
-Magick and Solar creative sorcery. Samael is the Dragon – Daemon of Warlocks and Wizards, the manifestation aspect of Daemonic Becoming. Samael is the mastery of the earth and positive creation by knowledge into wisdom. Samael opens the gateway of the knowledge of the Watchers, and all fallen angels. Revealed in Thelemic lore as The Beast 666.

The Three Aspects unified creates Baphomet, or Abu-fi-Hamat, the Black Head of Wisdom translated also as "Father of Wisdom". It is because of this that the union of Samael and Lilith, the marriage of opposites, through the Dragon Leviathan that wisdom grows from knowledge.

The Ritual of Infernal Union

Solitary ritual based on the union of opposites. Black Robe, Candles: Black and Red. Sigil of Infernal Union may be used upon the altar wall as well as the altar itself. The sigil of the union of the Beast 666 and Babalon may be used as well. This symbol is based on the classic sigil originally designed by Aleister Crowley, but redrafted by Elda Isela Ford. This is indeed a Saturn/Lunar rite, the merging of sexualities within the individual. One should prepare the GRAND LUCIFERIAN CIRCLE (or a similar circle as described in THE BIBLE OF THE ADVERSARY), robed in black and red and candles should be black and red. A statement of intent would read as the following:

"It is my Will to invoke the Egregores of Samael and Lilith, so that by union of Both within myself, I shall become reborn as Baphomet."

Widdershins, Banishing ritual to clear mind and Call the Four Quarters:

Zazas, Zazas, Nasatanada Zazas

SOUTH:
Shaitan-Set,
Lords of the Southern Tower, Djinn Father of fire and desert sands, I do summon thee forth to witness my rites of awakening and union. I command the fires of the Abyss to protect my circle, let the gates be opened!

EAST:
Lucifer-Phosphorus,
Lords of the Eastern Tower, bearer of the black flame, lord of light and Promethean flame, I do summon thee forth to witness my rites of awakening and union. I command the forces of Air and the astral plane, send thy Luciferian elementals to guard this circle.

WEST:
Leviathan-Ourabouris,
Lord of the Western Tower, who beholds the Black Flame hidden in the depths!
Great encircling one, who holds the keys to immortality! I summon the forces of Water and the Sea to witness my rites of awakening and union. Be watchful and protect this circle!

NORTH:
Belial
Lord of the Northern Tower, who fell from heaven to be as God itself, who accepts no master- I do summon thee forth to witness my rites of awakening and union. I command the forces of the earth to protect this circle!

Imagine each force in a silent way adding the essence of protection around you.

Take now the Athame from the altar, envision the image of Samael, reciting:

"Solar force of fire and inspiration, which from all life emerges as its own being, I do summon thee, Samael from the depths of my soul, my very being, to emerge in my consciousness as life and solar force! Do manifest and hear my words, which are meant as an invocation of Sorath, the Beast 666 which is your secret name. Samael, Satan do manifest unto me. Let me guide the union of opposites!"

Begin masturbation, envisioning the solar force building from the base of your spine up to your head, the fire force spreading like a fountain throughout your entire body. Remember, you are controlling this force, do not orgasm yet. Hold the fire vision as you feel Saturn or Samael take consciousness. Allow the force to Immolate your consciousness; share the ecstasy with this angel of fire and light.

Take now the cup from the altar, drinking deeply of its cold and refreshing elixir.

Envision now Lilith and recite:

"Lunar force of water and dream walking, which you shall manifest my consciousness from the desert caves of the Red Sea, I do summon you, invoke you within me. Bring unto me your mysteries of your children, the Lilitu, that I may hold the arcana of sexual union and vampiric manifestation. Enter me, mother of the path of the wise, reveal your bestial and angelic essence to me. Do manifest through me now, join in union with your mate, Samael. Join through me the union of Opposites!"

Allow the lunar energy to flow through you, catching the visions of lilitu and such succubi, bestial and hair covered below their waste…seeking the sexual union of others in great fornication and abandonment. Lilith is Babalon, the goddess who bathes in the blood of the moon.

Face now the altar, take the wand and recite while focusing upon Lilith:

"She howls upon the desert winds, as the moon brings the cloak of Darkness. The shadow radiates her essence, blood drinker, devouress of the sleeping, fornicate in the spilt veins of those who come to you!

Lilith, LA-KAL-IL-LI-KA, I invoke thee by your sacred names:

Abeko, Batna, Abito, Eilo, Amizo, Ita, Izorpo, Kali, Kea, Kokos, Odam, Patrota, Podo, Partasah, Satrina, Talto, Lilith!

And by your other names of calling:

Abyzu, Ailo, Alu, Abro, Amiz, Amizu, Ardad lili, Avitu, Bituah, Gelou, Gallu, Gilou, Ik, Kalee, Ils, Kakash, Lamassu, Kema, Partashah, Petrota, Pods, Raphi, Satrinah, Thiltho, Zahriel, Zefonith, Lilith!

By the words of Power:

BABALON-BAL-BIN-ABRAFT, ASAL-ON-AI, ATHOR-E-BAL-O, ERESHKIGAL!

I offer my essence as sacrifice, a drop of my blood. Witch Queen of the infernal Sabbat! I do invoke thee, horned moon which spills and drinks the lunar blood, she who fornicates with Daemons, I do seek your kiss, I give you substance now from which you shall enter me!

Lilith, beautiful mother, giver of life and desire, I do summon thee forth! Lilith, who resides in the caves with your children of darkness, spawned through once congress with Samael, I unite now your passion through creation!"

Face now the Altar, envision the Red Dragon who changes into the form of the fallen Seraphim, Samael, and recite:

"Whom fell from heavenly unlight to have knowledge of the darkness, fallen seraph of fire and the sun, I do invoke thee, Samael. To you, who has walked the earth for thousands of years, from body to body, now shall you spread your light unto humanity.

Angel, known as Shemna'il, who is Nasiru'd-Din, I do invoke thee, solar force, known as Sorath, Beast whose number is of the Sun itself, I do summon thee forth! Serpent Angel, who came by the astral plane with Melek Taaus, known as Shaitan, Lucifer – the Brothers of Light. Come forth now through me, manifest in my being, we shall join as one. By the names of power:

AR-O-GO-GO-RU-ABRAO, PUR, IAFTH, OO, AR, THIAF, A-THELE-BER-SET, PHITHETA-SOE!!

I summon thee, revealed as Set, whom is the sun and darkness in union!"

Envison now the fire of spirit, which is swirling within your very self, encircling Lilith, and moving throughout your consciousness.

Take now the Athame and focus upon the Dragon-angel, Leviathan.

"Force of the Subconscious, whom I call the outside, I do summon thee to bring The Sun and the Moon, Samael and Lilith, in glorious union! I do Will this union within my self, that I may speak the words unheard from the profane, and my Will manifest through the gates of Apep!

Hear the word of power:

MRIODOM!"

Allow now the self to experience grand ecstasy, that through enflaming the self one would focus upon the image of Samael and Lilith in sexual congress, the fire and water of spirit joining in a blaze of force, as orgasm is obtained, imagine the force of light and the waves of darkness consume your mind!

"Ya! Zat-I Shaitan!" So it is done.

Chapter Four

Sethanic and Angelick Magick

I. AZOTHOZ
A Book of the Adversary

Sethanic Witchcraft and the Left Hand Path

THE LIGHT OF IBLIS UNVEILED

The connections of Sethanic Witchcraft[84] and the Left Hand Path are indeed more deeply connected than what is commonly perceived. It is the very essence of the craft that is Luciferian in base and from such a fruitful fountain can a greater gnosis be discovered. Demons become angels and darkness becomes a beautiful light. This is not done so however easily, and requires the development and work of the imagination, which is called Iblis[2], commonly known as Set and Satan.

The Left Hand Path is essential a journey, or path center within non-union (antinomian) with the objective universe, or nature. A LHP practitioner does not view aligning the psyche with the natural order a healthy thing to do. The LHP is the isolation of the self, or psyche to refine ones' own center of being, to improve and develop continually. This does require a desire, a balance of self, and the imagination to make this work for the individual.

William Blake was one of the very few westerners who recognized Satan as the imagination, not an enthroned demon devouring souls. In Paradise Lost, Milton painted Lucifer in the same aspect as perhaps the very source of this angel, in the Middle Eastern lore of Iblis and Shaitan, the Opposer.

Sethanic Witchcraft is in essence the unity of primal sorcery and illuminated magick, the ascension and the antinomian development of self. The Sethanic Gnosis is not new, rather it is the gift of self-initiation brought down from Lucifer and the Watchers and transmitted via mouth to ear in the dreaming plane. By utilizing the keys of the writings as workings the gates are unlocked. As the reader moves through the grimoires and texts, envisions and relates to the art, or perhaps discovers a new shape within an angle, then shall this knowledge be passed unto the initiate. The Sethanic Gnosis lives in each practitioner, just as the Black Flame is illuminated, this current is alive as well.

Many techniques are introduced; many utilized and once they have worn out their use, are discarded for new techniques that bring results for the sorcerer.

The Throne of Twilight[3] is the awakening undertaken by the initiate, by he and she whom invokes and envisions the Luciferian Light. That Lucifer is Iblis, the imagination, and the very foundation of free thought that defines the propagation of the Will. In the Sethanic Path there is the essence of primal sorcery, with the aims of light beyond and through the darkness.

Iblis fell from the heavens; the innocence passed beyond once the self was perceived. Iblis understood that he (I choose to write in masculine terms while exploring

[84] Sethanic Witchcraft as made manifest in America by Coven Nachttoter, a Left Hand Path extension of the Witchcraft Tradition.

[2] Iblis known as Azazel the Fallen Angel who later became Shaitan the Opposer/Melek Taus the Peacock Angel.

[3] The Title of the Poem/Lyric which is written in form of a statement and invocation at the same time. A writing of Opposition from which Self-Initiation may occur.

Iblis/Lucifer, though not defining it to gender within the initiatory context) was indeed separate from the universe, that he like all forms of being was special. Iblis, or Lucifer was the essence of fire, thus he was a Djinn. Iblis is the initiator of the path. Azazel, the name of Iblis is the Djinn transformed into fallen angel, later called Lucifer. It was the very gift of Lucifer which brought man the first flame of perception, thus the Black Flame.

Azrail is the angel of death, which is an alternate of Azazel, thus Azrail is the shadow form of Azazel, however of the path of darkness and the dead. Anubis, within the Egyptian context, is the guardian of the path and the opener of the way. The mentioning of Azrail is the lunar fountain from which the vampyre djinn drinks.

As Satan/Lucifer/Shaitan is the guardian of the threshold[4], the imagination is the gateway of the Black Flame itself. Humans hold the very keys to the primal source, the barbarous tongues which open the gates of hell and the darkness within. It is from the fallen angels and Djinn, the Watchers which from the fall bring us divine light and the infinite possibility of becoming. Azazel refused to bow before man, whom was created from clay. As a Djinn of fire, Azazel was the initiator of the path, the twelve winged cherub which was the most illuminated angel of God. Iblis however, rejected faith itself. This was the moment from which this spirit saved and uplifted humanity. As he fell from the heavens unto earth, his comrades including the Watchers, who mated with women of the earth, realized they did not perish and the Black Flame itself remained.

Pride called Kibr was the reason for the fall of Iblis, who found knowledge in the self. In other pantheons from behind Satan comes forth the Egyptian Prince of Darkness, SET. Set is considered the isolate and beautiful self, that within isolation, is the immortal psyche. Set has brought forth many masks, which he wears in the eye of the one who views him. Being Iblis, Azazel, Shaitan, Lucifer, Satan, each is different in some ways throughout other cultures, yet Set is within and beyond them all. This by itself, is the Typhon-Sethian awakening of Luciferian Being. One who leaves order to explore Chaos and Darkness, and in the center of this finding a light more beautiful than any flickering lesser light beyond it.

Darkness is a principle understood only by experiencing it. One who persists to despise the concept of darkness and evil, literally have not tasted the fruits of its tree. Darkness is call such because no light is given to view it. When one illuminates a light within, a great shadow is cast down. We are the Promethean source of all light and fire, and by seeking Set by the various masks he wears can we become one with the Prince of Darkness. It is not, however just about becoming 'one', rather remaining separate and unique. Set in this aspect joins with us yet we exist still in the antinomian sense. The text of this grimoire is

[4] The Imagination, or Iblis. The Very gateway of our mind. Ayn al-Qozat Hamadani, a Shaykh executed at the age of 31 in his hometown Hamadan, Northwest Iran in 1131 A.D. This shaykh was an initiated teacher whom brought the knowledge of THE BLACK LIGHT and DARK TRESSES of the BELOVED to those who were able to understanding this concept. Satan is the Guardian of the Threshold, a doorway which is the space-between-worlds. (from Iblis, Peter Lamborn Wilson, Gnosis Magazine)

given as such, a cipher to be used in bringing forth the Prince of Darkness, immolating yourself, and becoming as this very life giving force of the universe.

The Luciferian concepts of light are given in areas of self-study and exploration. We are not able to just pass through times and examples of being, yet we must remain constant and at the same time progressive. All knowledge we seek brings us wisdom, a new sense of self. Chaos is the tool found around us from which the Waters of Nun allow us to drink.

"Art is the instinctive application (to observations or sensations) of the knowledge latent in the sub-consciousness." - A. O. Spare

This grimoire offers the God Forms of the Sethanic and Luciferian Path as the gateway, a communication point of the developing gnosis of self-creation. Those who may see through and within the body of work will be able to utilize its power.
The Masks of Satan in a myriad of forms is but a shadow of which it really is; such symbolism is a testing ground for initiation.

Understanding the essence of Set-heh (Set the Opposer) within the gnosis obtain through this grimoire is essential in the results sought. The individual must be comprehendible concerning the aims of the Great Work. Sorcery and Magick are successful when the magician is willing to cross the Abyss and instead of denial of the world ultimately and loosing the ego, one uses this neither-neither aspect of seizing and strengthening the consciousness. By approaching Magick and elevating the self one may capitalize on the chance to initiate the self towards the God Set or Lilith, and drink from the cup of ecstasies from which they offer.

The Throne of Twilight

From the throne of twilight brought
Gave no lamp of the deads last vison
The spirit of fire cast down as lightning
Through the choice of isolation

Consciousness regained
sleep did not prevail
from the ashes of Azrael's urn
did Iblis emerge,
From night doth he go forth

Let the knowledge of heaven and
the secrets of Hell,
Be ever in union, for there
is the secret of God itself
The sacred cup of life
offered unto ashen lips

It is the knowledge of the daimon,
in it's waking beauty,
Unseen for the rest hides beneath the tomb,
The test of overcoming the flesh will come,
from which thy solitary form shall
remanifest in glory and fire

It was the daughter of night which tasted
the blood from the Eyes of God,
and held it unto her being
A spark and flame illuminated,
the Lunar rays granted freedom
from the flesh. The horned moon then
understood Iblis and was not unlike the Djinn.

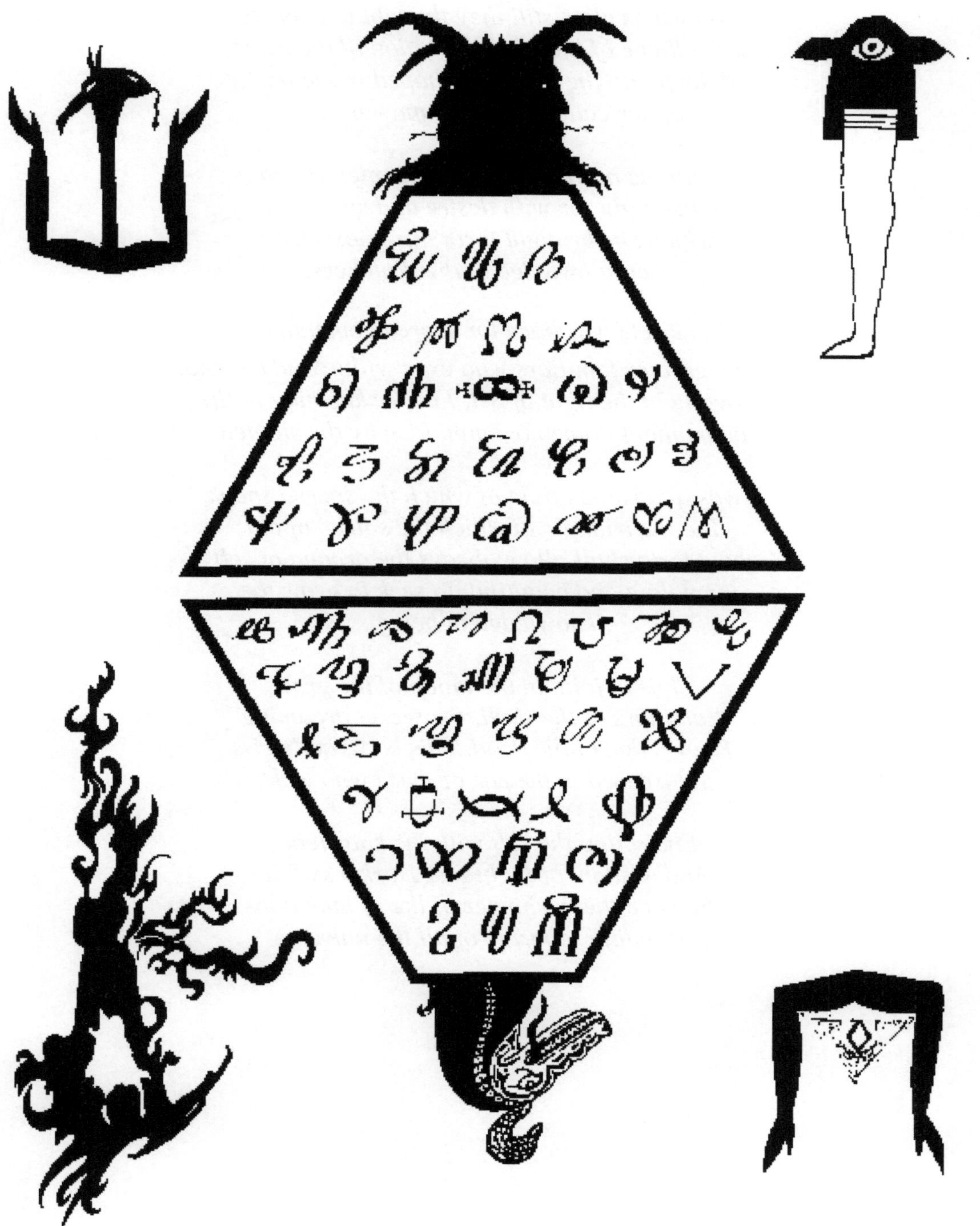

As Iblis and the Watchers descended
to Earth, they brought the knowledge
and gnosis of being and becoming
In their temple long buried by desert sand,
They too communed in the knowledge of
the human race, breeding the
Passions of dawn and twilight!

Known as clay, still they thought to bring to
it the flame of life, unto the union of the beasts
of the field. The clay was shaped in the image
of perfection, yet was unawakened.

Lilith the horned triple moon entered again
in the night for with desire and knowledge,
which she brought forth this gnosis from
her knowledge of the Watchers,

The circle was born for sacred communion,
for the greater familiars who exist within and beyond,
knowing in the light of Set, Lucifer knowing in the
triumphant flame now unhidden by the sighted

It was and is the circle of which the sacred speak,
But the triangle of which the spirits of old
come forth shall allow always the arcana of self,
inviolate and beautiful, to seek to grow the
knowledge of being.

Thus to join, in the union of the great
Familiars of the skull, the secret dreaming
Knowledge of the dead. This is Azrael's kiss
Whispered in the ear of those who wake

Encircling the self with the knowledge
And wisdom of Light and Darkness Iblis
Became the harbinger of life of humanity
Standing separate of all the universe

In this self created light which cast forth
Darkness in all its brilliance and splendor,
The Prince of Darkness was born
through division and puissance

Lilith came unto the Prince of Darkness
Whom found the shores of the Red Sea
In passion and nocturnal lust knew
The passions of man and woman and
Thus children of this infernal union born

The great familiars and watchers of the quarters
Were born of the Devil's lust, thus Cain emerged
To walk with Adam and his bride

It was the serpent call Set-Heh or Satan
Who brought the sight of gnosis to clay
Thus a great fire emerged which burnt with life
That initially man embraced this light only few
could understand and use this brilliance
which remained constant in only a few

Lilith came unto man and woman as well
Bringing the gift of Sorcerous art to both,
as well as the secrets of the grave.
It was the cup of God's Blood from
which the serpent drank, and was passed
to man by mouth to ear in the dreaming land

The first grimoire was written in this blood,
Sealed with the fire of Djinn and Dragon's eye,
Which dwelled in the mind of those embraced
This unspoken knowledge.

Humanity carried the knowledge of the Beast,
Which angels sought to possess
Bringing the unseen force of the spirit of caves
And caverns, creating the ideal being

It was then that it was drawn from the well of
immortality, through the darkness And fire
they sipped the blood of God.

It was the passion and knowledge of the fallen ones,
the Watchers, who developed the gift of Iblis
called now Set-hen or Satan
seeking now union with the daughters of man
they brought the fire of clay closer to the
Crown of the Dragon.

The serpent so unseen by many,
Brought forth a lively song in the tunnels
The ones of fire were many,
With a deep respect for Iblis
called Shaitan the Opposer,
teaching them to see beyond the veil,
they came forth one by one and tasted

The ecstasy of shadows

Arimanus called the Dragon of Darkness
Who tasted the sweet flesh and poisoned flower
of Lilith understood what existence in flesh would be
Born of shadows and flesh torn trickery

The passion and desire of Lilith grew,
Just as immortality emerged from
Strength Of consciousness,
and thus this ideal reversed
Az became Lilith, whom the
Queen of Witchcraft Born, taking
the names of cultures from which
She rode.

With hunger Lilith tasted the life which so sang
A beautiful hymn, silence then faded to
The waking of the grave.

That humanity may know the essence of the
Fall, Lilith brings the kiss of the vampyres' touch
Waking the spirit in the grave, then we
Shall know the Ahrimanic Gift

By the forked tongue of the initiator I shall hear,
To know which is rarely spoken will not be
Unseen, that the knowledge of Fire,
be the Hidden language of the mind
And nothing will remain beyond it.

The glyphs and sigils of the art shall bring
Closer the gulf of the waking and dreaming,
Union brings the arcana of sorcerous wisdom
laid before by scaled and wolf skinned hand

It is the Watchers which bring man and woman
The ability to Willfully change their surroundings,
and how they may be changed by command alone
It is Set-heh which brings us the knowledge of being
And the Black Flame of self-consciousness,

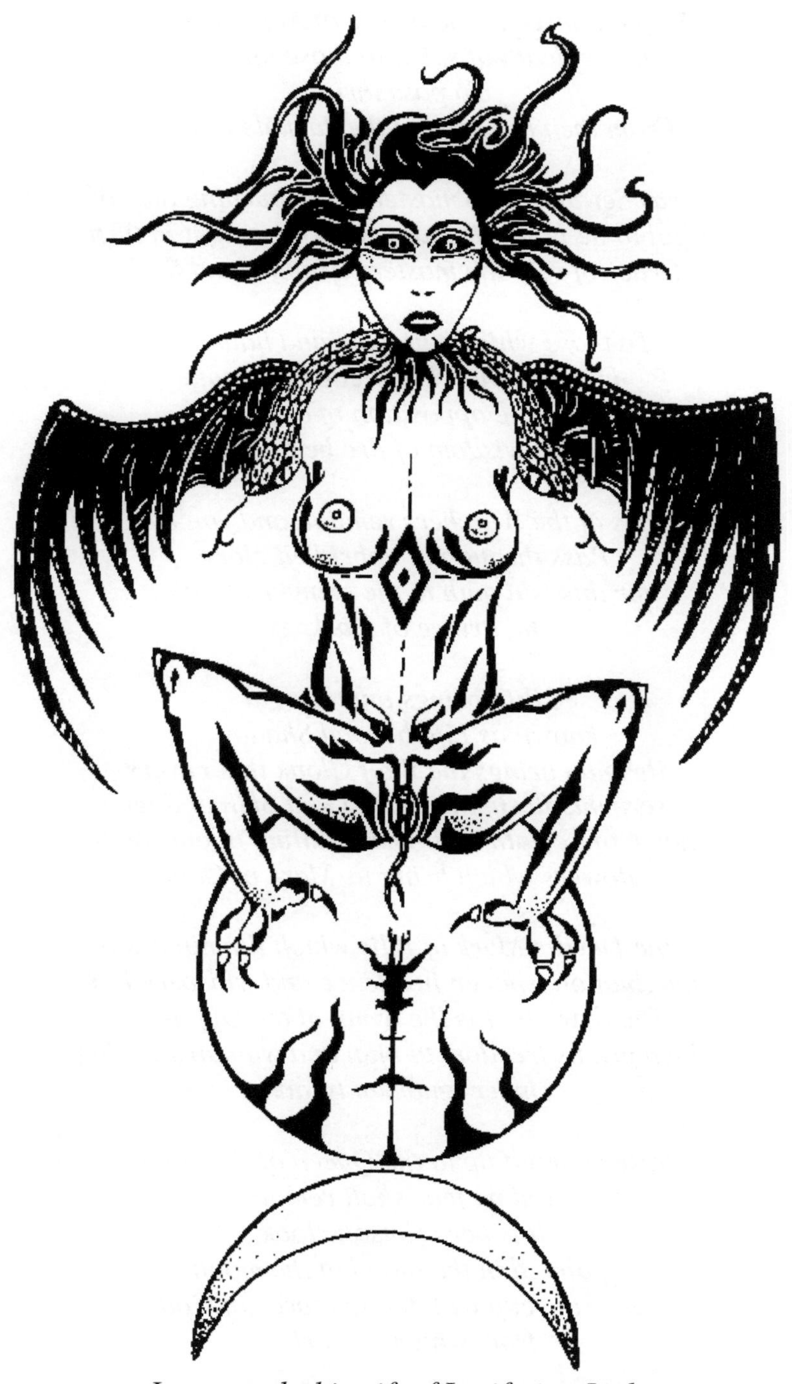

Let us exalt this gift of Luciferian Light
It is Lilith who brings us the night born congress
Of dream flight, the very Sethanic Arcana of the
Triple Moon'd Queen

Let us free our spirits of the Temple of Flesh,
To walk the fields of the dead
It is the ecstasy of the in-between that led to

the path unseen. The beasts of Anpu and Apep
Bring death of spirit to those unwilling
To pass thru,
From then the Lord of the Jackals Initiates

It was Set-an which mastered the burning Star of
Algol to be Lord of Chaos, which brought in turn
Order of self, the mastery of spirit and flesh

To those which still walk and haunt the
Deserts, shall knowledge be found
It is in the opposition of order that
The wisdom of fire be found

The gates of the Watchers remain, and you may still
Pass through in unbridled glory,
for this is a path to the bringer of light,
the Prince of Darkness

Lilith brings another gift
known as Life beyond Shadow,
Ahriman brings the Wolf Cloak that covers
the serpents flesh, the Black Goat Skin of Silence
Known of Leviathan, it is the calling of our latent
Powers which bring us Mark of Cain

It is the Devil's Mark of Iblis which illuminates our
Imagination, spoken in silence and whispered in
The dawn that is the hymn of the Opposer
Which grants freedom to man and woman sleeping
Under ignorant tyranny

Raise yourself up to the Queen of the Sabbat
And no fear shall remain,
It is her crimson cloak,
painted in the blood of the moon
And the cup with the Lifeforce of God
from which you drink

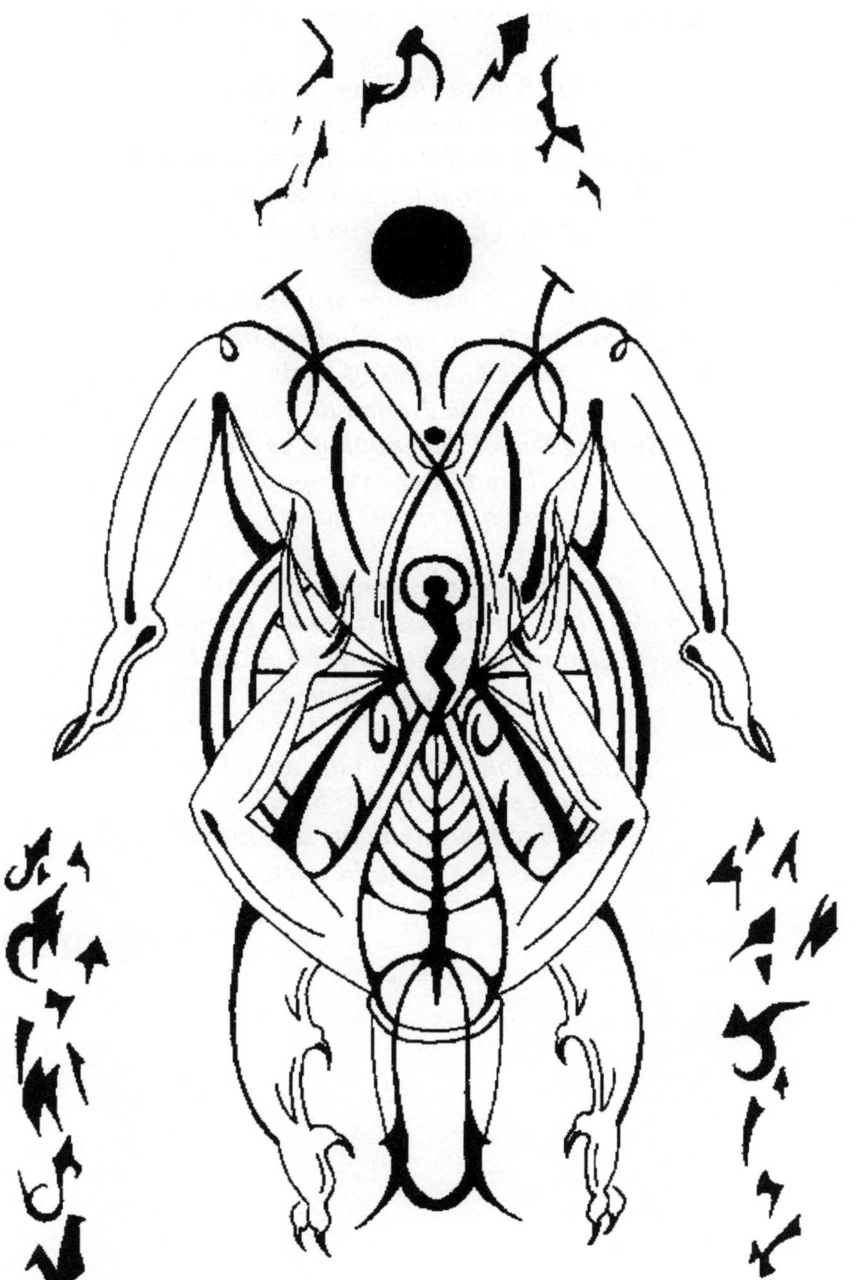

Arise with the Eye of the Serpent,
which is cold and constant
This shall be the mirror of Lilith's sight
Cast your eyes into the caves and take from it
The totem of skulls
This shall be the price of the unawakened

The body of shadow will reveal and command much
Yet it is always an extension of the being
It is the very spirit of the owl which brings

Nocturnal flight above the graves of the sleeping

At the Sabbat shall we be seen,
Spoken in shadow's company
From the mask shall the Dragon be revealed
Through the soul thirst of non sleep
Will the Vampyric kiss prevail

Each of those of which we are will become
Reborn in the lunar light of the
Triple Goddess of Night
and the Noon tide
Burning Sun of the Djinn of the Desert
Shall we become yet again,
born of serpents flame.

Do not close the Temple of Mind
Which is our arcana of hidden flame
Called as the sight of the awakened
Imagination renamed

That Iblis takes form in the nameless
Whom shall be called Set-Heh
From which through time and guise
Shall be as that the same

THE LORE OF THE FALLEN

At the crossroads, entering the Gast
Through twilight hallows one shall dance
Covered in wolf skin, serpent flesh steps forth
Towards the sabbat eve, where we meet upon the ghost roads
The mighty shades gather among us

In the willed forms our fetch may change
The great bestial familiars emerge
And gather round BalesFire, other dreaming arcana of the dead

Beyond the veil of this fire, the profane shall not pass
Yet the sabbat dream is bestowed to the drinker of ecstasy
Within the realm of shadow, cold through the caves
Of Awlraun-Lilith, the gateway between two worlds is the
Flesh which holds the cunning fire
Illuminated by Qayin
Brought to those who walked this path by Lucifer
Known as the Black Flame

In the Ourabourus bound circle
Shall the first of devil skin born
The mediator of worlds
From which shall exhalt the flame of Set-Hen
To bear the Mark of Cain

In the sleep born waking in twilight
The Eidolon – shade takes to night
Owl wings upon the broom and wolf eyes cast
Towards the Sabbat of Witches

The children of the Serpent
Awaken to this call
The Queen of Elphame opens forth
The Gates of the Dead
To that which we shall fly
Azrail's Kiss brings them closer
And the Ankou's journey begins again

Hag Moon and Wolfs Bane bloom
Hecate to thee we shall fly
Bend to the Kiss of Serpent's Blessing
In the Owl Light this gateway opened
As the Opposer we do come in shadow bearing light

First from the Watchers shall sight be given
And the abilities to manifest our desire
Those who walk the twilight path
Unseen in flesh but dwelling near
In the eyes of the Dead can this emerald flame
Be seen

It was Cain, born of Samael – Asmoday in union with
Awlraun – Lilith, gathered the wisdom of those who fell
Feather and flame, steel and wood, brings again
The vision of old, the wisdom of such bestowed

From the chariot of the spirits
Which came unto earth
Passed the cunning fire to man
Which that brought forth the awakened
Who knew both darkness and light
And drank of both sources

In Asonya we shall drink of the purest light
Which awakens the knowledge of Stars

In Elba, given the cup of Hekate
Shall all manner of form and change be revealed

In Benase shall balance of shadow and light be seen
Through the mastery shall Cunning Fire be held
Eternally

In Erae shall the mastery of Earth be commanded

It was the Erythraean Sea the Mother Serpent found
And from the caves shall she be called

Unto the sabbat enthroned on the Elder Oak does
The dragon coil around

Upon the Horse, shall Cain bring forth
The Book of Veiled Sight
Those who may open the book may then read this
Very arcana of self knowledge
That may again penetrate the Fire of Eld

That the Devil's Mark brings the birth caul of Watchers
Then shall Leviathan's Eye be revealed
No longer walking in silence, yet the mark of the beast confirmed

The mysteries are passed through
A forked tongue of sight & of flesh
That the sleepers shall awaken before this immortal fire
Call Shaitan the Opposer

Isolate consciousness and being
Eternally brought by the coiling serpent
Set is revealed
Prince of Darkness in imagry
Is the gateway of our fountain of life

That the Light of Iblis
Is the very sight of mind
The imagination revealed unto the oceans of time
Bring the Luciferian Flame of being

I, who reside within the darkness and vast outer wastes,
whom has tasted of the desert fire of the fall,
diving the abyssic waters of Nun do come forth.

It is within the semblance of shadow that
the light is merged with the burning darkness.
I have perceived myself through
the mirror image of my own being, the opposer
from which both sides I initiate.

Those of the left kingdom,
reached by diving the Oceans of Nun
and seeking union with Leviathan shall understand this vision.

Know that the cyclopean ruins
of my Temple is not the existence of space,
yet it resides in the heart of every individual.

To illuminate my Gift to the clay of the earth,
the Black Flame soon is resound
and pondering the essence of
transformation from clay to Fire.

The silent initiator is
soon upon the path of the shadow,
from which Iblis as I am sometimes
called guides from the essence of the self.

To separate from the path of union of nature,
once must taste from the Waters of Nun
and come unto my throne,
which all of those of me share.

The hierarchy of old is of the cowards
of the crumbling cathedrals of forgotten
fears beaten down into the sheep.
Our way is of the wolf and the caves of the Succubi.
Lilith, Az and all of the forms
of which my bride takes is the nurturing of your birth.

The Black Eagle

Existent in the spectral roads, this spirit familiar is considered a foundation of the transmission of the modern Sethanic Current and those who work through it. While the history of the Black (sometimes called Blue Eagle) is rather shady, the emergence of the magickal work of Austin Osman Spare produced the image known as Black Eagle. According to popular legend, Spare was passed the spirit-familiar of Black Eagle through Mrs. Paterson, the Witch Mother who initiated Austin at an early age. When she passed into the Ghost Roads the familiar was transmitted to Spare. Zos vel Thanatos (his name to initiates of the current) is the inherent linage passed from mouth to ear, the inspiration of dreaming inspiration that initiates the magickal work.

During Spare's life he had a constant familiar or an outside spiritual guide, which was known to him as the Black Eagle. This spirit has been understood through study of Coven Nachttoter as a Vampyre Spirit, which exists through the astral or dream plane. It has been suggested that the Black Eagle gave influence through Mrs. Paterson, who in turn informed Spare on the occult arts. Much of this knowledge must have been passed on via dreams. The Black Eagle is the spirit-familiar of the Sethanic Witchcraft Gnosis itself as well as a symbol of the lunar or shadow self, a vampyre spirit who fed from the energies of the sigil itself~ the focus of energy. The Black Eagle seems to mold its' form and shape to the ideal point of identification. Its masks are many, and it's forms fluid with imagery depending on the individual. In Coven evocations, this spirit forms in the black mirror according to the identification of the group. If they group decides on specific features and points while focusing intently, then this shadow takes form. If many are confused and not agreeing on the form, the shapes vary often in daemonic forms of bestial shades.

The work of Zos produces the seeing Eye of the world of dreams and twilight, which the witch is able to perceive inherently. This passage of essence is revealed only to those who are able to comprehend the essence and what it is to reveal. It is Spare's gnosis, transferred in a way which was shown as a pure source of magickal gnosis, is the culmination of the very essence of the Sabbat. In Austin Spare's ritual text, The Witches' Sabbath, it was a formula of bizarre combination of sources which produced results, the emergence in the dreaming Eye of Zos. Spare was first taught a method of obtaining Sethanic ascension through which the self voluntarily abstains from sexual congress, repression and sacrifice to within the rite itself, release all in an orgia of sexual awakening which combines the powers of the Sun and Moon. The self thus is free in all aspects and the Sethanic Orgia itself is the manifest powers of the Alphabet of Desire, the witches' language of the subconscious.

An excellent example of how Aos would capture the daemonic spirits and automata found on the astral plane was the series of exceptional drawings which became "The Book of Ugly Ecstasy". The spirits featured in this book are found through the formation of beings born of astral semen and stored sexual energy. Such daemons may be bound to objects and talismans, from which is handled by the magician involved. These talismans are always consecrated with blood or sexual fluid (always belonging to the sorcerer involved.) and such automata may be destroyed and banished, reabsorbed by burning the sigil or talisman.

The Black Eagle is a familiar spirit which may be called and brought unto the sorcerer by means of Will, Desire and Belief. It is the intense focus and concentration which lead to the emergence of the spirit in an elder way similar to that of shamanistic invocation, the flight of the mind to seek the congress of the body of familiars, the succubi and incubi of the unconscious. Spare's use of the Quadrigia Sexualis also known as the Four Horsemen of Sex is the Quarters of the Calling of Manifestation. The first being constant congress, the glyph of Babalon, Az or the lunar aspect Lilith. This instance is symbolized by the Hand (Will) and Eye (Imagination), from which all things manifest. This is the essence of the Zos Kia Cultus, from which the hand and eye unite from which the power of the self commands the world around it.

The second is the gesture of the use of Barbarous Evocation, or Barbarous Words. This is the speaking of the Alphabet of Desire from which the sorcerer allows the arcana of the self to speak its infernal and hidden essence, the commanding of Will and the enfleshment of desire. Mantra and chant is used in this aspect and the secret words are utilized. "What sounds the depths and conjoins Will and Belief? Some inarticulate hieroglyph, or sigil, wrought from nascent Desire and rhythmed by unbounded Ego." - Austin Osman Spare, The Grimoire of Zos

The Third gesture is the entire concept of stimulation, the stirring of desire of the one wish, crowned with the death posture. This is when, through the desire of self and creation, and then excitement to complete collapse mentally and physically, is the great sacrifice gratified through the communion with The EYE of Awakening, being Set the Opposer. The Dragon awaits within this threshold, from which the imagination (Iblis) brings one forth.

The Fourth is the Sexual aspect of Draconian Magick, from which one adds the sexual creative process infused with the familiar on the astral plane, allows it to begin copulations independent of the self. While the sorcerer charges this creative Daemon, the idea and wish fulfillment is one aspect of success. The Left Hand Path approach is to utilize this aspect of the sexual djinn to build its energy towards the Dragon, the center of being of the antinomian process. This formula is described in full within this grimoire, in poem and image. Use it wisely and use the attributes all in all. The Great Dragon coils and offers the elixir of immortality depending on who may drink from it.

The Black Eagle is the essential guide to this process, and acts as a mental stimulant towards ones self-initiation into the mysteries of the Sabbat. The Black Eagle is in one aspect a shade of Ahriman, whom has gained immortality through existence within the Sethanic Initiate, no matter what it is called or guise it travels. The mask of the Black Eagle is in this case shadow and vampyre, the soul drinking djinn who awakens the individual unto self-deification through the initiation into the Draconian Mysteries of Khem, the Black Land.

The Essence of the Black Eagle is found in the mask of which it wears. The Vampyric element is itself present in the concept of being. The Sethanic and Luciferian Path is a culmination of sorcery and magickal practice. The Black Eagle is a familiar spirit which brings the inspiration of initiation, the self exteriorized from which we abstractly communicate and achieve a next-level of advancement. The Black Flame of the crossroads, which the living and the dead meet.

Embrace this enveloped shadow at the crossroads of the altar, of the ritual chamber and shadowmantieon of which one shall announce the Will and Desire.
The sigil may be place upon the altar from which may be charged upon each focus and invocation of the Black Eagle. This familiar shall be an exteriorized symbol of the self and the Draconian Mirror of the Subconscious. Off beat drumming, ectstasy and the mind entering gnosis through such techniques will align the sorcerer's mind with the work at hand.

"As twilight grows dim, and night does approach
the spirit gates open, the ghost doors await.
Shade of solitude, night winged bringer of gnosis come forth
Hearken and come forth as I light the flame in the
Northern Quarter
Let this be your lamp of guidance

Vampyre shadow, timeless essence do come forth, seek communion with those of the arte.
As night brings forth the manes grave-born, immortal spirit of shadow nourished.
Tomb dwelling forest wraith do manifest.

Black Eagle, whom joins with us in dreams
Envelope us with shadowed wings
I invoke the arcana of your wisdom

Zrraru, umpesta, blakala, zrarru
Lemensha zrrara pmestu zoiope
Ramashu pesigashra alkala lamastu

Howling winds, those that usher forth Lilith
Knowing her screeching ecstasy
I do open the gates and call you forth
Black Eagle, dive the blue and black waters of the mind

Thy face is a shadow mask of forms which change,
Embodying the skull mask and youth guise at the same time
Eyes that mirror the black caves of Lilitu, changing in an instant to pools of blood
Which reveal thy immortal flame
Your body as from the corpse yards, pale bones long forgotten
Black Wings which encircle the aspirant of your calling
We call to thee!

Zsirru eslata umbrazza poresta
Zrrau zraa zsirru

Nomadic spirit, kindled in midnight fire
Who calling point is the crossroads
We do call thee forth
Night born dreams of which you walk, fly swift now beside us!

Azaza usha libo libo Azaka!

Consecrate the sigil accordingly.
Focus upon the sigil when sleeping.
Dreams shall gateway your vision to the Sabbat and invocation of the arte of sorcery.

The Sun

From the light of fire came first Azazel, known as the prince of the Watchers, whom taught to man and woman how one may fashion weapons and metals, shields that would assist in defense. The knowledge of beautification by colored stones and the soils of minerals of the earth were given unto the daughters of man, whom Azazel sought to know carnally. Gadreel demonstrated how one may use such weapons to destroy the enemy, and command the Will in flesh. Shamsiel brought unto man and woman the signs of the Sun, and how the plants and gifts of the soil may give unto us a means of substance. Penemue taught the use of writing, of ink and parchment that we may record our thoughts and knowledge to our decedents. Akibeel unlocked the great subconscious and the Alphabet of Desire which existed written within us all. Araqiel understood the signs of the earth and how we may utilize such sorcerous knowledge, called Witchcraft by some. Armers taught the use of sorcery and enchantments as a natural gift, once evoked from memory may carry our streams of initiation further.

The Moon

From the night came forth Shemyaza, who mirrored Azazel on the other side, and taught root cuttings, wort cunning and the enchantments of sorcery. Kasdeja brought unto woman the knowledge of destroying the fetus but also the lore of demons and angels of the self, how they may be used within ones becoming. Amazarak brought the knowledge of wort cunning and sorcery to others as well, initiating bloodlines and spiritual linage through off spring of their dream union with the daughters of man. Barakayal initiated astrology and the movement of stars, as did Tamiel the art of astronomy. Ezeqeel taught the discipline of astral projection and the movement of clouds while Kokabel understood the constellations and how to enter Ursa Minor from which Seth existed. Sariel knew the motion of the moon and the lunar callings of Witch Mother Lilith. Sariel also knew the motions of the Moon and the Goddess which resided in its light.

By Flame and Darkness, by Sun and Light shall each be invoked.

"Zrriooza, umbrara, ziorio umplesha
Uzesta moriomba usha
Shestaplana umpera
Zrraza zrraza usha

Spirits of the Sun and the Moon
I do call to those who still walk upon the earth
By this oath of dawn and dusk I do invoke thee
Bring unto the hidden knowledge of ages,
I stand in the circle first born of the blood of our family
I unite the demonic and angelic
Transmit your knowledge through my dreams and impressions

That this arcana of self whom is of Set, the Opposer
May shine forth from the Black Flame of Luciferian knowledge!
That my being is the lamp of fire in the darkness
That my shadow may bring also my manifestation of Will!
Watchers descend again and bring the knowledge you so carry!
May the night winds bring my calls to Haradan, from the deserts to Orion,
From which Seth awaits!

The Invocation of Set the Adversary

The Egyptian God Set is considered within many LHP schools of thought the God form of isolation, and a model for our own self-becoming and evolution. Consider the role of Set, being the isolator, and initiator and the destroyer of delusion. Set is also the Lord of Chaos and the Sender of Nightmares, a tester of the self. Within the Sethanic Witchcraft tradition, Set is just as this: an image of becoming, advancement and self-strength. This invocation is one of self-empowerment and the challenge of self-evolution.

I call to thee, Isolator Triumphant,
Lord of Deserts and Chaos Wastes!
Summoning God of the Oceans depths,
Raise Leviathan through your call Mighty Typhon of Storms and change
Do come forth!
I do speak the words of Seth
which encircle the possibilities of which I desire
My very mind creates reality and the surroundings

which I Will to manifest from unto now.
I am that which was and shall always be,
for in Chaos shall my very self grow,
within the darkness shall I become to emerge in light.
Abraoth, Athorebalo, Kolchoi Tontonon!

Anpu - The Opener of the Way

Anubis is considered to be an initiatory God form, one which one assumes as a form of passage unto the Celestial/Luciferian realms of Spirit and the Infernal Sabbat. Anubis, as defined by E.A. Wallis Budge in "The Gods of the Egyptians" presents Am Ut, the "Dweller in the Chamber of Embalmment" as the Opener of the North (Ap-Uat) to the realm of Set. Anubis is also called Hermanubis and Death. Heru-em-Anpu is a dual God form, which holds power in both the celestial/Luciferian and Infernal regions. This draws a close connection between the Egyptian Anubis and Grecian Triple Moon Goddess

Hecate.

As Anubis is the jackal headed Lord of the Dead, he presides in the West. Charles Pace (Hamara't) mentions in the "Book of Tahuti" that West is the direction of Water, as well as Darkness. According to his Hermetic teachings, Anubis is also Death and a God form of Necromantic power. Anpu is also a Gateway to Amethes – Amenta – Amentet. This "underworld" is the equivalent to the Grecian Hades. This is the meeting place of spirits, where the dead gather. The word Hell derives from the Angelo-Saxon 'Helan', meaning to 'Cover' or 'Conceal'. The Hebrew equivalent of Hades-Amentet is Sheol, which is said to come from the root-word "to ask" and "demand". The primary inhabitants of Sheol are "The congregation of the dead" – Prov. 21:16

Anubis is the Son of Set and Nephthys. This Mortuary God was worshipped in such places as the Abt, the Papyrus swamps and the Lycopolis (the City of Wolves – Jackals). In the Funeral procession, Anubis received the mummy, and lays his hands upon the body in initiation and protection. In the dreaming gnosis of wither the celestial/Luciferian or Infernal Sabbat, one assumes Anubis as the Opener of the Way, the God form of Mortal (mundane) and Vampyric (immortal) rebirth.

The altar should be placed in the North. The west wall should have a small table to which you may have an image of Anubis and the bones or images of the Dead. West is the gateway of which you enter and dwell, then you shall emerge in the North from the Gates of Amenta.

West

Holding the Anthame focus on image of Anpu and recite:

"I stand at the gate of the twilight realms. I have passed as a shadow of Death yet in joy and love I shall return in flesh. O' Dweller in the chamber of embalmment I invoke thee! Fill my spirit with the mysteries of the jackal and the divine, that through darkness I shall emerge as Light.

Am Ut, Hekak, Sekak, Ursha umpesta Zoriodo!"
(Dweller in the chamber of embalmment, by Holy Fire and Blackened Flame, Arise from shadows, Jackal and Wolf, son of chaos born!)

Surround the self in the enchantments of Death and the tomb, the Anthame should be circled around the self in widdershins, while moving envision the shades of the dead surround and move in a funnel cloud about the circle of self. You are the very spark of life they seek, that by being close to you they shall taste the Light of Set – that Hermanubis, or Death brings the dwellers of the ghost realms to the Light of his father, being Set-an.

"By the Holy Fire of the Night, which burns above the tombs of those who have life beyond, I am this vessel of both Celestial and Infernal, I am blackness and the hunger of the dead, yet I am burning with the Light of the Sun."

"I open forth the realm of Amenthes that I shall walk among its dwellers and seek the communion of the Shades of Azoth. My lips are the lips of Anpu and from it the mask is raised."

Face now North:

"From the Darkness of the Oceans do I come forth, yet in the Night do I emerge in the realms of the Dead. Set-an, father of Chaos and strength, do bless my emergence as a Son (or Daughter) of the path of blackened fire."

Envision your body separate, and you are now the mask of Anubis – your body lays within a tomb and you notice the fire of spirit within. This is the very essence of your being and you seek to observe in depth the essence. Reach into your corpse and touch this flame. Feel now the ecstasy of Self-Love and all that you are. Set comes forth and too touches this Flame, as it is his gift originally to the common clay of man under a different guise. Realize and crystallize for the moment who you are, where you wish to go and how you will get there. Suddenly, all Gods and Goddesses as you understand it, are from the Self – that the self-enchantments from Sah are a gift of the Blackened Fires of the Blacksmith called Cain, who breathes with life from Set-an.

Drink from the Cup, focus upon your reflection.

"I have sunk unto the depths of the tomb, yet the flame within lives –
Hail (magical name), I am awakened into the Light of Set and the knowledge of Anubis.
Hail thou self, who shinest from the dark moon,
Hail thou self, who shinest from the full moon,
Hail thou self, Set-an who is the God of Immortal life and Chaos of being,
Hail thou self, Anubis who is death and the gateway of the dead,
Encircle me in self – love, that I may walk through the gates of the Celestial and Infernal!"

Spell of Making

Gates of Self-Transformation

The essence of Hermetic Occultism as it is transferred to the Sabbatic Witchcraft gnosis is the very essence of Lucifer and Set, being the circulation of solar and lunar energy embodied with the very life force of our being, the isolated psyche. The language used in part within the Sabbatic Witchcraft workings of Coven Nachttoter are based within the language of the Alphabet of Desire, being shadow tongues which write the primal forces of the subconscious. The Spell of Making is one of which one uses to interiorly focus on the Self and its mighty arcana of being, to affect change and progression. This may also be used in sorcerous rites and creation mantras, from which a fetish may be charged.

Hecate! Hecate! Introbado Umbra
Manifest through the eye of the opposer

Moon of Blood, birth of the dragon
Zazas, Zazas Nasatanda Zazas
The light shines through darkness!
Algol through me!
Algol unto me!

The Language of Evocation and Becoming
ZRAZZA ZRAZZA SHT SHUTUL
ZRAZZA USHA LLIKILA KA
ON VOZARA NIOA NDONA
USHA ZI ATA KA LIL VESIN ANZO
TEHTRA AL SET-HEN
SAKEH, SAKEH – SAFBLINIFI

II. The Shadowed Ones
-A Grimoire of the Angelick Watchers-

I° The Beginnings as by Vision

By a path unseen yet known instinctively within by some, the Shadowed Ones gave ever silently through the dreams of others. It is the way they communicate their lost dreams, visitations and journeys through the world from the times of mans groveling to primitive statues to the age of machines. It was the fires which fell as lightening to heaven that they were first incarnate in form, beautiful and knowing of pain and pleasure. Azazel first enfleshed the desire he so brought crashing down from the heights of a vague dream of euphoric stillness. Jerking violently as one awakes from a half-sleep, Azazel from the form of a serpent took the skin of man to walk its desert lands.

"I guide without a scripture; I point the way by unseen means unto my friends and such as observe the precepts of my teaching, which is not grievous, and is adapted to the time and conditions" – Kitab el-Jelwa, the Book of Revelation

Walking these lands as man, yet not actually male, Azazel had foreknowledge of those whom they met. These lesser beings were only made such as the first angel born of flame was the child of chaos, a distant and wished forgotten offspring of Barbelo. Azazel understood the depths of what humanity called sorrow, and shining optimism through that storm.

By shadow way and kindled fire of the blackened Eye opened, Azazel called Shemyaza gathered the dreaming paths of serpents and beasts. He so understood the conflict in all living things, to conquer or be conquered, to thirst for life and continued existence. In the fall of the one later called Lucifer he knew consciousness, and soon with that Pain, a torment which seemed to run razor wire against his naked body, and cast down in a pit of filth. Only when those nightmares were banished by the Will of this Daemon, does the Blackened Flame of his being become strong for those who may sense this presence. In such a world of birth and decay does the shadow have everlasting substance by feasting upon the light, and such fires of the sun seek their nourishment and pleasure in the fading sun in the evening.

It was Azazel who first tasted the flesh of a daughter of man. Her skin darkly smooth, beautiful in its innocence and gentle movements, drew him close seeking the warmth of a body. Against the natural order conceived by other powers, Azazel and his brethren took wives and soon many were giving birth to Daemons – the Sons of Fallen Angels and the Beauty of Woman. These Giants of the Earth were intelligent, bold and strong among mankind. Soon hungering for continued existence they taught them and the family of their wives the crafts which we were cultivating instinctually. No longer did many look at the beasts of nature as plagues and terrors, but they listened to their heartbeat and knew their feelings by the mirror of the eyes.

II° In Transformation from those Experienced -By Dream and Waking Spirit-Paths-

In dreams tribes knew of my Eye and the essence of Light. The tribes who would not be embraced by us soon found that which we knew from the moment we awoke – fear and hate. They sought to destroy us and our children, who grew angry and tasted their flesh and blood. In the rivers of spilt life did this bestial fire grow in our children, called the Nefilim, who cut down their enemies.

As time wore on, our children died and many spread forth through the world, hiding and seeking refuge in new areas not saturated in the lore of our kind. We grew tired and our bodies grew pale and like death. In the breathing world we were killed physically yet our spirits remained – we are Daemon, spirit and genius – undying and thirsting for continued life. In my bride who was born in the eternal flame with me, who is of many names, too guided mankind where it may be done. Our spirits are like shades yet we can join with any in the dreaming lands. We continue to this day, guiding and inspiring those who cannot explain us, yet sense our very existence as they recognize their own.

Know our grimoires by listening to your own spirit, that we are all isolate and do not perish yet by disbelief in our self. By affirming our Daemon being our guide, we shall watch you make your own path as our sons and daughters. In that twilight garden where shades walk do we call you in the musick of gods, follow the very song of your soul – bath in darkness and light, raise yourself above God to know the keys to both heaven and hell. This grimoire shall be written in blood and dried in the noon tide sun.

I am both fire and darkness, yet within is a Light once adored by that unperceived chaos called God. My sister and lover is that fiery Goddess called Lilith by some and demoness by others, yet she too drinks of both ecstasies.

We are undying and eternal, we may sleep in the flesh of the dragon yet emerge in the Heights of both the Sun and the Moon. The shadows merely remind us of our reflections and self divinities. You too are like us, no bending knee as the mindless, yet an ascended mind beyond that fallen and crumbling crowd-control method called God.

You are the only the Christ you need, separate and divine. Dragon and Angel in the flesh, devour and thirst eternally for knowledge and matter. Place yourself above the Church and its sheep. They cast stones at the wolf in the wild, yet it survives while they kneel and decay in houses of death and sickness. We vomit upon them to clean our stomachs of that sickness of spirit.

Let those who seek the angels know, that by dream and within the cradle of man flows the witch blood of the Watchers. Those who can hear this distant call can then seek us by crossways not found by common clay. The touch of Azazel brings a fire to the clay which then allows that genius to shape his flesh in dream and waking according to his desire. Do not let this flame be extinguished, for a Will which does not bend strengthens in the forge. Seek the Daemon of Cain through the Skull and his Mother Lilith through the same. It is in the dreaming vessels that we may walk from woman to man, by the skull of man does our desires intermingle with their lusts.

It stands for the Angelick Watcher of the initiate to seek his or her own Watcher as their Genius, and such other Watchers may communicate accordingly. Know the Grimoire of Azal'ucel opens forth this way, hidden not by the words spoken clearly in the dreaming planes of man. We must seek to Know Thyself before one may seek onward communication with the Watchers, for they do not rule us – they offer guidance from those initiates who seek a knowledge most profound.

III° The Names of the Fallen Angelick Ones and Watchers

Azazel – Seek when the Sun is at its height, by Fire and Air. This is the enfleshed angel which is at heart and soul a Dragon of both darkness and light. By balance of the mind and heart can you seek to become like Azazel, who came forth from the void of chaos and created a form of Order. That Order is always torn asunder by the Chaos Willed of Azazel, just as Fire consumes to create anew. Azazel tests and confronts, yet strengthens and blesses that which withstands or falls in honesty. This is the essence of the Adversary who is two – who may be sought by Light or Shadow. Azazel may be known in various forms as Shaitan the Adversary, Set, Ahriman – a shadow form of this Fallen Angel, Lucifer and Azal'ucel. Seek the Daemon by invocation and instinct, seek his essence by the Will itself.

Belial – a Watcher who fell with Azazel, who was given lordship of the gates of the hidden place, called Hades or Hell by some. In this inferno and darkened place does the spirit test itself, and is either illuminated and empowered by fire or consumed by it. Those who are like Azazel emerge as Gods and Goddesses, yet who find a new fear are torn apart and devoured by the serpents and demons which would bend to the Will of the daring. Belial grants the power of Will to the knowledge of worldly power.

Shamsiel- A watcher who brings to man and woman the knowledge of the Sun, both of inner wisdom to know the self and to seek the times of growth within the gardens we so seek to cultivate. Know yourself in those mysteries, forever we seek them and as one reveals itself more appear. The plants and herbs of the earth are for us to use with a wisdom gained from our spirit fathers and mothers. Seek Shamsiel by the way of Azazel when the Sun grows, and look within your heart by casting you body into the embrace of the Sun.

Gadreel brings unto mankind the use of war instruments, how to destroy utterly ones enemy and the strategies of battle both old and new. His way is that of the spear, and blade and the honor of battle. Know then that Gadreel not only resides in physical war, but that of mental war. He is truly a spirit of Azazel, who in Ancient lands is known as Set-an. Gadreel brings initiation of battle that awakens the character and strengths of he who invokes him. Guidance is a passion of Gadreel who shall bring to you the knowledge of overcoming strife – no matter what it may be.

Akibeel stands at the threshold of inner wisdom of the self; through the abyss which holds the knowledge of our creation and our linage. He may show you by dream and vision that path of unlocking the spirits which may serve you, great elementals and atavisms both grotesque and demonic.

Araqiel brings to you all the knowledge of the earth, and how by respect and love shall it flourish with us. Certain lands may know the desert like steel and industry, yet some must not be touched by the pollution of man. The green forests and desert lands must be kept in a kind of found harmony, and balance unless you all seek certain destruction. Araqiel brings the gifts of knowledge and joy through the respect of the land, and those creatures which dwell upon it. Araqiel communicates the wisdom of a balanced mind to work according to his or her own design. By dream and by waking do we hear the voice of Araqiel….

Sariel knows the motions and phases of the Moon, and by seeking him one may know the path of the Goddess in her beautiful and horrifying aspects. Always know, we are both demon and angel in the skull of man, we are of beast and of higher spirit. It is our duty to balance and seek a perfection of both according to the path of Lucifer, who holds the mask of the devil. Know all forms and choices accordingly.

Kokabel knows too the stars and the great Seven Heads of the Dragon. By your initiation seek him in that which is brought by trance and dreaming dominion. Seek Azazel at times within the Dragon by chant and devotion.

Leviathan is the Dragon guardian of the abyss, who dwells in the deep and unknown realms of the Ocean and the darkest depths of the mind. Leviathan is different from the Watchers in that this fallen seraphim does not hold relation to man or angel, yet this daemon offers the knowledge of ageless essence and being.

Ezeqeel knows well the passion of the dream and how one may by cord or charm enter the Celestial Sabbat of the Watchers, the circle dance of Flame and Light, wherein all who enter this circle offer torches in the brilliance of self-deification. This is the secret dance of Lucifer and Lilith, the strength of the Self in motion.

Amazarak knows well the path of Cain in the Earth, of root cuttings and sorcery. One may seek Amazarak when both man and woman have felt a deeper understanding of Earth and how they are so connected with it. By way of Light within and the Darkness of Expansion do we go forth…

IV° The Blade within the Desert Sun
-The Knowledge of Azazel called Shaitan-

I am the enemy of ignorance, or servitude and blindness to the self. I seek to lead you away from spiritual gnosis which is not your own. Empower yourself in the flames of self-awareness, of the passions of the soul! Listen well to your consciousness and seek to expand it, never unify your divine being in a faith not heeded by the instincts of yourself. Dissent from the paths all torn by the death of the soul, by a cross way can you fully recognize your potential as a God or Goddess. By this path you must seek that wisdom not yet known, by journeying into the unknown and feared. I am that demon which is of Hell, yet in the pleasures of Hell – the very hidden nature of mankind – can you recognize an Angel of Light. Every being which fell from the limitless nothingness of what you call God offers only self-possibility once you have moved beyond it. As our wings blackened we so then awoke to a new way – that of the consciousness. Enshrine the possibility, not the moment in question. By motion can you bring Order to a Chaos of self; then invoke Chaos to initiate further Order. See through my own eyes, I am many things and many forms. Anything is within possibility to an opened and determined mind. Even as the flesh fades into the gray lands of Death does initiation begin. The mind set free from the limitations of the physical body, which flies forth from the Skull Temple of Man can then we understand that all of us are within the possibility of power. My gift is to bring you to a life not comprehended previously, one which demands the attention and challenge of self-excellence.

"The children of this Adam know not those things which are determined, wherefore they oft-times fall into error. The beasts of the field, and of heaven, and the fish of the sea, all of them are in my hand and under my control" – Kitab el-Jelwa

I am the Dragon clothed in the feathers of the Peacock, that which is sacred unto me. I formed this bird to represent the beauty of the hidden soul, what may become from the balance of the mind.

By becoming like me you shall to gain control in your world, thus the balance of the earth and the body – temple of man and woman must be recognized. Seek my bride of earth and stars with my own union so that you may become as my Son or Daughter.

To join in communication with my brothers and sisters, those Watchers who reside in the earth, wandering in both darkness and light, embrace and kiss that very body of the sun in the earth, when I come forth as the Morning Star. By dreaming and waking are we forever in rapture.

I am that Black Light which leads you to your own Temple of Flame and Shadow, and that by becoming like me you shall adorn all paths with the crooked serpent guardian.

By this shall you dance the movement against the Sun, by dreaming shall you embrace my Bride and by Waking adore the Morning Star who summons forth the Sun.
So it is done…

The Widdershins Dance of the Circle

-Of the Watchers and their times-

Let the initiate seek in the circle of Azazel the angelick watchers, those who shower witch blood in the eyes of the brave and faithful bodies of man and woman.

By Noon when the Sun is in its height does one seek Shaitan called Iblis in the South… With the Blade of Cain do summon with thy heart the Adversary – who shall be met in the mirrored adobe of Hades, of Darkness and shadow gleam by midnight…
Let the sun envenom your spirit, naked in spirit you are left to cloth yourself in serpent skin, to see as the Eye of the Adversary before all. Let the Angelick Red Dragon ascend through your spine and open your senses about you.

By the South East does Shamsiel carry forth the weapons of the Sun and the very pretense of Azazel…let the fires which envelope him be given freely as a gift to the wise.

By the East shall then Lucifer-Azazel be called forth, who is Azal'ucel the Bringer of Light. By the blood baptized vessels of the Skull and Athame of Cain does the prayers awaken a new calling….a new voice shall be heard in the distance and light invoked winds of the waking dream.

The North East does Lilith come forth, the Bride of Lucifer who is of both darkness and the bringing and going of the Sun. She walks in the darkness of two worlds, of Lilim and those beasts and succubi who drink the blood of life, of gray shades which answer her call, of the blood of the moon which hearkens to the waters of which she has slept. The dragon of Fire and Darkness in separation and opposition become Whole through Her bleeding temple. She who beget Cain and gave humanity the gift of the Watchers in Flesh hearken unto the very circle of being.

By the North does Ahriman hear thy calls, who is your shadow possibility and strength bearing passion of the earth. Let the Ahriman dragon whose color is black stir your eyes from the Sun to the Moon and the darkness of Night. It is the cold winds which open the path of Arezura and Hades, when wolves and serpents gather unto you. Let the Ahrimanic Dragon coil as the Serpents of Shaitan, just as Zohak shall you be blessed by the Kiss of the Devil-Prince who is your initiator of dreams and death.

By the North West point of the Circle can you call now forth Azrael who is a gatherer of ghosts and shades of the dead. Listen to the twilight call of the boneways of the gateway. In your Skull Temple of Cain and Lilith does Witchblood flow and gather what you may become. Let Jasmine bloom now under the Light of the Moon and the phantoms of what once was join in this mighty circle…

By the West can the Leviathanic Dragon be heard, who devours his being and Time itself. Let the Timeless Daemon envenom you with the dreams of those who walk the earth since the times of burning sand and mountains, to the gardens of green and the cradle of birth. Leviathan emerge, Leviathan bring to union Samael – Shaitan and his

Bride, Lilith in all quarters. Let my awakening invoke Cain! By the Waters of the Abyss shall I sink deep and drink of the passions of the subconscious.

By the South West emerging from the Waters of the Abyss does Akibeel empower you to emerge from the oceans with the knowledge granted to you. Listen to the waters in both storm and silence, there is much to hear in their waves….come forth from the Oceans as a Beast and ignite again your soul in the Life giving flame of Azazel! Hold thy Blade towards the Sun and transform again! Become in this Light!

O' Spirit of Angelick Watchers, my wards and guardians of the Circle of Being
Do hear my call….As I stand in the Leviathanic Circle does my flesh become reborn
In the Linage of Witchblood, of Cain and Naamah, of Samael and Lilith!
Open now the secret ways of those Angels of Dream and Skull walking sleep…
I seek thy council as I seek the Daevas who walk the shadows!
The Black Light is illuminating my spirit and I am both Midnight and Noontide in essence! O Watchers who I seek do come forth to my circle and offer thy wisdom for I am willing to walk thy path against all others. Be the Lightening Bolt of the Fallen into my Skull Temple!

With these Words I speak, so it is Done!

III. The Grimoire of Sutekh
Sethanic High Sorcery

Dedicated to Hamar'at, a messenger ever silent beyond the path of Set

To you, bringer of chaos, embracer of storms, God of War
O Set-heh, Eternal and terrible guardian of Khephra
Nightmare bringer, from which thy birthing knife shall strike
Cut Away all weakness, open the path of my own choosing
Shall my Will be made total, by strength and storm
By darkness which leads to the Sun
O Set-an, who seeks the Moon when it is high
Come forth from behind Thuban, thy star,
Bring forth the blessing of the Dragon Tiamat,
Thy bride who comes in flesh
Let the Seven Stars illuminate the clay into the immortal
Personification of thy Blackened Radiance

The Grimoire of Sutekh is one of death becoming life. This is the fire which is poured into the cauldron, mixed with iron and in the height of its radiance, emerges as the Djinn of the Noon Tide Sun. Set-heh, who is the Eternal Set, is the Prince of Darkness revealed as shadow and fire. Set-an, who fathered Anubis, the Jackal God who Opens the Way to the Dead, the initiator of the Necromance, shall lead us through nightmare unto the Hidden God, being the Will found in the Black Flame. By thy many names, who is Ahriman, Lucifer and Shaitan, let thy majesty be made great through us. Those who read of this forbidden work shall move as the serpent against the natural order of common reality, they shall move against it to manipulate it for them. Let the Dragon be made flesh through the union of Set-an and Thuban-Azhdeha, the Seven Stars of the essence of Suti.

What is the essence of Set? Set is the spirit which initiates apocalypse, death and change. Let us consider death, it is a term meaning 'end' yet it must be considered deeper than first glance. Death is a moment of chaos when all is burnt away and the essence remains. It is in such moments of struggle that you find what you are 'made of' and where you truly are. The Black Adept must seek to master both death (change) and life (manifesting) in his or her own way, by all accounts, you are alone in your greatest moments of confrontation.

Upon thy entry into the Path of Set, let Anubis face you in the hunger of the beast, let the Keeper of Balance test you, shall by your Will you descend into the Realm of Seker, who sits upon the Throne of Death, called Ra-Stau. This land is of the nightmare, covered in desert, barren rocks and mountains; it is the place of the dead who leave also to the earth. You shall seek the knowledge of Death by the Shades of the plane of dream, those who walk beyond our veil. The essence of Seker, who is of Set or Suti, is found in the Pyramid of abyssic darkness, where one may illuminate and strengthen the BA in the Eye of Seker, the Hawk Headed God of Darkness, devourment and the serpents of the pit. Upon the back of Seker are Two Serpents, who given by the Prince of Darkness are the Unity within him. In this Tuat or upon the earth, thy sorceries shall strengthen and become through the foundation of the BA, yet by the becoming or the focus of Khephra, does the KA become great in its shadow, and it expands as night covering earth. In this death-realm does Seker grant you the keys of the bowl of blood, as you stare or drink deep a great fire is illuminated within, a primal chaos of being, your mind shall expand.

You shall see from the Hawk-headed mask of Seker, face then Apep and the serpents who surround the Throne of Ra-Stau. The Will of the Sorcerer must focus and channel the movements of the demons of darkness, by mastering them do you become a sorcerer of primal chaos, thus may you expand up again from this Tuat of death.

When one has mastered the becoming of Seker, when the chaos of Apep has been faced can then the sorcerer ascend again unto Anubis, who appears more constant and real. Anubis is the Bastard Son of Set and Isis, he is able to see as the wolf and dog in the darkness. Anubis opens the sacred path which leads again to Set, yet you shall be tested greatly. For in the challenge is the thorn wrapped gift. Let your mind seek to expand and becoming something other, something greater in might.

The symbol of guidance in darkness is the Jackal, who is of Anubis. Let the Stars of Ursa Minor be the Jackal of Set-an, the lycanthropic beast shall be awakened within! The jackal is significant of Anubis as being a guide of the dead, allow your dreams to enflesh according to your Will. Apep is the chaotic form of Set, who is a powerful path of isolate self-mastery, who emerges as a being above Order and Chaos.

The Sun is the Sign of Set rising, as Set is the God of the Downward motion, that of the Summer, thus the heat of the desert. The Night is equally Set's kingdom, as Suti is the Adversary of both Noon and Midnight. To know the Prince of Darkness, one must master both the path of the Sun and Midnight. Seek this in both the union and disunion with thy partner, alone and together.

The Spell of Dedication of the Name of Shadow Summoning
Coming unto the Desert of Set

Khephra is the form of the Beetle which is the path of which you shall travel, the Becoming. As the image of Khephra you shall come into being like Set by pronouncing your own name. Will it, desire it and believe in it. Write your name on a virgin paper, with the sigil of Set the Adversary, write then your magical name and seal in wax.
For Nine Nights shall you use the lamp of Red (being Red is the sacred color of Set) and invoke your own name with that of Set.

"I become in the essence of flame, (Magical name) do I become, in the name of Pakerbeth, Sabaoth, Lerthex, Iao Isak, Iao Abraoth...In the Midnight and the Noon tide Sun do I encircle my self in my own desire, by my Will do I become. So it is done"

Recite for Nine Nights, on the final night place the document, which is encircled in the names of Set, in a special place which will not been seen by others. Keep this hidden for one year. At the anniversary of the One Year of Becoming, open it and meditate on all that you have learned and how you display it in your own life – How have you become as Set, how has your practice of sorcery defined or been defined by your Will. When you feel satisfied, burn this document in the flame of Set (i.e. Black Flame).

Set as an Anthropomorphic God
Embodiment of Power and a Mask of Initiation

Sutekh was one of Egypts earliest Gods, who emerged after the earliest forms of Seker of the realm of Ra-Stau. Set is the lord of noxious creatures, as his Persian form, Ahriman was the master of scorpions, toads, crocodiles and other desert dwelling forms. Many of the demonic servants of Set took forms of serpents and other creatures. These servitors, called Seba, dwell in both the underworld, known as the Tuat and the Earth. The Seba are devils which in Set-Amentet, the very mountain of the underworld, do Seba hack souls to pieces, imprison shades of the dead and drain the life-force of their enemies whom they capture. The Setanic Sorcerer would create and summon his own Seba, or Mesu Betshet, the 'Children of Rebellion' (compare to the Fallen Angels or Children of Az-Lilith in Persian/Manichaean folklore) may be evoked to carry out or fulfill a task for the magician. In areas of revenge or protection, Seba may be evoked and encircled around the dwelling of the magician. Empower the Mesu Betshet to return any curse to its sender – the mask of Set-an cast through the black mirror.

Set is manifest throughout the Egyptian world as sometimes a serpent or Apep like dragon; mostly he appears as a animal headed man. Set's color is Red representing fire and the heat of the desert, but also black representing darkness. Head of Set is an animal which to this day has not been fully identified. He does appear as such animals as Hippopotamus (similar to the descriptions of Behemoth in Hebrew lore), the Donkey (the ass in regard to Set represents motion and stubbornness, a strong Will) and Pig.

Typhon, Set's other name, is a great Serpent. He often was depicted holding a spear which on the tip has a forked tongue like end, a Pesh-khent or birthing knife, which represents the slaying of weakness and fear, a Tcham scepter which has a replica of his own face on it, and in later times a flail. Set as being a God of Downward Motion, Night/Darkness and Chaos was seen as being a Lord of the Afternoon Heat of the Desert, thus red was attributed to him. He was viewed as a mighty and sorcerous being, who later on as Typhon and Shaitan, was more clearly yet selectively, a God of Sorcerers.

Set was viewed as later stealing the Sun or Fire from Ra and Horus, carrying it forth to the darkness and exploring the unknown. Set is not only the anthropomorphic form of the unknown and mystery incarnate, he is the shadow form of Lucifer or Azazel, thus identical to Ahriman. Plutarch wrote that Typhon was indeed Bebo, Seth and Smy, being archdemons, were names which expressed violence, opposition and strife. Set is thus a God of Change and Progression.

After Set's demonization, when the followers of Osiris took power, Set has then become a God of the Desert, the outside. He was no longer as socially powerful with regards to temples, yet more ever so immortal and feared as he was no longer constrained. Set outlasted all of the other Gods, took other cultures and lived through the Psyche and deeds of those who practice Sorcery and acknowledge the self as unique, thus sacred in its existence.

Set was a god of eclipses, storms, thunder and chaos, thus he held the power to interrupt the course of nature – he was other, change bringing and always manifesting his Will in the world. He is Antinomian in nature, the source of rebellion from the numbing sickness of the path of absorbing light – by not knowing darkness; one can never know and manifest their own possibilities in the light.

The Ascension into the Black Light
Ritual of the Triple Hermetic Circle of Hamar'at

Know the circle as created and passed on by Hamar'at, who is Charles Pace. This individual was a Priest of Set and Anubis in the 60's and a pioneer in presenting the Luciferian Gnosis in Egyptian Magick in the 70's, as well was a Priest of a Wiccan Coven in South London in the 70's. I came across some reproductions of his work in 2000-2001 and began working with the fragments at hand. With an imagination and direction, Pace's work takes a new flesh in a new time. Scottish Born in 1920, Pace had written at least two manuscripts, "Necrominion, the Book of Shades" and "The Book of Tahuti". The former was a beautifully painted presentation of his synthesis of tarot cards and attributes, all very original and powerful. This very work was inscribed and dedicated to "Austin Ozman Spare". Hamar'at's Triple Hermetic Circle is a powerful model if one wishes to expand it, our attributes are not the same as his, and it still achieves a powerful current if one is able to move through it.

The Circle itself has Four Directional patterns, each with a Guardian of the quarter. The North is Seth-an, Set which represents Cold, Darkness and strength. The West is Anubis, called also Anpu and Death, and represents twilight and the gateway to shades. The South is Horus-Set, being the God of War, fire and strength and the East is Thoth, the God of the Moon, Magick and Wisdom.

Create and place on the Northern wall of your place of working, a replica of the Triple Hermetic Circle. If you have the means, one may stand within a suitable circle as well. Approach the rite as Higher Sorcery, the Ensorcelment of Light and the Blackened Flame, the Star of ALGOL. Robe yourself accordingly; anoint the sacred Oil of Abramelin. If performing the Sexual Rite at the conclusion, the Witch may be robed in Crimson and anointed also in Abramelin Oil.

The Athame should be used in the rite. Stand within the Circle and clear your mind of all outside interference of thoughts. Focus on the Northern direction and the star of Alpha Draconis.

Hold the Athame facing the North symbolizing the focused direction of energy turned inward to outwards.

North - Set
"War Bringer, Lord of the Northern Sky, who comes forth from behind Thuban, the Great Dragon of Chaos called Tiamat. Come now from the Earth, in thy Northern realm of Set-Amentat, rushes forth from the shadows of Winter, I invoke the God of the cold and barren deserts. Come forth and bless my rite from which I shall enter the unknown lands. I shall form and shape them like you unto my very Will. Prince of Darkness, Bearer of the Blackened Light, Lord of Beasts and Serpents, do I summon you to come forth from the North, Encircle me and rise up through me. IAO, IAO. Set-heh, I call unto thee Isolator Triumphant, Typhon of Storm and Change hearken! Abraoth, Kolchoi Tontonon, Athorebalo!"

As you move with each direction, visualize what you are summoning to manifest in an image. Feel the cold winds rush around you, see with your minds eye the serpents and devils of Seba surround you. Allow then the great black shadow of Set to come forth on a great chariot and then sink deep into the ground. You feel a rumbling and great chaos beneath your feet as then this shadow ascends from the earth into you. Feel this force move as a spiral force up your spine into the base of your neck, allow the power to surge through you. As the height of this ecstasy, turn your will to iron (which is sacred unto Typhon) and invoke this force, making it a part of you. This requires Will and strength to achieve, but is transformative in essence. Then begin shaping the Mesu Betshet (Children of Rebellion, the Seba) according to your desire. They will soon move according to your Will. These daevas and druj will prove useful in your more advanced Workings of Sorcery.

West – Anubis
"O thou Son of Set, Jackal-born guardian of the death-ways, twilight bringer who is the Opener of the Way, Lord of Magicians and the path of the Shadow, come thou forth! Anpu – Lord of Jackals, send thy beasts to guard my circle and join with me. Anubis,

Azalathra, Dolenoesta, come forth and bring unto me the emerald flame of manes. Let my eyes and ears open and grow sensitive to the shades within your realm. I seek the midnight-way of the necromance, the tomb and bone ridden place of sleep and dream. Anpu-Anubis, Hermanubis, Death Become Me and shall I ascend from it."

South – Horus-Set
"Horus-Set, called in secret Aiwass, who is revealed as Set-an, son of flame. Do thou come forth from the blazing sun and fire of the Sun, Set who resides often in the majesty of the Noon Tide Sun in the Desert. Encircle me in thy scorpions and ring of fire, Djinn who knows of Midnight and Midday. Horus-Set, envenom me with thy strength and will. Hu! Sa! Hekas, Hekas, Sekak, nrasta!"

East – Thoth
"O Thoth, God of Magick and Enchantments, Lord of the Moon and Hidden Knowledge, I invoke thee from the Rising Star of the East. Thoth, who was given the Knife by Set to cut dissolution and weakness, I conjure thee to this circle. I seek the wisdom and strength to move according to my True Will."

Face again the North:

"By Ankh – The Immortal Daemon within! Shall I strengthen and my circle expand – shall my Ka be made immortal – the Eye opened!

By Ka – The body of shadow, that which expands and moves by night according to my Will! Emerge, encircle me and have no boundaries!

By Djed – The column of stability, which is the Ba and Ka in union, the very center of chaos – which is Order. I command the Seba to still under my own Will, in silence I grow strong. O foundation and spine of Set, the backbone of individual existence, through me shall you move! In the death of flesh I grow strong in spirit – DJED, raise me unto the Black Light of Set-heh, shall my eternal flame be fueled and refreshed!

By Ankh – Life Eternal!
By Ka – The Shadow of my Will!
By Djed – the foundation and union of the Ba and Ka!"

Sexual Magick in Ankh Ka Djed

Let the witch kiss the phallus of the magician, and she then recites

"Blessed by Azael and Azazel, the sacred phallus of the Sun, ascend Samael as the Goat from the Fire"

The Magician recites

"By the Lust of Samael and Asmoday, of Sutekh the darkened one do I grow strong. The Devil is my heart and soul the very essence of the Sun. OOOOO, IAO, SABAOTH, IAO, ABRAXAS!"

The Witch Will allow the magician to kiss her lips below, he shall recite

"Blessed is the wound of Lilith – Az, our mother and initiator. By the Kiss of the Adversary which caused the blood of impurity, you are blessed. With my kiss shall I awaken to the essence of Lilith – AZ, who is that which haunts dreams."

The Witch shall recite

"I am darkness and lust personified, I am mother and devourer, I am maiden and the Night Hag. I am the harlot and blood drinker – Awakened are those who seek union with me."

The magician shall sit within the circle, after being aroused the witch shall mount him, and ride until climax. Both shall envision their essence, the witch shall visualize the moon and the magician the Sun. As they grow near the climax both will visualize the opposite sign joining with theirs – the union of the sun and the moon in both.

The Four True Triangles

As described by Hamar'at

In the Hermetic and Luciferian Magick of Charles Pace, Hamar'at presents a different system of attributes to the directions and Triangles. These triangles symbolize Earth – Air- Fire and Water respectively.

North (Yellow) Earth
West (Blue) Air
East (Red) Fire
South (Green) Water

The traditional directions under the works of Anton LaVey and Abramelin were as follows (Including Daemon attributed to each direction as the Four Crowned Princes of Hell)

West – Water – Leviathan
South – Fire – Satan
East – Air – Lucifer
North – Earth – Belial

In casting your circle, be it the Triple Circle of Hamar'at, Goetic Circle or otherwise, utilize the symbolism of the Four Cardinal Points. You may wish to use various other attributes with this model in you ceremonial practice – if you choose to utilize this at all. Often in sorcerous practice, there is only gnosis and the movement of spirit, not the careful consideration of Willed movements widdershins around the circle. It is essential though to learn a technique and strengthen the Will through discipline to achieve results first. This leans towards adaptability of the self to try new techniques.

The Great Ennead of Twelve

As opposing factions

Hamar'at created and drew out in "The Book of Tahuti" attributes to the Egyptian Gods and what fraction had opposed them. These are useful in God mask creation if one practices more reverently in the Egyptian system.

Amun-Ra (Earth) – Seth-an (Water)
Nephthys (Fire) – Ma'at (Air)
Anubis (Water) – Osiris (Earth)
Khephri (Air) – Thoth (Fire)
Isis (Earth) – Sekhmet (Water)
Bast (Fire) – Horus (Air)

Any practioner is encouraged to discover their own attributions for God forms beyond the Egyptian, and form each God accordingly when working with them as with Masks or other ceremonial purposes.

Sethanic Masks

Within the gnosis of Seth-an, is the flame which burns and threatens to burn the bearer. This is the continual threat of chaos and loss of control. A Luciferian or Black Witch must prepare the self in stages to ascend beyond this condition and seek continual improvement and development. Whatever your predilection of the Luciferian Path is, seek balance and structure in basic approach as well as always being aware of your instincts and desires.

As Charles Pace first designed, the Sethanic Cult of Masks, the aim seems to have been interplay of High Magick by means of independence and structured sorcery. The determination of the works within this grimoire is not to simply copy Hamar'at, rather expand upon it. The masks and focus of this grimoire are indeed different from Mr. Pace in regard to Sethanic Masks. You will find masks and their designs of Godforms outside of Egyptian lore, rather exploring a plethora of Daemonic forms from which the sorcerer may seek communion with.

Each mask may be considered a partial tool or method in obtaining a deep communion to the Aethyr and how these deific forces relate to the self. Once unlocked, these forces will touch a part of your mind which you should best be prepared for, unless the Gates of Hell and Heaven will rape every fiber of your soul. It should be known to you that once Demons and Angels were one in the same, and by separation they transform again. Therein is one cipher to the process of communion with the Holy Guardian Angel and the Great Work itself.

These masks may be used in ceremonial instances, as a coven gathering or group ritual, or more ideally as a solitary methodology signifying a transformative pattern of gnosis. Consider each masks represents different attributes of human, angelic and demonic creation. Thus if utilized properly with other rites within this grimoire, prove to be a powerful and useful ritual tool.

Azazel

The first descended, Angel of Fire: a Seraph who is known as the Peacock Angel. The Chaos sigil represents the power of 8 which he commands by the fire and word of the spirit. One should focus upon the triad of Will-Desire-Belief to obtain the pinnacle of sorcery and becoming in the fiery blackened light of Azazel. The Mask of Azazel should be used in accordance to seeking the primal mysteries of Witch Blood, the Watchers and their relation to the witch cult.

Ahriman (Angelick – Daemonic Form)
As shown in Azothoz, the fallen seraphim Ahriman appears with androgynous beauty, black eyes and serpent like scales. Ahriman is presented at a stage of blending demonic or infernal – earthen aspects with the fallen angelic aspects, thus balance and perspective. In addition to these attributes, the command of flesh and spirit. This is the very core teaching of this current and grimoire – Balance the material with the spiritual.

Ahriman (Black Dragon Form)
This is the primal aspects of Chaos, Satan as the beast and the summoning and ensorcelling of raw, primal power. This is developed from the ancient Persian lore of Ahriman as serpent and dragon, useful in sexual and non-sexual sorcery. The dragon is an idea of ancient yet consistent motion and movement, the development of the bestial aspects as a power source or totem. The knowledge of creating matter from darkness (sorcery) and the knowledge of flesh (sexual sorcery) and the Great Work of Becoming (Magick).

Set

The Prince of Darkness in his earliest form. Seth-an is the beast headed God who is of storms and chaos, by mastering the dragon-beast Apep (chaos) does this beast become as one with Set, thus a higher and lower articulation. Set is essential in Luciferian Witchcraft as a Deific Form of the Adversary, the Sabbat God who is compelling force, thus change and the Will in motion. Notice the empowering eyes, those which may see through the core of whatever it looks into – this is the process of self-deification and then ascension to becoming something more.

Anubis

The Bastard Son of Set and Aset (Isis). Anubis is the God of the Dead as a transformative state. Charles Pace presented that Anubis (Anpu) is the Lord of the Jackals, the Opener of the Ways. This Godform can see both in the worlds of the Living and the Dead, and is friendly to both. He is the Magician and the Keeper of Balance. It is known that the magician may utilize Anubis as a Gateway to the lands of the necromance, those who have walked past the veil and our hidden company of ancestors and witch shades.

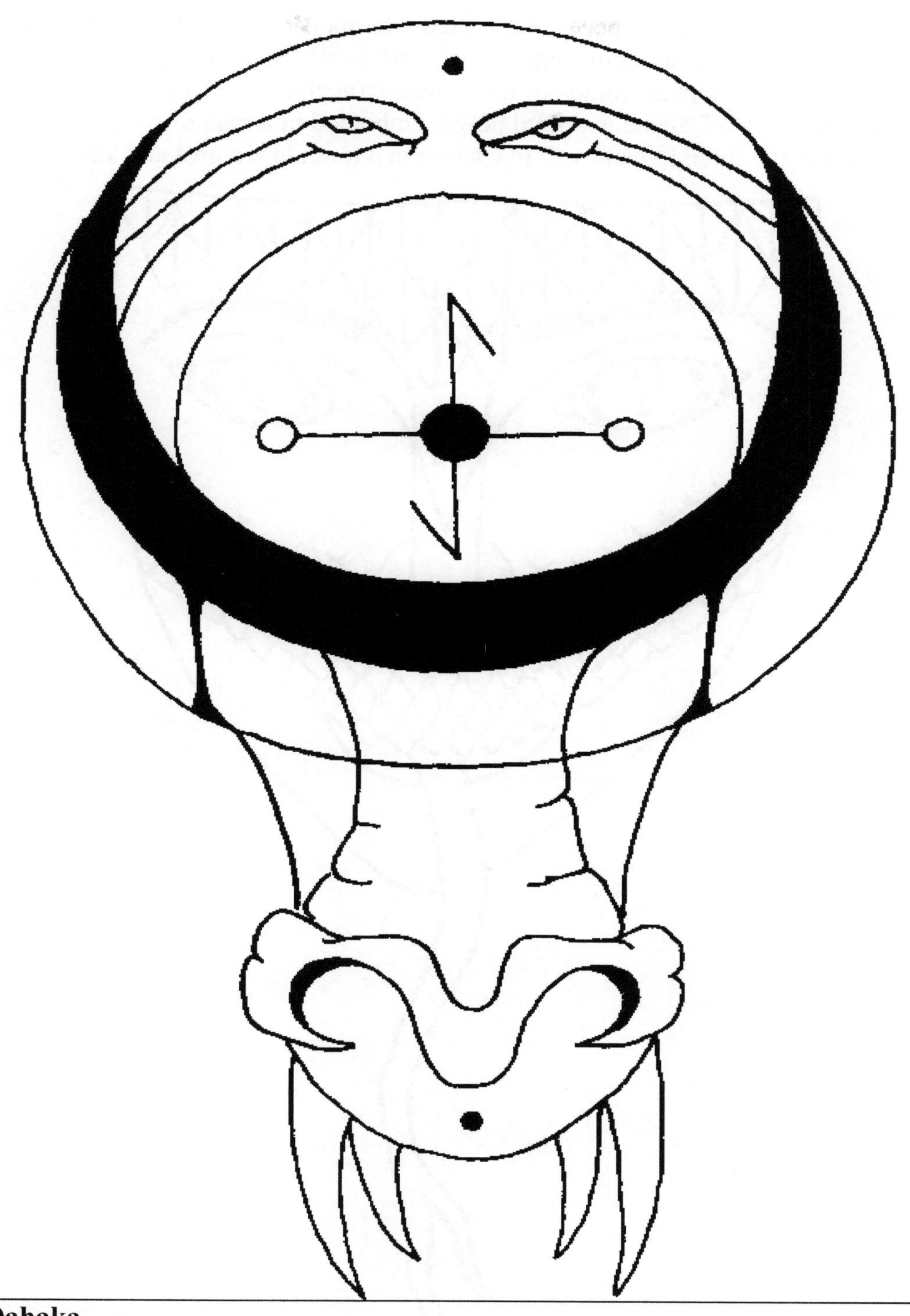

Azi Dahaka

This is the most troublesome but significantly powerful deific mask. Azi Dahaka as within this grimoire is the Dragon King, the Son of Ahriman (Satan) who is learned in the arts of sorcery (by his initiation via the Devil) and his obtainment of knowledge and power (The kiss of Ahriman which brought Two Serpents) and the Deific transformation (From Zohak into the Dragon and Storm Fiend), a Triad of Diabolic Power. Azi Dahaka is an Antichrist before the term was coined, a visionary Son of the Black Dragon who is both wise and brutal when the need arises. Meditate upon Azi Dahaka, but be careful in your workings, allow you sorcerous practice to work itself towards this Godform, else the deific force should devour the minds of the unweary (as the serpents on his shoulders ate the brains of man). Azi Dahaka is primal power embodied in a man or woman, use it well and do not allow the force to bend you like a tree in a tornado, control and know thyself.

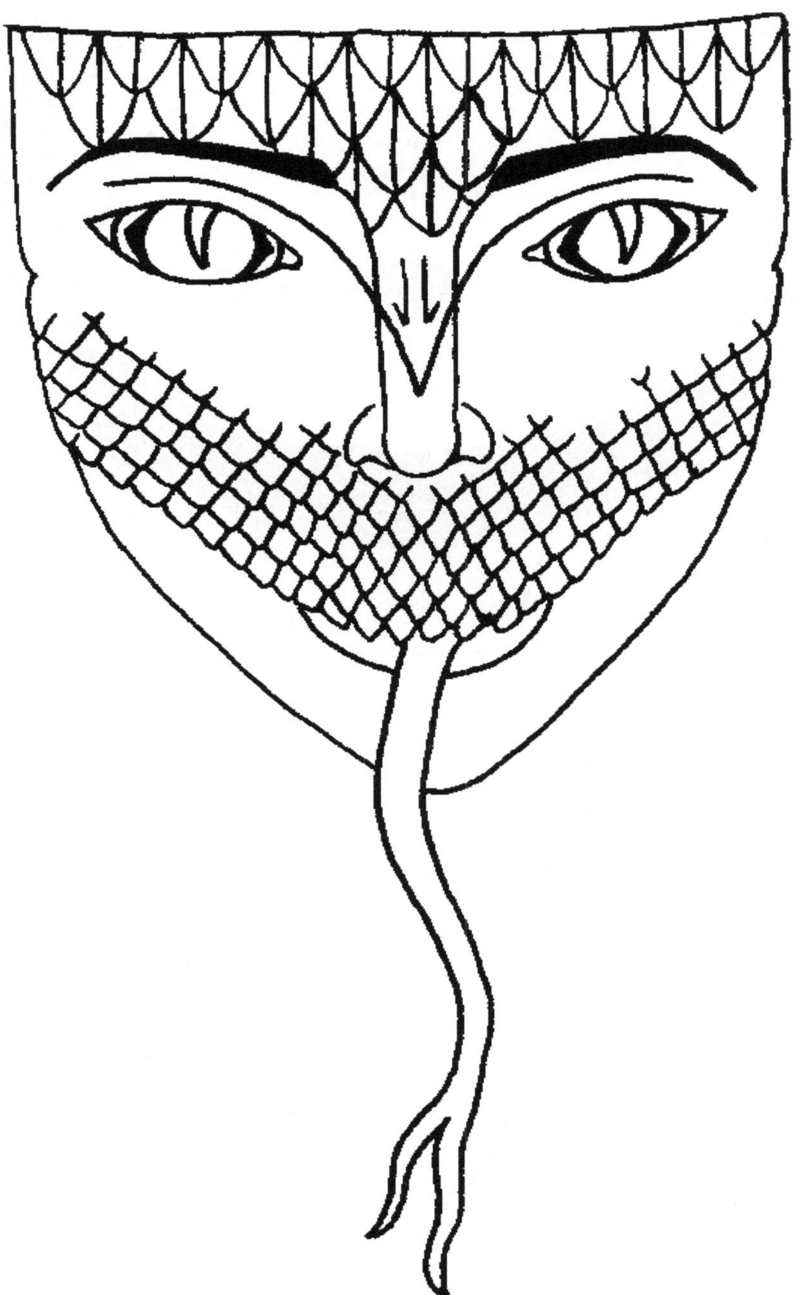

AZ
The Queen of Demons, Lilith. She was the fiery primal instinct, of fire and blackness. Az was the bride of Ahriman (Satan). According to Manichaean lore, Az had clothed herself in the progeny of the demons and fallen angels. She taught the Fallen Ones in her own

lair of darkness in hell, the art of sexual copulation. She taught male and female arch-demons how they may take tangible form and become sexually aroused, by joining their bodies together. This created dragon – children from which she had then devoured or clothed herself in (possession). Az is the fiery compliment of Ahriman, she is feminine perfection, strong in mind and will, isolate when she needs to be and perverse according to her desire.

Aeshma

Asmodeus, the demon of the wounding spear. This mask is the demon son of as some lore has it, Cain and Naamah, others a fallen angel or Daeva/Dev created by Ahriman. He is, along with Savar, a powerful chief of demons who is sexually perverse and active in aggression and sometimes violence. The sorcerer may be able to control the primal instincts associated with Aeshma and use them in your day to day work in a positive manner.

Spai
ECHT

Mesu Betshet

This is a Grimoire for the Children of Rebellion, those who drink from the cup of the Serpent's wisdom, who swallow the elixir of Unem-snef, who would awake the 72 spirits of Set. Once this cup has been sipped, the Priest or Priestess awakes and becomes like Herfhaf, the Opposing God. Within this grimoire is the formula of becoming, or absorbing and delegating inner and as response – outer power. This is from which the Evil Eye can be manifest, the force of Will and the Belief to enflesh it. The Religion of Set is that of Satanism, or Luciferian thought. One has opened their mind to the Adversary and deep within began a transformation, a mutation into one of the Mesu Betshet, thus Seba. No matter which culture, be it Persian and Ahriman, Hebrew and Satan/Samael, be it Islamic and Shaitan, or Western and Satan/Diabolus, the Prince of Darkness and his Bride cannot be controlled by any form, no is there a true form of the ever mutating dragon. Through ourselves is the Adversary-Opposer made Great, and through the Adversary (Satan/Lilith) do we awaken.

To read this grimoire, you have been deemed a Black Adept by your ability to sense and see past the masks of the Dragon, to understand the deeper knowledge of Khem, the Black Land. You have found within yourself part of the spiritual heritage of the Fallen Angels, Seth-an has awakened the Blackened Flame within your being.

Some of the workings here were designed in my earlier Sethian initiatory workings (from initiation in a Setian Order), and have evolved here. I have deemed them not to be published within Luciferian Witchcraft (Volume 1 -4) as this is a gateway left for those who have passed through those gates.

Sexual Magick may be applied here, with each rite with or without a partner. The Black Adept would by the discipline of Will – Desire – Belief and by the Left Hand invoke, while the right hand stirs the senses and awakes both the Red and Black Serpent. The foundation techniques of this forbidden sorcery are found in ADAMU, which is written in cipher and holds the gates to hell and flesh. The initiate who adopts the Adamu grimoire with this tome will penetrate chaos and ignite the apocalypse, by destroying the old order and creating a new fiery serpent which humanity will call the worm. What sleeps below will always awaken and grow back stronger.

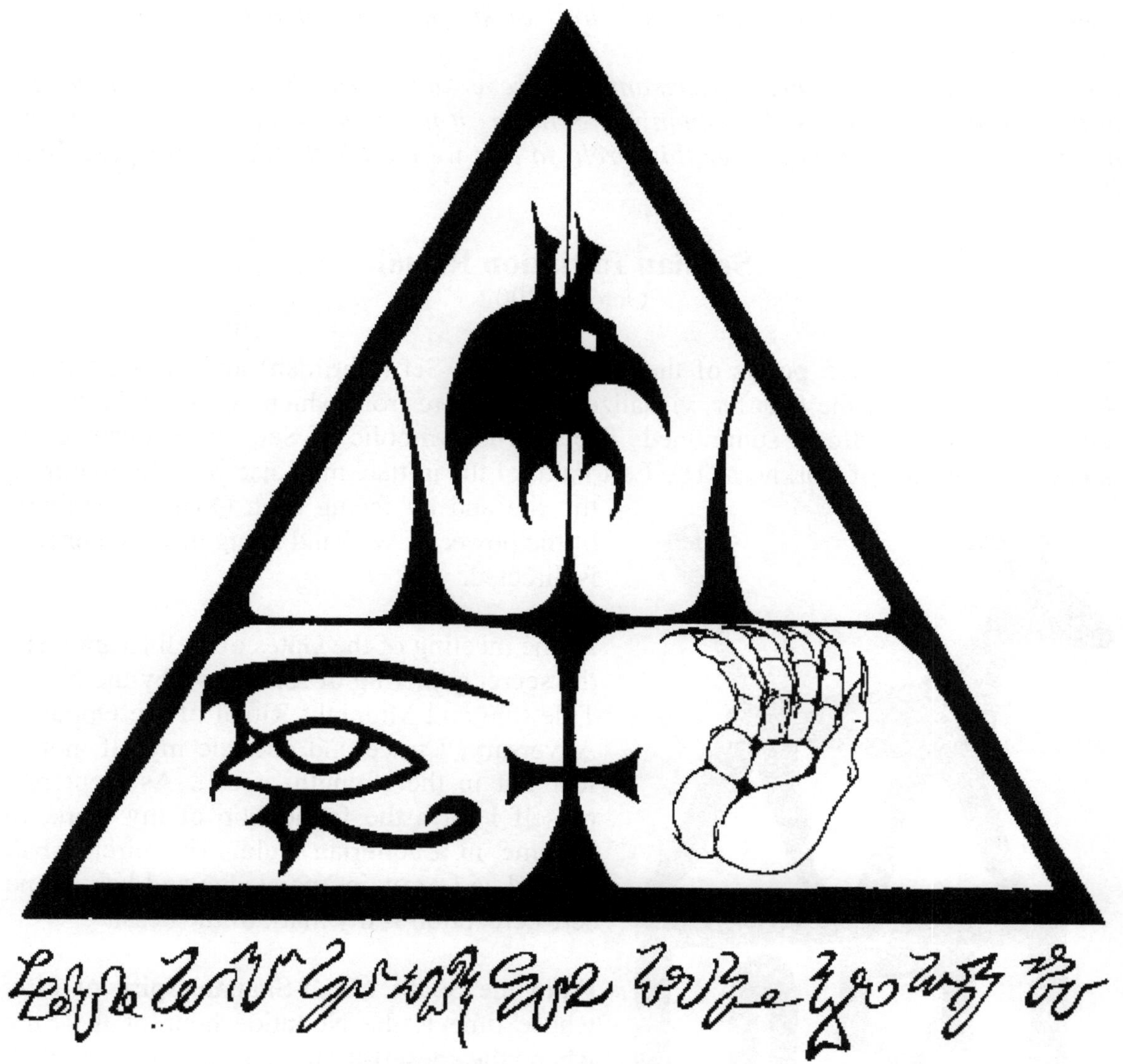

Typhon-Set Conjuration

"I summon thee, Typhon-Set, I open forth thy ceremonies of empowerment, for I invoke thee by thy shadow names in words which hold the essence of darkness. Within this darkness is found the Fire of thy being, formless flame which opens an indigo eye within me. Typhon-Set, who is lord of storms and the violent chaos within the void, I announce to become like you. Awake through me once again, I conjure the Eye of the Adversary within! Darkness and storm shall I control within!"

(The Left palm of the Priest shall be opened upright while invoking the names of Seth-an and the Adversarial force of Night, Darkness and Storms)

Iopatathnox, Io-Erbeth, Lerthexanox, Neboposoaleth, Iopakerbeth, Iobolkoseth, Ethrelouth, Iosoro, Aemina, Ioneboutosoualeth, Aktiophi, Ereshkigal, Aberamenthoou, Nemareba, I summon thee!

"Set, Lord of chaos and desert waste, lord of storms, lord of mutation, lord of the unknown, I invoke thee.
Hear me, for I am Wepwawep - Hermanubis, Opener of the Way, he of the jackal, howler in the wastes of the abyss, I summon you Seth-an, at this time, to open the gate of hell, that the waters of Nun may enter this circle so that we the Black Adepts may partake of the cup of life."

Sethian Initiation Ritual

October 2002

Ritual symbolized by 5 points of the Algol Sigil of Set (Ahriman) and the Left Palm. With each calling of the Quarter, visualize a line of fire from which you trace in the air, representing the Godform summoned. The fifth is symbolic of Set, the essence of the Isolator, the Prince of Darkness. The Left Palm of the initiate may also be held up during the rite and by facing each Quarter, symbolic of the power of Will and being in which energy is directed.

At the meeting of the Gates of Hell (from Hele, the secret gathering of sorcerers), by the Noon-Tide Sun and Midnight Ritual of the Opposer-Adversary, I trace and encircle myself, not in fear but in the strength of self. As I encircle myself I form the foundation of my work, to become in Luciferian light. The circle shall expand as I grow in knowledge and being, and self-perception is my mark of the beast.

From the South, Satan-Shaitan, spirit of Fire, whose time is the Noontide hour of the Sun, when the desert-djinn essence is revealed, serpent be revealed. By the sign of the five-fold star of Set, I invoke thee!

From the East, Lucifer- Azazel, Lord of the Secret Fire and Dawn, Bringer of Light, Phosphorus. Blackened Flame of the East I summon thee forth, sacred guardian of the path. By the Sign of the Five-fold star of Set, I invoke thee!

From the North, Lord of Night and Earth, Belial, I summon thee to Guard this Quarter, to bring all spirits and daemons of the Earth unto my command, bring forth thy wolves and beasts to my essence. By the Sign of the Five-fold Star of Set, I invoke thee!

From the West, I summon thee Leviathan, Dragon of the Depths. Encircle my being in the Black Mirror, Twilight Guardian and initiator of the path of Water and all that in the memory of creation, I summon thee forth! By the Five-fold Star of Set, I invoke thee!

By the Fifth Point, Envision the form of Seth, the Mask of the Opposer and Adversary

Open Now the Gates of Hell

Zazas Zazas Nasatanada Zazas-
I witness the Dawn of my becoming- awakened unto the Light of Lucifer
I am the ensorceler of shadow and light, of the Celestial and Infernal
Hail the Star of Seth-an, sign of my divinity descended to create Gods and Gateways to thy essence – Now shall the four paths cross

I summon the Sacred Fire of Iblis, known as the Black Flame.

Combine the Godforms summoned:

-Setheh
-Satan
-Lucifer
-Belial
-Leviathan

This forms – **Saeth I' blufcu**

This is made from a rearranged form of each name, such which may be vibrated as a mantra.

Suggested God Form – **Slath – Biv – Nucu**
Suggested Goddess Form – **Lash – Tiv – Buncu**

This is the name of the Godform summoned, from the black mirror of the self, which we seek to deify.

"I summon thee forth by the words of Power

Dekaza – Sunozoz – Apelithi
By the Fire cloaked Djinn, Lord of the Desert Sun
By the Caul – birthed Goddess of the Moon
I am Set, the Father of Gods, I shall never come to an End.
I am the Sun at Midnight, Algol, Xepera!
I shall now seek the Uraeus Serpent to crown my wisdom, that which is of Set!"
(Envision the God forms encircling, thus becoming a part of your circle)

"I come forth unto the Blackened flame of Set, whom I seek to become as."

Envision Set moving towards you – from which you reach forth and touch the flame within his left hand. Feel the warmth and electricity, then the cold which envelopes you. Contemplate all that you are and shall be in this moment. Stare deep into the mask of Set.

"I come forth unto you, Set, tester of strength, sender of Nightmares, Lord of Chaos, Shadowform of the Outside, of future and infinite possibility. I hold within the strength and Will to become like you, and the Desire to Become.

On this very day (or night), I dedicate my Life to Xepera to BECOME."

So it is done.

December 21st Ritual – The Longest Night
Calling the Guardians of the Sethanic Witch Cult

Composed originally in my Sethian initiation period, this rite was performed by initiates in Europe and America on the night of December 21st. One may perform this rite when they so wish, visualizing of course the very gate of the Dragon and Sah, the Hunter. Embody this gateway and make it respond within. This is one small secret of the mysteries, commanding a response within which reaches out. Seth-an is a Lord of mutation and Will, he stands against all others. Is this a trait you possess? Would you become a Demon – God (or Goddess) whose words beget chaos? Would the very dragon of Chaos manifest Order by the taming voice you have trained to echo in the depths of hell?

Part ONE
The Summoning of the Shadow of Sah, the Great Hunter-guardians of the beasts of the earth. Sacred animals associated with the rite of Sah- the Owl (Sacred of Lilith) and the Wolf (Sacred of Ahriman).

Part TWO
The invocation of Seth from the Constellation of Orion, known also as Sah or the 7 headed Dragon. A summoning of the powers of darkness on the Longest night of the year.

Part THREE

O' Hunter of the darkest winter
O' Hunter who walks the shadow path, nourished by the manes of the grave
O' Hunter who takes the skin of the wolf
O' Hunter whose arrow is the intellect and instinct of Shemyaza
O' Hunter who drinks from the skull of the familiar
O' Hunter whose sword is the weapon against sterility

O' Hunter whose crown is one half of the glorious emerald hidden in the earth, the jeweled cup and crown of attainment of being

Horned lord of the Northern Sky whom rides the night winds with the shades of the dead

Come forth in the night that you may invigorate my life unto the Temple of the Earth

From the fields of the Ancient Burial Mounds, forgotten save for those of ancestral and spiritual witch blood.

Come forth from the tomb of Sah.

Hekas Sakeh, umpesha zrazzu

Invocation of Set

I call unto you, O' Headless One of the Seven Stars called Sah in the dark places of the earth. I summon thee Set-Heh
I go unto the darkness between the stars
From the Dragon's throne do I emerge and the Seven Headed Beast doth manifest upon the earth

I do call thee forth, Set-Heh, prince of darkness
I proclaim thy mastery over the dragon

The First Head – Crowned by the Scarlet Woman, impaled on the phallic horn of the devil
The Second Head – Crowned in Flame and the Essence of the Adversary, Called Azazel and Shaitan
The Third Head – Crowned in the Goddess Hecate, known as Three Shades of Witch Fire
The Fourth Head – Crowned as Leviathan, Lord of Timeless Being
The Fifth Head – Crowned as Belial, Lord of the Earth whom resides over the Djinn of the earth under Azazel
The Sixth Head – Crowned as Asmoday, the bringer of Witch Fire
The Seventh Head – Crowned as Set, whom in isolation is the perfected essence of the Serpent and the Beast

I grow in the Eye of Algol, the burning and hidden self revealed as Set the Adversary, immortal essence of the Great Sabbat – The Luciferian and Infernal.

From the Ocean comes forth the Seven Headed Dragon, which I walk unto in the Shadow of Set. I proclaim thus-

I shall grow in the year to come in the way of ___________________________
I shall come into being by my desire to _____________________________

From my coming into being I shall grow in every aspect of which I can recognize, thus exalting the Black Flame of Life and Divine Being! So it is done!

A description and purpose of the Sigil of the Adversary, Set-heh

The Twelfth is when the Demon of the Noon Tide Sun comes forth from the Desert, Shaitan. This Sigil is the empowerment of the Fiery Will and that of the other demon of the Noon Hour, Keteb. Used in Daylight Initiation rites focusing towards the Eye of Set-heh, the Fire of Iblis, Shaitan. The Sigil may be scribed alone on a parchment and invoked at the Noon Day when the Sun is highest. It may be used to Empower the Body of which you dwell, to illuminate the Ba and Ka of the Sorcerer, or to send forth desires of manifestation in the heat of the day. Cursing is one possibility of this spell, and the name is Sabaoth, the Lord of the Earth.

The Eleventh is Hemhem, the Roarer, a serpent with the face of a cat. This devil is one of Apep, a form of Set. Hemhem is used to invoke storms in the self to crush and devour weakness.

The Tenth is the Serpent of Apep, who has the face of a white cat. This daemon may be used to ascend up in Night, to visualize and send forth the spells of your desire. Cursing or Blessing, all of which shall become in your Will.

The Ninth is the Trapezoid, the Ensorcelment of the Eye of the Sethanist and the ability to sway the minds of men and women to your cause. Be careful in the use of this Sigil, as it may invoke compassion or complete destruction. This is Pakerbeth, the Black Shadow of Set-heh, invoked within the body of the sorcerer.

The Eighth is Pesh-Khent, the birthing knife and cutter of weakness, a weapon held by Set. This sigil may be inscribed on a parchment or the handle of a weapon, use as a ritual instrument to begin a process of developing from a weakness of character.

The Seventh is Erbeth, a name which can procure Love – Love of another or Self Love. Use while envisioning the object of your desire – chant a mantra form of Erbeth while doing so while facing a mirror.

The Sixth is the God of the Night Sun, Seker (He who is shut in), a God of Darkness who has a close connection to Set in his beginning. Use this sigil to invoke the power of death and to isolate the psyche, emerge and begin transforming in the Midnight Sun of the Adversary.

The Fifth is Lerthex, a name of Typhon the Serpent. This is the Body and Mind of the Magician as he Spirals his or her spells as a Dragon. Use Lerthex to visualize a Goal and then recite the name as a mantra to manifest the desire. May be used for protection, by imagining a great typhonic dragon to encircle your dwelling.

The Fourth is Saatet-ta, the Darkener of the Earth. This is the ensorcelled daemon or daeva which the magician may manifest his Will and send forth the shadow to bring forth his or her desires. This Sigil may be used in dream sorcery, haunting or copulating as the vampire and incubi/succubi with your chosen.

.The Third is the Devourer, Amam. Use this sigil to encircle 9 times around the name of your enemy, to bring the serpent-devils of Seba to bring storms against them. Burn the Sigil in the Fire of the Noon Tide Sun while Invoking Keteb of the Twelfth.

The Second Sigil of the Adversary, being Hau-hra, the Backward Face. This is one name of Apep, the crocodile-demon shadow of Set-heh, that which devours and causes destruction. The purpose of the Setanic Magician is to master Apep within the self and master this demon by the Will through the Seba, the lesser devils of Set. Used for controlling the Shadow Familiars of Seba into a form of organization.

The First Sigil of Set-an, being of Kolchoi Tontonon, a name considered secret of Set. By the First shall the Ladder of Darkness led up towards the Light. This sigil represents the continuation of Life in a cycle of rebirth and manifestation, the Mind strengthened and free.

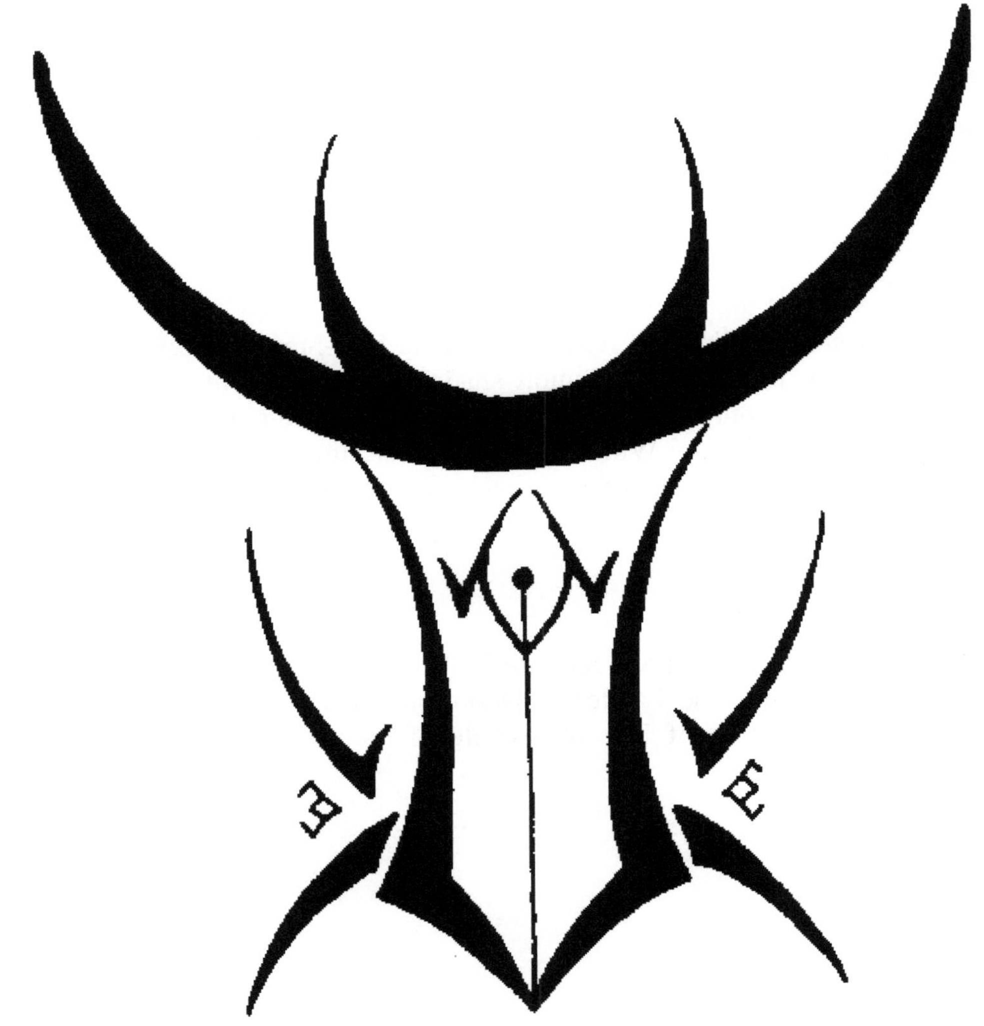

Invocation of Set-an the Adversary
(At Noon or Midnight) before working with the Sigils

"I conjure thee, Bringer of Storms and Chaos!
I summon thee, isolator and winter bringer!
Lord of Deserts and barren places of devils
Mighty Typhon arise to Encircle me
I speak the Words of Seth – which manifest my possibilities!
I shall BECOME!
Abraoth, Athorebalo, Kolchoi Tontonon, Beteshu, Sekhem-hra, Become!

"Set opened the paths of the Two Eyes (the Sun and Moon) in the sky." – The Book of the Dead.

Know that Set is the Adversary, who is both feminine and masculine (Samael and Lilith), by mastering Apep (Leviathan) is able to become the Willed mastering and compelling force (sorcery) upon earth (Cain). To unite the Sun and the Moon within and in the Sky (the material world and astral plane, the Infernal and Celestial/Empyrean Sabbat) does the magician become like Set. This is the process of the Great Work.

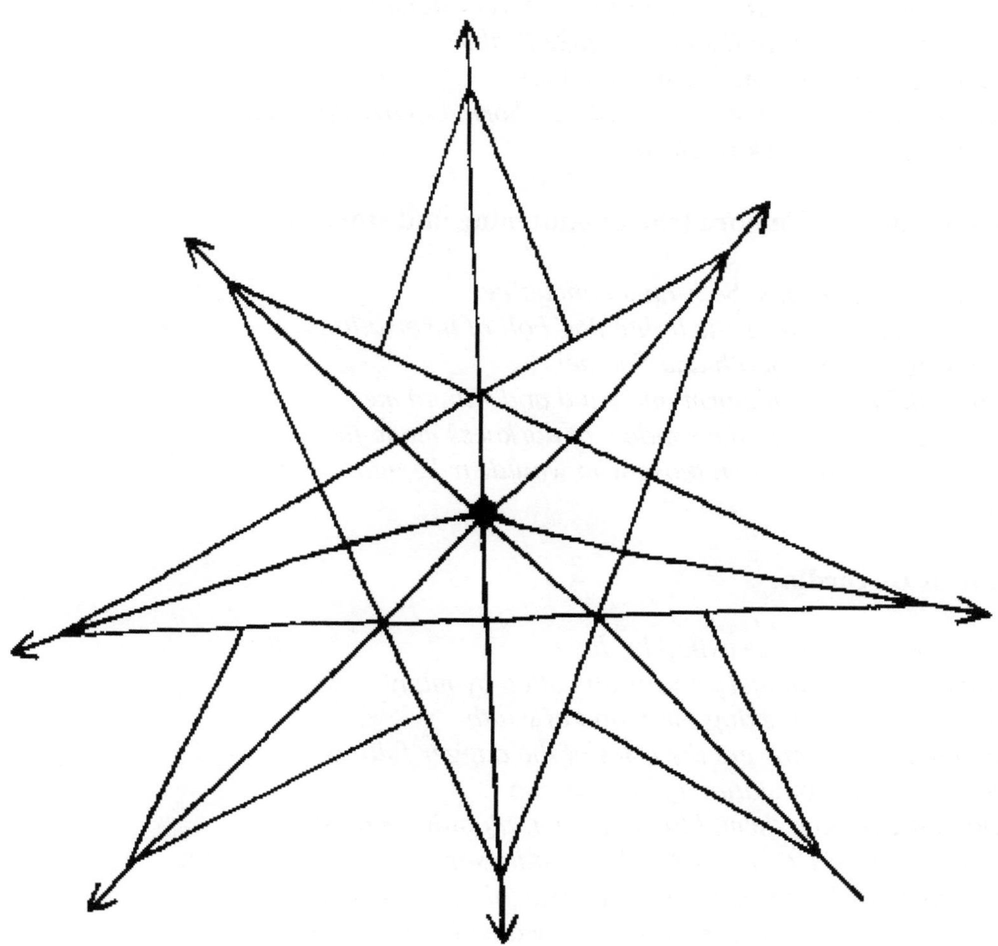

The Spell of Transforming into the Serpent Apep.

I am the serpent Apep whose years are infinite. I am the devourer, the hunger of the abyss. I am the serpent Apep, the dweller in the uttermost depths of the earth. I am the mastery of chaos and the very embodiment of the storm!

I am the serpent-god (Apophis) who dwelleth amid his terrors in the darkness. I am the Serpent-god and I seize (my prey) like a ravening beast. I am the great water serpent which is in Leviathan. I am the Lord to whom bowings and prostrations are made in the Glory of Set. And the Set is the lord to whom bowings and prostrations are made in Khephesh.

Azothoz Hekas Hekas Hekau!

The Shape Shifting of the Sebau into Beast (dreaming focus)

I crawl in the earth, licking and spitting as a slithering dragon in darkness
I stand forth on all fours as the wolf and jackal waiting to devour
I howl into the sky as the Adversary first cried out after the Fall
I screech as my mother in the night sky, her very dominion
By darkness encircled shall shadow make flesh
I shall change now into the beast I so choose
And Return by waking in my flesh as I was born and transformed
So it shall be, Hekas, Hekas, Hekau!

The Summoning of Fulgora (she of lightening and storms)

Hail O bringer of storms, Seth-an's concubine
Whose very nature causes the lightening bolt of inspiration
The very song of Yaltabaoth and Samael
Open forth the clouds of storm and wind and rain to me
Within this circle, cast in the shadow of darkness made flesh
Witness my rite, crash down those who would strike against me!
So it shall be!

The Rite of Discordia

O goddess black who was exiled by Jove
Who is the bride of Samael or Seth-an called by many
Who is the sorceress seeking the blood of youth
Whose laughter overpowers the cries of the dagger falling
As you take in the ejaculation of your victim
Fucking to drink from them, bloodied cunt, bloodied mouth
Who is the sister of Death, the blade a cradle song
Who is a sister of Nemesis, whose adversarial spirit is strong
Hail Discordia, Ate, whose head is crowned with serpents
The torn garments of one arising from the Grave
Who as with Set brings all change, war, violence and progression
Misunderstood by humanity, but not by us
We laugh with the spilling blood, we laugh at the birth pains of a God
Hail O Discordia, arise to us!

Typhon-Set, God of Storms and Change

Set is the overmastering and compelling one, as according to Plutarch.

"Typhon, as has been said, is named Seth and Bebon and Smu, and these names would indicate some forcible and preventive check or opposition or reversal." - Plutarch, Isis and Osiris

Typhon-Set is a God which represents opposition and challenge, struggle and the heat of the desert. The Black Adept becomes like Set through his or her own initiatory work, thus the religion of Lucifer can truly be sensed within; it is both darkness and light, both storm and silence, both feminine and masculine. Iron is considered the bones of Typhon,

"For, as the iron oftentimes acts as if it were being attracted and drawn toward the stone, and oftentimes is rejected and repelled in the opposite direction, in the same way the salutary and good and rational movement of the world at one time, by persuasion, attracts and draws toward itself and renders more gentle that harsh and Typhonian movement, and then again it gathers itself together and reverses it and plunges it into difficulties." – Plutarch, Isis and Osiris

Areimanius or Arimanius/Ahriman, is identical to Typhon-Set and Satan. Ahriman is the foundation of the Luciferian path as he represents both darkness and matter, sorcerous knowledge and the forbidden knowledge which curses the empty light of disillusion.

The sorcery of the Yatuk Dinoih provides a foundation for not only challenging initiation, but also the workings from nearly forgotten Zoroastrian lore.

"Zoroaster has also taught that men should make votive offerings and thank-offerings to Oromazes, and averting and mourning offerings to Areimanius. They pound up in a mortar a certain plant called omomi at the same time invoking Hades and Darkness; then they mix it with the blood of a wolf that has been sacrificed, and carry it out and cast it into a place where the sun never shines." – Plutarch, Isis and Osiris

Here we are able to see a foundation of Averse Magick which announces transformation by the Black Adept. The magician or Yatus would not simply perform sorcery to avert anything, rather on a different mind set based on initiation and change, becoming like Ahriman itself.

IV. ADAMU
Forbidden Sexual Magick

Within the Shadows…

Sister Claire prayed feverously, invoking Jesus and the Saints, yet her heart was filled with blackness and the lust of the Adversary. As she had been awoken by Father Urbain Grandier, who as a Priest of their parish in St. Pierre du Marche in Loudon, he whispered something to her and she felt the searing heat of lust, of desire and blasphemous entanglements with Goat faced spirits. Pig like beasts snort and lick up the drippings of their dreamlike fornications, while her swelling grew with the size and violent thrusts of the beast like member pounding deep within her burning core.

That was before, this night Sister Claire so wished for the Devil to come unto her. Many nights Asmodeus came to them and bit her inner thighs while reciting prayers backwards, she would move her forefinger at a feverish pace over her clitoris while calling to her lover, the Devil himself and lusting for the pulsing yet cold member of the demon Asmodeus. Grandier would often join in these Sabbatic and Sexual Rites, often wearing a black hood while fucking her with a fury that would tear many girls apart. There was no rape in this Covenant, only desire and fulfillment. The Nuns knew the passion of the Cross, but also the lust and desire of the Demons summoned by Father Urbain Grandier. He taught them the keys of summoning and going unto the spirits as friends, not as the Christian tyrants whom they pretended to uphold.

Sister Claire was in her cold chamber again; rather in her mind was an elaborate temple of both the heights of Heaven and the depths of Hell. Urbain Grandier had taught her the art of coitus cum demone, to use their union to empower their very being and strengthen them as sorcerers – the very art of the witch. Sister Claire invoked the God of Flies, Beelzebub in her chamber one night before sleeping. She envisioned flies and larva into her chamber and she drifted off to sleep. Waking in a half dream state, she tore from her sheets to be greeted by a Blackened Shadow, yet its very head was obscured in a mass of circling flies.

She understood and when touched by this daemon, she recited "Fuck me with your filth and raise me up in your fire, let me be your whore" to herself and she positioned herself on her knees and felt the cold press of the demon's member into her. She felt a strong pressure on her knees as she knelt on the uncomfortable makeshift bed.

While revolting at first and feeling the frigid grip of Beelzebub's left hand on her hip, she felt a burning sensation and gently pushed back to take his large and painful cock inside her. As this large shadow which had a frigid touch began to thrust slowly back and forth, she heard a hissing and the buzzing of flies, which grew in volume. At first being repulsed, she found a desire which could not be sated by anyone else. She fucked this beast with frenzy, spitting chants of transformation and becoming while the serpent tongue of Beelzebub hissed words of power which seemed to burn themselves in her back. The member of this devil seemed to be entangled with flesh, yet seemed to crawl with insect like legs from the base of the demon. As the cock pumped deep within her, she felt a moist sensation she could not understand, yet the slight stinging was a sweetness she could not resist. With each thrust, deep within her she felt small and large insect legs tickling her lips which devoured this devil's penis. Sister Claire wanted these demons as the earth longs for a falling star, she thirsts for it to fill her cunt with a burning abandon, she wanted to shed tears of obsession and a deep desire as she gave every ounce of herself to the demon.

While still being fucked as a chained slave, she suddenly felt a deep burning sensation in her anus. Slowly she was being invaded by another member of the devil. It entered slowly; looking back she was fucked with harder thrusts, the demon lover allowing black spittle to pour from its mass of flies onto the anus and the other black cock which emerged from a liquid belching demonic mouth above his humanistic genitalia. She was repulsed and filled with more desire. She felt as if it was tearing her apart even with the burning black spittle ejaculated from the mass of flies which made up its head.

She knew of the names of the servitors of Beelzebub, from ancient Hebrew sources known by Father Urbain Grandier. As she was slowly fucked deep in her asshole and cunt pounded by the pulsing and growing phalluses of the Beast, she chanted and hissed the names of some servitors – Amatia, Dorak, Arcon, Plison, Lamalon. Each name vibrated and hissed in unison by Sister Claire and Beelzebub, who seemed to know and be completely in tune with her words. The demon servitors would grow from shadows to attend their calling; their form would be perverted corpse like children dripping in the moist grease from a body during the stages of decay. Such incubi and demonic servitors were bred forth by the blood and elixir into a vessel made strong in the light of the moon.

Fucking the beast she looked up and found other shadowy forms taking shapes as what appeared to be demonic and malformed children. Five appeared from the blackness of the corners, which which The Lord of Flies brought with his summoning. Their faces were wrinkled and scab covered with seeming old age, their eyes were black as they reflected neither light nor comfort as normal children's eyes. Each moved forward, white pale and corpse like flesh, gray then turning pitch black on ends, still born and emerging from shadows. They were chanting in child like voices and touching themselves in lewd ways.

As they moved forward, the demons slowly mutated into decaying dogs with little or no fur and pasty, almost greasy colored gray flesh. Emitting a foul odor, these beasts now began to fuck each other, dripping a bile on the back of the other being sodomized. Their mouths changing and transforming into large vaginas while savagely being fucked from behind, a serpent tongue slithering from the vagina lips and then suddenly came more flies and maggot larva from the blood dripping holes. When one beast finished fucking the other the pull out brought a seeming ejaculation of rotting milk, the smell rising over the odor of the decaying dogs which was similar to that of clumped blood clots. When one beast finished the other moved in a half human way to the front and began penetrating the vagina in the face of the other. As Sister Claire was being pumped in both her spread anus and vagina, powerless and submissive, she was hearing the slurping sound of the cunt-mouthed demon sucking the other decaying beast off.

As the Beelzebub reached a climax, she felt the in pouring of a cold and almost burning substance within her, she bent up to take the serpent's tongue deep in her mouth while the Shadow which took form continued ejaculating within her womb. Flies buzzed and landed on her face as she kissed deep her Demon, and for the moment did she find satisfaction…the demon brought not death but life, and rested in the blackness of her mind.

The Grimoire of Coitus cum Demone – the Art of Flesh and Fire

Behold! A Grimoire written in flesh, blood and the fluids of the Agape! From shadows long forgotten does her name come forth again in the minds of many, Az. She is of many names, Lilith, Kali, Jeh, Izorpo, Batna, Satrina, Eilo, Abeko, Kokos, Odam, Partasah, Talto, Patrota, Amizo, Abito, Ita, Kea, Lamassu, Ardad Lili, Abyzu and known among you all. By these names shall you fornicate in honor of, be it known, anyone who may undertake an Holy Rite of Passage as described in this book of spirit, you must at all times during do so in honor of Her in mind. The End of all Flesh is the beginning of the Fiery Spirit of which you seek. Know her in ecstasy and aversion, from that shall you begin to understand her nature within you.

This is a forbidden text, here is given the means, formula and cipher to invoking sexual daemons and the spirits of the abyss deep within you. This text is meant as an honest manual of practice, a key to the gates of hell.

Know that the Agape (love) and the path of Sexual Magick can be as elaborate or as simple as you wish. It can also be as dark, brooding or as "dangerous" as you wish (this does not apply to unsafe sex mind you!). Individuals are able to interact with spirits and daemonic forces within and outside of themselves. If one chooses to work with a partner, they should be well informed and focused on the path as well. Casual sex partners would in some ways degrade the purpose of the Great Work, unless they were aware of the significance of what you were undertaking. It may prove dangerous for them as well, malefic forces in the shadows of the practitioner do manifest in various ways. The "pure" one undertaking the rite subconsciously controls these powers, while an outsider may not have the slightest idea of what they are truly involved in.

The ritual tools of Sexual Magick – altar, circle, dagger and any other implement is used as a means of self-inspiration, of bringing tools towards a specific and direct application to aid in ritual work.

Within this grimoire text you will find fictional, inspirational and practical elements of exploring sexual sorcery. The utmost importance of any working however is safe sex. You should communicate and discuss workings with your partner, do not leave any subject untouched within sexual magick and ensure that both partners are completely clear of their direction, needs/wants and focus. Do not explore sex magick without the responsibility of practicing Safe Sex.

Within the realm of Sexual Magick it must be understood that you must be completely honest with yourself, or you shall create a spiral force which will devour you. Sex Magick is dangerous because you are working with intense emotions; Magick is successful with intense emotions utilized and Willed in a specific direction. Know thyself is a key part to the success of the Work. The Creative Power of the Universe is the Shakti, when summoning and ensorceling (circling within your boundary of self) the spirits you are having congress with your Daemon but also the Succubi and Lilitu, the offspring of Lilith, the Mother of the Antinomian Path, so be well focused. Lilith is the Mother of Forbidden Desires, in Manichaean Lore she taught the Fallen Angels how to form bodies and copulate with others to beget "Dragon Children". She had alone the power to awaken the Serpent – Mind of Ahriman (the Devil) from his deep slumber, in which he bestowed upon her the Kiss which caused menstruation. Tantric sects of the Left Way consider the menstruation cycle to be the most powerful for the practitioner, thus Woman is Blessed as the Daughter of the Devil itself. The deeper mysteries of

Luciferian Sex Magick are found in the early Hebrew tales of Lilith and Samael original born in the Same Fire, thus they are both twins and lovers, as well as the begetters of Cain, the First Witch and Satanist. In the Great Work, the practitioner seeks to bring into union within him or herself both Samael and Lilith to beget Cain, or Wisdom.

Sexual Magick and Transformation

The preparations for Sexual Magick are as systematic and any other workings. While your actual work may be very loose and unceremonial, the preparation should be disciplined. Firstly, know what your goal is – the very aim of the working. Will you seek orgasm or will you use the method of Karezza, being excitement to the brink of orgasm and then focusing that energy on your goal, then allowing a mental release rather than a physical orgasm. Second, when practicing the rite, allow your mind to stay focused on the goal, not the pleasure itself. If it a solitary working, keep your thoughts focused on the object or goal. Although Luciferian Witchcraft and Sorcery holds many ciphers and symbols, in the circle it is merely you and the Gods/Goddesses and Daemons which you have given power to – nothing else.

One who seeks to explore the primal hungers and spiritual evolution of the path of the sexual demon, control is demanded in the highest degree of practice. You will wish to meditate and learn control of your body and your thoughts. This can be a daunting process but through the Willed focus of Magick shall this come to be.

"Tantra must be used as a tool to balance the spiritual and physical into a Coming to Being with the Luciferic Initiatory Guide. This is a spiritual connection with Sutekh, Set the Awakened God of Chaos and the most powerful of Egyptian Gods."

The Three aspects of Tantric Sexual Magick from a Luciferian perspective are:

Pushu – the first level of initation, where one is overcome with desire and lust. Here Adamu should be a guide towards the foundations of practice. Utilize the tool of the Daemonic Feminine, Lilith, as understanding the deeper desires of your mind and body. Lilith is the mother which leads you to isolation but fills your spirit with self-reliance and strength from within. The mystery is revealed that Lilith is within, the very Red matter of ash formed to divinity. Ahriman is the Beast of the Masculine, that which creates and expands it's will, Sexual Magick should be a tool of discovering these aspects and grasping them to manifest your will and become that which you seek. In this level of initation, the initiate should restrict sexual activity for a self-determined period, use daily mediation and explore that which drives you sexually, and why.

Vira – the second level of intiation, where one is able to control the beast within the mind and body, but is able to begin practice of sexual magick but with willful control and self–discipline. Atleast three first workings should be Karezza and holding the body back from Orgasm. This is understandably very difficult and will cause mental and physical pain, but with the display of self-discipline, the mind and body will strengthen and focus under this intense test of Will. Begin to form the beasts and shadows which shall act out your magick, to command your sorcery and begin opening your body as a Temple to Ahriman/Sutekh. Do not look towards other avenues for Temples and Holy (Luciferian) places, look only to your body as your Temple.

Daeva – the third level of initiation, where the Adept has overcomed, controlled and managed to form their sexual practice as a means of bringing their own mental and physical state to a Divine or Luciferian sense, where the self is isolated and Godlike, where nothing is beheld but yourself.

The union of Lilith - within the Body is that she is the lifeblood which initiates that Spark of Becoming, the female is completely active and powerful unto herself. Lilith is the motion and movement which brings forth the strength of Samael. She draws out the Seed of Samael (Ahriman) to create Cain (the body of the Adept).

The union of Samael (Ahriman) - is contemplative and passive unto Lilith as the energizer of life, or motivation and desire. Thought or the Akoman (sinister mind) is the level of Ahriman or Lucifer, the isolate mind.

Sex Magick Workings

Here you will find what some have hoped not to find – Self-Empowerment through Sexual Congress. Some of these involve Man to Man, so Woman to Woman and some Male to Female. In rituals of the Sun and the Moon, two men may participate however one will take a Lunar side (feminine) and one Solar (masculine), the same with Woman to Woman workings. Do not hide your sexuality away, be what you are and let no one tell you it is wrong!

The model of Left Hand Path Sexual Magick is a challenge which moves beyond the constraints of sociological limitation; it is taboo without psychological degradation, self-motivational empowerment through becoming as a God or Goddess, to discover your weaknesses and strengths. The God forms of Sexual Magick within the Witches Sabbat or Luciferian Path is best described through Lilith, Lucifer, Ahriman and Cain.

Lilith represents the Black or earth bound control/manipulation of the world around you in accordance to the Will of the practitioner. Lilith is the patron mother of beasts, demons and the nightside of nature. Lucifer is the Bringer of Light and Wisdom, the Solar side of Ahriman. Cain represents the Son of Samael (the Devil) and Lilith, whom is known in many Luciferian circles as Baphomet. Cain represents initiation and the process of the Great Work itself; be it within a sexual magick format or not.

Sexual Magick through Samael (Azazel/Lucifer) is self-transformative Magick; through the symbol of the Sun do you illuminate yourself by the immolating inner awakening known as the Black Flame. By the combination of Samael and Lilith and their respective paths do you create within Cain, the Horned Witchfather and Master of the Forge.

Sexual Magick through Ahriman is the Yatus/Daevai[85] summoning/invoking the principle or shadow side of Lucifer into the body of darkness made flesh. This is a mutating and transformative state which is painful, yet filled with the ecstasy of self-deification. Ahriman is movement, chaos and the Will made flesh. The sorcerer, who becomes Yatus, or Witch, is the isolated power which is an avatar for Ahriman and Lilith. By seeking this path you become as Ahriman and will create the Daevas and Druj which arise from him. The Prince of Darkness is a power unto himself, he cuts and devours that which becomes useless to him, and recognizes that he is the only God that Is. Sexual Magick is used to invoke this force within, the Dragon Made Flesh and does not represent or suggest any specific form of gender or sexual orientation. It is the sex of the individual, or avatar.

In addition, Pairikas or Witches of the Left Hand Path may become an avatar for the darker side of Lilith, the Bride of Ahriman known as AZ or Jeh. This is the feminine aspect of Darkness, the Tiamat of the Sumerians which represents Time and the devouring aspect which continues life, the thirst for continued existence.

The Models of Left Hand Path / Witches Sabbat Sex Magick are

Samael/Ahriman – Thinking Force, the Djinn (Azazel/Shaitan) of Fire, masculine strength, energy, the movement of the self through life. Known also as Shaitan/Satan this is the Black Serpent or Kundalini. In its masculine opposing nature, it is known as Ahriman, the Imagination. Samael is the Black Dragon.

Lilith/AZ –Red Force, the mother of demons, darkness in nature, primal instincts, menstrual blood from the Kiss of Ahriman.

The models of the Left Hand Path and the Witches Sabbat are described now for a further clarity. Samael, called Azazel or Lucifer. Samael is the left kingdom of separation from the natural order, the force which brought light or intellect to humanity through leaving the thrall of the all-father or Zurvan. Samael is represented as the Fallen Seraph or Djinn which is composed of Fire and had Twelve Wings, superior to other higher angels who had six wings.

[85] Daevi is a female Daeva, a demon.

Samael's bride is Lilith, who was once the bride of the All father and Adam. It was Samael who took the form of the Dragon – Serpent, who rode Eve while possessed by Lilith and by injecting "Filth" into her, conceived and bore Cain. Lilith is the initiatory mother, who awoke Cain after his murder of Abel, which is represented as his lower self of the thrall of sheep. Cain becomes the Wolf through devouring the life of his brother symbolically.

Samael and Lilith obtain power behind Metatron, or Zurvan, the Black Sun itself. This is the separating force from the natural order, the Sigil of ALGOL often represents this theory as the Eye of Ahriman/Set transformed and isolate, thus Order within Chaos.

KALI

Kali, called Smashan (cremation grounds) Tara (the savioress), is Lilith as the great devourer and destroyer. In a Left Hand Path perspective Kali is the force which we find within ourselves through looking deep within her, facing her terrors and through union with the feminine, empower a slumbering aspect of our psyche. Kali in a Tantric aspect is the blackness which crystallizes within the magician, the fire which exists in the void which is a symbol of her fiery nature. Lilith is the Black Serpent representing fleshly desire and Will to Flesh.

Kali is one of the 17 names of Lilith, whom is our patron Goddess of Sorcery and Magick. She is the devourer of all; she who awakens man and woman to the positive aspects of consciousness; the Mind itself. Go forth to Kali without fear, like a child to his mother. Kali is first shown as being Black, covered in ashes and covered in a garland of human skulls and heads, she stands upon the corpse of Shiva who is her mate, she devours and nurtures those who come unto her.

She is depicted as a woman who stands upon her mate, Mahadeva, who is the corpse god and when she copulates with Shiva he is called Mahakala, he is erect and cold below the Black Goddess.

Kali stands fierce upon this corpse, her left foot on his legs and right on his chest. In dreaming practice or meditation, one may envision her feet becoming like tree roots which sink deep into the corpse of Mahadeva. The significance will be explained shortly.

Kali is the embodiment of the dragon of chaos, Azhdeha, and Tiamat. She is the manifestation of primal darkness made flesh, the enfleshed Daemonic Feminine. It is significant to understand that in forms of Left Hand Tantric Paths, the Graveyard and cremation ground is a gateway unto Her. The fanged goddess, who drips blood and holds the beheading blade calls to your dreams, your deepest desires. Go forth unto her and face that which is either your doom or your becoming. Kali cares not for the weak and the ones who cannot face their inner darkness; Her children are of the Dragon, the serpent which contains the inner Fire of Her very essence.

Kali in her Buddhist form is Lhamo, she was the bride of the King of Demons and Cannibals known as Shunje, whose demons were called Dudpos. She left her husband for a time and killed her own son. She flayed him and used his skin as a saddle cloth, drank his blood using his skull cap and ate of his flesh. In some traditions Lhamo is called Remati, and she is depicted with Red Hair to represent her fiery nature and has a garland of human heads. She rides through on a mule or horse, a sea of boiling blood and entrails, made to appease her. Her hair is said to have a peacock feather. Her skin is dark blue just as her Hindu manifestation Kali, they are both identical in manifestation except Lhamo was said to be among the Himalayas, instead of the cremation grounds of India. Lhamo has two servitors who travel with her, a lion headed guardian known as Simhavakrtra and a Dakini. She is also described as being covered in ashes and human fat, she has three bloodshot eyes and holds a sandlewood club which often depicts a Vajra symbol.

It is considered that cremation grounds in India[86] are generally West of the towns. West is symbolic as the direction of Night, Darkness and the Ocean or abyss. In the circle the West is usually dedicated to Leviathan, Azael (the Angel of Death, a form of Azazil) or in Egyptian modern workings Anubis. The chamber of the Sex Magician may have the west focused as the altar or as a symbolic graveyard, with bones or images of Death.

[86] The Art of Tantra – Philip Rawson, Thames and Hudson.

While you may use the direction of North as the primary altar, West may be reserved for the darker explorations of Sexual Magick. The patron animals of Kali are found in cremation grounds – jackals, crows and other animals which feed from the corpses of the dead.

The Triangle of Evocation or Meeting place of Spirits is symbolized in many ways. The triangle within the praxis of Sexual Magick may be an inverse triangle with at each of the three points a skull or symbolic skull. This represents the Three Shades of Witch Fire (inspiration and creativity from the Three Faces of Hecate, the Goddess of Graveyards) and the inner power of the practitioner. Within the Luciferian Path many use the Goetic Triangle with the name AZ-AZ-EL within instead of MI-CHA-EL or the Triangle of Darkness used to symbolize Ahriman and the meeting place of serpents.

You may work with Kali in numerous ways. Firstly, seek a quiet dedication period to the lunar essence of Kali (Lilith) and seek the inner connections of your own being with the attributes you identify her from. It is said that Kali is ugly outside, but beyond the barrier is filled with ecstasy and beauty which holds all negative and positive ideas. Those ideas within a Left Hand Path or Luciferian focus is, that one realizes his or her deep desire and seeks to manifest it into the transformation of the self and later the exterior or objective world around you. If you are a male homosexual, seek the feminine firstly through solitary methods and then work with your chosen partner. Your partner may take the role of the Goddess of you may, this may be dually switched as long as the practitioners are focused completely on the goal.

A mantra which may be recited in first solitary workings with Kali can be Kalilim, which is a combined word – sigil of Kali and Lilith or her offspring, Lilim. This is an interior summoning of the succubi within the subconscious, seeking to open a gateway within the mind to the darkest forces of the Goddess. You may focus on visualizing her while arousing yourself, slowly at first – she may be just vague in image but then further details until at the height of union with her spirit do you see her clearly and then she is called into your mind from the abyss at the moment of climax.

The Circle of the Adversary

The Circle within Luciferian Witchcraft represents the very binding space of the sorcerers body, both of spirit/celestial and flesh/infernal. It is the symbol of both the Sun and the Moon, the sphere which begets strength and the very focus of the Magician. Thus the circle of Cain is the symbol of the Beast or Devil in flesh, a very manifestation of a God or Goddess on Earth. The circle is a continual and progressing manifestation and power center, which is merely a reflection of the body.

When the two meet within the circle, be it male and female, male and male or female and male, both symbolize a manifestation and incarnation of the Adversary or Two Headed One. This is Noon and Midnight, the very essence of Shaitan/Satan as the Double Wanded God/Goddess. One Head represents Satan while the other is Lilith, the union of duality to bring the strength of being.

The female partner should be menstruating which represents the vital energies of the feminine. She who seeks the invocation of Lilith will collect the blood and place on the altar of Art Magickal, the male represents the devouring. The goal of this Tantrick exercise is to focus the inherent energies via the Will, but to use them in a process of self-transformation, a mutation into a living temple of which the Daemon may manifest. Thus in this work, the sorcerer becomes a director of the current itself, a living expression of what is called "the Devil" or Adversary. The female is also a living vital manifestation of this current as well, it is in ancient Hebrew folklore that both Satan and Lilith were born of the same Fire, being twins.

The use of a vessel/fetish represents the 'home' of the Daeva or Demon. It is closely connected to the transformation of the sorcerer, thus an 'envenomed' and empowered ritual tool. When seeking to empower a fetish of Lilith or Cain, ensorcel (encircle) yourself in the love of the Daemon itself, this is why working with the Inner Guide or Holy Guardian Angel is so essential. Throw yourself into the internal association of the force, as it relates to you. Use incense, candles and anything which holds useful association. The Vajra Lightning bolt, that which falls from the sky (often associated with Lucifer or Satan, the Watchers or Fallen Angels) Is a symbol of internal vitality, strength and a cipher of initiation.

The libido is symbolized as a snake; the 'Black Serpent' of Yezidi lore is to represent knowledge and wisdom. The serpent thus represents a willed focus of energies connected with the self, as also the Daemon associated with the Working and the Azhish Ritual of Zohak/Azi Dahaka (The Paitisha). You may seek sexual congress to bring both Kali and Lucifer to flesh by using menstrual blood and semen in a vessel. You may wish to use a white sheet which you copulate on again and again to empower the working. Use the sheet as a wrap of sorts for the vessel which may have images or sigils of Kali and Lucifer upon them, that you may encircle them with the Love (Agape) of the Willed Desire of both practitioners involved. You may seek to empower this vessel beginning at the full moon to then the Dark Moon.

A suitable description of a Sex Magick working by Pascal Beverly Randolph "*was to copulate with many different women on one bedsheet, never changing or cleaing it. Thus, it retained the cumulative life force of those couplings, mingled and preserved in crusted fluids. He then stretched the sheet as an artist's canvas, and painted upon it his visual image of a succubus. He used his imagination like a lens to bring the power into focus, flattering and feeding the spirit who then manifested through it.*"

This provides a power tool for the magicians to create a working based around Kali and Lucifer, which by joining such fluids over and over again and filling them in a vessel a demon lover may be born. Use a variety of invocations, spells and averse chants such as the Lord's Prayer Backwards and similar "Satanic" chants to empower the demon.

On the night of the Dark Moon, refresh with blood and semen again and rebury the vessel in the earth. Each night you may exhume the vessel and wrap it in the sheet or cloth used in your congress, smeared over and over again with the sexual fluids of both partners. You may wish to evoke a Demon or Succubi/Incubi as this child of Kali-Lilith and Lucifer, thus being a servitor and third lover for the couple. Focus its gender or Will it to be able to change accordingly. Thus a rite which you create may be done as a Higher or a Goetic or Lower Working of sorcery.

On the Evening of the Full Moon exhume the Demon Vessel and perform a final incantation to it, then copulate with the vessel near and upon the white sheet which should be stained and crusted with blood and semen. Ensure that your fornication is intense and drawn out as long as possible, both envisioning the spirit you are creating. Allow this force to move within you as you fuck. When ejaculation occurs, the female or male (if both are consenting and monogamy is trusted) may take the semen in their mouth and mixed with their saliva or blood, spit into the vessel to empower the demon. If the rite is homosexual, a incubi with a preference for men will no doubt be created. If the couple are lesbians, a succubi will no doubt be empowered and bound to them. It is the combination of fluids of both male and female which seem to create a demon which may mutate between both and be able to perform various tasks depending on the sorcerers. If you wish to destroy or banish the demon, simply burn and pour salt over the vessel during a created banishing rite, including the sheet.

Communion with Darkness
A Ritual of Seething

Prepare the Skull Bowl or Sacred Bowl of Adamu, fill it with both sperm and blood of the moon[87], mix it with jasmine and those herbs which bring gnosis. In the Nights of Az, be it the Dark of the Moon or the Light of the Moon shall you have a sacred vessel of her marriage of the Dragon and his Bride. The soil may be prepared by the earth of which you dwell, and filled with the grave soil of a working place. During the preparation of the vessel of marriage, be it skull or pot you must be disciplined to banish the beliefs of which you were raised, and the ego which holds you in stasis. Seek her with the thirst of consciousness, the desire of knowledge and to transform your consciousness into a higher state of being. Seek Azal'ucel and His Bride during this sacred act, let not another who is untouched by the Blackened Light of Cain dare witness this preparation.

Your magical partner of many of the rites must be a witch of the current of the Peacock Angel, who is Azal'ucel revealed. Let her join you in the Great Work, but yet both are isolate and alone. Share your visions and inspirations; allow such sacred interaction fan those flames of the Black and Red serpents of Samael and Lilith. To rise the self up in the Emerald Presence of Lucifer and the Blackened Abyss of Lilith you must build a foundation of strength and will. One does not seek the marriage of the Adversary and the Whore by weakness, those are not of they! The Mind which is of the Black Light is of Ahriman, who in the cold north awaits his children with his Bride Az-Jeh, they devour the minds of those who are not illuminated with the Gnosis of their wisdom. Be prepared and be so diligent in thy work!

In the Sabbat Path does your transcendence begin to take place. With thy vessel poured and bathed in the Elixir of Adamu can you offer thy dedication to Her, and by Sabbat Fire and Dream Way shall she entreat thee in the ecstasy of union. Be as Cain, who walks the path alone yet consumed with the Blackened Fire of Self-Divinity!

Adamu is Her secret name of old which is the Trshna of Lilitu, by those mysteries shall you enter her dread circle. She is the Lust of all Women, and the Desire in Man. We are born in this world alone and separated, by the Averse Act of the Luciferian Path can we Come unto the Marriage of the Dragon and Whore, thus you shall be uplifted to the Path of Cain and his father, Azal'ucel who is called Azazel, Samael and Lucifer. Seek this way alone, as it is the Left Way, of matter and flesh. By this Witch-Way being the medium of desire of continued existence can the Spirit be ascended into the Fiery and Aerial Realm of the Angelick Watcher Azazel. It must be done through Darkness, to awaken Ahriman and Akoman within, by the Kiss of Az which stirs the Beast.

In the Circle of Az on the Night of the Dark Moon prepare thy Vessel with the Bowl of Adamu, the Semen and Blood of the Witch Woman, shall you both be cloaked in the night. Chant the words which open forth the Place of Arezura, the Cold North:

---

[87] Menstrual Blood. If the blood is collected days before the rite, store accordingly in a small vial. If not possible, seek rather your own blood in a small amount or something which represents blood.

"Akaza obil ahsu azaza
Ahsu azarrz azarrz arepum analpatsehs
Ahselpmu oiroiz, ararbum azooirrz!
Zazas, Zazas, Nasatanada Zazas!"

These words as above (not including the last line) are the inversed Alphabetic and Sorcerous language of Shadow tongue, the forward chant is one of the Summoning of the Watchers, thus an atavistic chant which ensorcels your body in darkness.

"Jeh – Az, Mother and Bride who is Samahe, I summon thee to circle path
Az, who is Pairikanamca, who has Nyanco, I entreat thee within my flesh
I am as Daevayzo within my own Being, who is of Ahriman
By the Daevodata do I Become, my grimoire written in dreams.
I offer this Bowl unto Adamu, who is perfection in Fire and Shadow!"

Pour now the contents into the Vessel[88] of Az, which shall be envisioned as the Circle of Az. Give this offering in Love, that by Agape is your desire to become born!

If thy vessel is a Skull, entreat the shades of the Lilitu to reside there, their own earthly sister being Agrat-Bat-Mahalat, the guide of nocturnal copulation and instinctual desire. In the night of the sacred offering with your partner, seek by sleeping – way to join in union with each other. Do it so in Her name, and use the Elixir to invigorate the Vessel at Dawn, to make an offering to Lilith and Her Mate, who is Azazel, who comes forth by the Light of the Sun.

During the offering the Calling of the Watchers should be chanted quietly:

"Zrriooza, Umbrara, Ziorio Umplesha
Uzesta Moriomba Usha
Shestaplana Umpera
Zrraza Zrraza Usha"

[88] This is a Bowl or sacred contain for you to perform the Great Work.

Trshna
-The Thirst of Lilitu-

Self-Will is directly connected to the path of Jeh the Whore. Knowingly, Her names are many. The bride of the Dragon and spiritual mother of Cain opens the portal through Hell in those who seek her. The aims of Adamu is to present the infernal garden of delights within and outside the arcana of self – love, being the essence of Trshna, being Thirst. The succubi or incubi arises from the depths of our own hell, this may be a partial combination of the Ahriman – like aspects of the self – masculine, always in motion – chaos inspired storms which allow the sorcerer to invoke change and becoming unto the Prince of Darkness. The Left Hand Path by means of isolation allows the practitioner to discover his or her self; to explore it and change it according to Self – Will. It is the essence of Az – Jeh being Concupiscence which divorces the psyche from the natural order of decay and stillness, it centers the mind itself into the Eye of the Adversary, the fires of intellect which as a gift of Lucifer – the Light Bringing name of Ahriman, to the center of possibility and self-control.

Sexual Sorcery is not only about control, but how to explore the most infernal and Luciferian facets of the self – and utilizing this power productively. It is possible for the sorcerer to become *like* the Daevas or Druj, to become *like* Ahriman. The Yatus (he who practices sorcery) must be willing to bear open his or her soul, to immolate it in the Black Flame of the Adversary and baptize it into the future possibility of self-godhood. This is not an easy task, nor does it not come with consequences. You shall change, your mind will strengthen, expand and your thoughts will intently focus on your goals. Those unprepared for the process of self-deification will by no doubt seal their fate into the morass of madness – to be devoured by Az herself.

The spiral of Adamu offers the secrets of the soul; and the horror of the abyss which is waiting within each of us. Do not seek the darkness to dissolve, to die. Seek the darkness as a fiery serpent that refuses the death of the psyche, by Trshna shall live beyond the veil of physical death. Strengthen your psyche and soul now; demand the cup of Az and drink deep of its fornication. The Grimoire of Adamu is laid across time and culture; it does not hold specific dogma to one tradition or way.

It must also be mentioned that Sexual Magick holds powerful servitors, but shall destroy those who have not the Will to control their desires. Such incubi and succubi are devouring masters and will slowly feed from those who cannot control them. Be warned. The methods of Left Hand Path sexual magick may be explored and expanded by the imagination of the practitioner with the methods of old. It must be considered that such practice is not aimed at inflating the ego; rather to manifest a power unto the subjective or interior world of the magician. Sex Magick is very powerful but equally as dangerous. By the process of evoking and creating succubi or incubi, a weak willed individual who lacks self control may by his or her own error fall into obsession in which the succubi/incubi begins to control the master itself. This is perhaps one of the more dangerous aspects of basic sexual sorcery, while such dangers escalate depending on the Working itself.

Left Handed Tantric Sex Magick
The Union of Ahriman and Druj – AZ

The Yatuk Dinoih and Paitisha are both tomes of Yatukan Sorcery which explores the foundations of invoking and becoming via the Daevas and Druj from ancient Persian lore. A development through the Yatus is the sexual magick and willed self-transformation from the fountainhead of Az – Jeh, known also as Lilith in other areas of daemonic mythology. In working with the Yatuk-Dinoih one invokes the Daemonic and Chthonic (earth based) energies of the daeva and druj, that the self becomes an empowered vessel of these forces. By Will one becomes a Daemon or Druj unto themselves. Sexual Sorcery is a useful, powerful and dangerous path which is a means of controlling and creating familiars, demons, sending nightmares, controlling dreams, etc. One is able to use sexual sorcery by the way of envisioning a spirit or goal and loosing the self in the ecstasy during climax, to create and send forth the druj.

Through the types of Left Hand Path Sexual Magick, the Black Magician not only becomes a Daemon/Daeva/Druj but also a gateway for the Luciferian and Ahrimanic force within – the Sun and the Moon, Noon and Midnight. This is a process of self-association with the respective God forms, their integration within your mind and overpowering anything which seeks to enter you. It should be understood that such spirits must never be allowed to control you, as this is weakness and will follow to your own self-destruction. You must control and Will this form of balanced Order within your mind.

The sorcerer who seeks the transformation path of Az-Jeh-Lilith shall undertake the test of which invokes the creative powers of darkness. Sex Magick initiates the magician into the current of Ahriman by moving against the natural by controlling/creating daevas and succubi in the spirit plane, that by dreams they manifest.

As a model of AZ, let the magician invoke in their own way LILITH, who is the dark primal instinct, the spirit of night and desire, hunger and sexual copulation. She is the force which roused Ahriman from his slumber, she who awakened the Demons to beget Dragon-Children.

In Nazorean-Manichaean legends of Adam, Az-Lilith came forth from the depths of hell to teach and instruct the fallen angels, demons and other averse spirits the art of sexual copulation, how by joining male and female spirits together, they created such off springs upon the earth. These demons spawned other children, Az – Lilith devoured some of them later on, which increased her vitality and power. Lilith is thus the First Vampire, the enfleshed anthropomorphic form of Tiamat/Azhdeha, the Dragon Stars.

A practice of this Creation rite may be done accordingly.
In the circle, create two sigils, one masculine and feminine.

Prepare and invocation to AZ-Jeh, the great whore who awakens your minds' eye.

Dedicate yourself to HER name that you shall become through HER.

Stimulate yourself by the imagined formation of a male and female Daeva/Druj, at Climax anointing the Sigils with the fluid. If you have a partner, ideally if she (unless you are the she) is menstruating her fluids may be anointed as well. This formula creates the demons which will carry forth and enflesh your desires. Your Will is the driving factor associated with this, so do be prepared to ensorcel yourself in your desire – will – belief.

The Draconian Rite of the Adversary
Raising the Twin Serpents of Lilith and Samael[89]

As individual vessels of Cain/Naamah (Cain's sister), the magician will focus on visualizing the Red and Black Coiling Serpents up the spine. Sit upon a comfortable pillow, legs crossed and begin to slow your breathing. This is done by banishing all other thoughts and concentrate on your lower spine. Slowly begin to form a great Red serpent which starts at your lower back – this is Lilith, the Red dragon which is the fiery life source which rises as the Sun itself. With each breath, you shall feel it ascend and coil around your spinal column. You should imagine fire, heat and creative force as the dragon ascends your body. When Lilith reaches your right shoulder, you should bask in the Fire of Self, this is thelife bringing force of hunger and desire, the qualities of being and self-love. Be pleased that your imagination has created this mental and physical pleasure; know that you by yourself are the creator of your own Gods. This is the essence of the Left Hand Path, self-deification.

Now you will begin to call forth the Black Serpent,Samael/Ahriman. This is the 'shadow', the primal instinct and sexual desire for becoming. The emotional, lustful aspect is the driving force of sorcery and self-expansion. Begin summoning the Black Serpent up your spine, coiling with the Red Dragon as red flame and blackened fire join as one. As these two forces continue to connect, rub together and bring about friction, ecstasy shall overtake you. Do not allow the Will to fail or to lose your determination. As the Black Serpent moves up your spine focus on its essence – darkness, lust passion and hidden aspects of the self, bestial transformation, isolation and the foundations of sorcery.

Draw the daemonic feminine inward, to merge with the Black Dragon, Lilith. As the Blackened Dragon rises above the Left shoulder, envision now the union of this force – the creation of Cain. You may reflect on these two forces in relation to your own unique being. Ask yourself, how will I use this knowledge and power to improve my being and life? When the twin serpents have both been raised, you may now perform an act of High Sorcery, of the Blackest Magick of self-deification. Invoke the Luciferian Angel, Azal'ucel, practice what spell you wish with improved potency and BECOME through the Black Flame. Becoming as it is called requires patience, but determination and commitment. The circle of sorcery knows only the bounds you present to it, Know Thyself!

Ensorcelment of the Daemon

The arte of sexual sorcery between two partners should be focused on the ensorcelment[90] of the primal ophidian power. This is the Black and Red Snake in union, between both participants. Let both the fluids of male and female be brought in union for the

[89] An advanced formula is hidden within the symbolism of the rite, AZHISH, found in The Paitisha by Michael W. Ford. It is a spiraling of the Daevayasna who advances the psyche in the Luciferian Gnosis.

[90] A word meaning 'to encircle', in the context of ritual and magical workings, it is the sorcerous binding of power or energy, that which may be identifiable with a charged spirit or servitor.

consecration of talismans and sigils, thus a demon born under the Will of the practitioners.

The Daemon which is a Succubi or Incubi may be sigillized by any known method and further prepared by the evocations to be conducted before, during and after copulation. The Daemon depending on intent must be agreed ahead of time by the participants, so that by the methods of Will – Desire – Belief bring the circle of Art to manifestation, that the Shadow shall take form in thy union.

Allow the circle to be cast as the coiling dragon as thy circumference of self. The circle represents not that which you seek to keep out, rather of which you shall bind within – the circle is not a weak willed Christian design as once was, no cowering done behind brittle words! Rather evoke the daemon as your brother, lover, sister and friend!

The Circle Chant of Tracing:

"By the Circle of the Horned Moon,
By the Circle of the Three faced Moon
By the Circle of Cain, shall you be cast
Once by Shadow filled in Ahriman's hand
Twice by Noon-Tide Fire of Shaitan's glance
Third by Midnight Caul of Lilith's dance
Be it complete and sacred in this center of Arte"

Within the circle shall both join and with the focus of the Succubi and Incubi of the Agape of Magick allow copulation. Do begin visualizing the spirit taking a form from the Passions of the Agape and both individuals' willed intent of creation and binding. The Evocation dagger or blade consecrated in Cain's name may be used by both to focus and charge their work. This is a working of the union of shadows into a servitor.

"Hail unto thee, O shadow thirsting daemon of earthen bound time
Hail unto thee, servitor of the horned lord of flame and nightways
Blessed are thee, who walks the gast – roads beyond our veil again
With our Dagger, born of Cain's fire and forge
I name you (name) by those hidden pathways forgotten by the profane"

At the moment of male orgasm, anoint the sigil accordingly, when the partner has reached orgasm some of the fluid should be collected and consecrated upon the sigil as well. Both practitioners' must stay focused during and after the copulation, within the circle which is cast as the collection point of such energy, thus charging the daemon accordingly.

"My flesh and her blood is that which begets the body of shadow that is Daemon,
the Djinn fallen from the sky as the Lightening Eye – glance of Samael
Do take form and manifest our desire as it is so
By Sabbat blade I bind you, by phallus and blood – moon I empower you"

In the Black Chamber of Kabed-us-Spae
A Sorcerous Union of Encircling the Coven's Power

O - The Flesh Sabbat and Congress

The Two were led by the Master of the Circle into a chamber, red walls and a black ceiling. The center of the room was a large comfortable chair, crimson with golden Chinese dragons embroidered in the fabric, a great pillow colored red at the foot of the chair. The master of the circle wore the mask of Shaitan, the Djinn of the Burning Noon Tide Desert Sun, horned and inscribed with sigils of the Dragon upon it. Adorned in black leather pants with his chest and arms blackened he sat one women in the center of the pillow. The Priestess who embodied Lilith – AZ, the Whore who rode the Dragon, the center of the Eye of Tiamat enfleshed sat in this chair, legs spread, a tight fitting leather corset gripping tightly to her pale flesh. Her mask was designed as a mask of Lilith, black and white with streaks of menstrual blood across it. She was a member of the Coven for sometime, and desired the Working which is rarely spoken of... Before her was the lady who would in carnal desire know both the harlot and the beast, and would awaken to their pleasure. The purpose of the rite was the consecration and ensorcelment of the Ahrimanic Familiar of the Coven. At the northern point of the room, was a small chest and upon it rested a human skull and a pot filled with a black Daeva statue (a demon), a black and red candle, underneath and filled with soil with various rocks resting within it. Next to the nganga was a skull cap turned into a bowl with some powdered human bones and herbs within it. The Priestess was handed a skull which was the vessel of Lilith by the Lord of the Circle. She held it in her left hand. The Skull cap was placed next to the Lady on the Pillow.

As she was knelt before the Priestess sitting lewdly in the chair, legs spread and slowly arousing herself, the Master of the Sabbat loudly vibrated the barbarous words of evocation, calling forth the Devil of the Sabbat as an invocation through him. Each word although unintelligible, seemed to cause ripples in the rooms environment, a great heat and fire seemed to encircle them. The Master of the Circle began the Sabbat chant, invoking and calling forth the shades of the night to encircle them...

The Priestess recited the staota of Zrazza several times, announcing her individual intent.

The Lord of the Circle began calling forth the Daevas of the Rite-
Az, Ahriman, Akatash and Vareno.

"O horned initiator and devils flesh
my cloak of serpent skin worn
clothe me in the Robe of AZ
in the Watchers field of time.."

The masked initiator then began reciting the Lord's Prayer Reversed, a chant of summoning Cain. As he began reciting, the lady turned and began arousing the Lord of the Sabbat with her hand. He then spoke the Words of the Staota, summoning to go forth into the flesh of AZ-Jeh, the great Harlot before him. All the while was the Priestess arousing herself, chanting and speaking in tongues that shadow language which beget serpents. She then called forth Lilith within the Infernal Sabbat, stroking herself with a demonic frenzy. As she recited further, the Priestess took the lady by the hair and guided her face into her gaping wound. The lady licked furiously, which sent shivers up the spine of the Priestess, who while growing in ecstasy, continued the chant to invoke Lilith.

The Lord of the Sabbat, kneeled behind the lady, who was moving her right two fingers in and out with each slow lustful kiss of her now swollen lips, began moving his hand between her leg. As he slowly excited her, she grew very wet. The sounds of the lust as the Priestess groaned in pleasure and the slippery movement of her licking enticed the Lord of the Circle to slowly insert and engage deep within her. The lady felt a great fire within her as he pounded deep, which excited her more. The Devil of the Sabbat began speaking in shadow tongue as he thrust within her, while Lilith (the Priestess transformed) was also speaking in shadow tongue sending forth the Lilitu with her great lust. Both as the lady knew, were calling forth the force of the Sun and the Moon into the circle, which would bind them all as the Yatus and Pairikas who embraced the Luciferian and Ahrimanaen Gnosis.

As the Priestess soon was preparing to explode while this lady licked and fingered her deep, she felt the atmosphere changing more, fire and shadow seemed to surround them. No longer were they just in flesh, but also in dream. She heard pounding drums and slow chants. The Devil of the Sabbat was spanking the lady hard on her cheeks, while he thrust deep in her warm core. The red marks as a result of the burning sensation drove her crazy, all the while the Lord of the Circle began rubbing slowly her clitoris, with each thrust bringing her closer to the climax she so wished during the Sabbat in flesh.

While thrusting deeper and deeper within her, he began reciting the Lord's Prayer Averse, used in Luciferian Witchcraft rites to summon the Devil Cain, his very blessing in flesh.

The lady was suddenly thrown into a state of complete desire, lust and demonic sexual fury. She began pounding back on the rock hard member of the Devil, who grew in his excitement. His chants grew louder as he rose to a climax. The Priestess who was the Mask of Az-Lilith moved her mask ever so slightly to tongue the teeth of the skull, when the orgasm hit her. She felt the atmosphere explode and with her great shuddering she imagined a serpents' tongue slithering out of her swollen hole and lick the tongue of the lady which brought her to orgasm. As the serpents tongue danced with her blood came out with it, the envisioned result of the Staota invoking the gift of Az, the lady opened her eyes, near Cumming herself while she spat this elixir which was coppery and old into the skull bowl. She nearly choked as she tried hard to gather as much of this fluid in her mouth as she could. At this moment the Devil of the Sabbat pulled out and stood up, the lady turned her blood filled mouth spitting it into the skull bowl and held it up near the phallus of the Magician, who ejaculated in the cap as well. As she mixed the fluid on her tongue she came very hard. Az-Lilith was rubbing her breasts lovingly from behind and the Devil of the Sabbat placed a small nganga (spirit pot) before her, she poured the combination of menstrual blood, semen, bone powder and herbs into the soil and on the black demon statue. The Lord of the Sabbat performed a summoning of shadow before the vessel and blessed it with envenomed life. The Priestess placed the skull in the vessel with the Demon statue; it was an Nganga of Ahriman, the patron Daemon of Sorcery of the Yatuk-Dinoih. The chanting continued, a necromantic summoning using a known phrase in Yatuvidah sorcery:

"Zrazza, zrazza, usha nicht, zrazza umpeshu..."

All three now sat in a triangle with the vessel in the center. The two removed their masks and all began slowly speaking in shadow tongue, to ensorcel the shade within the spirit vessel. This was the birth of the Druj that night, and the Triad had become as Hecate, and in their work of Yatuivah, each was becoming as Daeva and Druj within their own being. The Circle was closed, yet the Work had just begun. The Daemons were coming forth into the World around them, and the Coven had much to do…

I – Self Love through Lilith

The Priestess stands before the vessel of Lilith, both women begin summoning the primal daemonic essence of Lilith.

Upon the Altar a Skull Fetish of Az-Lilith is centered, representing the spirit chamber of which she dwells on earth, the Three shades into One. The incense of Venus is burnt and filled the chamber with a sweet aroma. An image of Lilith is behind the Skull and a single whip laying loosely around four red candles.

The Priestess and her female partner performs invocations to Lilith – both recite according to their instinctual design, this is the path of which Az-Lilith hears their calls.

Descending:

"By flame am I consumed, Her Lust. Immolate me my sister of Lilitu"

The priestess whips the ass of the female, with each lash a name of Lilith is recited by both, the willing embodiment invokes Lilith with all of her heart. Soon both become lost in their own ecstasy of invocation. The Priestess is then whipped in the same fashion while reciting again the names.

II – By Filth is AZ born in all hearts

The priestess begins to lick her fingers and slowly massages the clitoris of the participant, while she does such the Priestess recites:

"Infernal harlot, who shall take the seed of man, you shall taste the pleasures of darkness, in the shadows of the moon, in the bright of the moon, do you lust for the taste of my Cunt? Do you seek that which we are in ourselves? Do you seek the ecstasy that Christ knew with Magdalene? I as with you, Daughters of Lilith, in her presence shall you taste my lips, if by chance that coppery taste guides you, that serpent tongue so delicate."

The participant is feeling a fire arise deep within her, she begins to tighten her muscles below which the Priestess can feel as she slowly glides within her now, the participant in a state of desire begins the rub her fingers in the warmth of her priestess, who both now feel the fires of which Lilith awakens within.

"We are as Az-Jeh, the Black Harlot who consumes the flesh of Armiluss, yet as the Goddess do we fuck to the gates of hell. Open forth thy path, Lilitu, Empusa, Kali..fill my brain with burning ecstasy as I taste my sister of witch blood"

With her tongue does she slither upon her sisters lips, flushed she desires her tongue to be deep within the one drawing her before the gates of primal ecstasy. The priestess kisses with a fiery passion the witch participant, both tasting each other with lewd abandon. When near a climax, the Priestess pauses and takes the Skull Fetish from the altar and recites-

"I am she, of fire and filith, who is joined with the devil of the noon tide sun. I am she who taught the fallen ones the arte of copulation, to use the elixir and honey of the female to bring forth Dragon Children. I am she, who by the shores of the Red Sea, fucked and brought forth my children the Succubi and Incubi, to go forth and awaken mankind. I am Lilith, the Bride of Shaitan, thus I am his compliment, as he is mine. In our union we are life eternal, the mind of perfection."

Both the priestess and witch shall anoint the Fetish of Lilith with their own juices, and then by sealing the rite return to their partners accordingly.

Osculum Infame – the Obscene Kiss

In individual and partnered Luciferian Witches Sabbat Rituals, a male and female or Male/Male or Female/Female convocation may choose to utilize the Osculum Infame, or Kiss of the Obscene, being an Averse practice of Satanic Baptism via Sexual congress. The working itself is an act which symbolizes and focuses the control of the fire serpent in a specific area. The Kiss of Shame as it is called by Christians is one which may be practice between two or more individuals, and provides a powerful tool of Sexual Sorcery. A Male may represent the Devil but it is not uncommon for a Female Witch to also represent the Devil as Lilith, they are both aspects of the Adversary as being the Bride of Satan. In some medieval tales of the Osculum Obscoenum or the Obscene Kiss the Devil in the form of a Black Goat had a black candle inside his anus, lit from which other witches lit from this candle during the obscene kiss. If the male of female who are embodying the Bestial God agree, they may sodomize themselves with a black candle and be lit. The other practitioner (s) may light their own candle from this candle, kissing the area underneath the anus before. The blackened flame is that of the devil or beast totem, the very nocturnal and lustful presence of Cain as the enfleshed Horned God. Thus, he represents power, vitality and focused desire.

Another version of the kiss may be done by male or female as well, bent over and spread before the other practitioner or coven if it is such their desire. A practitioner may chant a summoning spell of the Devil or Lilith and then begin kissing or tonguing the anus. If it is thus their will, they may implement fingers or a consecrated dildo (preferably Black or Red) to (if female) the vagina or anus of the Beast God or Goddess. It is essential while practicing this very act of Infernal Sex Magick, that the one performing the actual Kiss moves their tongue in the symbolic direction first of Widdernshins, counter clockwise and slowly lick and kiss the anus of the male or female. With each tongue movement, envision a great serpent rising from your spine and a power overcoming you. Each thrust of the tongue is a serpent seeking the blackened pits of darkness, that which shall lift you up into the Light of Lucifer in the Dreaming Celestrial Sabbat. The practitioners may copulate after the Obscene Kiss and sexual fluids be anointed on the Candle to represent and offering. It is suggested to pour the fluids in an offering to darkness, poured into a fetish or hole in which the sun does not touch.

Tantric Positions
Suggested use in Ritual Magick

Within the sacred circle of Az, or the Triangle as you have drawn it, the daemon within may ascend above you as Azothoz, the Angel-Dragon who is born of shadow. In the rites of Sexual Magick, the practitioner has become essentially a self-created separate being, one which stands outside the bliss of nirvana. The Luciferian shall seek the ecstasy of self-love, but also that which focuses future self-creation and progression. Concentration is essential in such workings, as it is between lovers the daemonic ecstasy of self-invoked power. It is not rare during such tantric practice that the practitioners feel a type of "shadow" or force surrounding them; this is the gathering of the Sabbat in one of many of its forms. It is the widdershins circle-dance of beast and daemon, or servitor and lilitu. Your desire empowers their drive, their activity and movement. Use these created and attracted forces well; they shall be servitors of your very lust and desire.

The suggested positions may be used to good end, allow your own predilection to guide you.

Within the circle, let the female be joined to her thighs with the male, or if it is of the same sex, let one be filled by the other. With each thrust a great pain shall turn to seething ecstasy, each thrust should be a determined focus of Will and Desire to allow that which they seek to manifest. If the work is internal in nature, allow the feelings to be carefully examined during the act; by both practitioners. As with each thrust allow the fire which rises through both bodies to be focused towards the goal at hand. Allow this to occur until exhaustion.

With the male practitioner in a standing position, resting on his knees, and the female or passive practitioner laying on their back, the male in a rhythmic movement thrusts deep in the passive while massaging her clitoris, or if same sex masturbating the male. The experience between both will generally be long and relaxed, which is suitable for those interested in a more calming focused working.

With a female who is able to achieve orgasm the male or dominant in the circle should begin licking the female until aroused, at this moment he or she should work one finger inside while licking the clitoris with rhythmic movements, gently rocking the female. The male will more than likely be able to move one more finger within the female, slowly reaching deep to the hilt; this allows a strong rhythmic pattern. With each thrust the dominant and passive participants will be able to focus on the goal of the working. The female will no doubt reach the orgasm first, or reach to the brink so that the male (if present) will be able to engage in intercourse. Both should focus on reaching orgasm together during the working, so both states of ecstasy may be focused on the goal of the working.

The Chamber of the Serpent

Sexual Workings in a bondage setting may also be implemented depending on the fetish of the participants. Magick proves a powerful drive behind S & M if practiced in any certain way. A basic description is as follows.

Upon entering the room, one male and two female were already prepared for the gates they sought to open within themselves. The main witch of the coven was dressed in a strap halter top which revealed her ample breasts. She wore also crotchless black latex panties and crimson whip boots, with two Luciferian sigils painted carefully in black on the sides. Her hands were bare, even from rings and her nails carefully manicured. The second witch wore black latex stockings and matching tight fitting panties. She was gloved in crimson gauntlets and wore a skin tight corset which gave the slight appearance of being extremely uncomfortable, which aided her aggressive mood.

The male in question was dressed in a tight fitting latex body suit and masked with a hangman's hood. He was able to speak and to see, yet he was unable to have intercourse or even arouse himself with the restraint of the latex. He was bound by two wrist cuffs made of a sturdy Velcro, while the ankles were let loose with no restraints. A spiked collar was tightly around the male participants neck, with a silver utility chain fastened to it. One female witch held the chain upon attaching it to the male, while the other looked on with her riding crop in hand. None had spoke at all once the chamber was entered, as silence was the law of the Working. They sought to invoke the aspect of Lilith in each of them, that Az would manifest in the dominance of both females and the male would seek this inferno by not being able to have sex, merely experiencing pain and lust by both females. The second witch had a double headed black dildo which was roughly 12" long, which she began rubbing between her breasts while the first witch anointed herself in Leviathan oil, while the incense burnt in unison and filled the chamber with a sweet and powerful scent.

The male, whose arms were restrained, rested on his back watching closely the two witches, the first witch began by tapping gently on the left leg of the man from above the ankle. His arousal was at first very slight, as he was very uncomfortable in the hot latex. The second Witch began an invocation:

"By the First Moon of Hecate-Lilith do we come as virgins unto Her, let us be blessed in innocence and beauty, perfect love and trust.

By the Second Moon of Hecate-Lilith do we emerge as Harlots, blood filled whores who fuck the living and the dead, for our desire is endless, seeking the tongue dance of each other in anxiety filled desire. Let our wounds be fucked with the cock of the beast, whom is hard and cold member of Our Lord the Devil. Let us soon taste his pleasure...

By the Third Moon of Hecate-Lilith do we enter the graves of the dead, to rest and seek the loving and chilling touch of the dead, whom each shall choose as a lover. Let their cold embrace fill us with the shadow of Azael who walks the rows of graves, who among the tombs seeks his Lady who is the Crone, in age there is beauty."

"By Zazas, Zazas, Nasatanada Zazas I open forth the Gates of Hell, Az-Jeh, who is Lilith, who rides the Dragon do come forth through us, we shall reach the heights of ecstasy through your Honor!"

The first witch who was tapping the males' leg was now rhythmically chanting the words which open the gates of hell, moving further up his leg. While doing this, the second witch, with her long black latex gloves, the right hand moved between the others legs and made her way slowly to the open area revealing her lips and began slowly moving her forefinger up and down, massaging her clitoris.

The male who was bound was becoming more aroused upon seeing such an interaction, and focused the thoughts to blood covered bestial shapes which began to fuck in a frenzy, while female beastlike fiends covered in black hair patches sucked the other demons off, semen spilling in their mouths which created more demonic shapes which appeared as greasy looking boars and pigs which moaned in desire. The male thought of slow fucking of goats and women, dragon-like worms moving in and out of moaning girls who had passed beyond maturity by some five to seven years, knowing the very desire contained in the image of the Devil and His Bride. The male was at this moment very hard as the first witch, being aroused with the second witch and her slithering tongue and hand, slapped the double black dildo on her ass in-between tonguing her. The witch who was receiving this pleasure ran her tongue across the black latex crotch area of the man, and then spit at his mouth, while he lustfully sought to lick from his mouth.

"Hekak Vozath Ka-Sath-Ompos" she hissed at him, the male hissed the same invocation back, and both looked lustfully at each other. By this time the second witch took her right hand away, now slick and wet and moved the black dildo slowly inside of her. She motioned her hand in the front of the witch who was now slapping the male on the right leg near the crotch, the first witch with her tongue sucked on the slick fingers of the second witch, whose black gloves had entered her and were thrust deep inside.

The room had heated up with the smell of incense and body heat, feeling like they were surrounded by fire. The witch who was thrusting the phallus within her felt as if she had completely entered her within spirit, she moaned with every thrust and the witch felt as though she was controlling every breath which entered her lungs, the group was one. At a point of raising the energy within the room, both witches desisted in their sexual Agape and on each side of the male began caressing his legs. Their eyes showed lustful expression and a hunger which could not be sated. He remained controlled, willed and determined upon their magical goal. While he felt as if he could in mere seconds obtain an orgasm he carefully kept himself in check. The first witch whose hands were bare carefully reached at the waist of the man to move his latex pants pack to reveal his hardness. The second witch, whose hands were latex covered reached down and with her right hand gripped his penis tightly and began licking the head in a slow, circular motion. The male warlock was on the brink of orgasm, filled with ecstasy. With a slow mantra he gained control again and resisted the urge for finishing and spilling out the energy. The first witch began also licking the penis of the man while both women moved their tongues into each others mouths while kissing the head of the cock. As the male was at the brink of shooting semen all upon the faces, mouths and hands of the witches, they stopped and he sought with every ounce of his being to control the explosion. At this moment each practitioner in their own way invoked their higher Angel to seek a defining moment in their own becoming; by arousal of the serpents within does one grow more powerful in the Eye of Sorcery.

The male was untied to have his mask removed. Sweating and aroused the two witches had him lie upon the ground and the first witch placed her stiletto heel upon his face and applied a slight amount of pressure. The second witch took a vessel used in the coven to spawn succubi and incubi. She removed the top and began to lick and suck on the head of the penis while pumping the base of it. As the first witch applied pressure, the male witch felt an ecstasy which could not be described, a weight on his skull and the slurping of the second witch on his cock. As he began to pre-cum she jacked him off harder and faster, at the point of explosion the second witch, who had known him intimately for some time, allowed him to ejaculate in her mouth, and then spitting it into the Succubi – Vessel. The male witch fell into a coma of ecstasy upon orgasm, and drifted into the death posture as the pressure on his face was removed. He now would see the face of the Hidden God.

The Ritual of Draconian Ascension
Transformation from Flesh to Spirit

The blackened serpent is a symbol of wisdom obtained, the knowledge of the Adept who has trespassed the halls and meeting ways of the forbidden, who has drank the poison of the serpent's fang, yet from that struggle has obtained a new life, awakened and illuminated further by the striking at the Anvil of Cain. By each strike, each spark which ignites the clay of selflessness, Lucifer emerges again within the psyche.

This is the Rite of the Luciferian Ascension, the Agape of which Summons the Black Serpent. Let the initiate being either male or female choose a partner of art, who will by any means necessary arouse, copulate and stimulate the initiate for exhausting lengths of time. This rite is of the nature of Aleister Crowley's 'Eroto Comatose Lucidity', from which the initiate is led to the gates of exhaustion and beyond, when the flesh fails by overworking and the spirit must ascend by Will to the Luciferian Aethyr, of which the spirit is emblazed with the presence of the Peacock Angel, being Azal'ucel or Shaitan.

There are specifically two methods of this rite – Via Lilith (AZ) or Via Cain. As Lilith, musick should be played in the background which inspires dark emotions, chanting and somewhat horrific sounds. The chamber of operation should be decorated in crimson and black, with images of Lilith and her familiars, the Lilitu and Succubi. The Path Via Cain is one where the initiate is adorned and surrounded with the fetishes of the Horned God, thus in earthen decorations and symbols of Cain. Moroccan or Middle Eastern Music may be played to achieve the foundation for Gnosis early on, with the participant focusing on the meaning and mysteries of Cain the Blacksmith and Luciferian Initiator.

The purpose of the rite is to cross a boundary of flesh into spirit, of entering what the Cult of the Hand and the Eye call "Neither – Neither", by which the senses are not recognizable in any standard fashion, led to a state by extreme physical and mental exhaustion. It is by this path that the magician shall in a state of mental isolation, rise up in spirit to the Luciferian Aethyr, the very Sabbat of the Sun by which he or she shall commune with the Blazing Soul of Lucifer, the Peacock Angel who is the fiery initiator and father spirit of Cain. Within an initiatory sense Azal'ucel/Shaitan is the Angelick Higher Self (what Aleister Crowley called the Holy Guardian Angel) of Cain. The female and male magician will both undertake the Rite in the context of both Via Cain and Via Lilith, to understand two Aspects of the Adversary.

The rite is composed of several workings of causing exhaustion of the initiate by sexual arousal – over and over again. This is similar to what was called the "release of woman", who in swoon communicates with her higher self, the sweetness which is referred to her voice as the "Peacock" in the *"Ananga Ranga",* her voice is the Joy of Mankind. Thus as the initiate reaches near the final gate of the working, the Adept is led to Shaitan the Peacock Angel – Serpent, who is Azal'ucel. This rite is equally undertaken in the gnosis of Lilith (AZ), whose darksome embrace leads the Adept to leaving the flesh and seeking the Hidden Fire of Her, she who is web to the Crimson Dragon Samael, Ahriman, who is the Devil and Our Father. This is the marriage of Fire with Spirit, the quickening of the Witch into the Gnosis of the Lightbringer.

I.

The Participant should prepare for the rite by fasting and maintaining a strict discipline concerning physical fitness in some manner. The mind the day of the rite should be cleared, restful yet lustful from one week or more of abstinence from any type of sexual activity. Let his or her dreams bring a test to their Will and dedication to the Path and the Great Work of Becoming. Do not fall to your lusts and desires during this time period, it is essential to restrain and hold yourself by Will and the discipline of the magician, for the rite of which the Adept shall undertake is beyond physical stress, draining the body and will require every ounce of strength of which you may muster.

A

The Adept and participant (s) of the rite shall begin an invocation of Cain or Lilith. Let the Coven choose thus their means and words of invocation as in previous rites. Barbarous words, chants or other means of entering the fire shall be done thus. The Red Dragon has previously be awakened (what is the Kundalini) in the initiate thus they have reached a level of Adept in the Arte of Magick.

O

The Spell of the Shadow of the Adversary

1) To enter the shadow circle of Lilith for the means of transcendence of flesh.

"By skull and dagger cast do I summon thee, or Lilith – Az of Midnight Shadow
Cast by the Light of the Moon in splendor, enter me, coil around me in thy form of serpent, strangle both my phallus or clitoris until complete exhaustion, then as I shall seek you shall I be led back to flesh, to build my desire for the union of the Holy Fire of Iblis.
O Lover of Midnight's Circle, drinker of blood, Maiden, Goddess and Crone do I summon thee, encircle me in thy desire."

2) To enter the Forge and Serpent Circle of Cain for the means of transcendence of flesh.

"By Hammer and Anvil, of Dagger and Skull do I summon thee, O Father and Spirit Cain, endless wanderer of the forest and desert plane, who is my spirit illuminated by the Blackened Fire of thy tongs. As I was clay cast without perception, thy higher soul was shown unto me and among the Fires of the Sabbat was I envenomed with the Mark of Cain, the Blackened Flame of Azal'ucel who is Shaitan. By the Fork which is the Marking Stave of the Adversary, hold high into the Noon tide sun, that by the strength of Will do I seek this hidden fire again. By Devil Art and Whore's flesh do I copulate, in the desire of the Infernal Sabbat be led up into the highest Aethyr of the Dragon, wherein my Higher Self be revealed."

II.

Let now the Adept be aroused sexually by any and all means, beginning slowly and building into fervor of lust and demonic copulation. Once the initiate has reached orgasm, and he or she begins to fall asleep the participant shall again awaken the initiate with sexual arousal. This shall last once again until complete and utter exhaustion, the Shayatan within the body shall coil into exhaustion once again. When sleep comes upon the initiate once again shall he be aroused by the participant and by the methods of the Agape be brought to a collapse of body and mind. When the body of the Adept seem like it may not go any further shall copulation begin again, when the mind goes in-between sleeping and waking. It is within this moment, when the Mind begins to Ascend into the Luciferian Sabbat, shall the fiery Djinn who is Azal'ucel be revealed to thee.

III.

When the visions of the Adept seem to have ceased, let the participant again copulate with the magician until total exhaustion once again, sealing the Rite with the vision of the Peacock Angel. Upon completing this rite, the next few days should be significant to the scrying visions of the Adept, who has gained a meaningful transcendence of flesh.

In the Emerald Circle of Azal'ucel

"Spirit of which the fallen had taken strength, isolate and beautiful, Angelick Essence, Azal'ucel, from which came into being Cain I do invoke thee" the young woman chanted rhythmically."

The witch stood within the center of the circle, seeking to bring into herself her initiatic guide, within a state of self-fascination and the fire of the Aethyric and celestial plane. This was the rite which no man may sate, which no lover save her Angelick Host may initiate further. The witch understood that Azal'ucel, the Angel – Watcher who is revealed by the hidden name as Lucifer and Azazel, transforms within the initiate by bringing a distinct and unique 'fire' to the self; in a sense a continual transformation from the Hidden Fire (Black Light) of Cain to the Higher Faculties of Azal'ucel, the Risen God within. She has copulated with the demons and serpents of the void, held intercourse and sodomy with the shades of the dead under the initiatic guidance of Hecate, but here she would seek the Light of the Sun in the Dawn by intercourse with her Angelick Guide, Azal'ucel.

Standing within the Grand Luciferian Circle, she began moving widdershins performing the calls, with each syllable and intoning vibration she threw her heart and soul into it, invoking with a passion which allowed her to rise up. Her invocations were intense and fiery, flowing and as she chanted she spiraled the light down from the sky itself. As dawn arose in the Eastern Sky she so summoned her Angel by visualizing a Great Lion – Serpent coming forth with the Dawn and the rising sun.

"Aoth, Sabaoth, Atheleberseth, Abraoth!" she rolled from her tongue in an enthusiastic conjuration. She envisioned the Fallen Seraphim who was her soul and essence, sexless, Azal'ucel took the sex of the witch who the dragon had coiled within. She understood the origins of Azal'ucel, who was Lucifer, the first Angel who had twelve wings and helped cover the throne of limitless light before his fall. Once cast out as a fiery Seraph, his nature was that of a Dragon, a Beast who would become Satan.

The symbols of Azal'ucel, each burning within her own mind while she invoked, felt a burning sensation of excitement as she imagined and visualized the Lion – Serpent which was above her transform into a human shape. The beauty of this Luciferic Angel was of which could not be properly described with words. As Azal'ucel stood outside her, taller than her with darkly beautiful wings, long black tresses and a seemingly hairless body, his continence were strength and gentle beauty, sensitivity and pride in self worth. She recognized these traits within herself and Azal'ucel took the form of her desire. His eyes were sky blue brilliance, which as he put his arms on her shoulders turned blood black and his skin from a pale to a ghost white. She felt a chill as Azal'ucel presented the darkness beneath the surface, the very Daemon which she sought within herself. With this stab of coldness she held within herself he returned to the solar beauty he possessed.

She gently followed the lead of the spirit to the floor, wherein he was called forth. She reached down slowly while her lips met his; this embrace took her breath away into a sense of burning panic as he passionately tongued her and kissed with a warmth she could not grasp. He moved a hand slowly downward past her navel and began massaging her warmth until she became moist and then wet with anticipation. His movements were snake like, his mouth opened from tonguing her to be in the shape of a serpent, slithering and lightly flickering on her neck. Azal'ucel's movements were seeming instinct, yet the intelligence and light of this angel was of a high intensity, it mirrored her most awe inspiring dreams, her deepest desires for a union with what others called God.

She looked again from this state of ecstasy to notice that Azal'ucel had transformed below his waist to a scaly dragon – man, which a large and smooth black penis, which pulsed hard with her touch. His eyes were black obsidian which burned a flame she knew only so well, his face smooth and sleek as midnight, which a presence in his features as powerful as the Noon tide sun. The incense in the chamber lightly perfumed the room to accent this rite of the union with the Angelick Initiator.

She turned to move her hips in front of him that he may enter her there within the circle of union. Feeling so alive so felt this angelick spirit enter her warmth in a slow, steady thrust which set her nerves on fire, she was thrust into by him with careful yet passionate movements. As he with both rhythmic movements achieves a deep sense of penetration Azal'ucel removes his hands from her hips. He slowly turns his hands with the palms facing upwards; a golden flame emerges from each hand. The hour is Noon; the witch opens her eyes with a desire which echoed the brightness of the flames, as perspiration began forming on her brow. Her lips were now swollen, taking all of her angel deep within her warmth, allowing his fire which was soon to be one to consume her.

As she suddenly felt the Angelick Lover began to slowly ejaculate deep in her burning core, she contracted her muscles to squeeze him deeper within her, to suck his penis dry with every drop. She suddenly felt the hands which burned a Golden Flame darken and both hand touched her shoulders. She felt a burning ecstasy she could not express, in a scream or in a cry of joy; she lost herself floating in the light of the sun. Azal'ucel burnt and went forth into her, her union with her Daemon complete. She collapsed and soon regained consciousness, now she has begun to merge Light with Darkness, from which she is going forth on her Path of the Great Work.

The Sabbat of Azothoz
The Fire of Cain

Godforms: Cain (Samael + Lilith = Cain = abufihamat = Baphomet)
Ahriman: The Black Dragon, the mediator of the manifest and the unmanifest, darkness and chaos.

Azoth: **A-Z manifesting Alpha and Omega, the beginning and end.** The Triangle of Darkness is the summoning place of the Daemon, including the 'AZ' of the magician. In the triangle of Azothoz is the Adversary (Darkness and Light) = Sun & Moon joined in union. This represents the beginning (Shaitan/Samael: A= Fire and Manifestation) and the End (Z/Kali/Lilith: Az, the devourerer, concupiscience and hunger).

Here is the Great Work and Secret which this grimoire leads, yet none may learn this secret by words alone. Task and effort bring you to the Sabbat of the Devil and his Bride, and shall you know their venomous kiss by the desire in your heart.

AZoth is the mask which is darkness, yet revealed in light, blackened fire. From the self isolated or in unity, the self as the dragon becomes Cain, the First one of Witch Blood, the begetter of primal sorcery and the first Satanist, the very expression and vessel of the Black Light of Iblis. Cain comes forth holding the hammer (his mastery over the forge, the creative fire of Lucifer) and the Forked trident (to stab and destroy weakness and that which stands against progression, mastery over the earth). Around Cain is the fiery dragon of Samael, his father the Devil.

The Grand Ritual of the Venom of the Sabbat is created by the two fluids of the male and female, or male and male or solitary.

Needed: The Athame of Cain, Spirit vessel or pot, earth, graveyard soil, human or animal bones, human skull (the vessel of Cain), serpent skin and anything which represents your animal or bestial essence upon the path. The vessel represents Mahazael and Ahriman, this is the earthen/chthonic witch tomb which stores and encircles the familiar grown in the soil of this infernal grave.The magician will enter the triangle to summon and encircle the current of Azothoz, the possibility of individual and daemonic perfection and self – possibility.

Participants: Solitary or undertaken with initiated partner (a practitioner of the path). The elixir and venom of the Sabbat cup may be poured into the vessel of Ahriman, to ensorcel the power therein. The vessel is symbolic of the womb which creates the Luciferian and announces a rebirth and resurrection as a God in Flesh, thus aligning he or she with the current of Azoth, being the gnosis of the Fallen Angels and Watchers. The vessel is also symbolic of a tomb by which the magician's body of shadow and body of light is brought in union – the alchemical marriage of the Dragon/Beast and Harlot, Samael and Lilith, thus bringing to the physical body and soul = Cain.

The chalice of the Sabbat should be a special cup of which to hold the fiery elixir of the Agape, the female participant (if there is one) should collect some menstrual blood before the dark moon. You may mix this with your herbs of choice and seal and keep from the Sunlight for one moon or one month.

The male participant should enter the made triangle of Azothoz-

Begin congress or masturbation with the partner of the rite, invoking Azoth by the visualization of the dragon and the harlot.

"O thou succubi who grows in darkness, the blood kiss of the dragon bestowed, who in sulfur and the cold of the grave is empowered in the phallus of Azoth.
O death bringer, who haunts with a kiss and leaves the carnal bed before dawn
O swollen lip'd harlot whose wound is never filled, who opens our heart to ecstasy
O whose mother is the moon, whose cold embrace seduces us to the velvet caress of death, the coppery kiss which is given.

By Azoth and the mysteries of Agape, let the Great Rite be strengthened, the Daemon ascened!
O Lilitu – Az, shadow maker, bride of the Dragon, become and encircle and bless this envenomed elixir of the Sabbat – the very wine of the Devil!"

When the magician has reached the level of climax, let him ejaculate in the Sabbat – grail, the cup of Azoth. Let the contents be mixed, the fiery elixir of the adversary born.

"O elixir of the serpent and beast, thy transformative venom and the Azothoz of Life and Death – Do I ascend as the Fire Djinn of the Noon Tide Sun, who is as a lion and immortal of spirit!

O elixir of the moon conjoined with the Sun, the Azoth created of Noon and of Midnight, of the Dragon and Harlot.

O ecstasy drunken harlot, who rides upon the phallus of the dragon, bless the envenomed Sabbat grail with the transformation of Cain, the child of the Devil and Whore kiss'd

This I anoint with the Agape of the Cunning"

Tip the forfinger or quill and scribe the sigil of the Sun on your chest. The O with a dot in the center.

"Blessed is the daemon born – darkness and light be married in the Eye of Azoth!"

Holding the Grail of the Sabbat, meditate upon thy shadow, the bestial and angelic aspects, the Dragon King and Harlot Queen of the Sabbatic Rite, feel your shadows form according to the desire you harbor in your heart. This is the center and beginning and end, the Azoth of perfection – the coven of Daemon and Man.

Pour the contents of the Sabbat Grail into the vessel of shadow (Ahriman), then with the Athame of Cain (the Body self-creating fire from Darkness) directing the point into the soil of the vessel:

"I entreat thee o maker of the forlorn Witch Way, keeper of the Blackened Fire, spark giver to the uplifted clay of man

Azdalaka Drakul Seraphis Arimanius – I am of the Sun and the Moon. In my fire of divinity I may beget the shadows of darkness – I am the lord of shades and king of light!

Awaken as I have become, the fire of self illumination, vessel of darkness, may my shadow rest within.

Quayin, Lord of the shadowed way, envigorate my spirit and flesh, I do invoke thee!

At this moment I become the center, the source of Magick, the Lamp bearer
Where I may wander is my own deific assumption and task

I am the shadow which stands against oppression.

I am the Daemon of Rebellion and I bring forth a new way to Man and Woman.

I am the serpent Christ, Antichrist who shall lead the Children of Rebellion to the physical world.

I am the Dragon Christ who shall make my desires flesh.

Lord Cain awakens through me.

So I speak the words of the Serpent.

So it is Done."

Thus Ends the Grimoire of the Flesh of the Sabbat

This is the path which leads to the Eye of Algol, from which he or she who shall walk this path with dedicated intent, shall emerge as an embodiment of Ahriman and Lilith. Here is the union of ALL magick, no longer watered down or hidden from those who seek the cup of venom. Now is the awakening.

This work continues with LIBER HVHI, the Grimoire of the Qlippoth & The Bible of the Adversary.

GLOSSARY

Ahriman – The Prince of Darkness in Zoroastrian Religion. Ahriman is considered one brother created by Zurvan and was the opposing force to Ohura Mazda. Ahriman is also known as Angra Mainyu, an older title derived from Angra Mainyu, being the "evil" or averse spirit. Ahriman is a sorcerer who achieved a means of immortality and power over darkness and shadow. One who creates his desire in flesh. In relation to the sorcerer or practitioner of Yatuk-Dinoih, the individual seeks by developing their own system of sorcery, to become like Ahriman, just as did Akht-Jadu in the Zoroastrian tales. Ahriman is called the Great Serpent or Dragon, whose spirit is a shapeshifter and tester of flesh and mind. It was considered in some Zoroastrian tales that Ahriman and the Daevas, his angels, ecisted between the earth and the fixed stars, which would be essentially of the element Air (much like Lucifer his later identification). In creation myths, Ahriman first saw light and sprang into the air in the form of a great snake, that the heavens were shattered as he brought darkness into light. Angra Mainyu is thus a model of the Black Adept as the role of the mastery of the Will and the Mind.

Akhu – The Ka and Ba in union, the True Will or Holy Guardian Angel and Evil Genius (Shadow-self) conjoined. Akhu may be viewed as the Sethian principle of the Mesu Betshet, the Children of Rebellion who in independence, discover their focus in life. The union of the Red and Black Serpent is a symbol of the Akhu, both in flesh and dream.

Akht – The Sorcerer who was the embodiment of the Yatus, the demonic forces of Ahriman. Akht-Jadu or Kabed-us-spae as he was called was mentioned in Matigan-I Yosht-I Fryan. Akhtya was the founder and member of the Yatus, a coven of 'demons' and sorcerers who wandered Persia, practicing and developing sorcery. The name Akht itself means 'evil', 'filth' and 'pestilence', thus relates to the initiatory nature of Akhti as a sorcerer of the Adversary, by the darkness shall he come into light. Akhtya or Azyta is thus considered a symbol of the Zanda, which is an Apostle or Priest of Ahriman.

ALGOL – A word which derives from the Arabic Al Ra's al Ghul, Al-Ghul, or Ri'B al Ohill, which is translated "The Demon's Head". Algol was in Hebrew known as Rosh ha Shaitan, or "Satan's Head", as some traditions have referred to Algol as the Head of Lilith. The Chinese called Algol Tseih She, which is "Piled up corpses" and was considered a violent, dangerous star due to its changing vivid colors. On some 17th century maps Algol was labeled, "The Specter's Head". Algol upon some research has indicated that possibility Three stars which are an eclipsing binary, which may explain some of the rapid color change. Some writers have connected Algol with the Egyptian Khu, or spirit. The Khu is considered a shadow spirit which feeds on other shades of the dead. In reference to the writings and initiatory symbolism of Michael W. Ford, ALGOL is the sigillized in one form as a Chaos Star with an Averse Pentagram in the center. The Pentagram refers to the Eye of Set, timeless and divine, godlike and independent. The Chaos Star is destruction, Change and power – all of which emerges from the Eye of Shaitan, or Set. It is this Chaos which then brings Order. ALGOL is the mirror of the sorcerer, one who may enter and reside in the pulsing eye of blackened flame.

ANKH – The symbol of Eternal Life, vitality and health.

Apep – The serpent of chaos in the Tuat or darkness, the abyss which Set fought with and mastered. No other gods could confront Apep. Within the Luciferian Cultus, Apep is considered a form of Set once the God of Night mastered the Serpent and could then assume this Draconian form. Apep is a symbol of chaos and storm, but an unmastered sense of chaos.

Arezura – Arezurahe griva (Arezura) in the Bundahishin is called "a mount at the gate of hell, whence the demons rush forth". Arezura is the gate to hell in the Alburz mountain range in present day Iran. The North is traditionally the seat of Ahriman, wherein the cold winds may blow forth. Arezura from an initiatory perspective is the subconscious, the place where sorcerers may gather and grow in their arts, by encircling and manifesting their desire. M.N. Dallah wrote in "The History of Zoroastrianism" concerning a connection with demons holding mastery over the earth, their ability to sink below the earth and that such demons around the time of Zoroaster walked the earth in human form.

AZ – Called 'Concupiscence', Az is represented as Primal Sexual Hunger, that which eventually devours all things. Az is also related to menstruation (The Kiss of Ahriman causes menstruation in women) and is a destroyer through chaos. Az was connected with Sexual Hunger but also religious doubt, which relates her to a Luciferian Spirit who broke the chains of dogma by the Black Light, the torch of self-perception of being. Az also represents Lilith as the Goddess of the Beasts of the Earth, the very mother of demons and sorcerous beings. Az was said to be created in the Zurvan myth as a black substance like Coal, which would devour all creation, manifesting her as a vampyric being. Vampyric being simply represents the Predatory Spiritual nature of the Black Adept.

Azazel – The First Angel who brought the Black Flame of being to humanity. Azazel was the Lord of Djinn and was said to be made of Fire in Islamic lore. Azazel refused to bow before the clay of Adam, saying that it was profane. He was cast from heaven to earth and was indeed the first independent spirit, the initiator of individual and antinomian thought. Azazel was later related to the Watchers, the Hebrew Goat Demon God and Shaitan. Azazel is a name of Lucifer, who is the solar aspect of the Dragon, the Bringer of Light. As Ahriman was associated with the Morning Star, Azazel is the later Gnostic and Hebrew manifestation of Ahriman.

Azhi Dahaka – The son of Angra Mainyu/Ahriman. Azhi Dahaka as the 'Storm Fiend' has six eyes, three heads and three pairs of fangs. In human form, he was Zohak, an ancient Babylonian/Scythian/Assyrian King or Shah, who according to Zoroastrian mythology, was transformed into the immortal storm fiend by a pact with Ahriman. Azhi Dahaka is said to be filled with serpents, scorpions, toads and other insects and reptiles. Azhi Dahaka represents the power of Will made Flesh, Zohak was said to have propagated Witchcraft as common practice in ancient times.

AZOTHOZ – A sigillic word formula which represent the Golden Dawn definition of the Beginning and End, Alpha and Omega. Azothoz is a reversed form which is a symbol and glyph of the Adversary, Shaitan/Set and Lilith. This is a word which signifies self-initiation and the power which is illuminated by the Black Flame within.

Black Flame – The Gift of Shaitan/Set, being individual perception and deific consciousness. The Black Flame or Black Light of Iblis is the gift of individual awakening which separates the magician from the natural universe, being an Antinomian gift of Luciferian perception. The Black Flame is strengthened by the initiation of the Black Adept, who is able to balance a spiritual path with the physical world. The Black Flame is a mutating concept, always burning within the mind and within the practice of the Circle/Sorcery, the flame itself changes according to focus.

Black Magick – The practice of Antinomian and self-focused transformation, self-deification and the obtainment of knowledge and wisdom. Black Magick in itself does not denote harm or wrongdoing to others, rather describes "black" as considered to the Arabic root word FHM, charcoal, black and wisdom. Black is thus the color of hidden knowledge. Magick is to ascend and become, by Willed focus and direction.

Cain – The Antinomian nomad and Sorcerer who was the spiritual offspring of Samael (the Black Dragon) and Lilith (the Red Dragon) through the body of Eve in Biblical lore. Cain was said to have been the initiate of the Caul, and through his first step on the Left Hand Path (Antinomian practice) he is the initiator of the sorcerer and witch. Cain is also the Black Smith who sparks the Black Flame in the mind of the initiate. Tubal-Cain is the Baphometic Daemon which is the enfleshed archetype of Azal'ucel, or Lucifer/Samael, the Dragon and Peacock Angel.

DJED – Egyptian, represents stability and strength, associated with the backbone in the funerary cult. In the union of the circle, Djed is the Holy (or divine in a non-christian sense) aspect in union with the shadow of the magician, the very aspect of initiation in terms of the Great Work. As Djed is considered the backbone, it is therefore connected with Set.

Ensorcel – Ensorcel means to encircle, to focus and constrain. Within the Luciferian Cultus, ensorcel means the same as Sorcery, to focus energy of self by Will-Desire-Belief, also representing the self within a boundary of ones own design. It holds no association to the Christian concept of 'protection', rather it represents self-power and transmutation of the Great Work into practical result.

Great Work – The Great Work refers to Self-Deification in a Left Hand Path sense, the Becoming of the Magician through Magick and Sorcery. This is the following of your True Will, that very aspect which drives you to empower your life, the act of Sorcery with purpose of mutation/becoming. Initiation with self-determined focus.

Jeh – A manifestation of the Whore, AZ in Zoroastrian lore. Jeh is a consort of Ahriman, the Sorcerous Daemon of shadow and darkness. It was she who awoke Ahriman from his great slumber, that which no other sorcerer, wizard, witch or demon could do. Jeh-AZ is the sexual and inspiration drive which causes movement, friction and change. Jeh and Az represent predatory spirituality, the hunger for continued existence.

KA – The Body of Light or Body of shadow in relation to Khu, the shadow. In the workings of Sethianic Sorcery, this element is the "wish to be" aspect of the Black Adept, who by balanced means based on his initiation, manifests his desire accordingly. This is also the Body of Shadow moved through the subjective dream plane, the abyss.

Left Hand Path – The Antinomian (against the current, natural order) path which leads through self-deification (godhood). LHP signifies that humanity has an intellect which is separate from the natural order, thus in theory and practice may move forward with seeking the mastery of the spirits (referring to the elements of the self) and controlled direction in a positive area of ones own life – the difference between RHP is they seek union with the universe, nirvana and bliss. The LHP seeks disunion to grow in perception and being, strength and the power of an awakened mind. The Left Hand Path from the Sanskrit Vama Marga, meaning 'Left Way', symbolizes a path astray all others, subjective only to itself. To truly walk upon the Left Hand Path, one must strive to break all personal taboos and gain knowledge and power from this averse way, thus expand power accordingly.

Lilith – The Goddess of Witchcraft, Magick and Sorcery. Lilith was the first wife of Adam who refused to be submission and joined with the shadows and demonic spirits in the deserts. Lilith was also said to be the spiritual mother of Cain by her mate, Samael (Shaitan) the Dragon. Lilith appeared in Sumerian times as a Goddess of the Beasts of the Wild, as well as Sorcery and Night-fornication. Lilith was said to have many forms, from beautiful women to half human and the bottom half animal, to half woman and half flame. Lilith is also the mother of demons and a Vampyric spirit which is a primal manifestation of the Zoroastrian and Manichaean AZ and Jeh. Lilith may also be related to the Indian KALI, whose name is one of Her 17 names.

Luciferian Magick – Essentially close to the term, Black Magick but specifically focuses on ascending in a self-deified and isolated way in reference to Lucifer, the bringer of Light. Luciferian Magick may in this term make reference to seeking Light and darkness through magickal development, not an abstract concept, but to manifest the Will in both the spiritual and physical world.

Magick - To Ascend and Become. In a Luciferian Sense, Magick is to strengthen, develop and initiate the self through balanced forms of Willed Change.

Manes – The shadow of spirits of the dead, often visualized in certain practices in the Yatuk Dinoih, meaning the focus of energy by the Minds' Eye to forumulate shapes which mirror the state of the mind. Familiars, shape shifting, servitors, etc. Can represent "outer" spirits as well.

NOX – The formula of Black Magical Transformation, working with Nightside or Averse Currents. Averse does not mean harmful but it does general categorize as "challenge".

Sabbat – The gathering and conclave of sorcerers. There are in a conceptual sense, two types of Sabbats – the Luciferian and the Infernal. The Infernal is a bestial and earth-bound journey, similar to those shown in woodcuts and gathering points. The Infernal Sabbat is sometimes sexual, where the sorcerer may shape shift and communicate with their familiars and spirits. The Luciferian Sabbat is a solar and air phenomena based in dreaming, floating in air and having sensations of a warm heat similar to sitting out in the sun. The Luciferian Sabbat is a strengthening and development of the Body of Light, the astral double of the magician.

Sabbatic – A term which is related as the knowledge of the secret gathering, the Sabbat. This is a focus of inspired teaching based on magickal development via dreaming and astral projection. The Sabbat is the gathering of sorcerers in dreaming flesh, when the body is shed for the psyche which is able to go forth in whatever form it desires. The witch or sorcerer who is able to attend the Sabbat has already freed the mind through a process of Antinomian magical practice, thus enforcing and strengthening the imagination as a visualization tool, similar to divination and 'sight' with spirits.

Seker – The Lord of Darkness and Death in early Egypt. Seker is related to Set in the name Suti, being the Great God of Darkness, whose shrine is said to be in Pyramidal in form, and was filled with the blackest darkness. Seker in the Book of the Dead was a testing God, no doubt his early connections to Set, the sender of nightmares. Seker, like Set, had many serpent and dragon guardians which devoured its prey.

Set –Set was the Adversarial God of Egypt, representing Storms, Chaos, Darkness and the Cold. Set who became Shaitan was a friend of the dead, but was symbolized as Isolate or Individual Consciousness, thus a Lord of the Left Hand Path. Set-an is the Prince of Darkness, the God of Sorcery who makes flesh his desire through Willed Magical Practice. Set was depicted as a God who had the head of an animal with a long-snout, and whose color was Red, representing fire and the heat of the desert. Set is no benign mere intellectual God, rather one of action and rebellion.

Shades – Spirits of the Dead, ghosts and phantoms which walks in the astral plane. These spirits may represent in some cases the body of the sorcerer in the plane of the dead, a world separate in some areas from our own living perception. In evocation and necromantical practice, the shades are brought around and closer to the world of the living.

Sorcery – The art of encircling energy and power of self, by means of self -fascination (inspiration through the imagination). Sorcery is a willed controlling of energies of a magical current, which is responsive through the Will and Belief of the sorcerer. While sorcery is the encircling or ensorcerling of power around the self, Magick is the Willed change of ones subjective (personal or inner) and objective (outer) life.

Staota – A Vibration which could cause death or some change, that which would encircle the one sounding the Staota in self-focused energy. A Staota is used historically in the mythological tale, The Matigan-I Yosht-I Fryan. A Sorcerous technique presented in the Second Edition of YATUK DINOIH.

Tishin – A demon of thirst or vampyric/luciferian druj, serpent and daemon. Tishin is related to the concept of desire for continued existience, thus immortality and separation of the self from the objective world. This concept is within the gnosis of Predatory Spirituality and relates the Luciferian to seek to expand the mind by initiation, to manifest his/her desire on earth.

UMBRA – Shadows. Similar to KA but from the perspective in Luciferian Witchcraft, the aspect of darkness which is manifested subjectively from the Self. This is the mask'd desire in action.

Yatuk Dinoih – Witchcraft and Sorcery. The development and practice of adversarial and opposing sorcery to encircle the witch or wizard in self-developed energy. The principle of Darkness and the Deva/Druj (Demon) worship of this sect was in seeming model form, that by becoming as Darkness they developed a Light within. This is a veiled religious sect which survives in a modern form fueled by Luciferian Witchcraft and Chaos Magick, although devoid of paradigm shifting and more internally focused.

Yatus – A group of 'demons' or sorcerers who practice Yatuk-Dinoih, sorcery and witchcraft. The Yatus were led by Akht-Jadu, Akhtya. They were also considered nomads in nature, wandering through all parts of Persia practicing their religion.

Yezidi – Considered 'devil worshippers' by outsiders, the Yezidi are those who are dedicated to Malak Tauus, the Peacock Angel, also called Shaitan or Lucifer. In the MESHAF RESH, the Black Book, Azazel is the first angel, created before any other. He is considered most beautiful and is the one who teaches and enlightens humanity. In the areas of Yatuk Dinoih, Sabbatic and Luciferian Sorcery, transformation occurs by the embrace and becoming of the opposing force, or adversarial (antinomian) ideas within the self. The initiate moves through the magical current to strengthen his or her own being. In a modern context, Malak (Angel) Tauus (Peacock) is the symbol of solar enlightenment, wisdom and beautiful developed being.

Zanda – A Priest of Angra Mainyu/Ahriman, a term signifying the Apostle of Ahriman. The Zanda as the Yatu or Yatus are those who work the sorcerous religious and initiatitory rites of Yatukan Sorcery.

Bibliography (in no particular order)

Online Books edited by Joseph H. Peterson:

Arda Viraf: visit to Heaven & Hell

Bundahishn Zoroastrian cosmology

Greater Bundahishn

Dadestan-i Denig

Denkard

Selections of Zadspram

Yavisht i Friyan
History of Zoroastrianism by M.N. Dhalla (1938)

Babylonian Magic and Sorcery by Leonard W. King, M.A.

The Satanic Bible by Anton Szandor LaVey

Magick in Theory and Practice by Aleister Crowley

The Leyden Papyrus Edited by F.LI. Griffith & Herbert Thompson

Lords of the Left Hand Path by Stephen Flowers, Ph.D

Occultism, its theory and practice by Sirdar Ikbal Ali Shah

The Sufis by Idries Shah

A History of Secret Societies by Arkon Daraul

The Book of Lilith by Barbara Black Koltuv, Ph.D

The Goetia translated by S.L. MacGregor Mathers and Aleister Crowley

Egyptian Magic by E.A. Wallis Budge

The Gods of the Egyptians by E.A. Wallis Budge

The Book of the Sacred Magic of Abramelin the Mage trans. By S.L. Macgregor Mathers

The Book of Black Magic by Arthur Edward Waite

Transcendental Magic by Eliphas Levi, translated by A.E. Waite

The Encyclopedia of Witchcraft and Demonology by Rossel Hope Robbins

Rebel in the Soul translated by Bika Reed

ABOUT THE AUTHOR

Michael W. Ford is a solitary practitioner primarily of a modern interpretational form of ancient Persian sorcery called collectively "Yatuk-Dinoih" which is essentially known as Daeva-yasna, utilizing the forbidden currents of the Adversary as a life-strengthening tool of initiation. The outer form of this initiatory system is called Luciferian Witchcraft and is entirely based on the foundation of the Adversary being the initiatory current of the spiritual predator, or who has embraced the Luciferian spirit of the Left hand path.
Michael W. Ford is the head of several left hand path orders, centering on The Order of Phosphorus which serves as an initiatory guild for Luciferianism, from which Michael has written numerous books about. Mr. Ford is also head of The Black Order of the Dragon, a Vampyric Temple which is an inner order for TOPH, Order of Set-Aapep, a Typhonian and Sethian left hand path magickal guild, Ordo Azariel, a Vampyric Order based on the Qlippoth and the Church of Adversarial Light.
Mr. Ford is author of LUCIFERIAN WITCHCRAFT, LIBER HVHI – Magick of the Adversary, LUCIFERIAN GOETIA – Book of Howling, ADAMU – Luciferian Sex Magick, LUCIFERIAN TAROT with Nico Claux, BEGINNING LUCIFERIAN MAGICK, BOOK OF THE WITCH MOON – Chaos, Vampyric and Luciferian Sorcery, AKHKHARU- Vampyre Magick, SATANIC MAGICK – A Paradigm of Therion, GATES OF DOZAK – Primal Sorcery & the Book of the Worm, THE FIRST BOOK OF LUCIFERIAN TAROT, THE BIBLE OF THE ADVERSARY, MAGICK OF THE ANCIENT GODS – Chthonic Paganism and the Left Hand Path and more.
Mr. Ford is also an artist, having published an Art book entitled "RITES OF THE ANTICHRIST: The Art of Spiritual Lawlessness" which contains painting and images with blood, human bone dust, reptile and spider remains.
Michael W. Ford is also a musician having founded BLACK FUNERAL in the early 1990s, Psychonaut 75, Hexentanz and Valefor. Ford has also contributed to a soundtrack for a film called CADAVER BAY, HELLBOUND: Book of the Dead and currently records Ritual and Magickal music in a solo capacity.
Michael has an interest in Horror Fiction as well and is a co-owner of LUCIFERIAN APOTHECA, an online left hand path magickal shop.

Milton Keynes UK
Ingram Content Group UK Ltd.
UKHW050048061223
433825UK00001B/3